Women
in Iran

Recent Titles in
Contributions in Women's Studies

From the Field to the Legislature: A History of Women in the Virgin Islands
Eugenia O'Neal

Women and Domestic Experience in Victorian Political Fiction
Susan Johnston

African American Women and Social Action: The Clubwomen and Volunteerism
from Jim Crow to the New Deal, 1896–1936
Floris Barnett Cash

The Dress of Women: A Critical Introduction to the Symbolism and Sociology
of Clothing
Charlotte Perkins Gilman, Michael R. Hill, and Mary Jo Deegan

Frances Trollope and the Novel of Social Change
Brenda Ayres, editor

Women Among the Inklings: Gender, C.S. Lewis, J.R.R. Tolkien, and
Charles Williams
Candice Fredrick and Sam McBride

The Female Body: Perspectives of Latin American Artists
Raysa E. Amador Gómez-Quintero and Mireya Pérez Bustillo

Women of Color: Defining the Issues, Hearing the Voices
Diane Long Hoeveler and Janet K. Boles, editors

The Poverty of Life-Affirming Work: Motherwork, Education, and Social Change
Mechthild U. Hart

The Bleeding of America: Menstruation as Symbolic Economy in Pynchon,
Faulkner, and Morrison
Dana Medoro

Negotiating Identities in Women's Lives: English Postcolonial and Contemporary
British Novels
Christine Wick Sizemore

Women in Iran: Emerging Voices in the Women's Movement
Hammed Shahidian

Women
in Iran

Gender Politics
in the Islamic Republic

Hammed Shahidian

Contributions in Women's Studies, Number 197

GREENWOOD PRESS
Westport, Connecticut • London

For Roohi and Nahid
sisters, teachers, and *friends*
with love and gratitude

Library of Congress Cataloging-in-Publication Data

Shahidian, Hammed, 1959–
    Women in Iran : gender politics in the Islamic Republic / Hammed Shahidian.
      p. cm.—(Contributions in women's studies, ISSN 0147–104X ; no. 197)
    Includes bibliographical references and index.
    ISBN 0–313–31476–4 (alk. paper)
    1. Women—Iran—Social conditions. 2. Women in Islam—Iran. 3. Sex role—Iran.
    4. Patriarchy—Iran. I. Title. II. Series.
    HQ1735.2.S53   2002
    305.23'0955—dc21   2002016099

British Library Cataloguing in Publication Data is available.

Library of Congress Catalog Card Number: 2002016099
ISBN: 0–313–31476–4
    0–313–32482–4 (set)
ISSN: 0147–104X

First published in 2002

Greenwood Press, 88 Post Road West, Westport, CT 06881
An imprint of Greenwood Publishing Group, Inc.
www.greenwood.com

Printed in the United States of America

The paper used in this book complies with the
Permanent Paper Standard issued by the National
Information Standards Organization (Z39.48–1984).

10 9 8 7 6 5 4 3 2 1

Copyright Acknowledgments

The author and publisher gratefully acknowledge permission for use of the following material:

Extracts reprinted by permission of Sage Publications Ltd. from Hammed Shahidian, "Gender and Sexuality among Iranian Immigrants in Canada," *Sexualities* 2(2), 1999: 189–223.

Extracts from Hammed Shahidian, "The Iranian Left and the 'Woman Question' in the Revolution," *International Journal of Middle East Studies* 26(2), 1994: 223–47. Reprinted with the permission of Cambridge University Press.

Extracts from Hammed Shahidian, "The Education of Women in the Republic of Iran," *Journal of Women's History* 2(3), 1991: 7–38. Reprinted with the permission of Indiana University Press.

Contents

Acknowledgments

Many have assisted in the completion of this project, appearing in two independent yet interrelated volumes, *Women in Iran: Gender Politics in the Islamic Republic* and *Women in Iran: Emerging Voices in the Women's Movement*. I would like to thank my cohorts in the Sociology/Anthropology Program at the University of Illinois at Springfield for their support and friendship. I am also grateful to Nancy Ford, Executive Director of the Institute for Public Affairs at UIS, for her encouragement and support.

Deborah Kuhn McGregor, Michael Lewis, and Nastaran Moossavi number among the people who read both volumes. Several colleagues read chapters of these books at various stages—my thanks to them all: Ali Akbar Mahdi, Nasser Mohajer, Shahrzad Mojab, Ali Pourmand, and Robbert Schehr. Many activists inside and outside Iran read all or parts of the manuscript. They wish to remain anonymous. I would like to express my warmest appreciation to them for sharing with me their experiences, and extending their cooperation and trust. My special thanks to Ethan Lewis for believing in the importance of my work, for his warm support, insightful editorial comments, and his valuable friendship. I wish also to thank Kris Jagusch of the Center for Teaching and Learning at UIS for her editing of several chapters.

My family has been a great source of continuous love, kindness, and friendship throughout my life. To them I am particularly indebted for teaching that a passion for justice and human dignity is indispensable to a meaningful life. I am most grateful to them. Recognizing my debt, however, is surely insufficient compensation; but recognition at least testifies that I remember.

Note on Transliterations

I use Farsi, rather than Arabic, pronunciations as the basis of my transliterations (e.g., nafaqeh rather than nafaqa). For the most part, I use a modified version of the system recommended by the *International Journal of
Middle East Studies*. I have avoided diacriticals with three exceptions: (ʿ)
for ʿeyn, (ʾ) for hamzeh, and (â) for long "a" (similar to the word *car*). I
use (q) for the Farsi gheyn or ghâf. Whenever common transliterations
exist, I use them to avoid confusion (e.g., Iran instead of Irân, Hashemi
instead of Hâshemi, Ali instead of ʿAli). I also use existing English spelling
for proper names when available. I transliterated Farsi and Arabic words
as they are pronounced by Iranians, not as they are written, in order to
both ease the reading for those not familiar with these languages and to
more accurately reflect how the majority of Iranians use these words.

1

Introduction: Gender Politics and Revolution

He said: "My wife must be honorable and modest *(najib)* ... and I have heard a great deal about you in this regard. Of course, coming from a respectable family is also an important condition, which you do. She must also be family-oriented, interested in family life . . ." [And more nonsense of this sort.] I interrupted him: "What you say is too basic, too general. This is not an interview. Go to the heart of the matter." "You're an educated woman, and that's very important for me. Of course, in our possible future life—pardon me for saying "possible"—management will definitely be implemented–though not too strictly—but input will also be solicited." I thought: "Great! The mister will allow me to say 'yes' or 'no'!"

A young medical doctor relayed to me this conversation with a young, devout man. Her supervisor told her that his friend was interested in her, but too shy to speak with her face-to-face. She knew her answer even before talking to the man. The whole idea of someone seeing her from afar and deciding that she was "wifely material" repulsed her. Besides, he was a hizbullah, too distant from her beliefs and lifestyle. "He is one of those men who have no respect for a woman. He sees her not as a human being, but as a weak creature, good for nothing except providing sex, breeding, cooking, and suffering—the kind of man who as soon as he comes into some wealth, marries a second wife. I was disgusted." But the exchange is quite telling about gender relations in the Islamic Republic of Iran (IRI).

Note, for instance, how the subject of the sentence is concealed, as the man lays out his ideal familial relations in the passive voice: "Management will be implemented"—not "*I* will manage *you*," or even "*I* will implement management." He is appealing to a divine command in verse 34 of the sura *Women* ("Men have authority over women because Allah has made the one superior to the other, and because they spend their wealth to maintain them"), codified in the IRI Constitution. His expression sounds passive, for, after all, an ordinance is merely being implemented. But he is also laying down the foundation of a family, where his authority must appear as *benign management*. One thinks of the opening line of Shakespeare's Sonnet: "They that have power to hurt, but will do none." He prefers that her acceptance be volitional, without making him resort to an unequivocal pronouncement of his divine "duty." This way, the couple can live happily within a relationship that, though clearly defined, is also immensely subtle.

Subtlety is essential when a man wants to exercise authority over an educated, financially independent, and intractably free woman. In a society where education is a source of respect and financial security, the difference in the man's and woman's educational level complicates the situation even more. He has a Bachelor of Arts degree in management, whereas she is a medical doctor. But several factors work in his favor. He is a man in a system that puts him in charge. Regardless of her financial independence, it is still *his* responsibility to provide for her. And with that "responsibility" comes status and power. He is also a believer, a soldier of Islam with shrapnel in his side, proving his devotion. Then, though not as educated, he holds a sensitive post in an office whose exact nature he reveals only in the strictest confidence to a woman he tries to woo.

Indeed, a new cloak is spread over the power arrangement of their "possible future" relationship; he reveals secrets that paradoxically accentuate his strength and disclose his vulnerability. Notwithstanding his position, "sometimes, when no one is around, I sing songs"—anathema for a hizbullah of his stature. His confiding in her is supposed to create a bond, a trust that only a man and his woman can share. It makes him exposed—presents him as an ordinary individual, not a family despot—in a relationship in which management is miraculously "implemented." His status is concealed, but it is also saved from her anger.

But none of these are concealed before her eyes. He can hear that in her sharp responses, in her quickness to set his boundaries right from the start. At the beginning of the conversation, he addresses her familiarly, using her first name. Before even responding to his greeting, she tells him, "Please address me by my family name, as Ms.—" And then throughout their short conversation, she reminds him of the difference in their backgrounds, values, and lifestyles. He comes from an uneducated family, while her parents, brother, aunts, and uncles are college educated. And as he tells her that the women in his family all wear the châdor, as he expresses joy that she, "too," comes from a "moral, respectable, religious family," her mind wanders to a picture of her mother, her aunt, and her cousins, in low-cut dresses and miniskirts.

Her comments disclose irritation while listening to, and relating about, him. Her reflection that he wants not an equal partner, but a breeding cook, sets their disparate worlds on a collision course, despite his efforts to create an amicable union. Yet, she believes, the mere fact that she felt compelled to speak with him upon her supervisor's "recommendation," and that the man has the audacity to approach her as his future wife, make her vulnerable. Her unavoidable condition tells her that, save in her private milieu, she does not receive the recognition she deserves: "I felt sorry for myself. Why was I, raised in a family that respected my rights, denigrated so much? I considered that an insult."

The above exchange demonstrates the interaction of gender and cultural politics. Discussions in future chapters will explain the politics of gender articulations in pre- and post-revolutionary Iran, the emergence of divergent gender relations, and the changing power relations between men and women. This first of a two-volume work presents the circumstances that the second volume treats. *Gender Politics* studies the tension in the patriarchal structure of Iran from the 1960s, especially since the 1979 revolution. The pre-revolutionary attempts to move the locus of patriarchal dominance from the home to the public sphere—a project that yielded certain, though limited, advantages for women—met with strict Islamist opposition. The new regime sought to revive private patriarchy in all its tyrannical forms. Yet the government did not altogether succeed. Patriarchy under the IRI has bifurcated between private restrictions and praxes that, though public, are immensely influenced by domestic mores. Coercion has proven integral to the Islamic state's gender politics. Coercion testifies that the IRI is still winning; resistance points to intensifying tensions between public and private patriarchies and women's autonomy—and to potential for genuine change far beyond the limited reforms instituted by the Shah and even by the so-called Islamic feminists.

In *Women in Iran: Emerging Voices in the Women's Movement*, the liberating possibilities alluded to above and the barriers to their achievements are detailed. I discuss the emergence of Islamist women's reformism—broadly defined as gender politicking in the context of Islam and the Islamic state's teachings and laws. This trend I consider a bargain with public patriarchy whereby women become visible in society and history and their grievances against patriarchal relations receive recognition. Visibility secures some women an active role in various spheres of public patriarchy; in return, these women spare patriarchy, somewhat, by limiting the reach of feminist politics to the most blatant forms of discrimination. Reformist bargaining with patriarchy appears to be a step forward, especially under such conditions as the Islamists have attempted to impose on Iranian women. Under closer scrutiny, however, reformism diverts feminist attempts to fundamentally alter gender relations. In Iran, for example, reformists have espoused an agenda that reflects the interests of middle- and upper-class, professional, gainfully employed, heterosexual (Muslim) women. Though weaker and less ideologically and organizationally consolidated than reformist women, many secular feminists have drawn attention to workingwomen's rights, and have sought revision of such key issues as morality; sexuality; and the relations between individual and community. These activists and authors question the very assumptions of existing political culture, and reject prioritizing sociopolitical objectives that relegate gender to peripheral significance.

In what follows, I will lay out the theoretical terrain. I remark how gender and sexuality interact with culture. I explore patriarchy as an adaptive system, influencing women's grievances and their movements' articulations of demands and objectives. These discussions are followed by a summary of the book.

THE SOCIAL CONSTRUCTION OF GENDER

Gender refers to cultural ideals that normatively order images and expectations on the basis of socially defined masculinity and femininity (West and Zimmerman 1987; Acker 1992). Gender plays a pivotal role in the ordering of a society through various forms of "doing gender" (West and Zimmerman 1987), refashioning of structures of patriarchy, contestation over gender roles, and struggle over sexuality and its use as an identity marker for the collective. Gender also involves organizations and institutions (Acker 1992; Lorber 1994). As Judith Lorber puts it, gender is "a process of social construction, a system of social stratification, and an institution that structures every aspect of our lives because of its embedment in the family, the workplace, and the state, as well as in sexuality, language, and culture" (1994: 5).

Emphasis on gender's social and cultural construction has traditionally distinguished it from sex, determined solely by biological difference. Recent scholarship, however, has grown critical of this distinction that ignores how sex is also socially and culturally constructed (Epstein 1988; Butler 1993). Social identification of sexes, then, is important primarily as a reflection of how a society construes and constructs sex and gender. Both sex and gender are contingent and relational categories, constructed through an intricate, interactive multiplicity of such factors as class, ethnic relations, race, religion, education, and economic power. Gender relations and the meaning of gender identity change as men's and women's access to various social resources alters. Gender, as Butler has argued, is neither an "essence" nor an objective, external ideal to accomplish; it is, rather, performative, that is, created by the very acts of gender. Gender is "a construction that regularly conceals its genesis" (Butler 1990: 140).

Because of its contingent, relational nature, gender is not always acted out consistently; socially acceptable gender identity is never fully attained. Socially defined gender denotes power as central to making gender relations and identities. Power operates through multiple mechanisms, and is never completely unidirectional. Opposition and resistance are concomitant with domination. In interaction between the sexes, power is often negotiated through the articulation of specific gender definitions.

As a construct that conceals its social nature, gender appears "natural." Yet whether deemed natural, divine, or social, gender is "assumed" a permanent component of social life—we have no choice but to become men or women. Gender is, in other words, teleological. Individuals are believed to merely act out who they are supposed to be, to fulfill suprarelational tasks, apparently natural, ideological, or just "common-sensical." As a social institution, gender survives by projecting models of ideal man- and womanhood. Gender operates as if perfect genders exist, thereby establishing hierarchical relations not only between genders but also among members of each gender. Yet "ideal genders" rarely—if ever—materialize: genders intertwine with class, ethnicity, race, sexual orientations, beliefs, and ideological commitments. Within the larger pyramid of gender, there are smaller ones (Barnstein 1998: 146).

"Ideal genders" are constantly contested and fluid; they are nonetheless pivotal for preserving gender as a social institution, as well as promoting preferred versions of man- and womanhood. Gender is coercive, aiming to safeguard both dominant gender hierarchies and its very institution. Since they are constantly contested, systems of domination always rely on some form of overt or covert violence. Feminist scholars have discussed extensively how patriarchal domination breeds male violence against women (Millett 1970; Benjamin 1980; Dworkin 1981; Binney 1981; Stanko 1985; Walby 1994). We can expand these discussions, arguing that any gender differentiation is coercive. The symbolic representation of gender as natural, inevitable, or legitimate perpetuates inequality through what Pierre Bourdieu calls "symbolic violence." It is, of course, conceivable that gender differentiation would be based on a "different-but-equal" principle. Yet the arbitrariness of gender would persist even under such conditions. Even when men and women would perform equally valued masculine and feminine roles, gender distinctions would still remain arbitrary. The arbitrariness of gender, the assumption that one *cannot but be* male or female, makes gender coercive. Fluid, constantly changing genders are *genders* nonetheless. Gender relies on this symbolic representation of reality as natural and justifies its reproduction.

Gender rituals—daily practices, codes of appearance, ceremonies, invented traditions, etc.—do not just assert gender identities; they often also remind involved individuals about the power dynamics of gender relations. Consider *nafaqeh* in Islamic family law (see chapter 6). A husband is legally responsible for fulfilling his wife's basic needs, regardless of her financial power. *Every morning* he is supposed to pay her that day's *nafaqeh*. This daily ritual is also a daily reminder about power division within the family. It reinforces for women and men what is already defined in their relationship as gendered individuals: "Women shall with justice have rights similar to those exercised against them, although men have a status above women. Allah is mighty and wise" (Koran 1988: 356, sura *Cow*, v. 228). That couples may—and many in fact do—follow a much more "respectful" economic arrangement does not negate the reality of their interaction. His option is there; the hierarchy is stipulated. Though not easily discerned, the pressure permeates like air.

Gender involves reading grandeur, even sacredness, into the quotidian. Manhood, for instance, symbolizes a nation's strength; womanhood, its purity. This process is accentuated in theocratic or nationalist systems with expressed ideological commitments. In such systems, mundane gender behavior and appearance acquire a transcendent, even "sacred," character. Gender expressions involve cultural border-making that requires "essentializing" and overgeneralizing "proper" and "improper," "good" and "evil," "us" and "them." Men and women are presumed to embody not just individual characteristics, but all that is honorable about "us," as distinct from "their" not-so-reputable traits.

CULTURE AND CULTURAL INNOVATION

Social life without culture is as impossible as social life without production. Culture gives meaning to our actions, enables us to become cognizant of our lives. Without culture, our behavior would be "a mere chaos of pointless acts and exploding emotions" (Geertz 1973, 46)—instantaneous and isolated deeds deprived of any shape and meaning. To Clifford Geertz, culture consists of patterns of meanings embodied in symbols transmitted through generations. We use symbols to communicate, preserve, and develop knowledge about our world and attitudes toward our life. To understand a culture, we must go through different layers of meanings to uncover the complexity of cultural symbols. Geertz writes:

Undirected by cultural patterns—organized systems of significant symbols—man's [sic] behavior would be virtually ungovernable, a mere chaos of pointless acts and exploding emotions, his [sic] experience virtually shapeless. Culture, the accumulated totality of such patterns, is not just an ornament of human existence but . . . an essential condition for it. (46)

Culture is a productive force that affects society's every aspect. Culture is not merely a reflection of social relations; it is also a window through which we look at our world. In other words, culture outlines what we see "out there." Marx taught us that social life is founded upon objective material relations, not abstract thoughts. We must add to this lesson that culture shapes the way we understand and organize our objective social relations and pursue our interests. Max Weber comments about the interweave of objective interests and subjective values: "Not ideas, but material and ideal interests, directly govern men's [*sic*] conduct. Yet very frequently the "world images" that have been created by "ideas" have, like switchmen, determined the tracks along which action has been pushed by the dynamic of interest" (Weber 1981, 280).

Culture then both reflects and articulates material interests. This means that culture is not indifferent or benign. Social groups that control economic production and have political leverage also control the means of cultural production. Yet cultural domination cannot be explained merely by ideological dominance from above. Cultural hegemony is always accompanied by various degrees of conscious and active acceptance by the masses. Hegemonic concepts and values become the staples of "common sense" and popular beliefs. These concepts shape how people see their surroundings and explain their world. Dominant groups attain their cultural hegemony through shaping how the populace views and explains the world. It is, therefore, vitally important for political movements—the women's movement included—to redefine existing values and concepts, or create new ones.

Divergent class and group interests indicate that societies have not one, but several cultures. Different social groups have distinct cultures, their commonalities with the dominant culture notwithstanding. As Raymond Williams (1982) discusses, sociocultural beliefs stemming from old relations make up the "residual culture" while ascending groups and classes and flourishing social relations give rise to the "emergent culture."

Certain periods create favorable conditions for cultural innovations and the development of new sociocultural horizons. New cultural patterns surface at times of chaos (Swidler 1986). Cultural innovation is a social process; the best ideas will be relegated to oblivion if they fail to attract popular support. New trends do not enjoy equal success. Yet there is no doubt that social movements can and should propose new cultural notions and social values congruent with their goals. These innovations are rooted in emerging sociocultural patterns. Social actions are articulated in the context of these structures of meanings. A social event is distinguished from a simple incident by its relation to a host of interrelated meanings and social institutions.

SEXUALIZING CULTURE AND POLITICS

Gender functions dialectically with sociocultural arrangements. Laws and policies determine men and women's access to resources, while gender intervenes to set up priorities. In this regard, *how* social actors define transformations of gender relations is as crucial in understanding their political agendas as the actual developments. Culture defines gender relations. It also provides an outlook for interpreting gender relations. Even when available cultural interpretations are not acceptable, culture defines the parameters of new interpretations, as well as the concepts and vocabularies of the new discourse. This second function of culture is particularly significant for the study of social movements since it influences the extent to which these social processes distance themselves from the very structure they oppose. Nonetheless, not much is achieved if an analysis is limited to depiction of the myriad forms of cultures popping up here and there. Instead, I believe, we should investigate further how gender relations shape the very cultural patterns that give meaning to them. This follows Butler's keen analysis that gender constantly conceals itself.

We thus need to enhance our analysis of gender beyond formal rights (e.g., family law, educational regulations, employment rights, political exigencies, and cultural policies) to encompass the broad perspectives and paradigms that shape cultures and define priorities within which gender is construed. Since gender is teleologically defined, its investigation in any social system must include a study of that system's proposals about the nature and dynamics of its ideal order. Examining gender in sociopolitical movements must be concerned with political agendas, but also with "metaphysical" explanations and assumptions behind those agendas. How is the universe perceived? How is society defined? Where do human beings fit into the grand scheme of things? Such questions create the context within which any gender politics must be understood.

This is not to say that gender relations are fixed in their ideological articulations. Gender and its interpretations are negotiated, since they must operate within confines of possibilities. Variety, nevertheless, does not preclude common axioms and imposing rationales. It is also true that individuals do not sheepishly follow their culturally defined roles; they bargain with hegemonic cultures, negotiate components of ideologies. Yet cultural explanations often direct our train of thought and action along pre-laid "tracks" (Weber 1981: 280). I analyze Islamic gender ideology in this book, not because it mirrors the realities of people's lives, but because it delineates the context of gender policies. Only by understanding that background can we compare Islamic policies with the daily experiences of Iranians, the depth of reforms, or the radicalism of different trends within the women's movement.

Assessments of women and politics—women in social movements or in existing political systems—have focused primarily, if not exclusively, on men's and women's gains and losses. I believe we must move beyond— move beyond, not jettison—these pragmatic concerns and opt not to merely achieve gender equality, but to obliterate gender distinctions altogether. Gender politics must emphasize that equality is achievable only when arbitrary gender differentiation is left behind. Gender identification willy-nilly requires some degree of essentializing the self, giving the self some fixity—no matter how fleeting—that only hinders its development. It is undoubtedly impossible for men and women to be prisoners of their gender identities—gender is rarely a total institution. But gender *is* a prison nevertheless. It creates boundaries and parameters within which we have to survive. We then need to be cautious about any movement—right, center, or left—that offers the alternative of a "better" gender structure.

Sexuality is a key factor in the negotiation of gender identity and gender roles. "Sexuality," writes Foucault, "must not be thought of as a kind of natural given which power tries to hold in check, or as an obscure domain which knowledge tries gradually to uncover. It is the name that can be given to a historical construct" (1979: 105). Sexuality is a historical construction, which brings together gender identity, physiological traits and capacities, needs, desires, and fantasies. Gender relations "script" our sexual behavior, serve as "blueprints" for the "whos, whats, whens, wheres and whys of our sexual gratification" (Gagnon 1977: 6). Yet appropriate behaviors are not always neatly defined, or exhaustively followed. As culturally accepted, but constantly contested, ways of responding to and satisfying bodily pleasures and desires, sexuality is political to its core (Weeks 1986). Sexual identities are individuals' choices in the context of what is historically available to them. But sexual identities also indicate resistance and opposition (Weeks 1981). In this regard, the possibility of defining oneself in sexual terms brings into focus several hierarchical power relations, including gender, sexuality, nationality, and class.

Sexuality is tied to gender roles and the symbolic and actual reproduction of nations. Institutionalization of heterosexuality not only predefines sexuality proper as heterosexuality, but also reinforces existing gender relations. Stevi Jackson argues that the institution of heterosexuality is inherently gendered, since it is founded upon "the assumed normality of specific forms of social and sexual relations between women and men" (1999: 5). My analysis of gender relations in the IRI supports Jackson's contention. In the IRI, heterosexuality ensures proper gender behavior. Confinement of sex to marital relations supposedly secures the nation's health and strength (there is strength in numbers), and defines the context of gender roles. The family becomes a "natural" foundation of society, both creating and being created by a heterosexual couple whose gender roles shape, and are "necessitated" by, that family. Deviation from the "natural," "proper" heteromarital sexuality is intolerable, unless it somehow contributes to the perpetuation of "proper" sexuality. Homosexuality, for instance, is "overlooked" only insofar as it remains a compensatory outlet and does not interfere with the divine duty of marriage. Heterosexuality, then, reproduces and regulates the nation.

Forced heterosexuality not only exposes homosexuals to persecution, it also exposes those powerless within the intra-gender hierarchy to violence.

This is so, especially where women are not readily available and homosexual sex is regarded as compensatory sex. Young males, especially those with limited means of support, may find themselves most vulnerable. Numerous "unofficial" reports from Iran relate stories about poor adolescent males providing sex for older men in exchange for a place to stay and something to eat. Poverty-stricken boys are particularly in danger of being forced to male prostitution for *bachehbâz* or pederast clients.

As in gender, class plays a crucial role in creating sexuality. Classes define respective sexualities differently. Kathy Peiss (1983), for instance, demonstrates that in the late nineteenth and early twentieth century urban America, working-class women benefited from dance halls, theaters, and the workplace in organizing their premarital sexuality. She argues that earning money and living in large cities allowed these women to alter the meaning of premarital sex, the social manner of sex, and the pool of potential husbands. Suzanne Staggenbord (1998: 103–4) similarly contends that, at the turn of the twentieth century, middle- and working-class men experienced masculinity differently. Working in bureaucratic positions with little room to express autonomy and individuality, facing the threat of competition from women and immigrant men, middle-class American males felt threatened. Fearful of feminization, middle-class masculinity was defined in contradistinction from femininity. Heterosexual liaisons reaffirmed their sexual identity as men. Working-class men, however, proved their manliness by supporting their families through hard, physical labor, affording these men more freedom from heterosexuality.

We must also pay attention to the cultural politics of class and sexuality. As Michael Lewis (1993) suggests, the culture of class inequality prompts individuals, particularly of middle-class background, to emphasize their "privilege" and "superiority" compared to those beneath them, rather than dwelling upon their "lacks" and "subordination" relative to those above. This psychosocial mechanism conceals the social nature of class difference by falsely presenting such a divide as resulting from individual attributes, rather than socially conditioned constraints. Comparing downward while gazing upward allows people to explain their place in the social hierarchy in terms of "accomplishment" rather than "failure" in a system that defines class and status as personal achievements. Had it not been for such cultural interpretations of inequality, depression and feelings of inadequacy would have been rampant. This mechanism also helps to maintain class division— again, especially among the middle class—through what I call "class scare": a well cultivated fear that should class distinctions disappear, people would lose their privileges and become "just like those beneath them." This scare is then used to control other social behaviors by emphasizing the "threat" they cause to class stability.

The class scare plays a pivotal role in the construction of gender and sexuality. In post-World War II United States, for example, nonmarital sexuality came under fire as men faced greater difficulties in fulfilling their "manly duty" of providing for their families. Family life symbolized social stability, thus not only creating a bastion against the "Communist threat," but also reaffirming middle-class concerns for economic success. Fear of the loss of manhood prevailed; male homosexuality, as well as inclination toward communism, were interpreted as failure to be a man (Kimmel 1996: 237).

The class scare is also functional for controlling sexuality when class inequality is under attack. The Iranian Left, for instance, looked down upon transgressions of heteromarital sexuality as a decadent bourgeois deviation that distracted militants from labor politics (Shahidian 1996a; 1997a). Under the Islamic Republic, with its self-laudatory commitment to the poor and downtrodden, sexual deviations are often persecuted as subversive attempts by the "wealthy" enemies of Islam (see chapter 6)—this, though that regime's economic policies not only benefited many of the rich, but also encouraged the emergence of a new stratum of *Muslim* rich.

PRIVATE AND PUBLIC PATRIARCHY

By patriarchy I mean a social structure that allows men's subordination and exploitation of women. Gender and patriarchy are not synonymous; patriarchy is "the salient feature of gender as a social institution in many societies" (Lorber 1994: 3). Sylvia Walby (1994) suggests that patriarchy consists of not one, but multiple structures: paid work, domestic production, state, male violence against women, sexuality, and culture.

Studying the transformation of patriarchy in British society of the nineteenth and twentieth centuries, Walby (1994) delineates a movement "from an individual to a more collective form of appropriation of women" (179). In private patriarchy, men are the direct oppressors of women and beneficiaries of sexual inequality in their positions as husbands or fathers. Patriarchy, she suggests, underwent a series of modifications in the past two centuries, partly in response to women's demands for equal status in society, and partly in order to increase the control of the state over all aspects of social life. In the area of employment, women are no longer barred from certain professions; they are instead confined to jobs segregated from and valued less than those of men. At the same time, women (that is, upper- and middle-class women primarily) have become less constrained by household production. The exclusion of women from political and cultural realms has been replaced by their subordination. That is, though female sexuality is recognized, double standards and objectification of female sexuality persist. The control over female sexuality has shifted from the exclusive control of a father, brother, or husband to that of a broader public arena. In public patriarchy, therefore, the expropriation of women has been effected more collectively than by individual patriarchs. The household has remained a site of patriarchal oppression, but it is no longer the exclusive loci of women's presence and male domination. Women are not formally excluded from any sphere; but that indicates not emancipation, but a movement "from an individual to a more collective form of appropriation of women" (179).

Walby contributes to the ongoing debate about the dichotomy of private and public spheres. Michelle Rosaldo's (1974) discussion of the bases of sexual inequality suggested that men have successfully subjugated women by barring them from the public sphere, while themselves controlling both private and public domains. Feminist scholars held the exclusion of women from the public sphere to be universal. This exclusion constituted the ground for the universal presence of male domination. Recent studies of women in both Western and non-Western societies, however, have cast doubt about the applicability of the dichotomy of public and private spheres. Studies of the working-class families of the West reveal a more permeable border between the two spheres (Gamarnikow et al. 1983). A number of studies about immigrant families disclose a similar inconsistency between the theory and the actual experiences of immigrants in the West (see, for example, Moallem 1991; Kibria 1993; Dallalfar 1994). Scholars of the Middle East similarly argue that dichotomizing public and private domains generalizes based on Western experience. In the study of gender relations in the Middle East, we should pay attention to the inextricable nexus of public and private, especially respecting the private's influence upon the public (Nelson 1974). Rosaldo (1980) and Lamphere (1997) have concluded that the hypothesis of the public-private dichotomy overgeneralized based on the nineteenth century social theorists' reflections about the European paths of industrialization.

Walby's analysis extends this debate. Her formulation rids us of dichotomous reasoning in our gender analysis. It shows the flexibility of the patriarchal system, by demonstrating how different structures of patriarchy enable it to vacillate between private and public without being confined to either. Private and public patriarchal structures are ideal types, classifications that aid analysis. In real life, drawing clear dividing lines is not always possible: old and new structures coexist for some time before the former is completely replaced by the latter. Walby finds both private and public spheres present in both forms of patriarchy. In effect, patriarchal relations in the public arena are crucial in shaping patriarchal relations within the household. What distinguishes private and public forms of patriarchy, then, is the privatization of women's experience of patriarchy in the latter. In the private form, the immediate beneficiaries are also located in the household, while in the public form, the appropriation of women's labor and services takes a collective form.

Furthermore, the shift in the site of sexual domination from private to public is accompanied by a change in patriarchal strategy from exclusion to segregation and subordination, whereby women are no longer barred from economic, cultural, and political institutions, but the domains of their involvement are segregated from and graded lower than those of men.

Deniz Kandiyoti's (1988) analysis of classic patriarchy in North Africa, the Muslim Middle East, and South and East Asia (particularly India and China) resembles Walby's assessment of British private patriarchy, especially in the concentration of women's responsibility in domestic production and men's authority over women.[1] Kandiyoti's classic patriarchy is characterized by patrilocally extended households, engaged primarily in rural production, in which senior men have authority over family members, including younger men. Daughters are married off at a young age; they move to households headed by their fathers-in-law. Brides live under the control of their fathers- and mothers-in-law, until they themselves become mothers-in-law and exert authority over a subservient daughter-in-law. Women, writes Kandiyoti, "have access to the only type of labor power they can control, and to old-age security, through their married sons" (279). They consequently opt to ensure their sons' lifelong commitment: mothers aim to subordinate sons' conjugal affection to duties toward the family of origin (while brides work hard to sidestep mother-in-law's control).

Structures take shape amidst constant cooperation and resistance by those who people them; patriarchy, too, must reckon with women (and men) who create it and whose lives are in turn shaped by it. Women, who bear the brunt of male domination, do not passively surrender; they resist patriarchy, forcing it to compromise. They design their defiance, however, within sociopolitical conditions that emerge when such factors as gender, class, ethnicity, race, nationality, and culture intersect. Women's and men's real living conditions, as well as their subjective accounts of their lives, reflect omnipresent coercion and defiance.

Women's absence from nondomestic production, especially among the well-to-do, is celebrated as a status symbol. Their exclusion is often accompanied by discriminatory practices and institutions such as purdah and hejâb (the veil). Yet women tolerate, even revere, these institutions to maintain family status. "They would rather adopt interpersonal strategies that maximize their security through manipulation of the affection of their sons and husbands" (280). Kandiyoti calls this process of subservience and manipulation under classic patriarchy as *traditional patriarchal bargain*, through which women maximize their life chances and gain "limited security" in exchange for economically advantageous options.[2]

Through patriarchal bargain, women create conditions for themselves that guarantee their relative well-being under male domination. This condition gives the false impression that life is fine, save in those rare instances when women become victims of unfortunate circumstance. The normalcy of the quotidian makes an oppressive relationship appear natural and, in-

deed, fair. It is no surprise that some women who negotiate a secure arrangement in such conditions may end up supporting the very arrangements
that oppress them.

Capitalist expansion and women's struggle lead to a crisis in the traditional bargain. The number of women in the formal sector increases; facing
economic hardship makes many men, especially those from the working
classes, unable to be their families' sole breadwinner. Men and women can
no longer meet their obligations under the traditional bargain.

The crisis that ensues brings patriarchal coerciveness to the foreground.[3]
Cultural "switchmen" (in Weber's term) guide men and women in understanding the changing environment and defining their interests. While symbolic violence effects the *acceptance* of private patriarchy at times of
"normalcy," it can muster a strong *defense* for that system at times of crisis.
As public and private lives change, many men feel that they are losing
control over "their lives." They feel threatened because their power is challenged. Since family relations in a private patriarchy are based on men's
authority, limiting men's influence in the family appears as the destruction
of the family. They see cherished values on the road to extinction, without
having a clear picture of what the future holds for them. The breakdown
of the traditional bargain for many women marks the demise of traditional
patriarchal control; many others, however, do not welcome the change. As
classic patriarchal bargains enter a crisis phase, observes Kandiyoti, the
system's "internal contradictions" are revealed and participants in the system are forced "to take up new and seemingly contradictory positions"
(Kandiyoti 1991: 35). Many women of the transitory generation find themselves between a rock and a hard place. They are not completely freed from
the hardship of the past and, at the same time, cannot claim the benefits
of the new order.

The ambiguous conditions that arise from such social transformations
explain women's strong presence in conservative, antidemocratic, even patriarchal movements. In the late nineteenth and early twentieth century
Western Europe and Northern America, for example, "maternalist" movements venerated women as caregivers and challenged men who frequented
bars and brothels to be inspired by women's moral commitment (Koven
and Michel 1990). As women met their Victorian obligations, men, too,
were coerced to fulfill their responsibilities. To secure their positions in a
patriarchal family, in other words, these women reinforced the same family
system that had subjugated them to a domestic life and offered men economic, social, and moral dominance. Similarly, National Socialist women
interviewed by Claudia Koonz (1987) informed her that they enjoyed the
Nazi system, despite its strong patriarchal practices, because they believed
that as mothers, they contributed a vital role to the strength of the "fatherland." Analyzing the late twentieth century "kitchen table backlash"
against feminism, Jean Hardisty (1999) demonstrates how the United States

"Right's message of a return to 'traditional values' has tapped the public's mixed feelings about recent changes in the role of women, and in the process, organized political opposition to feminist reforms" (70–71).

What we can conclude from these examples is the active presence of a female agency that, *in the name of women*, calls for a revival or restrengthening of traditional gender relations. This is not surprising, as culture reinforces gender relations and conceals social inequalities. Commenting on "official language," Bourdieu writes that "the system of concepts" members of a given group use for representation of their social relations "sanctions and imposes what it states, tacitly laying down the dividing line between the thinkable and the unthinkable, thereby contributing towards the maintenance of the symbolic order from which it draws its authority" (Bourdieu 1977: 21). Such "systems of concepts" displaces, diverts, camouflages, and legitimates "through oversights and omissions, and in their deliberately or involuntarily complicitous silences" (188–89). That those suffering from inequality may indeed misrecognize (to use Bourdieu's term) the injustice of their situation is amply commented on in the feminist literature (see, e.g., Elster 1983; Narayan 1997).

Identification with the collectivity and the belief that they are engaged in a crusade to save "their people"—nation, race, the Islamic ummat (the community of believers)—affords these women added strength. They serve the collectivity; but, more importantly, they themselves become more powerful because they embody the purity, power, and commitment of their community. This heightened self-worth empowers women and "emancipates" them from barriers that have hitherto confined them (see Rommelspacher 1999: 56). Identification with the community expands these women's "range of activity and responsibility." They deem their struggle to be going far beyond meager advances in the family or the workplace; they believe that they are indeed, as Birgit Rommelspacher puts it, "liberating themselves from the constraints of the family and also from a relatively self-referential existence" (56).

Identification with a cause also allows these women to defy family authorities and transcend traditional gender role constraints. Muslim women from traditional families, who may rarely perform public functions, participate in street demonstrations, even if their husbands disagree, because they are serving Islam. The call of the faith supersedes a husband's authority. Allegiance to Khomeini (and later, to Khamenehii), the Prophet, or Shiite Imams and saints, expressed in passionate pleas of love and fidelity, create a higher patriarchal power that outranks husbands. Rommelspacher (1999: 56) cites a similar pattern among Nazi women who, in the service of the *Führer*, resisted the orders of their husbands. Nazi women thusly identified with "male grandiosity" which, in turn, enabled them to "devalue the concrete husband."

Tanika Sarkar and Urvashi Butalia (1995) make similar observations about women's participation in the radical Hindutva movement in India. The discourse of the Hindu Right legitimizes women in their own eyes as valued players in "public and even political demonstrations of Hindu fervour and faith" (9). This is achieved by the "careful erasure of boundaries" between private and public spaces. Hindu nationalism offers these women "a vehicle for redressing their experiences of gender inequality and for transgressing sex-typed roles" (Basu 1995: 164).

Yet, in a seemingly paradoxical manner, linking the family with patriarchal "grandiosity" strengthens patriarchal gender relations. Bourdieu (1977: 190–92) suggests that "direct domination," that is, domination between two individuals, often takes very subtle, romanticized, disguised, even "enchanted" forms. In this way, two individuals can live peacefully, side by side with each other, and even affectionately, while one has a clearly domineering relationship with the other. The covertness of the relationship makes the coercive nature of domination disappear (just like in the vignette that began this chapter, "management will definitely be implemented"). Violence takes a gentle face (since management is not "too strict" and "input will also be solicited"). Indeed, as Bourdieu puts it, in this kind of relationship, violence "is never recognized as such." Furthermore, the pressure of family life becomes even greater because families represent imposing, ideal orders—they are not just families; they are Hindu, Islamic, or German families. Conjugal relationships consequently become more than ever "enchanted." To be worthy of collective identifications, husbands and wives are expected to exemplify their community. Fair and benevolent, men are to avoid overtly acknowledging their authority and, unless left with no other option, must refrain from overt violence. Women are to loyally perform their sacred wifely and motherly duties in private or public. Leaf through any Islamist treatise on the family, and one will fail to find one instance where the husband is not enjoined to be kind, concerned, and, above all, judicious. (Remember how, in our vignette, the man's revealing of his secrets made him simultaneously vulnerable and stronger.) The reliving of private relations in supraindividual entities, *disfigures, hides, and protects* the relations of male domination in the traditional patriarchal family.

GENDER, PATRIARCHY, AND SOCIAL MOVEMENTS

As a constantly reconstructed identity rather than a fixed character, gender is a constitutive element of social movements as men and women struggle to define their collective identities through ideological constructs, symbols, and meanings. Social movements entail not only a reaction to oppression (real or perceived), but also a preference for a new social order. Conceptions of ideal social order invariably have to address not just political and economic issues, but also general moral and philosophical outlooks. They involve, in other words, a restructuring of polity and economy as well as the social and cultural fabric of the quotidian. Family and gender relations occupy a prominent position in this regard and thereby make visions of new gender roles and sexualities integral to any vision of future society.

In times of social unrest, daily activities presume new meanings in the emerging and all-enveloping political context. During the American Revolution, for example, the consumption and production of many commodities, such as textile products, took on political significance because of the relationship they suggested with Great Britain. Women played a particularly key role in this respect through providing "a protected market for domestic goods" (Kerber 1980: 43–45). Iranian women played a similar role during the Constitutional Revolution. After the Qajar king gave the concession of tobacco to the Regie Company of Britain in 1890, Iranians protested in great numbers and decided to close down shops to refuse the sale and consumption of tobacco until the concession was abrogated. Women often made up the majority of picketers who forced many merchants to close their shops and join the strike; "their shops would have been subject to the plunder of women" otherwise (Teymouri 1971: 152).

Modes of participation in the revolutionary movement are also gendered. Temma Kaplan (1982) argues that in the 1910s, Barcelonan women became inspired by their traditional roles as housewives and mothers (what Kaplan calls "female consciousness") to take political action against inflation and inadequate food supply. Peteet's (1991) study demonstrates that women's mobilization in the Palestinian nationalist movement has been structurally diffused, crisis-oriented, weak in theoretical perspective and practical strategy, and closely related to a women's stage in the life cycle. The movement had to reconcile its goals with the cultural norms of female propriety. Because of this imperative, women had to gradually ease into resistance organizations.

Women may also strategize on their familial roles to maximize their political strength. Simona Sharoni (1997) remarks that some Israeli women activists have used the language of maternal care to mobilize broad public support for peace. At the same time, participation in political movements modifies existing gender roles. Rema Hammami (1997) and Carol Bardenstein (1997) observe, for instance, that in the process of the Palestinians' struggle, the definition of a "good mother" has changed from the provider of family services and shelter to one who offers a martyr. A similar redefinition appears among Iranian hizbullah women whose family role encompasses keeping the family intact *and* willingness to selflessly offer loved ones to martyrdom for Allah (see chapter 7).

Gender also influences how authorities persecute activists. Kaplan (1997) argues that in the Aba Women's War of 1929 in Eastern Nigeria, soldiers were ambivalent in their reaction to fighting women, since their idealization of motherhood barred them from using physical force against women. Iranian political activists similarly remarked in their interviews with me that IRI authorities were initially puzzled by female revolutionaries: they could not believe women could have political opinions of their own and remain loyal to their convictions at the expense of destroying their family lives. Yet such misconceptions seem too feeble to withstand the test of time. The same political prisoners informed me that their jailers soon realized their mistake and treated them as they would any other political foe. And the history of the IRI persecution supports this observation. Noteworthy, however, is the impact of how female opponents are treated by observers. One of the students assaulted by hizbullah vigilantes in the August 2000 confrontation in Khoramâbâd was quite perplexed that their assailants did not show the slightest mercy "even" on women: "These people, who constantly recited holy words, did not even show pity on the sisters on the bus and assaulted them." More than physical abuse, however, vigilantes' compromising of "the sisters' " honor seems troubling. Vigilantes likened the women on the bus to an exiled woman who, in a summer 2000 Berlin lecture event by reformists and pro-Khatami intellectuals, danced in protest: "Beating and kicking the sisters, they shouted: 'You are like . . . [that whore?] who danced in Berlin. You must be eradicated" (*Hayat-e-no* 28 August 2000). When pro-government militants compromise the honor of a Muslim sister, disbelief about the government mounts, though assumptions regarding gender are not necessarily revisited.

Revolutions (re)construct gender through reinforcement of mythical or real interpretations of women's roles. These narratives in turn prescribe women's roles in post-revolutionary society. Hufton, for instance, shows that analyses of the role of women in the French Revolution relegated women to a conservative supportive role (Hufton 1992: 133–54). Deemed superstitious, ignorant, and under the intoxicating clerical influence, women were denied the right to vote, for fear they might subvert secular and liberal ideology.

The tension between cultural constructions of gender and revolutionary movements becomes particularly manifest when it concerns sexuality, a domain highly charged with deep-rooted beliefs and values. Recent contributions to the study of nationalism underline interrelationships between national identity and sexuality (Anderson 1991; Mosse 1985; Parker et al. 1992). They point out that nations more often than not are presented as virtuous, considerate, daughterly, or maternal women. As women become the symbolic expressions of nations, so interactions with other nations are expressed in terms parallel to sexual morality and feminine virtues. Protecting the nation comes to mean protecting the virtue and purity of the women of the land, especially when the nation is facing an imperial power (Burton 1992). For example, an iconography from the time of the American Revolution portrayed America as a vulnerable, naked woman. As America lies on her back, the British author of the Boston Port Bill hovers over her, pouring tea down her throat, while one of the politicians surrounding peeks up her skirt (see Kerber 1980: 40).

The metaphorization of nations as women is grounded in patriarchal relationships. Consequently, the female body becomes the battleground not only for countries and their enemies, but also for competing definitions of "national identity." Preserving a pure national identity becomes equivalent to protecting and controlling women's sexuality. Liberating sexuality from this bond offers individuals the chance to become autonomous agents who act on their own behalf—with whatever affiliations they might choose—not as sacred symbols of the state. Thus, challenges to the dominant sexual "order" become important not only for the emergence of new sexualities, but also for challenging hegemonic gender relations. In the Islamic Republic of Iran, as I will discuss in chapters 7 and 8, sanctification of sexuality, the identification of national purity with femininity, and the determination of national and religious lineage through the male have serious consequences for men and women. Relieving sexuality from the dominance of sociocultural norms and Islamic values is an important step toward the secularization of sexuality.

The struggle for constructing gender and sexuality is actor-centered and involves both politico-economic relations and everyday practices. Politico-economic changes may shift the primary site of women's oppression, the mode of patriarchal exploitation, and patriarchal strategies—hence, immensely shaping identities of men and women of different social backgrounds: for some, introducing new opportunities; for others, limiting consequences; for some, providing new avenues of expression; for others, proliferating crises in meanings and values. These developments are rendered meaningful only in a cultural context. The language, concepts, and values used to articulate these changes both reflect the hegemonic culture and simultaneously shape and reshape it.

GENDER AND SEXUALITY IN IRAN

Gender relations in Iran have been markedly influenced by the assumption of the complementarity of roles within a heterosexual family. The two sexes are created differently and should accordingly assume different responsibilities in public and private spheres. Men and women are dichotomously identified with rationality and emotionality. Though both sexes are regarded as sexual in nature, women are deemed in need of male supervision as female action is supposedly dominated by emotion. As family is considered the only proper locus for the expression of sexuality for both sexes, regulation of female sexuality becomes a main preoccupation of the male family members.

The regulation of the behavior of family members primarily falls on the shoulders of the father who is responsible for the maintenance of his wife and children. (Other male members of the family, especially sons, exercise similar restrictions on their sisters and, in some cases, mothers.) Men's economic power, their right of divorce, albeit conditional, and automatic custody of children puts women in a vulnerable position. As "queen of the house," however, wives are also responsible for maintaining the house, which includes supervising children's behavior. Sons and daughters are raised in this atmosphere to assume similar roles as grown-ups. Daughters grow under their mother's wing and are supposed to be properly trained for assuming the roles of wives and mothers in due time. Sons, on the other hand, learn their roles primarily by emulating their fathers. Parents are responsible for rearing their children in a manner that would best position them in the marriage market. Sons should be raised to assume their economic responsibilities in the family as well as their authoritative role of the patriarch; daughters are raised to be honorable, chaste, and skillful in managing the household. Their upbringing should qualify them to find suitable marriage partners. In either case, their performance reflects their family background and upbringing.

Power relations between women and men in the domain of sexuality have been based on the "traditional bargain." Under the traditional bargain, "good women," that is those who have complied with the social codes of chastity and virtue, would have men's respect and protection. Those who have failed to comply would be deprived of social respect and protection. Because of their presumed vulnerability, daughters (or any female member of the family) need closer supervision. In an ironic twist, therefore, the recognized sexual nature of women becomes the basis for the control of their sexuality. In that sense, hejâb becomes not an external cover, but an *internal* one. Whether the woman wears the veil on the outside or not, she should conceal her true nature from others, and at times even from herself. Women's "chastity" and "virtue" have been essential elements of Iranian cultural identity. Sexual pleasure has had supposedly little—if any—bearing on the life of an "honorable" woman. She is to protect her "capital" by remaining a virgin prior to her marriage (Vieille 1978: 454). After marriage, she is to offer sex to her husband to fulfill her "marital duty" (*vazifeh-ye zanashoo'i*). Furthermore, men's categorization of women into "saints" and "whores," along with identifying marital sex primarily with procreation, places wives above "mundane," if not unclean, carnal pleasures. Though the woman is believed to have as much sexual desire as her husband (if not more), she is expected to conceal it from herself and others. "The man [perceives] himself as revealer of the latent erotic powers of the woman" (Vieille 1978: 463). Thus, despite the fact that the family serves as the legitimate locus for the expression of sexuality, marital sexual relationship assumes a sacred, asexual character. "True love" stands beyond the physical pleasures of the body.

To be sure, women are not passive victims. They exert some degree of power in familial relationship through offering or withholding "sexual services." This maneuvering power, however, is limited in a system that regards sex a marital duty and assumes women as men's property and object of pleasure. Though men have an obligation to satisfy their wives' sexual needs, modesty may prohibit women from expressing concern over sexuality. Besides, the overwhelming power that men enjoy in divorce makes women vulnerable to men's emotional and physical violence in sexual relationships. Emotionally, she is reduced to a sexual object that is not *supposed* to enjoy sex; physically, she is exposed to marital rape or, at best, to boorish sex in which she cannot learn to enjoy sex.

Despite the seeming dichotomy of gender roles, masculinity and femininity, as Sedgwick demonstrates (1995: 15–16), are often defined not at opposite poles of the same axis, but rather as orthogonal to each other. Patriarchy provides sexes with a range of acceptable behavior. Within this range, men's behavior could be modified without altering the structure fundamentally (Morgan 1990). As Homi Bhabha explains (1995), choice can induce anxiety for men. Thus, masculinity is *"always* in crisis" (Solomon-Godeau 1995: 70). In the context of gender relations delineated above, Iranian men, too, experience ambivalent roles. Though men do enjoy more freedom of mobility that enhances their freedom for sexual encounters, they are expected to portray a respectable image of themselves. To prove their sexual prowess, they feel the pressure to have sexual relations at all cost, but to gain social respect as a "decent man," they ought to maintain their chastity. To be a *man*, they should prove virility and sexual appetite, to be a *good* man, that is, a desirable husband for somebody's daughter, they should prove "innocence," aversion to sexual temptation outside the confines of marriage. Men also learn that women, too, are sexual, and as men, especially as *good, respectable* men, they are expected to protect their women from the machination of other men. This expectation not only makes all men watchful of each other, but also encourages men to be fundamentally suspect of women. They are seen as either innocent victims of conniving men or constantly plotting to lure men while maintaining a socially acceptable image. Virginity then becomes not only a sign of chastity, but also of a matured discerning ability. The traditional patriarchal division of women into wives, mothers, or daughters and whores also becomes a division of wise and gullible women.

Ample evidence testifies to the limitations of this description of gender relations in Iran. Though there is not yet a thorough analysis of the histories, ideologies, and practices of sexualities in Iran, personal and social-scientific observations as well as common sense indicate that among many Iranians—women and men alike—sex is neither postponed till after marriage nor experienced solely within matrimonial relationships. Bauer (1985a), for instance, shows how working-class women in Tehran offer

alternative explanations of moral codes to suit their experiences and responsibilities. Friedl (1991) also cites incidents of pre- and extra-marital
relationships in rural Iran. Accounts of individual Iranians, too, reveal that
many people either have themselves experienced nonsanctioned sexual interactions (holding hands, necking, petting, oral sex, anal or vaginal intercourse), or know of people who have had similar experiences.[4] Beliefs and
ideologies of this sort, as Gramsci noted in his discussion of hegemonic
cultural order, "serve to cement and to unify" an entire community (1971:
328). Yet they also function as a "mask" "over the underlying cracks in
the social fabric and hiding them from view" (Thompson 1986: 30). In
other words, the sexual ideology described above not only presents an ideal
picture of a collective identity, but also reflects the aspirations of a dominant social and cultural order rather than the realities of people's everyday
lives. Social values and beliefs, however, form the content of people's consciousness. As individuals internalize these, the cultural order becomes not
only constitutive, but also *regulative*. These values function, therefore, as
mechanisms of social control by forming the criteria for evaluation of self
and other people's behavior. They serve as a basis for labeling those who
do not comply with imposed gender roles and sexual norms as "corrupt"
(*kharab*), "licentious" (*harzeh*), or "Westernized" (*qarbzadeh*).

Unfortunately, however, this vision of sexuality remains popular. Cases
that contradict this vision are considered isolated aberrations, not modes
of living. Several scholars have pointed out the serious complications arising from women's two contradictory sexual roles before and after marriage—chaste, disinterested in or even unaware of sex prior to marriage,
and seductive and kind or lenient after marriage (Saadawi 1981; Shaaban
1991; Zakaria 1988). Yet little attention has been paid to individual and
social behavioral implications of unwed women who are not supposed to
be interested in sex, yet find themselves seeking sexual pleasures.

GENDER AND CULTURE IN THE IRANIAN REVOLUTION

Gender relations in Iran underwent extensive transformations under the
Pahlavis. Proponents of the Pahlavis have praised these changes as emancipatory (see, for example, Afkhami 1984), while critics have censured as
all negative and detrimental for the Iranian "masses" (Az 1981). These
changes are neither, as I discuss in chapter 2. First and foremost, I think
they indicate a process of shift in the form of the Iranian patriarchy from
private to public. With the increase of women's education and employment
in the formal sector of the economy, the home, as the bastion of men's
dominance over their women, was perceived to be losing its significance.
Initial steps through legal reforms to limit men's power within the family
reinforced that fear, especially among the clergy whose traditional role in
the judiciary was undermined. Yet the reforms did not end sexual discrim-

inations. Exclusionary practices began to decline, but segregation in social and economic spheres persisted. Violence and sexual abuse of women moved beyond the four walls of the home, to streets and workplaces.

Though these changes were by no means uniform or inclusive, they resulted in further development of relations of capitalist production, a zeal for secular and scientific analyses, apathy toward religious thinking, and a crisis of traditional values among segments of the urban middle class. As I argue in chapter 3, these developments contributed to a crisis in gender relations in Iran. Increase in women's participation in the formal sector of the economy, the spread of literacy among women and their access to college education, as well as revisions in family laws had profound impacts on gender relationships, especially in urban areas (Mirani 1983; Moghadam 1993). Routine contacts between the sexes in the workplace or college, changes in social practices (such as the increase in age when initially married) and values (such as criticisms of arranged marriage or debates about women's rights), led many people to the realization that Iranian gender and sexual mores were outdated.

The gender crisis coincided and coexisted with a general politico-economic crisis of the Pahlavi regime. Participants in the revolution of 1979 have affected and been affected by this coexistence, yet the dominance of the politico-economic crisis overshadowed concerns about gender relations. Issues like class, gender, oppression of nationalities, and political freedom were articulated at the politico-economic level, especially at the state level, while personal, "private" experiences of gender and sexuality were deemed secondary. In other words, the Iranian Revolution was male-defined not just in its answers to problems or in its agenda for the future, but also in that it focused merely at the level of political economy, targeting the state, vying for political change.

Yet all participants of the revolution had a vested interest in reshaping gender relations. The religious opposition to the Shah articulated their agenda clearly since they saw the disorder in gender relations to be symptomatic of a more fundamental problem that threatened their existence. As the writings of the Muslim clergy make abundantly clear, gender crisis was considered to stem from secularization of society and a spread of scientific fervor that created apathy toward religion among the youths. The clergy viewed in these changes a conspiracy of non-Islamic, foreign power against Islam. It was, then, not surprising that women became the target of the newly established IRI quite early (see chapter 4).

While the religious opposition to the Shah articulated emerging gender relations at the juncture of public and private, both the women's movement and the Left have addressed gender relations primarily in politico-economic terms. Prior to the reforms of the sixties, when issues like veiling, education, sex segregation, and female employment could be addressed amidst the politico-economic conflicts, both the Left and the women's movement had proposed progressive agendas. But after these issues were partially and formally resolved, ambivalence and confusion grew.

The Left continued to endorse women's rights in certain areas—opposing mandatory veiling under the IRI, the law of Retribution and its treatment of women as worth half of men, and the exploitation of women workers. The Left, as I demonstrate in chapter 6, subsumed women's struggle against patriarchy under struggles against monarchy and imperialism. To make the matter worse, some of the Left's radical lexicons seeped into the Islamic oppositional ideology—"cultural imperialism," "imported culture," "responsible art," and "oppressed," to name but a few. The common use of these terminologies made it difficult to discern the differences between the Left's analysis and that of the Islamists. The impact was twofold: the Left could neither realize the incongruity of the two analyses nor could it articulate its own discourse on culture and gender as autonomous or qualitatively different. Besides, since the Pahlavi state claimed to champion the rights of women, the Left did not want to be identified with the government's efforts.

The women's movement also underwent a period of confusion and ambivalence. If the demands of the movement were met by the Pahlavis, if mandatory veiling were lifted and women's presence in the educational and labor spheres was increasing; if, in short, the state was championing the cause of women—what else then could the women's movement ask? This confusion was augmented by the lack of free dialogue in Iranian politics. The Pahlavi state's monopoly over women's organizations and the eventual dissolution of all women's organizations into the Women's Organization of Iran obliterated the possibility of grassroots women's movements. Lack of political freedom left little room for women to discuss their issues in open, public forums. Meanwhile, changing gender relations constantly challenged the daily arrangements of gender roles. The "private" problems of gender relations remained outside the political discourse. Accomplished women participated in political debates as sexless, politicized beings. That is why the numerous women active in science, art, literature, and the like challenged the Pahlavi state on political grounds more strikingly than they have challenged Iranian-Islamic patriarchy. Save for a few exceptions like Forough Farrokhzad,[5] in most cases women intellectuals articulated their cause predominantly as politico-economic. Consequently, women participated in the anti-Shah movement with unfocused demands. They took part in the movement, but defined their participation and demands predominantly in terms of independence, freedom, and class equality. The woman question was considered a "natural" appendix to those demands. Women's activism emerged only after the newly established IRI launched its assault on women.

The revolution has profoundly changed the ideology and practice of all political groupings—the IRI, the women's movement, and the Left—regarding gender relations. Islamic gender analysis, as delineated in detail in chapter 6, presumes the world as a purposive system. An individual's sex is predefined with assigned roles, deemed different but complementary for men and women. Sexuality plays an important role in creating a harmonious world. Intimacy enhances happiness and tranquillity in a family and, more significantly, reproduces healthy human beings. Gender teleology thusly connects sex, gender, and sexuality. The mission of the Islamic state in Iran is to create proper conditions in which men and women can accomplish their holy duties. Since the family is regarded as a microcosmic society, the IRI has considered it pivotal to "strengthen the family," that is, to emphasize the primacy of the domestic role for women and secure men's position as heads of households.

Predefined gender identities have rigid models of private and public expression. The appearance of Muslim men and women is crucial for IRI ideologues, because it ensures the society's Islamic characteristics. The ideal gender look and behavior also creates a gender pyramid. In this hierarchy, devout men occupy the highest position; the more removed men are to this ideal male, the lower their position. Women are allotted a precarious status: collectively, they have less power and fewer rights than men, but Islamist women, especially those with political power, could wield considerable power over others, even non-Islamist men.

I argue in chapter 7 that the IRI initially attempted to shift gender relations in Iran back to a private patriarchy. Soon, however, the government realized the impracticality of that agenda. Women's massive resistance has proven too strong to dismiss. Furthermore, some structural changes in pre-revolutionary Iranian society have prohibited the implementation of many exclusionary policies. Finally, economic hardship under the IRI leaves no choice for many families other than reliance upon two incomes (and often, more than just one job per partner). As long as the Islamic regime is unable to meet these economic demands, it has no choice but to yield. Thus the initial *exclusionist-protectivist* orientation was replaced by a *segregationist-protectivist* approach. Both approaches are similar in their fundamental assumption that women need to be protected. To accomplish that, the latter proposes seclusion. The former, however, calls for a "safe," regulated social space for women. The new, Islamic household appears a gentler, kinder home. Popular guidelines for better homes and marriages emphasize the importance of paying attention to wives' economic, emotional, and sexual needs. The goal is to create a family life attractive enough for women to either prefer to stay home, or at least value the "sanctity of the family."

There has been a decline in women's overall labor force participation in the IRI. An increase in women's participation in unpaid family labor has led to a considerable decline in women's employment in rural areas. The more the market moves toward skilled labor, the fewer the employment opportunities for rural and urban poor women. While skilled laborers of the industrial sector have a low share of the employment, government workers, particularly teachers, maintain the highest employment rate among workingwomen.

Women's political participation in IRI politics is at best tensional, especially because sexuality and domesticity cause restraints for women's political participation and make their determination questionable. The IRI has mobilized lower- and middle-class women into street politics, especially in using a "sentimental connection" to gain support for the war against Iraq. The Islamic regime has also involved a limited number of women in formal politics, a considerable number of whom are relatives of Islamist statesmen. A number of nongovernmental organizations (NGOs) have emerged after the 1995 Beijing conference. Most NGOs, however, are state-sponsored and activists express concern about the autonomy and freedom of action of these organizations.

As argued earlier in this chapter, the social construction of sexuality entails control over individuals, especially women, in private and public. "Proper" gender behavior often requires close monitoring of sexuality. In the IRI, popular resistance to Islamist ideals has made coercion integral to gender relations. Gender policing—preoccupation with men's and women's appearance and behavior—and sexual policing—ensuring the legitimacy of sexual contacts—have been intertwined. The restrengthening of men's power within the family justifies family violence, and in particular, spousal abuse. Furthermore, imposing Islamists' rigid conception of gender on a heterogeneous population that includes different shades of Muslims, non-believers, and non-Muslims has proved impossible without the use of overt force. Post-revolutionary Iran has been the scene of contentions between Islamists and the public over major issues of human rights and democratic freedom as well as such minute details as wearing sunglasses or make-up, or the interaction between men and women. The hejâb especially has turned into a battleground. Women have resisted the regime's stringent dress code, negotiating dress color and style. Though the ambiguity of Islamic law on "proper hejâb" creates possibilities for negotiating "proper gender behavior," it also puts women in a vulnerable position as the definition of "acceptable dress" could change easily. Especially at times of political or economic crises, the IRI has used this uncertainty to increase pressure on women as a symbol of its prowess.

To be sure, the IRI is not a cohesive system; there are many discrepancies among officials regarding gender policies. But what divides them is rather less significant than their commonalities. These commonalities include the determination of keeping women, women and men, men; maintaining the patriarchal family; upholding a patriarchal moral order; and assigning exclusive gendered spheres—be it in social or spatial settings, or both. These concerns are pursued through a union among patriarchy, Islam, and the state, as I discuss in chapter 4. This patriarchal triad aims to restrengthen men's position in family and society through a traditional sexual division of labor in which genders are defined as complementary opposites.

No component of the patriarchal triad is static or monolithic. Quite to the contrary, as my discussion shows, each is a dynamic historical institution. Women can at certain historical junctures pressure one or the other institution to "serve" in their interests. The "moderate" faction of the Islamic state claims to favor a more active social and political role for women. These proposals are backed by some IRI theologians who call for provisions that afford women higher degrees of mobility and social presence not available in the stricter interpretations of their fellow Islamists. Though the women's movement should–and indeed does–benefit from these cracks and fissures in the patriarchal structure, it is nonetheless imperative not to substitute these limited benefits for the far-reaching goal of eradicating the male supremacy of the patriarchal triad. Experiences in other parts of the world (see e.g., Ray 1999: 146–148) and in Iran prove that states can—and indeed do—co-opt demands of the women's movement, and amend and modify existing laws, without effecting any qualitative difference.

The success of the Islamization of gender is not uniform. The Islamic regime has been relatively successful among the faithful, especially in rural areas or among urban lower classes. The safety of a sex-segregated Islamic society for women of these groups has meant new opportunities. Firm believers, for instance, who refused to send their daughters to Pahlavis' educational centers, now feel more comfortable with female education. Furthermore, as in other revolutions, the Islamic revolution has effected the emergence of new political and social spaces into which an unprecedented stream of popular mobilization is channeled. Skocpol (1994) argues that revolutionary states are particularly apt in mobilizing their popular supporters in warfare. In the Islamic Republic of Iran, too, women believers were mobilized to promote the political agenda of the state, especially in displaying support for the Iran-Iraq war. Nonetheless, coming to terms with Islamic gender ideology is not easy, even for Islamist women (see *Emerging Voices*). These women are elated by a rhetoric that claims acceptance of women's capabilities and promises to elevate their status in society. In practice, however, these believers face the limitations of a gender ideology that rests on fundamentally patriarchal premises. Among the rural or urban poor, this conflict becomes more pronounced for younger women as their access to education and new social experiences increases their expectations.

The Islamic revolution was supposed to create an Islamic republic; it was supposed to enjoy the active consent of the majority of the population. By that standard, the experience of the IRI has been a failure. I contend in *Emerging Voices* that, since its inception, the IRI has had to deal with considerable popular resistance. Even when systematic challenges to the state's legitimacy have been absent, a considerable portion of the population has always demonstrated a disbelief in and rejection of the IRI—in toto or otherwise—to create an oppositional atmosphere. By oppositional atmosphere, I mean a rejection by the public of the dominant politico-cultural structure.[6] That attitude, however, is disorganized and does not have a uniform, institutionalized, or nationwide formal representation. Periodic strikes by various social groups, episodic social protests, daily forms of resistance in such social sites as schools and workplaces, and the struggle over symbolic means are all "weapons of the weak" (Scott 1985) and diverse manifestations of the oppositional atmosphere. This oppositional view can be expressed through a variety of media, including "off the record" comments, jests, cynicism, clothing styles or other appearance attributes, ideas expressed in private, underground literature, or the "subversive" flow of information between inside and outside.

Also, a new stratum of upper class has emerged under the IRI with considerable economic and political strength. These people call for a more active public presence for women and relaxing the control over them in segregated spaces. While disapproving of the "immorality" and "laxness" of the Pahlavi upper class, the Islamist upper class is interested in Western commodities and such leisure activities as skiing, horseback riding, and wearing brand-name clothes—pastimes previously denounced as decadent. These men and women, then, have a conflictual relation with the more orthodox interpreters of Islam(ism).

The IRI's seemingly paradoxical ineffectual victory is rooted in the ambivalence of gender relations in pre-revolutionary Iran. Standing at the edge of a transitory movement, the hegemonic culture of the Pahlavi Iran contained both residual and emergent trends, both resistance against and support for developing gender relations. If there were concerns for the "virtue of Iranian woman," there was also increasing understanding, at least among the educated urban population, that men and women could work side by side without having the ignitable interaction of, as a Farsi saying puts it, "fire and cotton ball." If there were concerns for "women's modesty," there was also acceptance—even encouragement–of women's unveiledness. If there were concerns about promoting "authentic Iranian values," there was also acceptance of Western fashion.

These "contradictory" tendencies account for much of the confusion and ambivalence of anti-Shah activists during the revolution; to a great extent, these contradictions also explain the gender politics of post-revolutionary Iran. Among the urban middle and upper classes (that is, the non-Islamist upper class), Islamic policies have limited appeal. Women show their resentment of and resistance to hejâb on a daily basis. The severity of punishment for transgression indicates the limited appeal of the Islamic ideology among a significant portion of urban dwellers, particularly those in metropolitan cities. Thus, in discussing gender politics under the IRI, we need to distinguish between dominant and hegemonic cultures. Though Islamists share some beliefs, norms, and values with many Iranians, their dominance is achieved through the imposition of their ideals on society—and, at least so far, with the use of brutal force.

RECAPITULATION

In this chapter, I provided a general overview of the theoretical foundations of my work. Culture—historically accumulated and transmitted patterns of symbols and meanings—is an indispensable productive social force, blended in the totality of social life. Culture enables us to interpret our surroundings, rendering them meaningful and intelligible. Like a switch operator, culture leads us to define and pursue our interests along certain tracks. Though all social groups participate in the making of cultures, all do not have equal power in shaping their content and development. Social groups that control economic production and have political leverage often also control the means of cultural production. Cultural politics refers to the process of incessant conflict between dominant and oppositional cultures for gaining hegemonic power. Both residual and emergent cultures oppose dominant cultural patterns; the former, to ensure the continuous validity of cultural and social residues; the latter, to secure the development of new socio-cultural lives.

Dominant groups can attain cultural hegemony when they enjoy the active consent of a major segment of the population. Consequently, certain fundamental beliefs about society, economy, polity, morality, and culture appear as "natural." The persistence of dominant culture, in other words, lies in "common sense," popular beliefs, and language. These domains become crucial terrains of social struggle. For a movement to claim victory, it is essential to define its continuity with and separation from popular beliefs. Movements must be concerned not only with political processes, but also with language, common beliefs, and values—in a word, culture.

I emphasize a distinction between hegemony and dominance in cultural fields. While hegemony involves consent, dominance is achieved through overt and covert coercion. To be sure, just as hegemony entails force, dominance also relies on popular beliefs. Yet it also forces cultural patterns that differ or oppose popular consensus. Though cultural dominance depends on force, it may not withstand popular resistance. On the other hand, dominance can also be prolonged through hegemony by resignation—giving up the search for alternative social orders.

Gender functions dialectically with culture and society. Culture shapes the context within which gender is defined. Culture also provides us with the tools to articulate gender identities and act out gender roles. Gender refers to cultural ideals that normatively order social interaction on the basis of socially defined masculinity and femininity. Gender also involves organizations and institutions. Thus, gender plays an important role in stratifying society. Embedded in all private and public institutions, gender is a key component of socio-cultural existence. While social policies regulate access to resources, gender, along with such other social institutions as class, race, and ethnicity, defines priorities for the allocation of resources.

Gender is teleological: it projects models of ideal man- and womanhood, operating as if such ideals exist. Through this mechanism, hierarchies are established both between genders and among members of each gender. Yet socially acceptable gender identity is never completely realized; "ideal genders" are continuously contested. Gender involves coercion, be it overt or covert. A particularly significant form of coercion is symbolic, involving the presentation of gender as a "natural," inescapable differentiation. To combat this perpetuation of social inequality, I propose to enhance our critique of gender beyond instances of unjust distribution of resources, and include the very coercive nature of gender.

Sexuality is a key player in the negotiation of gender identity and gender roles. As socio-historically defined ways of responding to and satisfying bodily desire, sexuality is a political field wherein individual choices and historical circumstances converge. I particularly emphasize the dialectical relationship between enforcing "proper" gender and "proper" sexuality. Sexuality, and, more specifically, heterosexuality, reproduces gender differentiation by predefining "normal" sexuality between members of two "different," even "opposite," sexes. Sexuality is also intertwined with symbolic representation of nationality. Class similarly plays a crucial role in creating sexuality. Classes define respective sexualities differently. But social class does more than give differing expressions to sexualities; it also regulates how sexualities are defined and shaped. "Class scare" has an important function here: it uses the fear of losing class status to ward off "deviant" sexual expressions. Sexual "deviation" is associated with the unruly practices of lower classes that, if not regulated, could bring anarchy to the "respectable" and "safe" mainstream society.

Gender and sexuality perform in historically specific structures. I discussed private and public patriarchy as two forms of patriarchal structures. Both are structures of male control, but through different mechanisms. In private patriarchy, women are primarily confined to domestic production and controlled by specific men. Women's seclusion in the private sphere is replaced by their segregation in certain fields and levels of social activities in a public patriarchy. Male control over women is exerted not only through individual men, but, more importantly, through such public channels as the state or the media. Patriarchal domination is countered by women's resistance, resulting in bargains that delineate men's and women's responsibilities and entitlements. Women gain some assurance of relative well-being under male domination through patriarchal bargain. But this "agreement" also produces a false impression that the status quo reflects the interests of men and women equally, that the patriarchal system is functional, though unfortunate "instances" of abusing power may occur.

A shift in patriarchal relations from private to public threatens men's and some women's privileges and values. Men experience a loss of control, though for many women, the demise of private patriarchy marks the opening of new avenues of opportunity. For others, these changes mean losing the status and protection they have had in the traditional bargain, without benefiting from emerging gender relations. Some women have become active participants in right-wing movements that aim, among other things, to restrengthen the patriarchal family.

Just like private patriarchy, public patriarchy functions on the basis of a bargain. The modern bargain concedes women's qualified public presence and their relative autonomy, as long as changes in gender relations do not undermine patriarchal domination in its entirety. Patriarchy recognizes sexual injustices and undertakes to increase women's social and economic roles to even higher echelons of political and economic institutions. But these policies affect only some women, since recognition of sexual inequality is not accompanied by a commitment to distributive justice.

In the chapters that follow, I will analyze gender relations in Iran using the theoretical framework delineated in this chapter. I will emphasize the tensions of refashioning patriarchy from private to public. Chapter 2 describes the refashioning of patriarchy from private to public forms under the Pahlavi monarchs. The changes can be summed up as the attainment of liberal feminist ideals, ideals that have been taken up once again by reformist Islamist women. Chapter 3 delineates Islamic reactions to changing gender relations of the Pahlavis, particularly following the reforms of the 1960s. Gender politics in the revolutionary days is taken up in chapter 4, where I emphasize women's mobilization and the immediate consequences of the rise of the IRI for women. Chapter 5 assesses the strengths and weaknesses of the Left's gender and cultural politics. Gender relations in the Islamic Republic are traced in chapters 6 and 7. First I limn the articulation of gender and sexuality in post-revolutionary Iran, arguing the centrality of coercion in the Islamization of the society. Then I study vacillations in the IRI's gender policies concerning employment, education, and politics. I will discuss struggles against patriarchy in *Women in Iran: Emerging Voices in the Women's Movement*.

NOTES

1. These systems have obvious differences, most notably the key role extended family plays in "classic patriarchy" in determining inter- and intragenerational and gender relations. Resemblance, in other words, does not denote sameness.

2. Kandiyoti (1988) compares sub-Saharan African women's strategy of autonomy and protest with Middle Eastern women's subservient and manipulative tac-

tics. Different socio-historical circumstances, she contends, made each strategy plausible for the women of these societies.

3. On movements reacting to feminism, see Chafetz (1989).

4. Studies of other Middle Eastern societies reflect a similar trend. For examples, see Davis (1993) and Shaaban (1991).

5. Forugh Farrokhzad (1935–1967), a leading figure of modern Iranian poetry, discussed emotions, sexuality, and intellectual concerns in her poetry.

6. My reference to the "oppositional atmosphere" is inspired by Marshal and Orum's discussion of the "climates of opinion." Based on C. Wright Mills' argument that the power of the United States ruling elite in the post–World War II era was in part preserved due to the "prevailing public mood about nuclear war," Marshal and Orum refer to public moods or "climates of opinion" influencing policies that affected the women's movement in the United States (Marshall and Orum 1986: 22). Though "difficult to assess in detail," they contend, climates of opinion "carry considerable weight, and serve to influence the actions of even the most independent of legislators." "Oppositional atmosphere" refers to a similar phenomenon.

2

Refashioning Patriarchy: From Private toward Public Patriarchy

I am referring here to the Iranian woman of the past who, as some stories testify, was at least a good housekeeper, understood kindness and purity, or at least sacrificed herself selflessly for those dear to her. Today's woman is even losing these simple humane characteristics; she has learned from the West how to be indiscriminate *(be-band o bâr)* and totally out of control *(lejâm gosikhteh)*. After she put aside her *châdor*, she has taken a leap with the least authentic face in order to catch up with the front line of cultured women of the world; and we can see how after her leap . . . she has fallen to an absurd and meaningless abyss and slime has been covering her.

The nostalgic disappointment of the poet, novelist, and literary critic Reza Baraheni (1972: 16) voices a common assessment of women's conditions in pre-revolutionary Iran. Critics of both religious and secular wings viewed the changes in gender relations with considerable suspicion. Were legal provisions against polygyny, unilateral divorce by men, or early marriage positive steps toward a better society, or merely superficial reforms to promote the Shah's persona as a modernizer? Was women's increasing access to education beneficial for them, or simply a ploy to make Iran further dependent on the West? Neither secular nor religious oppositional forces had uniform answers to these questions, of course. Nonetheless, they shared a deep distrust of governmental policies. The changes were dismissed as icing on the cake. The opposition charged that little had changed, for the reforms had little impact on subaltern women. Indeed, the opposition deemed a dictatorial regime incapable of implementing positive measures.

At the other end of the political spectrum, advocates of the monarchy praised both Pahlavi monarchs for "emancipating" Iranian women. The reign of the Pahlavis entailed a steady procession of women toward freedom, or more accurately, a steady procession of women *being led* toward freedom. The position of women alone, they argued, was solid proof that the Pahlavis would lead Iran, as Mohammad Reza Shah himself put it, to "the gates of great civilization."

Contrary to the denial of the opposition, the changes were real. Yet despite the jubilation of the royalists, the changes were by no means extensive or fundamental enough to "emancipate" women. Neither Pahlavi king had such an agenda. It was hardly Reza Shah's intention to do away with the sexual division of labor; nor did he believe the abolition of this kind of division of labor beneficial to women and society. His son best describes his idea of emancipation:

Reza Shah never advocated a complete break with the past, for always he assumed that our girls could find their best fulfillment in marriage and in the nurture of superior children. But he was convinced that a girl could be a better wife and mother, as well as a better citizen, if she received an education and perhaps worked outside the home long enough to gain a sense of civic functions and responsibilities. (Pahlavi 1961: 231)

Insofar as the last Pahlavi king is concerned, he himself, in an interview with Oriana Fallaci, said that in his opinion women's accomplishments throughout history amount to nothing: never have they offered humanity a single great personality—not even "a great chef" (Fallaci 1976: 272).

Yet the change was real. Gradually, but steadily, women were shifting the boundaries of gender roles and assuming an undeniable presence in public life. Education opened new avenues of self-expression for middle- and upper-class women. These women had to improvise and innovate methods of manipulation of, adaptation to, or outright confrontation with age-old internal and external convictions in a changing environment both as students and as skilled laborers. Despite the limitations through discriminatory policies, many women attained preeminent positions in science, humanities, literature, and art.

Forugh Farrokhzad has been by far the most controversial figure of contemporary Persian literature. Her poetry was a candid testimony of her independent and rebellious personality. The free expression of sexuality in her first three books created much uproar among her readers. Love and sexuality, of course, are no strangers to Persian poetry. This time, however, a *woman* was boldly admitting that she not only has a sexual self—that is, she presented *female* sexuality to Persian poetry—but was also willing to commit "sin" in order to gratify her desire (Hillman 1987; Milani 1992).

Women's creativity was not limited to poetry. Simin Daneshvar, Shahrnoush Parssipour, and Mahshid Amir-Shahi are among the well-known short story writers and novelists of contemporary Iran. Mehri Âhi and Lili Golestân have translated Dostoyevsky, Turgenev, Lermontev, Oriana Fallaci, and García Márquez into Persian.

In music, for instance, pop singers like Pourân, Elâheh, Googoosh, Râmesh, and Giti had an undeniable and, to date, unsurpassed presence. Sheidâ Gharache-Dâqi, Pari Zanganeh, Simâ Binâ, Parissâ, and Hengâmeh Akhavân followed the example of their predecessors such as Ghamar, Marzieh, and Delkash, and established themselves as serious performers of classical Iranian music. In cinema and theater, too, attention should be paid to women actresses like Farzaneh Ta'idi and Fakhri Khorvash. Farzaneh Ta'idi performed in over eighty movies and plays and received awards for her acting. Her critical views on the cinema industry's exploitation of women became known through her numerous interviews. In an exclusive with the widely circulated daily, *Ettella'at*, for example, she criticized Iranian cinema for presenting "an insulting picture of Iranian women" (Golestan 1988). Among others, attention should also be paid to Mahin Oskoo'i. Oskoo'i studied theater in Moscow and founded the famous Anahita Theater after her return to Iran.

Among academicians one can refer to Homa Nategh and Simin Daneshvar, to name but two nationally revered examples. Daneshvar taught aesthetics at the School of Music, the School of Fine Arts, and the University of Tehran. She published essays, short stories, a novel, and served on the editorial boards of several journals. Daneshvar has also translated several novels and plays into Persian, including the works of Chekhov, Shaw, Paton, and Schnitzler. Nategh was a history professor at the University of Tehran. Though she intended to avoid politics on the university scene, she realized that the scope of censorship in Iran was broad enough to include even her analysis of Iran's history. Muslim fundamentalists called for her dismissal when she referred to the nineteenth century Babi movement as progressive and revolutionary. Shortly after, she published *Az Mast keh bar Mast* (*No One to Blame But Ourselves*) in which she discussed Iranian intellectual history during the Qajar period and criticized the religious attack on critical thinking and modernity. The book caused the rage and furor of the traditionalist scholars and provoked libelous articles in national newspapers.

I will discuss in this chapter how the sixties' reforms in gender relations, part of the so-called White Revolution of the Shah and the People, were to refashion Iranian patriarchy. I use Sylvia Walby's private and public patriarchy models, discussed in chapter 1. I do not intend, however, to present a systematic discussion of Iranian patriarchy here, nor do I follow the specific structures identified by Walby. What will follow is not a comprehensive account of the patriarchal structures in Iran; it is rather a sketch of the changing gender relations in Iran in order to highlight the refashioning of Iranian patriarchy in the decades preceding the 1979 revolution. I will argue that educational, labor, and legal reforms gave women easier access to the public sphere and afforded them greater mobility. These measures also challenged men's patriarchal prerogatives in the family and society and brought family relations more under the control of the state.

Changes in women's participation in the formal sector of the economy and their increasing access to education similarly challenged the exclusive control of the patriarchal family over women. Still, *emerging relations had instead subjected women to new forms of patriarchal control.* These changes, then, profoundly affected how men and women related in their daily lives as well as in public. As opportunities arose for new gender relations, "assumed" rights and responsibilities of men and women were questioned; certainties of the past gave way to ambiguities of the future. These developments led to a crisis in the "traditional patriarchal bargain," based on which "good women," that is, those who have complied with the traditional sexual division of labor and the social codes of virtue, would have men's respect and protection.

A NOTE ON PRIVATE AND PUBLIC PATRIARCHY

The refashioning of patriarchy in Iran was neither conspiratorial nor emancipatory. It involved, rather, what Walby (1994) calls a transformation of patriarchy from "private" to "public." Though her work is based on the example of Great Britain, Walby's approach to patriarchy as "a system of social structures and practices in which men dominate, oppress and exploit women" (20), a system composed of multiple structures, grants us a way out of the dichotomy of progress or regress. Regarding the political discourse of pre-revolutionary Iran, Walby's approach enables us to go beyond labeling reforms emancipatory or superficial and allows us to see patriarchy as more than a specific arrangement of, say, labor force, education, or sexuality. I am particularly critical of equating increase in women's socio-economic roles with women's emancipation. Both the proponents of the Pahlavi regime and its opponents—especially among the Left—shared this vision. Advocates and critics alike considered that educated, employed women symbolized progress, regardless of the sexual division of labor within the family, male violence against women, women's control over their sexualities, and the persistence of patriarchal norms and values. Monarchists accentuated women's gains to laud the services of the Pahlavi kings; opponents dismissed the changes to justify opposition.

After the fall of the monarchy, one confusion among the Left related to classifying various political forces in binary categories of "progressive" and "reactionary." "Progressives" supported women's social roles, "reactionaries" wanted women confined to domestic chores. But this classification only created further quandary: where does the Shah fit in this assortment? To avoid condoning the Shah, activists had to resort to another explanation that identified gender inequality as a "superstructural" problem, that is, the spread of the imperialist culture, or the Pahlavis' leniency toward traditional beliefs.

THE "WHITE REVOLUTION" AND WOMEN

In the early 1960s, the Shah solicited the United States for assistance in response to a heightening economic crisis. The impending election, however, made the White House extremely cautious, particularly because the Democratic Party was critical of the Republicans' support of the corrupt regimes in the Third World. To the Shah's dismay, Nixon lost the election and John F. Kennedy moved into the White House in 1961. The new administration was not willing to extend its support of the Shah unless signs of "liberalization" became apparent (see Bill 1988: 131–53; Katouzian 1981: 213–33). The combination of these political economic factors forced the Shah to implement some overdue reforms. In January 1963, the Shah announced the six-point series of reforms. On January 26, 1963, the series was put to vote and, not surprisingly, 90% of the population voted in its favor—and hence the names: "The Shah's and People's Revolution" and "The White Revolution." The fifth point of the program was the enfranchisement of women. Women "participated" in the "national referendum" (the government referred to their wholehearted participation, though their vote had no legal worth) (Bamdad 1977: 118; *Iran Almanac* 1977: 528).

During the sixties, three concomitant initiatives in education, labor policies, and jurisprudence offered women a progressively higher share of the public sphere under the Pahlavis. Women found more opportunity to pursue professional careers than they had previously. As the revolution of 1979 approached, nearly 2,000 women were employed as teachers in institutes of higher education and universities, 800 as engineers. Women composed one-twentieth of the skilled workers in factories and one-third of the nation's college students. There were additionally significant numbers of female doctors and writers—though here, as in all fields, those numbers proved disproportional to the population. I will outline below these general trends.

EDUCATING WOMEN FOR THE PUBLIC SPHERE

The right to an education has been a major demand of the Iranian women's movement from its formative days in the mid-nineteenth century. Women activists considered access to education a vital means for overcoming social barriers. Limited numbers of women did receive formal education either through their relatives or by going to *maktab*, the traditional school in which boys, and occasionally girls, learned reading and writing. Readings included classical Persian literature, the Koran, and other religious texts (Bamdad 1977: 19–22). The transformation of Iranian education to a modern school system began with the vote of the Parliament in 1926 to devote one half of one percent of land revenues for public elementary education. Though girls did not receive a fair share, the change was notable. According to Colliver Rice, there were 1,200 girls in 10 free primary schools by the early 1920s (1923: 154). According to *Le Journal de Teheran* (18 Feb. 1936), by the early 1930s, that number rose to some 50,000 students enrolled in about 870 schools (quoted in Woodsmall 1983, 146). Most schools were private and founded by liberal intellectuals who believed education to be a necessary step toward women's emancipation (Sanasarian 1982: 61). The University of Tehran, the first Iranian university, was established in 1934. Two years later, the first group of Iranian women enrolled in an institution of higher education.

A similar trend existed during Mohammad Reza Shah's reign. According to the *Population Census of 1956* and *Population Census of 1966*, the literacy rate among girls seven and older rose from 7.3% in 1956 to 18% in 1966; the literacy rate rose drastically among urban women, from 20% to about 40% in one decade. In rural areas, however, changes in women's literacy occurred at a much slower pace—in 1966, less than five percent of rural women were literate as opposed to one percent in 1956. The improvement in literacy among rural men was much higher. The literate rural male population increased from 11% in 1956 to about 26% in 1966. In 1971, close to half of the urban women were literate, as opposed to less than 10% of the rural women. The literacy rate was about 70% among urban men, compared to less than 32% among rural men (sample survey of 1971). In the academic year of 1973–74, girls constituted some 38% of all primary school students. A more considerable change occurred in the women's share of secondary education—from less than 25% in the academic year of 1955–56 to over 35% in the academic year of 1973–74. During the same period, the number of girl students multiplied by 14 times—from 40,454 to 587,556.

The sharpest increase occurred in teacher training programs, from 12% in the academic year of 1955–56 to 51% in 1973–74. This drastic change had a pronounced impact on the sexual composition of the teaching profession. By the mid-1970s, more than half of the primary school teachers and about thirty percent of the guidance (junior high) and secondary school teachers were women.

The sexual composition of college students remained relatively the same from 1968 to 1975. In the 1968–69 academic year, women constituted 26% of the total 58,000 students. The ratio reached its highest in the 1972–73 academic year (29.9% of the 115,000 students).[1] In 1974, women accounted for 49% of the total number of graduates in medicine. In law, humanities, education, and natural sciences and mathematics, female students had a significant share. Women's entry into other areas rose steadily.

The percentage of women who studied engineering doubled from four percent to eight percent between 1971 and 1974. Some 28% of law students in 1974 were female.

Women's share of education, nonetheless, was far from satisfactory. In the mid-1970s, less than 35% of girls of school age attended school, of whom only 25% would receive a high school education.[2] Still fewer would succeed in getting a higher education. According to a report prepared for the Women's Organization of Iran, "at best, only 1 in 7 and as few as 1 in 10 doctors in the country are women; of 12,000 existing engineers whose sex is known, less than 350 are women; out of nearly 1,900 lawyers only 316 are women" (Kayhan Research Associates 1975: 8). Women's higher education followed the traditional sex role. In the 1973–74 academic year, for instance, 40% of all women graduates majored in human sciences, constituting 53% of students majoring in human sciences. Natural sciences and mathematics numbered second, with 17% of all female graduates and 40% of all students in these fields. Agriculture and law had the lowest ratio of female graduates (close to one percent each; about ten percent of all agriculture students and 28% of all the law students).[3] Women were barred from studying mineralogy.

According to the data for the academic year of 1974–75, women were also underrepresented in the teaching staffs of institutes of higher education. Although nearly half the teachers in the pre-college level were women, in colleges women constituted less than one-fifth of full-time professors and about 12% of part-time and hourly faculty members. In the same academic year, however, nearly 35% of all college students were women.

Despite its limitations, the trend of women's education clearly indicates increasing access to the public sphere, be it as "educated" spouses and mothers or as members of a modern society gaining qualification to participate in its affairs.

WOMEN IN THE FORMAL ECONOMY

The gradual decay of the traditional economy and rapid expansion of capitalism after the reforms of 1962 increased women's participation in the formal sector of the economy. Data prepared by the Plan Organization indicate that from 1956 to 1972 the number of workingwomen increased by about two-and-a-half times, from 573,000 to 1,400,000. Following the Fifth National Labor Conference in 1974, the Ministry of Labor was required to provide equal employment for men and women. The Women's Organization of Iran was to assist the Ministry in implementing this policy as well as providing women with vocational training and determining their labor skills (*Iran Almanac* 1975: 417).

Out of Iran's 33,581,000 estimated population in 1975, 16,374,000 were women (49%). In the same year, the number of employed women was 1,775,000, the majority of whom were employed in agriculture (1,084,000). Women's participation in dentistry, law, and engineering was the lowest—248, 316, and 350 women respectively (*Iran Almanac* 1976: 351). Some 490,000 women were engaged in various forms of industrial activities. Over 85,000 were employed in government services. Seventy-four thousand women were self-employed. Fifty-five thousand were schoolteachers and over 1,500 were university professors. Though the nursing profession was mostly staffed by women (20,100 women nurses), only 880 women were employed in other aspects of the medical profession. The percentage of workingwomen in the economically active female population (women ten years and over) also increased. In 1956 some nine percent of the economically active female population was employed. According to the 1966 Census Report, this percentage increased to over 12 in 1966 and was expected to exceed 14 in 1978.[4] This percentage is indubitably lower than the real percentage, for although a sizable portion of women work on the farms, their participation is rarely recognized.[5]

Women's entry into different branches of the formal economy was by no means uniform. In 1972, approximately 500,000 women were employed in industry, mining, and transportation.[6] Composing almost two-thirds of the economically active female population, they were mainly concentrated in areas such as textile, clothing, food industries, packing, and electronics, which were continuations of traditional sex roles.

The service area likewise absorbed female labor. Secretaries and clerks accounted for the major portion of this category of female workers. Women did, however, staff shops, department stores, and supermarkets. Their participation in marketing, traveling, and tourism also increased. The service sector, despite ranking second in number of female employees, boasted the major *increase* in number of women employed; while the number of women in the social and domestic services rose from about 55,000 in 1966 to almost 225,000 in 1976, numbers in industrial activities rose by merely 2,000 (140,000 to 142,000 in respective years).

The teaching profession also attracted many women, as mentioned earlier. Nursing was virtually an exclusively female profession. Women also worked as medical aides, laboratory assistants, data collectors, bookkeepers, and architectural and mechanical assistants.

The state retirement plan, which covered all government employees, made the state a favorable employer for decades.[7] The security of governmental employment gradually translated into a cultural value which inspired many people to seek employment with the government, even at a time when the government paid lower salaries than the private sector. Women's employment followed the same path and nearly 30% of all employed urban women were hired by the government.

There are no reliable data on wages and salaries. In her examination of women's employment in Iran, Kar (1994: 120) remarks on the existence of two general trends: first, a considerable increase in the overall wages and salaries in the one-and-a-half decades preceding the revolution; and second, a discrepancy between male and female wage increases. She suggests that younger women seemed to receive wages comparable to their male counterparts of the same age or experience—yet as the age of employees increased, so did the pay difference. These findings are credible, considering the general economic boost after OPEC (Organization of Petroleum Exporting Counties) and the legal provision that prohibited underpaying female employees. The growing pay difference as the years on the job increased could be attributed, as Kar herself suggests, to the difficulties women faced in climbing the occupational ladder.

The 1966 census reported over 22% of all economically active women employed in agriculture. This percentage decreased to about 11% in 1972, a drop indicative of both an alteration in the employment trend of Iranian women and a general shift away from agriculture toward the modern sector. According to the 1979 census, 20% of rural women were economically active, 67% were housewives, and the remaining were either unemployed, students, or provided with private income. These figures, as mentioned earlier, are much lower than the real percentage of rural women who, except among the rural elite, work until old age. This is, indeed, a reflection of the widespread opinion that only women who participate in cultivating and harvesting are economically active (Benería 1982). This factor became particularly important after the land reforms that forced many women to become engaged in unpaid family work. Moreover,

when the husband must answer for his wife during the census or other interviews, he may only perceive his own activity and may consider his wife as formally economically inactive since she is "only an unpaid family worker." Similarly, since she has not received wages for her labor, and most likely classifies her main activity as tending to her household and children, she may not perceive herself as being economically active. (Touba 1980: 55)

Inflation and the inability of fairly primitive agricultural industries to compete with the developed industries of the cities have caused the emigration of villagers to cities. More often than not, men's migration to urban areas left their women, children, and old relatives in a poor economic condition. According to the census of 1965, 6.5% of heads of families in Iran were women. 56% of these lived in villages, 44% in cities. Bad economic conditions also made women emigrate from rural to urban areas and work in the worst conditions. In a case example documented by the Fedaiin, a 13-year-old girl moved northwest from her hometown, Mashad in northern Iran, to Tabriz in search of a job. She made about 5,000 to 6,000 sun-dried bricks with her hands. She said: "My father and brothers brought me here because we are poor and all of us must work to earn enough money for the family" (OIPFG [Organisation of Iranian People's Fadaiin Guerrillas] 1979a: 64).

As the sketch above shows, the one-and-a-half decades preceding the 1979 revolution put a decisive end to the seclusion of women from the market. Women's presence in virtually all aspects of the economy increased. Though this increase might not appear substantial, the mere fact of the increase in women's participation tells much about changing gender relations in pre-revolutionary Iran, changes that later made it impossible for the IRI to implement exclusionist policies and to revive private patriarchy thoroughly. The seclusion of women was replaced by their segregation in the labor market: a considerable number of women were concentrated in a limited number of occupations, such as weaving and sewing, services, teaching, and nursing. These occupations extended the traditional sexual division of labor beyond the private sphere.

TOKEN WOMEN IN POLITICS

Women's presence in formal politics also rose after the 1960s. Here, too, a seclusionist policy was abandoned in favor of a segregationist one at once more compatible with modernization policies and more responsive to women's demands. Before women could claim a presence in formal politics, however, they needed to be recognized as a political entity, as citizens with the right to elect and be elected. Women demanded the right to vote for decades before they were "granted" the right as a component of the Shah's White Revolution. Women's right to vote was argued in the Second Majlis (the Iranian parliament) in 1909, and rejected due to stiff opposition by Muslim clergy.

In 1959 the Majlis once again debated the issue. This time, the Iranian government, in response to women lobbyists, initiated the dialogue. The government proved too weak, however, to withstand the combined opposition of the Muslim clergy and other conservative Majlis representatives. Realizing the weakness of the Parliament, Iranian women demanded a prime ministerial decree granting voting rights in provincial and town assembly elections. Yet the coalition of women and the Prime Minister still couldn't topple the opposition; the plan failed.

A series of events from 1959 onward encouraged the government to proceed with the fifth point of the reform. In 1959, the Iranian Majlis entered into a debate concerning women's right to vote. The combined opposition of the clergy and secular reactionary representatives forced the government to retreat. Three years later, in May 1962, a woman who was running for the Isfahan City Council was disqualified due to the pressure of traditionalists "even though the municipal election law as it stood at the time was unqualified (as in the Persian language) by any distinctions of gender" (Bamdad 1977: 116). Shortly after that incident, Prime Minister

Assadullah 'Alam issued a decree which granted women the right to not only vote but also run for provincial and town assemblies. But, "owing to the still strong influence of reactionary elements opposed to women's progress," the government postponed the implementation of the law.

With the failure of that gambit, the government utilized the various women's organizations to show women's dismay at the opposition to women's rights. Therefore, on January 7, 1963, under the auspices of the government, women's organizations refused to celebrate the occasion of unveiling by Reza Shah. Their notice of cancellation read:

In view of the continuing denial of legitimate rights to women, and in particular the government's failure to hold the local elections in which the right to vote has been given to women, the Women's Associations of Iran advise the male and female public that as a sign of protest the usual joyous celebration on 7 January will not now be held. (117)

On January 24, 1963, women teachers, women employed in the civil service and private institutions went on a one-day strike. The referendum of the Charter of the White Revolution was two days later. A few days after the referendum, women staged another demonstration in front of the Senate and demanded women's suffrage in all elections. The Shah accepted their demand.

In January 1963 women finally gained the right to vote. On 27 February, addressing an economic conference in Tehran, the Shah noted that although both Islam and Iran's Constitution emphasize women's rights, Iran ranked women with the insane and the criminal, and deprived them of their basic civil rights (*Iran Almanac* 1970: 528). Shortly thereafter, six women were elected to the Twenty-first Majlis and two were appointed to the senate. The first female Minister of Education was designated two years later, in 1965. In 1971, the first woman diplomat was deputized by the Iranian Ministry of Foreign Affairs to serve four years as an attaché in the Iranian embassy in Algeria (*Iran Almanac* 1972: 566). Even so, these were token appointments. Women were grossly underrepresented in high political offices, both as women and as one-fourth of the total government employees (*Iran Almanac* 1976: 351).

In October 1965, about 2,000 women from various women's organizations gathered at the first Iranian Women's Conference. The Conference called for thorough revisions in laws regarding marriage and divorce and demanded the annulment of laws that prohibited women from holding judicial offices. In 1966, the government, which was now gaining increasing power, supervised the dissolution of all women groups into a pro-government Women's Organization of Iran (WOI). The Shah's much-hated sister and an important figure in the coup of 1953, Ashraf Pahlavi, directed the WOI, and the Queen's mother served in the administrative cabinet. In so doing, the government sought to not only present a progressive image of itself to both national and international spectators, but also to control any opposition from the women.

When the 1979 revolution approached, women had token presence in various echelons of Iranian political life—from the judicial bench to ministerial posts. The trend shows once again a change in patriarchal policy from seclusion to inclusion, yet still with women's presence in formal politics only token and closely supervised.

STATE FEMINISM

The emergence of women in Iranian formal politics is tightly linked with the state effort to control and shape women's presence in society. One objective of the Pahlavi dynasty from inception entailed curbing any popular expression of will. In place of the genuine, grassroots women's organizations, Reza Shah organized a few state-administered women's groups. Kanoon-e Banovan (Women's Center), for example, was established and extensively funded by the Ministry of Culture in 1935. Reza Shah's daughters, Ashraf and Shams, were present in most of the meetings. There was no indication of any feminist demands in the activities of the Kanoon. The organization's goals included "mental and moral" education of women, instruction in child-care and housekeeping and philanthropic activities to support "indigent mothers and children having neither parent nor guardian" (Bamdad 1977: 93–94). The last women's organization to be closed by the government was the Tehran branch of the Patriotic Women's League in 1932 (see Sanasarian 1982: especially 67).

The vacuum of power following Reza Shah's abdication in 1941 gave a breathing space to progressive forces. Besides the Women's League, which in the absence of its royal patron became progressively isolated, a few women's organizations came into existence. But the coup d'état of 1953 brought with itself a new reign of terror and suppression. Heavily supported by the United States after a CIA-engineered coup, Mohammad Reza Shah gained the upper hand following a decade of challenge between the court, the clergy, nationalists, and leftists.[8] A massive wave of repression and persecution swept the nation. The subsequent consolidation of power by the Shah meant the end of any organized popular movement for years to come. As Sanasarian correctly characterized this stage of the women's movement,

The women's rights movement entered an institutionalized and legitimate sphere of activity in which demands were still made upon the authorities, but in this instance the changes asked for were in accordance with the ones received. In other words, women's organizations did not make demands that could not or would not be met;

their activities were quite compatible with the government's stand. (Sanasarian 1982: 79)

The women's organizations which came into existence in years immediately after the coup were either charity societies (the Charity Association of the Shah's second wife, Soraya, or the Welfare Council for Women and Children)[9] or professional associations (Iranian Women's Medical Association and Iranian Nurses Association).[10] A couple of the old organizations also continued their activity, but they had to change their names to conceal their past. Nevertheless, the government was not content even with the limited independence that these organizations enjoyed and tried to exercise ultimate control over them. Three years after the coup, fourteen organizations joined and established the Federation of Women's Organizations which "served as the center of contact for exchange of information, joint planning of lectures, meetings with visiting leaders and consultants" (Woodsmall 1960: 77). In 1959, seventeen organizations joined to form Showray-e 'Aly-e Jam'iyat-e Zanan-e Iran (The High Council of Iranian Women's Associations). The High Council replaced the Federation, with the Shah's twin sister, Ashraf, as its honorary president. At this point women's organizations still maintained a legal status provided they accepted the leadership of the High Council and became a joint member. The activities of the High Council, like those of its predecessors, revolved around charity works (though on paper it was also supposed to provide opportunities for better education of women by forming special classes and training women to staff them, and by establishing rehabilitation facilities for female ex-prisoners).

In 1966 the High Council was replaced by Sazeman-e Zanan-e Iran, The Women's Organization of Iran (WOI), chartered to raise women's status and advise them on their rights and social duties. The Organization was also responsible for assisting Iranian women in carrying out "their social responsibilities and in playing the important role of a woman as a mother and wife" (*Iran Almanac* 1972: 569; WOI n.d.). It coordinated women's economic, cultural and social activities, especially in the fields of education (including the campaign against illiteracy). The WOI functioned further as the liaison with international organizations like International Association of Women Lawyers, International Association of Teachers-Parents, International Women's Club, International Council of Jewish Women, and National Society for United Nations.

During the 1970s, the Organization lobbied for significant reforms, particularly in family law. It pushed for increased financial support for divorced and abandoned women, higher inheritance shares for females, revised custody rights, and restrictions on polygamy. It campaigned against laws restricting women's freedom, like the Passport Law requiring married women to present permission from their husbands before leaving the country. The Organization reported, further, that even existing laws, such as that which guaranteed comparable wages, were not being enforced.

Whether the WOI initially proposed these reforms or simply followed behind the government's desire, it enjoyed the government's permission and stamp of approval. It was especially vital for the Organization to have the approval of the Shah since, as Mahnaz Afkhami, the Secretary General of WOI puts it, convincing the Shah was always "one phase of legal action" (Afkhami 1984: 333).

The WOI had no intention of undermining the patriarchal authority of men. In effect, its discussions were based on the assumptions of the traditional sex roles. One WOI legal counselor, for instance, in her discussion of a couple's mutual marital obligations approvingly quotes Islamic edicts and limits her criticisms of the law to lack of proper wordings and adequate provisions. If, as Sanasarian claims (1982: 89), there were "a few feminists" in the Organization, their feminist convictions and demands should be considered as aberrant with no substantial bearing on the overall practices of the Organization.

The Organization set up a network of Family Welfare Centers in 1967 to provide services for women in the areas of education, health, day-care and legal counseling. According to official sources, in 1975–76, over 100,000 women completed literacy and vocational classes in these centers (*Iran Almanac* 1977: 422). There were also about 120,000 reported visits to family planning clinics in 1974 and over 70,000 in the first six months of 1975 (WOI n.d.: 4). In 1974, the Organization undertook a yearlong functional literacy experimental project. The Saveh Functional Literacy Project was to teach women reading and writing as well as know-how in areas such as agriculture and home economics (Homayunpour 1975).

In 1969 the Organization additionally established a School of Social Work at Varamin, a neighboring town of Tehran. The SSW offered a degree equivalent to an Associate of Arts degree. About 100 students graduated from this school each year.

The WOI also undertook research about various aspects of women's life in employment, environment, and education. Its studies discerned that though an increasing number of women joined the workforce, only a small percentage (13%) were gainfully employed, with a great portion of these concentrated in the traditional "female" fields: handicrafts, weaving, agriculture and secretarial work. On January 2, 1976, the twelfth regional seminar of the Organization passed a resolution calling for equal pay for women as well as full implementation of the compulsory educational law. It also called for an alteration in the content of textbooks regarding sex roles (Homayunpour 1975).

That said, it is important to bear in mind that the Organization could never afford even the above mild criticism of the regime had it not had the permission of the establishment. An appendage of the establishment, it lacked the militancy of a grassroots women's organization. Its function and characteristics were best summed up by Minou Reeves, the Head of Foreign Secretariat in Empress Farah's Private Office and the Director of Public Relations in the Organization for the Protection of Children. The Women's Organization of Iran, she writes,

became increasingly institutionalized and mainly attracted opportunistic and profit-seeking women who, inspired by Savak, became the female demagogues of the regime's philosophy. As the organization lost its appeal to genuine feminists, it degenerated into a cozy bourgeois social club. (Reeves 1989: 98)

"A cozy bourgeois social club" had little appeal for middle- and working-class women. Its purpose, as part of the state apparatus, was to control and confine the women's movement rather than contribute to or lead its progress. This aspect of the Women's Organization becomes vivid when, for instance, in an internal memo it gives "members permission to engage in political activities" (*Iran Almanac* 1971: 560). "Engagement in political activities" became even more important in early March 1975 when the Shah announced the creation of the Resurgence Party *(Hezb-e Rastak-hiz)* and required the participation of all "loyal" Iranians in it. Thus, WOI's 1966 Constitution was changed; the new one called for a more active participation in politics.

Furthermore, WOI's organizational hierarchy indicates a high level of political influence exerted on it by the Pahlavi Court. At the very top presided Ashraf Pahlavi. Farideh Deba (the Queen's mother) was the vice-president of the Organization. The secretariat was next, composed of the Secretary General and her personnel. The secretariat was responsible for project proposals and coordination of the Organization's 361 branch offices and over 70,000 volunteer workers. The Secretary General was appointed by Ashraf Pahlavi from the members of the Central Council. The Central Council had eleven members, six of whom where appointed by the President of the WOI. Finally, there was the High Committee for Co-operation. The High Committee planned programs and discussed legislation related to women. It consisted of eight cabinet members including the Minister of State for Women's Affairs (Mahnaz Afkhami, who was also the Secretary General). The High Committee, not surprisingly, was headed by Ashraf Pahlavi (WOI n.d.: 16). The class composition of the local branches hindered an effective control from rank and file. As Sanasarian puts it,

in many towns and cities wives of affluent and influential officials would monop-olize the branch. Year after year, they would elect one another to leadership posi-tions in the organization. They would systematically prevent the election of—or a higher rate of participation from—the working-class women. (1982: 92)

The Organization also depended financially on the Pahlavi regime. Though WOI officials denied any such dependency and "argued that the entire membership of the chapters and the WOI's leadership work were on a voluntary basis" (Sanasarian 1982: 86), there are reports of a hefty budget—anywhere between $20 to $50 million (*New York Times* [Supplementary Materials], 7 October 1978: 24) (Friedan 1975)—unlikely to have been provided by membership dues, service fees, and donations.

Sanasarian points correctly to "a close relationship between the government and the organization" and rejects the official claim of a quid pro quo relationship between the two. Yet it is an oversimplification to dismiss the WOI as a mere window dressing organization. It was a manifestation of the activities of the women of the ruling class. Its concern was to legitimize and safeguard the new opportunities that were becoming gradually accessible to urban middle- and upper-class women—but, due to its attachment to the government, the WOI failed to effectively mobilize even the upper strata of the bourgeois women. Number of membership does not truly reflect the degree of WOI's popularity since, as Sanasarian argues, most of these alleged members "were professionals . . . whose associations belonged to WOI, making their membership automatic" (1982: 85). Many (especially from the Left) argue that since WOI was not concerned with improving the lives of the poor and downtrodden women, it cannot be considered a *women's* organization. But, to be a women's organization is not the same as being the militant representative of women of every class and nationality. As a "cozy bourgeois social club," WOI never aimed at altering the status of *all* women. Nor does being politically active require an adherence to radical changes. The activities of the Organization were narrow and WOI was content with the crescive improvement in women's lives within the existing structure. That should come, however, as no surprise since it never adhered to feminist principles.

WOMEN'S MOBILITY

Whether to get an education, go to work, or participate in formal politics, women needed to have freedom of movement. A series of legislative reforms granted women legal support against "unwarranted" restrictions imposed upon their spatial mobility, dealing another blow to the traditional bargain that governs private patriarchy.

According to the 1935 Iranian Civil Code, if a husband did not approve of employment for his wife, he could simply notify her employer and prevent her from working. The woman then had to take the matter to the court and prove that her employment would neither bar her from performing her familial duties nor harm the family honor. Husbands' reluctance about their wives' employment was not as serious in the rural areas or among working-class families, where women's work is a financial imperative, as among middle-class families wherein female employment was considered indicative of fiscal problems. The middle-class mentality and patriarchal relations socialized both men and women to dislike female employment. In accordance with the Islamic shari'ah, the Marriage Law of 1931 entitled the wife to control her property. She could make contracts, and possess or dispose of property without her husband's permission. The husband, however, was legally considered head of the household. Maintenance of the family was the responsibility of the husband, although the law could not force his obligation if he refrained. A wife could apply for a divorce and should the husband refuse either to provide or divorce her, the court could imprison him from three months to one year. Consequently, a woman holding a job outside the home insulted her husband's (or father's) pride as it implied his inability to provide for his family. Women often shared this pride, thus showed reluctance to suggest any family economic trouble by working outside the home (Pakizegi 1978: 223).

The Family Protection Law of 1967 accorded the woman independence to seek a profession. Under the new law, if the husband sought to terminate his wife's employment, he had first to prove in a court of law that her employment was incompatible with the family's best interest. Only with the court's permission could the husband restrain his wife from having a job ('Araqi 1977: 147, 179, and 222–26).

Furthermore, following the 1975 revisions of the Family Protection Law, the woman, too, could ask the court to impose the same restriction on her husband. The court would make such a decision provided that it would not interfere with the maintenance of the family.

Another legal reform to grant women more mobility was the Passport Act of 1972. Prior to that year, women needed their husbands' permission to travel outside the country.

Like other reforms of the sixties, the revocation of men's control over women's employment and spatial mobility affected primarily upper- and middle-class women. Yet the new regulations constituted a significant step toward bringing seclusive gender relations to an end. Individual men's control over the female members of their family was questioned in favor of a wider control by the market and the state. This new locus of control also opposed the specific edicts of the shari'ah, which explicitly make women's departure from home contingent upon permission of a male guardian. The reversal of this law after 1979 and the renewal of a father's or husband's permission as a requirement for issuing passports for women indicates the significance of the pre-revolutionary legal reforms in this area.

GENDER RELATIONS IN THE HOUSEHOLD

Deeply tainted by Islamic discourses on gender and sexuality, gender relations in Iran have been historically constructed on the basis of comple-

mentary roles. These roles are predetermined for men and women, supposedly on the basis of their natural makeup and capability. As rational
creatures, men are heads of households, responsible for the maintenance of
the family. Essentially emotional beings, women on the other hand are "by
nature" assigned the nurturing role. Household chores then are defined as
"naturally" a part of women's familial role.

The dichotomous definition of gender roles thereby not only obfuscated
the economic nature of women's household chores (see, for example, Delphy 1984), but also concealed the fact that many women were involved in
generating incomes for their families from the home. Women's participation in many areas of the cottage industry has been located within the
household. Furthermore, women's salaries were often considered a part of
family property, belonging to, or at least controlled by the men. Women
only received money from the head of the family as an allowance. (This is
in spite of Islam's recognition of women's entitlement to their income and
wealth.) This practice, noticeably, was changing, especially among urban
middle-class families. Younger middle-class couples sometimes pointed out
her control over her money as a sign of the "modern," "egalitarian" nature
of their relationship. For instance, although women's income was also used
for life necessities of the family, statements like "I do whatever I want with
my money" denoted her emergent economic independence.

Like many other societies, the inclusion of women into Iran's formal
economy did not drastically alter their household role. Though there are
no reliable statistics on household chores, double shift was a dominant fact
of life for the majority of women. Since women's employment was still
considered by many an aberrant venture, dedication to "the family" and
"familial responsibilities" was often deemed a prerequisite to women's
seeking an outside job. Indoor plumbing and the gradual introduction of
electrical appliances made the accomplishment of some tasks easier for
women, but as Walby (1994: 61–89) indicates in her study of British
women, technological development in household industry often changed
the form of women's household work, or even added to it, rather than
decreasing it.

In short, though we cannot detect a drastic change in gender relations in
domestic chores, there were definite signs of expanding relations, albeit
limited in scope and conflictual in nature. Women's education and employment affected their confidence in themselves and how women were
treated in the families.

MIGRANT WOMEN: NEW CHALLENGES AND FRESH OPPORTUNITIES

A concomitant circumstance of capitalist development has historically
been the migration of the poor and landless peasantry to cities. Iran was

no exception. The majority of landless peasants who did not benefit from the agrarian reforms were faced with two choices: they could either stay in the village and work as agricultural labor or migrate to cities in quest of a job. The waves of the migration began shortly after the reform (Brun and Dumont 1978). The majority of these newcomers settled in the slums and formed an underemployed proletariat; many of them became Khomeini's followers at the time of the revolution. Nonetheless, considering that they were coming from conditions which were by no means better than those of life in the slums, the attractions of the cities continued to draw the migrant poor (Kazemi 1980).

Many migrant women were caught between their traditional and urban lifestyles. They felt alienated and deprived of protection, both as newcomers to city life and as women who felt their dignity violated by urbanites. Women whose families settled in relatively "better" areas had a different experience. A study of women in the city of Isfahan shows that despite the existence of greater potentials for change in the city, migration increased women's seclusion and limited their economic activity:

[T]he urbanization of the migrant women has resulted in no immediate or discernible lessening of the domestic seclusion to which they were already accustomed in the villages and which is the characteristic environment of the native city women as well. Indeed, the seclusion may have been intensified because of the possibly greater threat posed by the large mass of urban strangers. Economically active females under age 30 are less frequent, relatively, in the city of Isfahan than in its rural surroundings. (Gulick and Gulick 1978: 510)

Individual women responded to the new situation in different manners. While some acquiesced to the increased restrictions, others showed "strong self-assertiveness" (502). For many, however, the experience of urban life was an occasion to become aware of the cultural changes permeating the country. They came to believe that education was an important prerequisite of upward mobility. They aspired to a better and higher level of education for their offspring (518). Difficulties facing a struggling working-class family, however, often thwarted their ambitions and hopes. The children of many migrants had to work and could not take advantage of the educational opportunities as much as native boys and girls could: "The differences were made up for by the fact that more of the migrants' sons and daughters were working. The relative frequency of working sons and daughters increased among the 13- to 18-year-olds and more so among the migrants than among the natives" (511). Of course, this "compensation" does little or nothing for the individual—does nothing for the son or daughter who would be laboring in the fields anyway, does little for the son or daughter given the opportunity they would not otherwise have had to work in the fields. In the case of girls, early marriage continued to be a "reliable" alternative.

Migrant women's struggle revolved around making sense of the changing environment, adapting to it, and ultimately improving their status, as well as the day-to-day battle for survival. They utilized networking and informal gatherings, disseminating information through interpersonal communication to cope with their environment. The absence of men during the day relegated more authority to women over decisions regarding daily matters. Urban women, especially those educated, were more likely to defy male regulation of their conduct and resist physical abuse. The increase of the age of women at the time of the first marriage (Bauer 1985b: 180) also affected the relationship between the sexes—the smaller the couple's age difference, the greater the likelihood of female assertiveness. From her study of migrant areas of southern Tehran with which the migrants had incessant contact, Janet Bauer provides some examples of women's resistance:

Cobra Xanoom discussed with her friend, who had just returned from Mecca, how to bring pressure to bear against her own husband who was not supportive of her plans to go on the *hadj* (the pilgrimage to Mecca). When Miriam was angry she refused to sleep with her husband and Khadijeh constantly nagged her husband to take the family on weekend outings, although he never did. (173)

The changes were particularly discernible for the women of the second-generation migrant families. Going to school played an important role here by broadening their horizons, especially through association with a new and larger group of peers. Furthermore, education and familiarity with the urban environment offered them a better chance to exercise their will, the reason being that education not only equips "people [with] basic skills but it also gives them a certain status and aura which very often affords them even more autonomy in social interaction" (169). Bauer finds "exceptions to restrictions on women's traveling alone, talking or working outside of the home according to the level of the woman's education and her familiarity with how to deal with new situations" (173).

CHALLENGING ISLAM IN QUESTIONING MEN'S PATRIARCHAL PREROGATIVES

Individual men's control of women was not threatened only in relation to employment or traveling. In order to effectively refashion patriarchy in Iran, family relations had to undergo profound changes. Through the modernization efforts of the Pahlavi monarchs, the institution of the family gradually surrendered some of its previous functions to the state and its functions became progressively limited to procreation, consumption, and childrearing. Through this "policing of the family"—to borrow a term from Jacques Donzelot (1979)—the state assumed heretofore traditional responsibilities of the male-headed family, such as the children's education. These measures not only restricted men's power within the family, but also challenged Islam in some important manners. First, the introduction of the modern legal system under the Pahlavis meant the progressive marginalization of the clerical establishment from legislative processes. Second, some legal reforms, especially in the realm of family law, undermined crucial aspects of Islamic shari'ah that acted as a constitutive component of the traditional legal system.[11]

The marginalization of the clergy from the legislative system took place through a number of policies, dating back to the early days of the Pahlavi dynasty in the mid-1920s. Prior to the Constitutional Revolution of 1906–11, the Iranian judicial system was composed of two systems of laws: shari'ah, or the Divine Law, and 'urf, custom, known also as qanun. Shari'ah, which was based on Islamic jurisprudence, regulated individuals' social behavior. 'Urf, on the other hand, was the administrative law and was based on a series of precedents or regulations. In principle, the 'urf courts had jurisdiction over matters which involved the state. In practice, however, unstable political conditions relegated virtually all judicial authority to the shari'ah courts (Banani 1961: 68). In 1925, under the aegis of Reza Shah, a committee within the Ministry of Justice undertook responsibility for preparing the first volume of Iran's Civil Code and presenting it to the Majlis. The Civil Code consisted of two parts. One component was a secularized version of the shari'ah and the second was a translation of the *Code civil de français*. In 1932, the Muslim clergy were legally prohibited from registering legal documents. This decision not only limited the clergies' public function (as they were until then in charge of registering all transactions concerning property, marriage, and divorce), but also deprived them of a considerable source of revenue. The lack of well-defined procedures and skilled personnel meant that in practice the clergy, not the *nazmiyeh* or civil court, remained in charge of registering these transactions. They also maintained their jurisdiction over matters regarding marriage, divorce, writing wills, and guardianship of *vaqf* (religious endowment).

The introduction of the Family Protection Law of 1967 and its revised version of 1975 further increased the role of civil courts. Though the legal reforms of the sixties and seventies never directly revoked male status as the head of the household, they challenged men's unilateral power in such pivotal areas as polygyny, temporary marriage, and divorce. These measures were in direct conflict with the Islamic laws.

Verse 34 of the sura *Women* of the Koran makes men heads of households and advises them on how to exercise their power:

Men have authority over women because Allah has made the one superior to the other, and because they spend their wealth to maintain them. Good women are obedient. They guard their unseen parts because Allah has guarded them. As for those from whom you fear disobedience, admonish them and send them to beds apart and beat them. Then if they obey you, take no further action against them. (1988)

The Laws of marriage in the Iranian Civil Code of 1925 were essentially the same as those of Islam. The Civil Code considered marriage a contract between two "freely consenting adults" who, as long as they remained within the boundaries of Islamic law, could set their own terms. "Freedom within the boundaries of Islam," of course, meant that a woman who was to be married for the first time had to have the approval of her father or, in his absence, another male guardian. The Civil Code differed from the shari'ah in one respect. The Code considered a man and woman's expressed intention to be married sufficient for regarding the couple legally married. However, secular marriages were extremely rare and in practice the *mullah* had to administer the marriage in accordance with the principles of Islamic law.

In 1967, the Ministry of Justice drafted the Family Protection Law to modify some regulations that were blatantly injurious to women. The 1967 Law did not formally repeal any articles of the Civil Code, but where the two statutes came into conflict, the new law would prevail. In 1975, a revised version of the Family Protection Law was passed, stating the repeal of any prior law that conflicted with the new ones. The Family Protection Law of 1967 imposed some restrictions on men's rights in marital life, but "fell far short of [women's] demands for equality. The government had attempted to placate women without offending the religious establishment" (Afshar 1985: 54).

Under the Civil Code, men were legal heads of the family and had guardianship of their children and wives. Therefore, in the name of family honor and interest, they could impose limitations on women's movement and had the right to forbid their wives to set foot out of the house, to seek a job, or to obtain a passport. Men were also entitled to a wide range of services such as cooking, sewing, cleaning, and sexual relationships. Islam holds a woman's sexual availability to be an important part of her duty in a marriage. She should always comply with her husband's orders and satisfy his sexual desires, unless the shari'ah or custom explicitly allow her to refrain, for such reasons as medical problems, menstruation, or the performance of religious duties. Taking care of parents and next of kin at the time of need is also a family obligation.

According to the specifications of the Koran (sura *Women*, v. 3), Muslim men can marry up to four wives at a time if they can be impartial to their wives and "maintain equality among them." The Family Protection Law of 1967 did not outlaw polygyny; it merely restricted its practice. The reason for this conservatism was that Article 2 of the *Supplementary Constitutional Law of Iran* prohibited any law contrary to the precepts of Islam. The Family Protection Law of 1967, however, differed from the shari'ah in some respects: it neither distinguished between permanent and temporary wives nor mentioned a third and fourth wife—in other words, it limited the number of co-wives to two. Based on the new regulations, a man seeking to marry a second wife needed to obtain the permission of the court. The court reviewed the man's financial capacity and his ability to act impartially before granting him the permission. The court was not obliged to consult the first wife, though the law recommended it. Failure to obtain the permission of the court for a second marriage was punishable by imprisonment from six months to one year for the man, the second wife, the *mullah*, and the notary involved in drafting the marriage contract. The marriage itself, nonetheless, was valid. It also constituted grounds for the first wife to seek a divorce. On January 7, 1975, the Minister of Justice announced further restriction on taking a second wife by making the permission of the first wife mandatory. As before, the first wife could divorce her husband if he took a second wife.

Another restriction placed on male privilege involved temporary marriage. Traditionally, two kinds of marriage—permanent and temporary marriages—have been available to men. Temporary marriage *(mut'a, siqeh,* or *ezdevâj-e movaqqat)*, an acceptable form of marriage in Shiite Islam (see Haeri 1989), is a legal contract between a man and an unmarried woman. The period of the duration of the marriage—which can be from one hour to 99 years—and *mahr* or *mahriyeh* (a sum of money or goods; dower) should be specified in the contract, otherwise the contract will not be valid. At the end of the specified period, the marriage automatically dissolves. Temporary marriage is a personal contract between eligible, consenting couples. It requires neither family approval nor the presence of any witness. There is no limitation in the number of temporary wives for a Shiite man— this is, of course, in addition to the four wives to whom *all* Muslim men are entitled. A woman, on the contrary, can be married only to one man on either a temporary or permanent basis. After the dissolution of a temporary marriage, the man can immediately engage in a new contract with a different woman. The woman, however, must keep *'iddah*, a waiting period of forty-five days or two menstruating cycles. She does not inherit from her temporary husband and is not entitled to alimony. Yet, the children born into a temporary marriage are entitled to the same rights as those of a permanent marriage provided the marriage was registered. Contrary to the Civil Code, which recognized and sanctioned temporary marriage, the Family Protection Law made no provision for it. In a circular of January 3, 1976, the Ministry of Justice informed all offices of notaries public that any man intending to register his temporary marriage had to declare that at the time of taking the temporary wife he had not been married to another woman (*Iran Almanac* 1976: 351). Since there was no law requiring the registration of temporary marriages, it is hard to determine how widely it was practiced. Based on the statistics of the Ministry of Justice, however, temporary marriages, or better said, registered temporary marriages, peaked between 1965 and 1967. The registration, if not the practice, of this kind of marriage declined in subsequent years (Haeri 1980: 228). This decline can be traced to a change in the attitude of the people and to reluctance to register temporary marriage due to its legal ramifications.

Divorce is another area in which men have traditionally enjoyed unlimited power. Because of its conviction that family is the basis of social life, Islam approaches divorce with considerable resentment. The Prophet is said to believe that "of all the permitted things, divorce is the most abominable with God" (Esposito 1982: 29). The Koran (v. 1, sura *Divorce*), nevertheless, accepts divorce as a last resort, but makes provisions to curtail its frequency. It advises the couple to seek a reconciliation. Part of the Islamic divorce procedure is the appointment of a council, composed of trusted relatives and friends of each side, for the purpose of inciting and overseeing a negotiation prior to the finalization of divorce.

Islam considers divorce the absolute right of the man—he can at any time repudiate his wife and by a simple pronouncement of "I divorce you"—even if the pronouncement comes in jest, or when drunk, or under duress—at once terminate the marriage. The woman, on the other hand, can divorce her husband only under specific conditions, such as insanity, impotency, or castration. After a divorce, the man can marry another woman immediately but the woman has to keep *'iddah*, which in the case of a permanent marriage is three menstruating cycles. Considering the amount of freedom the Islamic divorce law entitles Muslim men, one should not be surprised by the degree of difficulties faced by Muslim countries in their attempts to revise it and grant women the right to dissolve their marriage. Yet, it is true that "the most urgently needed reform . . . was to restrict the husband's unfettered power to repudiate his wife at will, for this power represented an even more serious threat to the welfare of the Muslim women than her own lack of the right to seek a dissolution of her marriage" (Coulson and Hinchliffe 1978: 42).

The divorce law reflected in the Iranian Civil Code was a modified version of the Islamic command. The Civil Code gave the man the permission to divorce his wife at any time he wished without specifying any reason, if she were not in the middle of her period, or in the "clean" period immediately after intercourse. The Code also specified a series of grounds for divorce for both parties. Among the grounds for divorce on the husband's part were any deformity or defect causing leprosy, paralysis, blindness of both eyes, or insanity. A woman could divorce her husband if he was insane, impotent or castrated at the time of marriage or after. She could also stipulate in the marriage contract the permission to divorce him under certain conditions.

The Family Protection Law of 1967 provided other conditions as grounds for divorce. Those conditions were: the conviction of either the wife or the husband to five years of imprisonment; any harmful addiction; marriage of the husband with another woman without the consent of his present wife even if it was approved by the court; desertion by either of the parties; the conviction of either of the parties of a crime detrimental to the prestige of the family, or the other party.

Before making a final decision that the marriage had irretrievably broken down, the court had to send the application first to a board of arbitration chosen by the parties as the last attempt to reconcile the differences, unless both parties agreed to divorce. If this attempt failed, then the court would issue a "Certificate of Irreconcilability." This procedure was supposed to limit the man's power in the matter of divorce and place the final decision in the hands of the court. However, even under the new law, the husband could divorce his wife any time he so desired. The divorce had to go through the court, but, whether there were justifiable reasons or not, the court was unable to reject divorce applications filed by the husband.

It should be noted that laws of divorce changed at a considerably slow pace. The slow absorption of women into the formal sector of the economy limited their ability to maintain themselves and their families. Unjust divorce settlements, inadequate alimony, and the failure of the law to provide mechanisms which would guarantee the payment of alimony or *mahr* made divorce a difficult choice for many women. Many mothers stayed in bad marriages because they did not want to be separated from their children—a problem that to date haunts Iranian women. The stigma against divorced women even further reduced a woman's chance of initiating a divorce. In effect, patriarchal relations have often capitalized on the idea that, as a Persian saying puts it, "a woman enters her husband's house in a white wedding gown and leaves it in her white burial shroud."

Women, however, availed themselves of even minute changes in order to create new possibilities, especially in large cities like Tehran. Studies show an increase in the number of divorces immediately following the passage of the Family Protection Law of 1967. "This," as one scholar observed, "to a large extent, reflects the fact that before the enactment of the Family Protection Law women would tolerate any conditions arising out of their relations with their husbands because they knew quite well that they could do nothing short of using sheer force to make him agree to a divorce" (Saney 1974: 19). Iran has a high rate of divorce—one in every four marriages ended in divorce in the 1970s. Research conducted at Tehran University placed Iran among the first five nations with a high rate of divorce (*Iran Almanac* 1975: 418). Available figures pertaining to marriage and divorce in Tehran show a high share of divorce—53.3% of all divorces in Iran in 1349 (1970) took place in Tehran (*Kayhan* 26 April 1971)—is indicative of Iran's divorce pattern. In 1968 (one year after the introduction of the Family Protection Law), 217 per thousand marriages ended in divorce. By 1973, this number increased to 289 divorces per one thousand marriages. The divorce rate declined after 1973 (Vajdi and Fathi 1978).

In conclusion, though the legal reforms of the Pahlavis were limited in both scope and depth, they did introduce some revisions in familial power relations. Men's role as heads of families was not disputed, but many sources of their power were either taken away or limited. These measures obviously were not tantamount to an "emancipation" of women; quite to the contrary, they subjected women to more control of the public patriarchal order. Considering the tight intertwining of Islam with Iranian legal, political, and social life, these measures also threatened clerical control over women's (and men's) lives.

COMPROMISING THE SACRED SEXUALITY

Changes in the social relations of the sexes, especially among the upper and middle classes prior to 1979, effected a crisis in the dominant sexual ideology in various ways. The exclusivity of family as *the* domain for the social and sexual interaction of the sexes was challenged. Increased women's presence in public—as students, office employees, or housewives—provided social space for less restricted interactions between females and males. This interaction was also enhanced by the commercialization of leisure and the rapid increase in social spaces: restaurants; movie theaters; discos; youth cultural houses (*khaneh-ye javanan*); institutions for extracurricular activities such as music, theater, painting (indeed, one euphemism for dating was being involved in *fa'aliyât-hâye fouq-e barnâmeh*, or "extracurricular activities"); classes for learning languages or preparing for college entrance examinations. Furthermore, a dominant trend in the socio-cultural development of Iran under the Pahlavis, especially Mohammad Reza Shah, was the increasing involvement of sex and the market. Sexuality was portrayed more frequently and vividly in the media; there was more discussion of interpersonal relationship, including sex. Sexuality was tied in this manner with consumerism and the spread of fashion. Sexuality was being recast in a new way. It was gradually moving away from a sacred manifestation of marital blessing to a more secularized human need. The distance between traditionalism and the bedroom was increasing, though the latter remained at the edge of the former's horizon. One can consider as an example that even though virginity maintained its strength, much of the ceremonial aspect of proving a bride's virginity at the time of marriage—the night of *zefâf*—was replaced by private recognition between the couple, especially among the urban middle and upper classes. The couple, then, could have the liberty to engage in premarital sexual intercourse.

The media played an ambivalent role in the changing sexuality. There were, on the one hand, pronounced expressions of new forms of sexual behavior. Love affairs of unconventional sorts—for example, the unmarried couple—were frequently presented in short stories, popular songs, movies, or TV series. In this regard, the media presented many with a *surrogate mode of expression*. In a society where sexuality was still an uneasy subject, where love had to be concealed, the depiction of love in the media reflected a personal experience of love and sexuality, but was also distanced enough to express such emotion in a noncompromising fashion. Individuals could, indeed, hide in the nonpersonal aspect of these representations, and express their experience of love vicariously through them. On the other hand, however, the media also offered a contained representation of love and sexuality. Though inundated with references to sexual contacts—from holding hands, to embracing, to commenting about the enchanting body of the lover, to spending a magical night together—unconventional sexuality was also represented in the context of deception. In the movie *Beta*, for example, Betâ (played by the famous pop singer Googoosh) was the beautiful, but intellectually challenged, daughter of a respectable family who was deceived by a lecherous, pompous writer. In her illusions, she believed that they would soon get married. So, she slept with him. Eventually, Betâ realized that the man she loved had no serious intentions about a shared future. The movie ends when after a police interrogation for suspicion of prostitution, a stranger picks her up in the wee hours of the morning in a lonely street.

I do not want by any means to overemphasize the scope of these changes that were primarily limited to urban, middle- and upper-class scenes. Yet they are noteworthy because they caused a crisis that gave rise to possibilities for redefining gender and sexual identities. In the early seventies, research carried out among Tehran University students (a group particularly relevant to the present study), indicated that tension with "old customs and traditions" counted for over 50% of "youth problems." Ten percent of the problems was attributed to "difficulties of social intercourse, friendship and marriage," 53% to "prejudice and family adherence to old customs and traditions" (*Iran Almanac* 1973: 415). At the time, 55% of the Iran's population was 20 or younger, 40% of whom lived in urban areas. The Iranian government set up a number of seminars and organizations in response to the "youth crisis." In March 1973, for example, the police also set up a Youth Guidance Organization to monitor the activities of young men and women. As a result, a number of cafeterias in large cities like Tehran were closed down by the police, "since the boy and girl students instead of attending their classes, used to gather there" (*Iran Almanac* 1973: 415). In smaller cities, too, the police were particularly attentive to young men and women meeting in "suspicious" places like back alleys with little traffic. In such cases of "impropriety," the deviant could experience degradation; she would have been released to the custody of her male elders, he would have part of his hair shaved off. "Among our youths," psychologist Saheboz-Zamani expressed in his radio program, "a significant portion of life, education, time, wealth, and energy is devoted to the crippling problems of sexuality" (1965: 236).

Changes in notions of sexuality are also reflected in public discourse. For years, impersonal expressions functioned as euphemism for "having sex." These expressions included: *hammam raftan* (going to the public bath), *hendel zadan* (to start the engine with a handle), *khâk bar sari kardan* (to do the damned thing), and *sofâl posht-o-rou kardan* (to turn a tile upside down). Sex was also expressed in vulgar terms like *gâ'idan* (to fuck), or the binary *kardan* (to do) and *dâdan* (to give), respectively. These expressions presume an active and proud task for the male, a passive and shameful reception for the female.

Gradually, other phrases regarding sexuality, some part of the Persian vocabulary for centuries, were introduced into the public discourse: *nazdiki* (closeness), or more explicit ones like *hamâqushi* (sharing an embrace), *hambestari* (sharing a bed), *hamkhâbegi* (sharing a bed), *'eshqbâzi* ("love playing"), or *'eshgvarzi* (love making). These expressions of course reflect more a linguistic reconstruction than an actual practice. Their romantic connotation does not translate into passionate foreplay. Still, the very acceptance of sex as an affectionate event between two partners *is* implied by these linguistic nuances, and points up a major change in thought.

To summarize, the revision of public and private boundaries following the reforms of the sixties provided more legitimate social spaces for men and women to interact. Furthermore, the media portrayed sexuality more frequently and vividly than before. Increasingly, urban middle- and upper-class families admitted that men and women socialized, developed amorous relationships, and responded in various degrees to their sexual impulses. Of course, men and women involved in these relationships were not judged equally; double standards remained powerfully in effect in a society that saw family honor tightly intertwined with female sexual morality. State intervention in forming and regulating sexuality also increased. Encouraging "modern style" socializing of men and women, Pahlavi state was directly involved in developing new discourses of sexuality. At the same time, however, the state also acted as an ultimate father figure in regulating the morality of the youths, especially the female youths.

VIOLENCE AGAINST WOMEN

The various forms of male violence against women—rape, sexual abuse, wife battery, sexual assault, sexual harassment—emanate from unequal power in gender relations. As such, male violence is a form of social control, an integral part of male domination. Hammer and Saunder (1984) convincingly argue that the state policies perpetuate male violence by denying women the necessary resources to distance themselves from abusive relationships and by remaining indifferent toward many forms of violence against women, especially those taking place within the family. Violence against women is often attributed to the mischief of *some* men against their women, de-emphasizing thereby its scope, frequency, and institutionalized character. In Iran, not unlike other societies, conventional beliefs have denied the very existence of some forms of violence among women. Fear of negative publicity and humiliation, for instance, has forced most victims of rape, incest, or sexual harassment and their families to silence. Such crimes are conventionally seen as deviations that exist in the corrupt and sexually obsessed West. Eastern societies that continue to emphasize moral values are deemed unexposed to such immoral conducts. When such occurrences were acknowledged in Iran, they were reported as rare phenomena. "Rape is not a significant problem in Iran," states an Iranian woman scholar (Mirvahabi 1975–76: 397). Non-consensual marital sexual relationship was never recognized as rape. Wife battery, though by no means rare, was considered merely the abhorrent act of unenlightened men.

The pre-revolutionary developments in gender and sexual relations created a paradoxical situation. Changes in gender roles influenced women's assertiveness and invited revisions in sexual beliefs: sexuality, even female sexuality, gained implicit and explicit recognition. Even so, relaxed interaction between the sexes led to a crisis in the traditional bargain. Women frequently experienced various forms of public harassment such as unwanted sexual advances, pinching and other forms of physical assaults, and sexual slurs *(matalak)*.

A particularly harsh form of violence against women, sanctioned by the law, was related to adultery *(zena)*. The Penal Code, an amalgamation of Western (Italian) laws and the shari'ah enacted in 1940, defined adultery as an illegitimate sexual relationship between a married individual and a person of the opposite sex. The punishment for adultery was set to be six months to three years of imprisonment. In addition to this punishment by the law, the Penal Code granted the husband the right to kill his adulterous wife and her paramour. The punishment could also be meted out against the woman by her father or a brother. This punishment was indeed harsher than what Islamic law suggests. In the shari'ah law, the husband must *first*, in the presence of four witnesses and before an Islamic judge, prove that an illicit sexual relationship did exist between his wife and another man (Mirvahabi 1975–76), though in reality this requirement has not protected women against raging men. The woman, of course, is not protected by the same provision if her husband commits adultery. During the last years of the Pahlavis, the legal sanctioning of this form of violence against women came under criticism, but the law remained in effect till the end of the reign of the Pahlavi dynasty (Mazluman 1994).

Male violence against women remained a forceful source of sexual oppression. In post-1960s Iran, women who defied conventional criteria of proper moral behavior in their appearance or conduct became victims of verbal or physical sexual harassment. The existence of some forms of violence such as rape or incest was often denied or underemphasized. Others, like marital rape, was never recognized as violence. The increased public presence of women both marked a triumph over male domination of the public and made women more vulnerable to male violence. Some forms of violence, especially crimes of honor, were explicitly or implicitly sanctioned by the state.

RECAPITULATION

In this chapter I provided a sketch of the changing gender relations during the sixties and seventies. Based on Sylvia Walby's discussion of the private and public forms of patriarchy, I suggest that educational, labor, and legal reforms reconstructed the Iranian patriarchal system from private to public. In doing so, the site of control over women had been broadened to beyond the four walls of the home and the individualized control of men. These changes affected gender relations in the quotidian. Albeit gradually and unevenly, public patriarchy attempted to remove obstacles that excluded women from public life. Increasing women's participation in the formal sector of the economy and their access to education contested many of men's patriarchal prerogatives such as control over women's social and spatial movement, marriage, and divorce. Education increased women's access to the sources of knowledge and enabled them to claim a new position in family and society. Increasing participation in the labor force not only provided women with a new social space, but also offered them economic independence. Legal reforms similarly introduced further rights for women within the family. Though men maintained their position as familial patriarchs, their power became limited. Domestic division of labor did not change drastically. Employed women remained the primary family caregivers and had to bear the burden of both job and household tasks. Changing gender relations also effected some modifications in the realm of sexuality. Public interaction of unmarried couples gained some legitimacy. Dating as a prelude to marital relationship became more acceptable among educated, urban families. Double standards, however, persisted. Emergent gender relations made women indeed more vulnerable to various forms of sexual transgression in public. Male violence against women remained high and, for the most part, unreported.

Changes in gender relations did not challenge men exclusively; women, too, shared the confusion and ambivalence of living amidst outdated beliefs and practices and emergent relations. Changing gender relations were the source of a gender crisis that played an important role in shaping the 1979 revolution. But, as I will discuss gender relations in post-revolutionary Iran (see especially chapter 4 of my *Women in Iran: Emerging Voices in the Women's Movement*), the consequences of refashioning patriarchy continued to shape Iranian politics throughout the IRI history by effecting the development of a "dual society" in the Islamic Republic.

The gender crisis was heightened because the reforms of the sixties affected the clerical community both through the increasing threat of marginalization of their role in the public sphere and by repudiating Islamic laws concerning gender relations and family life. Thus, the consequences of the changes in gender relations should be gauged not only in the actual changes implemented, but also in their symbolic implications. Exploring the actual and symbolic dimensions of this gender crisis is the subject of the following chapter, where I will discuss how Islamists viewed changing gender relations advantageous to two adversaries of the Muslim community: the infidel without and the chaos within.

NOTES

1. Information based on *Statistics of Higher Education in Iran*, published by the Institute for Research and Planning, Ministry of Science and Higher Education.

2. See the 1976 census and the statistics published by the Iranian Ministry of Education for the academic year of 1975–76.

3. Information based on *Statistics of Higher Education in Iran*, published by the Institute for Research and Planning, Ministry of Science and Higher Education.

4. There is a slight difference in database for 1956 and 1966. In 1956, persons ten years old and over were considered economically active members of the population. In 1966, this membership was twelve years and over.

5. In 1973, for instance, over forty percent of the economically active population of Iran participated in agricultural activities while only seven percent of the rural female population was reported as active.

6. Information based on the *1972 Labor Census* of the Ministry of Labor.

7. According to this plan, employees who worked for a certain number of years (usually 30 years) were entitled to a retirement pension. Government contributions provided part of the fund used for the payment of retirement pension. The other source of the fund was the dues deducted from the salaries of the civil servants each month during the course of their employment.

8. For examples see, Abrahamian (1982: ch. 9), Bill (1988: ch. 3), Cottam (1979: chs. 15–17).

9. See Mehrangiz Dolatshahi, in an interview recorded by Shahrokh Meskoob, 15 May 1984, Paris, tape 4, Iranian Oral History Project, Harvard University.

10. For a list of different organizations active in this period, see Woodsmall (1960: 80–83).

11. These were compounded by a third measure developed by the Ministry of Education that suppressed the clergy's role as educators in the traditional schools.

3

Gender Crisis: Preventing the Future

My dear, honorable brother, this land in which we live, away from our own country, which is quite beautiful with its mansions and apartments, has many deficiencies in its spirit. In this society, boys and girls receive the same education; appear together in dance balls and theaters. In this society, women work in offices and men waste their time roaming the streets. There is no law; nobody's rights and duties are limned. Lustful, bribe-receiving, conniving people are admired, the subjugated and the poor die of starvation. The wealthy spend a life of vice and promiscuity, oblivious to the poor. Shameless prostitutes spread harlotry and corruption and no one cares. This society mimics foreigners in all aspects of life. It shows no respect for education and morality. No one trusts another; friendship is absent. Wickedness, abuse, and injustice rage rampant. Such a society undoubtedly will hold no value in my mind.

Fakhriyeh, the protagonist of Mostafavi's *What Every Young Girl Must Know*, expresses this scathing criticism (n.d.: 15–16). She is the daughter of a wealthy Iranian family, living in an unspecified Eastern country. The family migrated to avoid the tyranny in Iran. She is endowed with the beauty of both the spirit and the body (her name denotes pride and honor). Everybody in town knows of her and holds her in high respect. Yet despite her high morality—or more accurately, *because of* it—she is not a good judge of character. She assumes other individuals are as innocent as she. After all, a woman will always be her emotional self, regardless of her breeding or cultural background—"A woman is always and everywhere a woman; she will not become a man no matter how hard she tries" (46). She is befriended by Jamâl, the son of another respected Iranian family living in that city. Infatuated with Fakhriyeh, Jamâl showers her with compliments. "Sometimes he wrote exciting and sentimental letters to express his intense emotion" (7). He knows that until she breaks free of her brother Eftekhâr, whose name denotes honor and pride, it will be impossible to "tame" her. Through a mischievous plan, he attempts to sever the relationship between the brother and sister. "The beautiful Fakhriyeh, the all-kindness and fidelity Fakhriyeh, the good-natured Fakhriyeh, fell prey to Jamâl's poisonous propaganda and gradually developed a mistrust for her loyal brother and other relatives" (8). Her wise brother patiently observes until an opportune moment to warn her about her socializing: "Avoid evil-natured people who claim being righteous, loyal, and upright" (9). Though at first apprehensive, Fakhriyeh eventually realizes the wisdom of her brother's guidance.

In reaction to her mistake, she becomes reserved and reclusive. Eftekhar expresses concerns for his sister's changing mood. She responds that her experience with Jamal has led her to rethink her surroundings, who she is, and how she should live. She realizes the corruption of that society. She then spells out what she sees wrong about the society in which she is forced to live. In her ideal society, a woman's place is clear and where she is by nature assigned to be:

A woman has a special place and designated duties in a family. Housekeeping and raising the children is a woman's responsibility. If a woman deviates from this path, family life and household affairs will be in shambles. If a woman is constantly roaming around, she will undoubtedly fail to do her duties. A woman who is preoccupied with other tasks not only does injustice to herself, but also ruins the organization of the society and her family. She will paralyze men, disabling them from doing their work. A woman must learn about purity, morality, and housekeeping. She must learn how to attend to her husband, children. She must learn about hygiene. Her visions must be limited and not go beyond her special domain. (22–23)

But her metamorphosis is not yet complete. Fakhriyeh and Eftekhâr have to visit their paternal uncle and she surprises her brother with yet another change. She appears veiled. She has realized that only the veil can safeguard a woman from the hunting eye of men. The brother is not convinced. Their discussion soars after they arrive at their uncle's—a law professor who is referred to as the "Doctor." Pleased to see his niece veiled, he explains the significance of the veil: "In a society, if women are veiled, there will certainly be a decrease in disease, lust, emotional distress, prostitutes, and other vices. Experience proves that seventy percent of all the robberies, murders, crimes, and treacheries are due to the lax morality and showing-off of defiled women" (30).

The rest of this short book is devoted to defending the Islamic position on hejâb and a comparison of Muslim and non-Muslim women's rights and privileges.

Mostafavi initially published *What Every Young Girl Must Know* back in 1952, after a turbulent decade regarding gender relations in Iran.[1] A second printing appeared around the Revolution (the book does not have a publication date; my estimate is based on the fact that I purchased a second edition in the fall of 1978). The author characterizes the book as the "amusing and sweet story of an honorable Eastern young girl." The book is an obscure one. There is nothing significant about it to stand out amidst the religious penning on women. Despite all the self-congratulatory remarks by the author, his is a weakly constructed and poorly written religious-political manifesto. Yet it is exactly its run-of-the-mill character that makes the book interesting: it is one of many, written with no scholarship, yet reflective of the concern and agony of many Islamists. Written more than a decade prior to the period with which we are concerned here, the book bears an uncanny resemblance both in form and content to much of the religious social criticisms of the post-1960s. The author obviously recognized the similarity, for he chose to reissue the work shortly before the 1979 revolution. The author is male, though a woman utters the ideas. The book is addressed to women. It is presented as women's and society's last chance for salvation:

Dedicated to you young girls and mothers who have not yet surrendered the riches of your purity and chastity to satanic and lustful thoughts of some ferocious evil-doers.

Dedicated to you, guardians of the land and religion, who witness day and night the corruption and misery of this distressed people. (Dedication page)

There is also a feeling of distress, of social estrangement, in the text. The family is dislocated to avoid dictatorship. But their host society is hardly different from their native: it has the same social anarchy that inspires Fakhriyeh and her uncle to look toward Islam. "Foreigners" are being imitated "in all aspects of life." There is a strong dismay about the changing order of gender roles. Women in particular are held culpable for social disorganization.

In the post-1960s era, too, it appeared to many as though something had torn asunder the very fabric of Iranian society. Iranian society was perceived preoccupied with consumption. Children had evidently fallen victim to parents' self-indulgence. Youths were seen standing at the edge of catastrophe—drugs, promiscuity, Westernization, and alienation. Men were deemed brainless bureaucrats, indifferent to social issues. Women looked most vulnerable of all, and thereby, most guilty for being vacuous, self-consumed, and rootless. Though women were not seen as the cause of the problem, they were surely represented by many authors, mostly male, as symptomatic of all that was going awry in the development of Iranian society.

Things fall apart; the center cannot hold.

William Butler Yeats so quoted John Donne to reflect on the eve of the Second World War. The same feeling resonates in the religious writings of the pre-revolutionary era. The Iranian authors' concerns were of course shared by many others, though not necessarily to the same extent nor expressed with the same sense of urgency. What was going on, one wonders, in a society that notwithstanding the supposedly horrifying chaos, exalted itself for its humanity, sanity, and firm belief in virtue and family honor? How was the reshaping of gender relations from private to public interpreted to evoke such reactions? What were the cultural politics of the Islamic authors? How did they propose to settle "the gender crisis," defined according to men's interpretation of the crisis? These questions shape this chapter.

I will propose that gender politics be viewed in the context of overall social changes that the reforms of the 1960s initiated, accelerated, or deepened. The emergence of public patriarchy signified to religious authors a thorough change in how individuals, particularly individual women, defined themselves in the universe: moving away from prescribed molds of the past toward new possibilities. These definitions were not drawn according to Islam. To the religious opposition, a return to normalcy required restoring men's power in the family by returning to private patriarchy. In the process, however, they realized that change was inevitable and that their discourses, too, should reflect compatibility with the new order. The Islamic discourse on women was subsequently moderated in the theories of Ali Shariati and his followers.

GENDER AS SYMBOL

People reify their society through "imaginary" boundaries in perceptions of "authentic indigenous identity" of a community (Anderson 1991; Cohen 1995). In times of social change, when the foundations of a society are "dismantled or become anachronistic," when the plasticity of norms and values becomes evident, those foundations are replaced by "cultural bases expressed symbolically" (Cohen 1995: 81). Gender becomes a major element of contestation at times of rapid change. As groups side with or against change, changing gender roles become the sign of progress or the symbol of demon. The family often symbolizes social stability and "authentic," traditional values (see, for example, Staggenborg 1998). Women and their social and familial roles become the battleground of divergent politicking.

But in modern times, continuity of or rupture from the "indigenous" lifestyle is contested in the context of global society. Political considerations and international laws may confine borders, but political entities do not necessarily coincide with the multidimensional spatial realities of our time (Soja 1989). The electronic media, Meyrowitz suggests (1985), has subverted the "situational geography" of social experience. We increasingly become the "direct audiences" of performances that happen on distant shores. In this way, what takes place in one society comes to forewarn of the future of another. The multidimensionality of time and space in modern time is then important to understand how changes in gender role go far beyond their immediate consequences.

In Iran, the refashioning of patriarchal domination concerned political criticism at two tightly linked levels. One, as discussed in the previous chapter, regarded the actual change that reshaped, though admittedly in a limited way, gender roles in family and society. The other was symbolic. From this vantage point, the change was much more far-reaching than it appeared. The ideal genders of the private patriarchy symbolized order; the suggestion to change them was tantamount to subverting the order of life, "the natural order of the universe." This generalization became possible by the nature of the modern age. The globalization of life under modernity has in many ways made the borders obsolete. The media brings everything close to home; what happens in "other places" could easily become "our" future. Who are "we" mimicking? The West. Then does that not mean that their life today is our destiny tomorrow? In this respect, then, the strategy of the clerical opposition to the Shah was preventing the future. Their solution was to reestablish order by securing once again men's prerogatives in the family and restoring women's jeopardized morality.

Understanding how gender was construed in a multidimensional time and space is essential for any discussion of cultural politics in prerevolutionary Iran. It is only from this perspective that we can account for the sense of urgency evident in Islamic texts. This sense of urgency is clearly visible in virtually every line of religious texts published in prerevolutionary years. Mostafavi's dedication of his book to those women "who have not yet surrendered" their "purity and chastity" to diabolic forces clearly reveals this desperation. It is due to the same realization that Muslim authors point out so emphatically the quality of their works. Mostafavi, for example, lists questions to be addressed and states: "These are truths and issues that will all be discussed in the most eloquent and mellifluous manner in the following pages" (Mostafavi n.d.: 86). Mostafa Zamâni writes that "wise people who want to secure their happiness and make a haven of their house, have no choice but to implement what is written in this book, words inspired by the generous and bountiful source of Islam" (Zamâni 1970: 19). Fahim Kermâni states the purpose of his book to be an attempt to save Islam in the face of the attacks directed against it:

The aim of compiling this book is . . . to reattract the attention of the younger generation, and especially those who seek knowledge of the great concepts of Islam, who have been attacking the religion [of Islam], or have grown indifferent toward it due to dominant ideas in our society or some illusions and incorrect thoughts. (Fahim Kermâni n.d.: 156)

From Motahari to Shariati, one can clearly detect the echo of this urgency, this last chance, in their pleading with the nonbelievers, "Just listen to us," "Don't be too hasty to judge."[2] These authors did not see changing gender relations as isolated. In their eyes, the changes were part and parcel of a continuous attack launched on Islam by its enemies (the Shah, foreign powers, and secular intellectuals). They understood ongoing social changes, and to some extent rightly so, as an attempt to limit the influence of Islam. The writings of the Islamic theologians in this period conveyed anxiety and concern about the future of Islam. A cry of hopelessness and helplessness dominated their writings, in which frequent references were made to the general apathy of the younger and educated generation toward Islam (e.g., Shariati n.d.-b: 470–71).

Much of the debate (especially within Iranian intellectual circles) about gender politics in Pahlavi Iran has been paralyzed by an exclusive assessment of "what exactly happened" under the Pahlavis. Yet the reforms of the 1960s, and chief among them the refashioning of patriarchy, are not noteworthy simply because of their immediate results, but also for the upcoming directions they suggested. Social movements react not simply to their immediate environment and their present conditions, but also to what "happens" in their environment in some future time or vicariously through other places. Herbert Blumer warned sociologists that ignoring the meaning behind actions falsifies the behavior under study. "To bypass the meaning in favor of factors alleged to produce the behavior," he wrote, is "a grievous neglect of the role of meaning in the formation of behavior" (Blumer 1969: 3).

To the clergy, one aspect of the assault on Islam was overt: the clerics had been gradually stripped of their traditional judicial and educational responsibilities from the turn of the century and especially following the establishment of the Pahlavi dynasty. Their economic power was also weakened (see Akhavi 1980). Severe as these detriments were, however, they were never intended to do away with religion in toto; they were temporary and subject to the political atmosphere. The restrictions imposed upon opposition political organizations were often more relaxed with respect to religious circles (see Faghfoory 1987; Floor 1983).[3]

The religious writings of this era acknowledge two sources of fatal enmity toward Islam. One is the scientific discoveries and the spread of literacy which created doubts regarding religion; the other is the attempt to undermine the divine order of the universe primarily through the destruction of the family and the "natural" division of labor between the sexes.

Subjecting religious teaching to scientific scrutiny induced many educated individuals to jettison their religious beliefs. As James Bill observed during his research in the late sixties,

[The result of education] has been a sharp move away from this most basic of value systems which organized all phases of a Muslim's life. Thus, a mujtahid stated in 1967 that whenever he spoke and worked with university students, he left his 'ammamah (turban) at home and wore only a plain suit. The students of today, he pointed out, had little respect for the cleric. (Bill 1972: 61)

Of course, the clergy's approach toward modern science was not a unified one. Some vehemently rejected any technological innovation as "impure" and the creation of the pagan non-Muslims, while the reformists within the religious hierarchy accepted Western technology to the extent it could be utilized in accordance with Islamic standards.[4] The problem then, as formulated by Mortezâ Motahari, is not if we should completely accept or reject modern science, but rather to accept technology as a means of improving human societies and to reject the corrupt sociopolitical structure that enslaves science (Motahari 1983: especially 19–29).[5]

The relationship between religion and modern science, however, is not so simple. (Had the question *been* simply whether the loudspeaker is the "Satan's horn" [Motahari 1983: 111] or whether the stranger who appears on TV can see his Muslim female viewer.) A clash between scientific and religious paradigms, as Mohammad ʿAbduh (the Egyptian Muslim thinker of the nineteenth century) foresaw, is inevitable since "faith, by its very nature, cannot be touched by science: the two have separate orbits and each must keep within its own" (Rahman 1982: 51). The threat did not escape the attention of the Iranian clergy. Morteza Motahari plainly expresses this fear when he writes that

The recent scientific modernization in Europe has caused a peculiar consternation, anxiety and discombobulation by shaking thoughts and refuting age-old axioms and beliefs about the universe and nature. . . . Definitely, it has also generated doubts and uncertainties about . . . religious matters. (Motahari n.d.-a: 29)[6]

Islam is a religion based on a strict hierarchical order: a masculine God on the top, angels next, followed by men and finally by women (Sabbah 1984). An opposition to a part of this hierarchy of order and power is construed as an attempt or, worse yet, a conspiracy to subvert the order of Allah Almighty. Gender, and more specifically the "woman question," thus becomes an integral part of any Islamic critique of society. Any such critique could become a political issue questioning the entire system. The clerical critics of the Shah's Iran disliked the Shah's government because the development of capitalism and, what was known among many Iranians as "westoxication,"[7] was a threat to the very existence of Islam. In that sense, the attack of the religious opposition on the existing society was the appeal of a dying force to be given a chance to survive.

It is noteworthy that unlike the perpetual preoccupation with the problem of female gender, Islamist authors wrote sparsely about masculine gender role. There was, of course, concern about lustful, deceitful, uncontrollable men[8]—but there was nothing new about this view of men that would reflect a "crisis" of manhood. Men are assumed to take the role of a protective provider for women. Though that point is clearly discussed in Islamic texts, there is no direct reference to the fact that independent, wage-earning women create a crisis for this notion of manhood. Nor are men called upon to rise up *as men* and reclaim their manliness. When men are addressed, they are merged in or, more accurately, stand for the broader concept of "nation" (*mellat*) or "Muslim people" (*mardom* or *ummat-e mosalmân*) who are called upon to fight against the enemies of Islam. The crisis in manhood was due to men's failure to be alert, to resist the temptations of immorality. One could argue that rescuing the nation was predominantly a masculine task in which women *also* participated.

SAVING ALLAH FROM THE ENEMY WITHIN

In her study of male-female relationships in Islam, Fatima Mernissi indicates that the Muslim system constantly confronts two threats: "the infidel without and the woman within" (Mernissi 1987: 43). In the eyes of the religious critics, contemporary Iranian women embodied not one, but *both* threats; the enemy without recruited women in their fight against Islam. The key to this analysis is Islam's view of sexuality and humankind's relationship with God.

Islam considers sexuality a genuine human need. It not only approves of it but also encourages it in its legitimate context, that is, within the family. "No celibacy in Islam" is an Islamic dictum demonstrating approval of sexual gratification. Despite the recognition of human beings as sexual subjects, Islam does not grant them the right to seek sexual gratification as an end. Sexual relationship is merely a means to create tenderness between the couple and secure the Muslim family. Distinguishing between lust and love, Motahari argues that free sex is not conducive to deep and passionate love. In societies where free sexual liaison is practiced, "women are degraded and there is room only for evanescent lust and promiscuity" (Motahari n.d.-b: 81).

But we do need sex and thereby women to survive: "Ever since human-kind appeared on this planet and started community life, it has been in need of the female sex for both physical reproduction and social life; the man has never stood independent from woman" (Tabâtabâ'i 1979: 1).

In this cosmology, the woman is to reproduce the human race. Civilization is assumed to be a masculine product.

Though men do need women for survival, it is also men who use or abuse women, who denigrate them or lead them to freedom. Tabataba'i states that with respect to the treatment of women, human societies have passed through three stages. In the first, prior to the advent of any religion, men subjected women to numerous mistreatments. Deprived of any rights, women were little more than laborers, porters of heavy loads, providers of sexual services, and caregivers to the young and the ill. Woman was no more valuable than a four-legged animal (9). In the second stage, the Babylonians, Romans, Greeks, Egyptians, Chinese, and Iranians developed laws and religious regulations. But these mandates subjugated women, denying them independence, autonomous personality, property, and inheritance. In these societies, woman was treated as a child who had to remain under man's control for her whole life (13–14). The third stage coincided with the advent of Islam, the age of real liberation for women (17–21). It is only at this stage that sexuality and sexed bodies find their true function: the reproduction of Allah's children. The family becomes the breeding place; the only sphere in which legitimate sexual relationship can be established in the Islamic world is the family. This assessment, it is noteworthy, not only does not rely on any anthropological evidence, but also contradicts much of what we know about the history of gender relations.

Even within the confinement of the family, however, sexual life should not divert the devoted Muslim from the worship of Allah. Thus, as Sabbah convincingly argues, one of the characteristics of the Muslim Deity is "a relentless and systematic hatred of the believer's family, especially a polarization of that hatred around the wife and children, identified as the enemies of the system" (Sabbah 1984: 103). In other words, no kind of sexual pleasure—and for that matter, nothing in life—should beguile Muslims into abandoning Allah. "Men are tempted," the Koran (sura III, v. 14) warns us, "by the lure of women and offspring, of hoarded treasures of gold and silver, of splendid horses, cattle, and plantations. These are the comforts of this life, but far better is the return to Allah" (Koran 1988).

That is, however, exactly the kind of threat which refashioning patriarchal relations and the demise of traditional patriarchal bargain have posed for the present day Muslim community. A pivotal component of this threat is women's assertion of their sexual self. Undoubtedly that was not the first time in history when Muslims had engaged in sexual relationship solely for its pleasure. Indeed, issues pertaining to sexual relationship are dealt with such enthusiasm and are presented so illustratively in religious handbooks

(*Towzihul Masâ'el*) that they often turn the ascetic manuals into what Gellner (1984: 27) calls "theoporn." Nonetheless, while past aberrations were limited and isolated—or at least the Muslim community so believed—they became more prevalent and, thereby, more perilous in the contemporary society. The government, albeit implicitly, condoned a more lax attitude toward sexuality. Furthermore, constant contact between men and women in offices and universities was interpreted as an ever-present source of temptation. Had the associations been made under Islamic directions, there would have been of course no reason to be alarmed. But in a society that gradually but steadily distanced itself from the Islamic tradition, any proximity between the sexes was deemed a source of corruption. This anxiety toward sex and sexuality—what one could call "sexophobia"—explains why Khomeini looked aghast at the Iran under the Pahlavis and saw nothing but a huge whorehouse.[9] To the clerics and faithful believers, women constantly lured men into fornication by rejecting the Islamic dress code and appearing unveiled in public—in essence, to the devout Islamists, nude. "The phenomenon of nudity," writes Motahari (1969: xxii), "is without a doubt *the* disease of our time."[10] Besides, advancement in the making of contraceptive methods and their widespread use enhanced women's control over their bodies. Thus, although Islam does not forbid birth control, Muslim clergy were apprehensive about its popularity. Motahari, for example, cautions us against its contribution to the corruption of sexual morality and the weakening of the family (1969: 76–77; 1978b: 260; n.d.-b: 31). Therefore, the fruit of decades of change in the lives of Iranian women affirmed the Islamic belief of women as a source of *fitna*, chaos and derangement, which qualifies them as Islam's internal enemy.

Therefore, the damages that an independent assertive woman causes to Islam are twofold. In the first place, she defies the wishes of Allah Almighty and destroys the "natural" order of the universe. In other words, the woman who ventures to redefine her position in the universe and to affirm herself as an independent being supplants Allah. In the second place, she incites others to disobedience both by setting a precedent and, more dangerously, by luring them away from the worship of Allah.

Claiming control over their biological function, women defy the divine order in yet another way. The supreme creator and owner of the universe is, of course, Allah: "To Allah belong all who dwell on earth and in heaven. Those that worship false gods follow nothing but idle fancies and preach nothing but falsehood" (Koran 1988: 69). "To Allah belongs the kingdom of the heavens and the earth. He creates what He will." This means that the woman merely carries the fetus, but it is Allah who conceives, deposits the fetus in "a safe receptacle," and gives birth to the new generation: "He gives daughters to whom He will and sons to whom he pleases. To some He gives both sons and daughters, and to others He gives none at all" (158). And: "Allah created you from dust, then from a little germ. No female conceives or is delivered without His knowledge" (179). Or, "Did We not create you from an unworthy fluid, which We kept in a safe receptacle for an appointed time? All this We did; how excellent is Our work" (54).

The concerns and worries of the divinity, however, are merely reflections of the anguish and torments of the mortal man. The Islamic deity is no exception. So, the earthly meaning of the clerics' preoccupation with the usurpation of Allah's rule over humanity was in effect the fear of the patriarchal system of assaults on its foundations.

RESTORING ORDER IN THE PATRIARCHAL FAMILY

Family is a system of property that involves, among other things, rights of sexual possession and household labor. Heterosexual marriage creates a relationship of erotic property between members of two genders and sanctions and limits partners' rights over their property (Collins and Coltrane 1995: especially ch. 2). Marriage establishes the legitimate context for sexual gratification. Family systems with unilateral sexual possession rights grant men exclusive possession over their wives, while men themselves enjoy great freedom to have sexual liaison with others. The family is an economic unit, a business specializing in running a household, that shapes and is shaped by gender relations (Coltrane 1998). Sexual possession and economic property are integrally linked in a family. Consequently, any change in gender role can profoundly affect how men and women relate in family settings. As social resources available to each party alter, the property arrangement undergoes renegotiations. That is why social change, and especially changes in gender roles, creates so much anxiety about "family values." What is often objected to is a subversion of patriarchal gender relations, not the "family value" per se.

The decline of private patriarchy in Pahlavi Iran implied revisions in the dominant gender relations within the family. Men's customary prerogatives were to become limited or repealed. Throughout history, Islam advocated servility and obedience as the best qualities in a woman. Imam Bâqer has reportedly said that the duties of a woman to her husband include "being obedient, not defying him, not giving his riches away without his permission, and surrendering herself to him in bed" (quoted in Nuri 1964: 129). A constant component of the clerics' critique of Iran under the Pahlavis was the changes that plagued the "sacred institution of the family" and women's place in it. The severity of the complaint can be understood only if one takes into consideration that the "Muslim family is the miniature of the whole Muslim society and its firm basis" (Nasr 1966: 16).

That the family is a system of property in Islam is abundantly clear in the writings of Islamists. In effect, it is exactly on the basis of this notion of the family as a business enterprise, a "sacred company" (*sherkat-e mo-*

qaddas) (Zamani 1970: 21), that Islamists promote gender relations within the family, based on a traditional patriarchal bargain. From this perspective, women and men enter the marriage market with different objectives. A woman wants economic provision and security. She wants to pursue "her love for children," create a center for autonomy away from parental rule, and satisfy "the need for a kind companion and a sacrificing protector" (22). A man is inclined toward the "sacred company" also to achieve certain goals:

A warm kind bosom that once in a while would caress him, would make his sorrows disappear, and would comfort and console him. The feeling of loneliness pushes him toward marriage, hoping that thereafter he will be surrounded with liveliness and commotion: that is what inspires him to have children. Another factor is his excitement for the marital act (*'amal-e zanâshou'i*) and gratification of lust. (22)

Notice that her primary concern is being provided, having economic security. To achieve her goal, she resorts to such means of finding a husband, *showharyâbi*, as coquetry. And after finding him, she does everything to "keep her husband and attain her goals" (22). Also notice that he is primarily concerned with having company—in living room and in bedroom—having someone to create a refuge from the crazy world outside.

To have a long-lasting "sacred company," husband and wife must obey its regulations . . .

Interestingly, after this point, the focus of writing in Islamist literature changes. Men are advised hurriedly that they should be mindful of their wives' needs, respect their wives, remain loyal, and be generally nice and kind to them. Women, on the other hand, are advised to understand that *they* have the primary responsibility of making a marriage work (see, for example, Zamani 1970: 197). Remember that in Islam, men's jihad, holy war, is to fight against the enemies of Islam; women's, to attend to their husband's needs. Women are instructed to understand men and be aware of special circumstances in men's lives. If men do something that may not appease women's sensitivities, there must be a good reason for that:

We cannot overlook this point either, that for a man, his wife is like a treasure, especially if they are newlyweds. She is a precious gem, a valueless treasure chest. He does not want anyone else to know of his treasure and to covet it. If he learns that she leaves the house [alone and without his permission], he will object because of the intensity of his feelings: Why did you present yourself to others to watch? This objection is caused by his love. But shortsighted women sometimes attribute this to their husband's suspicion or, worse yet, accuse their husband of jealousy. They are seriously mistaken. Instead of thanking their husband, they traverse a false path that leads to the destruction of their sacred company. (148)

The above illustration—one of many—is particularly interesting because it clearly underlines the sexual property aspect of the Muslim family. The example is fully understood only in the context of women's resistance to the ideal Islamic family relations. One can understand how the change from private to public patriarchy, from a system in which individual men control their women to one in which such a control is limited and regulated, could cause agony and frustration.

The increase in women's participation in the formal economic sector made her economically independent. Providing for the family has been considered men's duty and it was in part as a compensation for this "hardship" that Islam granted them privileges in, among other things, inheritance (e.g., Motahari 1978b: 232), not to mention sexuality. Women's independence, therefore, limits men's authority in the family. Besides, granting women the right to divorce their husbands and making men's desire to repudiate their wives contingent upon the decision of the court was in direct violation of the Islamic doctrine. That is why Khomeini proclaimed any divorce based on the rulings of a secular court illegal and any woman who marries another man pursuant to such a divorce, an adulteress (zenâkâr) (Khomeini n.d.: 463–64).[11]

Motahari provides an explanation for the unequal familial rights of men and women. He bases his analysis on a duality of social and familial rights. In a society, he argues, all people are created equal. Gradually, however, due to differences of talents and character, people acquire unequal rights. This acquired inequality becomes in turn responsible for social differentiation (Motahari 1978b: 150–51). The laws of nature, on the other hand, govern families. These laws place family members in different positions. Men and women are, therefore, born with different rights, abilities, and needs (151–53).

Another concern for religious authors related to women's spatial mobility. According to Islamic law, a woman cannot leave the house even for the purpose of visiting her family unless she obtains her husband's permission. Khomeini writes:

A woman who is permanently married ('Aqd-e da'emi) should not leave the house without her husband's permission and must surrender herself to him for any joys and should not disincline having intercourse with him unless for some excuse valid based on the shari'ah. . . . If she does not do these and disobeys her husband, she is guilty (sinful) and does not have the right to enjoy the food, clothes, house, and intercourse. (Khomeini n.d.: 386)

There was no doubt that women's education and employment outside the house decreased men's control over them both inside and outside the house. When women refuse to seek a man's permission to leave the country, to which the reform in the Passport Law testified, it is only a matter of time before they cease to ask men's permission at all.

Mohammad Ali Shâdkâm pays lip service to the Pahlavi government for liberating women, but condemns the flood of misguiding advertising, contact with Western women, and blind imitation of Westerners' "unreasonable" lifestyle. The result, he writes, has been outstanding.

Unfortunately, a large number of young women and girls took advantage of the charter [of the White Revolution concerning women] and used it as an excuse so that, in the name of liberation, freedom, and equality with men, they could follow a path in which, by inappropriate and immoral behavior, promiscuity, wandering about in the street and imitating those corrupted women—often appearing on movies, TV, etc.—they would throw themselves with no clothes on like a crazy person into the arms of strange men and over and over do the filthy, shameful deeds of the sort which are contrary to women's natural greatness and their social virtues. The continuation of this situation, the excessive contact of [Muslim Iranian] women with non-Muslim nations, especially their polluted and corrupted women, and finally a series of unreasonable and unacceptable social intercourse and imitation of the deeds and behavior of these propaganda dolls and statues who pour into Iran and into the women's circles from the most remote part of the West as models and fashion promoters, gradually attracted some of the healthy [i.e., uncorrupted], and pure women to this rapidly increasing group of airhead, weak and so-called modern and liberated!! women. Now, the spiritual value and the natural greatness of [the Muslim Iranian] woman are sacrificed for Westerners' devious and profit-seeking purposes. (Shâdkâm 1976: 185)

One wonders, Shâdkâm continues, if the misguided women who ask for women's participation in social and political matters, who "ignore women's definite responsibilities regarding internal family life and childrearing" (187), know about the negative result of women's social liberation in other countries.

The heart of the problem, of course, is the future of the family. First, what happens to the "natural" and "definite" division of tasks in the family? With both man and woman out on the job, who is going to take care of the children and household chores? Some may consider childcare centers as a possible answer. But can these centers really provide a child with the tender love "nature" bestows upon women? The assumption is that even if the woman goes to work outside of the family, she is responsible for domestic duties—after all, the natural order of things cannot be tampered with.

Second, the fear of divorce haunts the writings of this period. The Family Protection Law and the debates around it signaled for the religious leaders and concerned Muslims like Shâdkâm that the traditional family was in jeopardy. Shâdkâm wonders if "the ladies who support freedom and equality of the sexes, who consider the establishment of Family Protection Court to be a reasonable solution," have pondered the consequences of the alarming rise in the rate of divorce (187)?

There are other disconcerting issues, Shâdkâm points out. One day the media advocates the omission of the husband's approval in order to get a passport. The next, they reject men as the head of the household. And the day after, demand the abolition of men's control of their women's movement (188).

INDIVIDUALITY, SEXUALITY, AND HEJÂB

The transition from private to public patriarchy creates for women, as we discussed in the previous chapter, some room for self-expression. The autonomy women earn through education and employment, as well as the changes that condition men's control over their lives, give women an open space for self-identity. Promoting individuation is indeed a dominant trend in modernity, a process by which individuals can think and act as individual actors (Giddens 1991; Melucci 1996b). Individual identity becomes not a finished fixity, but an ongoing, reflexive project. Individuals are afforded the social space necessary for articulating their social and personal lives as autonomous, albeit not severed, from institutions such as family, kinship, religion, class, and state. This process affects cultural frameworks surrounding gender relations, especially in the area of love, marriage, and sex. As individuals probe different options, uncertainty substitutes the certainty of bonds of traditional love and marriage. Love was to flow naturally from the innate need of men and women to live in union and, more importantly, to procreate. When individuals engage in interpersonal relationship as self-reflexive partners, however, considerations external to the relationship lose their regulating power. Commitment to the relationship becomes contingent upon loyalty to oneself.

Sex, especially for women, was deemed to be confined to the marital bed. Though men did enjoy more than one bed, disloyalty in women, even in the isolation of their dreams, was a serious transgression that threatened the core of their lives. The transition from private to public patriarchy subverted that order. As delineated in the previous chapter, this transition affected traditional sexual morality particularly through secularization and liberalization of sex.

To the Islamists, individuality is reprehensible because it breeds idolatry. In effect, Islamic doctrine rests on the idea of collectivity. The Islamic ummat is a community of believers who are led by an Imam to creating a society based on Islam. Essential to the construction of an ummat is its members' oneness of thought *(towhid-e fekri)*. No aberration is tolerated since only the leader knows what is best (see Rose 1983). Shariati comments on this aspect of the ummat as follows: "The members of an ummat—from whatever family, society, or race they might be—think in one way, have a similar faith and are dedicated to carrying society to perfection—and not happiness and prosperity *(sa'ādat)*—under one social leadership" (Shariati n.d.-b: 520).

Shariati's Islamic critique of liberalism culminates in the individual's loss of identity in the community which then becomes the basis of a "monotheistic classless society," a community of believers with no individual identity. "Classes" disappear because there is no difference of ideas and lifestyles—"one can breathe the oxygen of Islam everywhere" (Shariati 1977: 23).[12]

Sexuality and hejâb constituted other significant sources of clerical anxiety. As I mentioned earlier, Islam recognizes sexuality as a part of all human beings. Men and women, however, enjoy sexuality unequally. While men are permitted to marry up to four permanent wives and, among Shiites, an infinite number of temporary wives, women can be married to only one man at a time. The reason, Muslim authors contend, is that men are oriented toward conquering women sexually whereas women are the prey and derive their satisfaction from being overpowered (Motahari 1978b: ch. 7). The Koranic verses demonstrate this tendency by asserting that women were created to secure a joyful life to God's male creatures: "By one of His signs He created you from dust; you became men and multiplied throughout the earth. By another sign He gave you wives from among yourselves, that you might live in joy with them, and planted love and kindness in your heart" (Koran 1988: 193); or, "Allah has given you wives from among yourselves, and through them He has granted you sons and grandsons. He has provided you with good things. . . ." (Koran 1988: 309).

Islam's notion of women's sexuality is a contradictory one. On the one hand, women are acknowledged as sexual beings and on the other they are characterized as passive individuals who seek pleasure in being chased by men. Fatima Mernissi refers to these tendencies as Islam's "explicit" and "implicit" theory of sexuality:

Moslem society is characterized by a contradiction between what can be called "an explicit theory" and an "implicit theory" of female sexuality and therefore a double theory of sex's dynamics. The explicit theory is the prevailing contemporary belief, according to which, women are passive. The implicit theory is epitomized in Imam Ghazali's classical work. He sees civilization as struggling to contain the woman's destructive, all-absorbing power. Women must be controlled to prevent men from being distracted from their social and religious duties. (Mernissi 1987: 32)

This vision of passive female sexuality is reflected in the following verse of the Koran: "Women are your fields: go, then, into your fields as you please" (1988: 356). The passive woman, the "field" that awaited fertilization now makes demands. The heart of her demands is the recognition of her identity not as a projection of male desire, but as a being in her entirety. This is unacceptable in Islam since, despite its claims to honor women and to bow down before their grandeur, an individual woman lacks an identity of her own. Women are all the same; having one is the same as having the other. The Prophet himself sanctioned this notion. It is said that "the prophet saw a woman. He hurried to his house and had intercourse with his wife, Zeynab, then left the house and said: 'When the woman comes toward you it is Satan who is approaching you. When one of you sees a woman and he feels attracted to her he should hurry to his wife. With her it should be the same as the other one" (quoted in Mernissi 1987: 42).

Another aspect of female sexuality according to Islam is its strength (Brooks 1995). Motahari not only admits this aspect of femininity but also argues that it is even stronger than that of men. This characteristic would not threaten an ideal Islamic society since women, in search of true love, can control their sexual urges. To the contrary, this strength should create sexual harmony. The Muslim family, according to Motahari, satisfies women's sexual and emotional needs and obliterates any reason for seeking illicit sexual fulfillment. In modern society, however, women are deprived of Islamic protection. The deprivation is harmful both to women and to their environment. Motahari writes:

Contemporary society, in the name of freedom for women—or, to put it more boldly, freedom of sex—has corrupted the soul of young people. This kind of freedom, instead of assisting women to blossom their capabilities and potentials, has wasted human energies and capacities in unprecedented ways. Women have left the household, but where did they end up? In movie theaters, beaches, street corners, and parties! Today's woman, in the name of freedom, has ruined the family, without fixing a school or a center of the sort [which can be helpful to society] in its stead. I dare saying that she even ruined [the already existing] schools. (1969: 203–4)

What lies beyond the chivalrous dedication to upholding women's honor is a concern over men's exclusive right to their wives. Securing this right is one reason for the highly regarded women's virginity.[13] Saving Islam from women, that is, from one of its most dangerous internal enemies, requires a tight control of the female body and sexuality. Therefore, a woman's laughter, for instance, is regarded as an amorous call. When a woman's body, except for her hands and face, is viewed as a sexual organ (*'aurat*) which, "like a house without surrounding walls," is in need of protection (Motahari 1969: 229), there will be no room for free expression of the self, sexual or otherwise. Only men should initiate sexual relationships and actively seek gratification. The woman should not display her desire independently. As Paul Vieille puts it, "the man conceives himself as revealer of the latent erotic powers of the woman" (1978: 463). This extremely passive notion of female sexuality represents itself in the daily life of the people and plays a major role in women's denial of their sexual urges and men's sexual dissatisfaction with their "frigid and disinterested" wives (see, for example, Azari 1983b: 53–54).[14]

Undoubtedly there is a more relaxed notion of sexual relationship among the professional middle and upper classes and the intention here is not to claim that there is one idea of sexuality common to the entire Iranian population. The point is to emphasize that despite its claim to the contrary, Islam has systematically denied female sexuality and, considering its role in the formation of Iranian culture, it has effectively prevented open discussion of sexuality by belittling it as preoccupation with the "bestial" aspect of life. Turning sexuality into a taboo, Islamic ideology fettered the growth of women's (and men's) knowledge of themselves and the development of a sexual polity that liberates women's bodies as well as their minds.

Hejâb plays an important role here. As Motahari points out in his book, *The Problem of Hejâb*, the central issue regarding hejâb is not whether a woman should be covered. It is rather concerned with the husband's sexual property rights:

[Hejâb relates to whether] a woman and a man's use of her should be free of charge: should a man be permitted to seek pleasure from any woman at any setting or not?

Islam's . . . answer is negative. Men can take pleasure in women as their legal wives within the sphere of family and after accepting great responsibilities. But [outside the family relationship and] in public, seeking pleasure from strange women is prohibited. Women, too, should be prohibited from giving men pleasure, in any possible way and form, outside the family structure. (Motahari 1969: 66–67)

Motahari cites several benefits of such a relationship. Less exposure to sexual stimuli means less sexual pressure on individuals, thus creating psychological comfort. He quotes Imam Sâdeq, a Shiite leader descended from Mohammad, commenting as follows on the perils of looking: "Seeing is a poisonous arrow that comes from Satan. Many is a look that causes long-lasting sorrow and misery." And: "Looking is the adultery of the eyes" (223). One should keep in mind that even though there are some dress codes for men, the most detailed laws and regulations on how to present oneself in the presence of strangers concern women alone. Hejâb also contributes to the stability of the family. "In the system of free sexual relationship, marriage puts an end to boys' and girls' freedom and forces them to be loyal to each other. In the Islamic system, marriage puts an end to their deprivation and waiting" (75).

In addition, hejâb keeps men and women out of mischief and leaves no question as to the identity of a child's real father. The third benefit of hejâb is the stability of the society. "Bringing sexual relationships into the public sphere weakens social energy for labor and [other kinds of productive] activities (77). Finally, the most revealing argument is that hejâb creates respect for women; it makes them more valuable. Since women gain their respect through men's hearts, "Islam encourages women to take advantage of this opportunity. Islam particularly emphasizes that the more modest, dignified, and chaste a woman is, and the less she displays herself for men, the more respectable she becomes" (80).

But if men and women are equally prone to the "poisonous arrows" of the eyes, as Islam does believe, why is it that the responsibility for covering is specifically women's? The reason:

a woman is the symbol of beauty and a man is the symbol of infatuation. Naturally, a woman—and not a man—should be told not to expose herself. Thus, even though the order to cover oneself is not for men, when men leave the house they are more covered than women. For, a man's inclination is to see and gloat, not to show off. On the contrary, a woman is more inclined to show off and not to gloat. A man's inclination to gloat stimulates a woman to show off more. Women are less inclined to gloat, thus men are less inclined to show off. (128)

Contrary to men, who are rational and thoughtful beings, women act more on their instincts and emotions, making them more susceptible to men's deceptions and tricks. Thus, it is up to society, that is, men, to make sure that women's virtues remain intact. Men are after each other's women, and since their sexual desire is uncontrollable, women must be kept hidden to prevent men from attaining each other's possessions. The restraints are not on men's desires and the ways of satisfying them, but on the object of their desires.

THE PERILS OF AN EDUCATED WOMAN

Another dimension of the gender crisis was disturbing the hierarchy of knowledge and undermining men's monopoly over Truth. Allah as the or-organizer of the world conveys his will and guidance to His creatures through male prophets: "The apostles We sent before you were no more than men whom We inspired" (Koran 1988: 297). Men receive Allah's words and transmit them to women. As Sabbah remarks (1984: 70–71), the Koran addresses women directly only when worship is concerned:

Enjoin believing women to turn their eyes away from temptation and to preserve their chastity; to cover their adornments (except such as are normally displayed); to draw their veils over their bosoms and not to reveal their finery except to their husbands, their fathers, their husbands' fathers, their sons, their stepsons, their brothers, their brothers' sons, their sisters' sons, their women servants, and their slave girls; male attendants lacking natural vigour, and children who have no carnal knowledge of women. And let them not stamp their feet in walking so as to reveal their hidden trinkets. (Koran 1988: 216)

Or in a verse which the clergy often cite as a proof of the egalitarian approach of Islam toward men and women, "Those that do evil shall be rewarded with like evil; but those that have faith and do good works, both men and women, shall enter the gardens of Paradise and receive blessings without number" (Koran 1988: 166).

Women disappear from the audience, however, when issues of law and administration of the Muslim society are concerned. In sura IV, which incidentally is about women, for instance, men are advised on the legalities of inheritance, divorce, and incest.

Men's monopoly over knowledge is threatened not only by women's claim to education, but also by their assertiveness. To be sure, Muslims have always claimed that, as the Prophet says, education is a duty of all Muslim men and women. Indeed, many considered education to be an essential factor in keeping youth attracted to Islam and away from atheism and communism (Motahari 1987b: 183). Nonetheless, there is one fundamental limitation on the Islamic zeal for knowledge. Knowledge can be pursued as long as it does not dissuade us from religious beliefs. "There is no doubt that science alone does not guarantee society's happiness and prosperity," writes Motahari. "Society needs both religion and science. . . . Islam wants neither a nonbeliever scientist nor an ignorant believer" (179).

The horizon of women's adventure in the realm of knowledge, however, is much more limited. As many scholars have pointed out, Islam firmly believes that the sexes complement one another (e.g., Nelson and Olesen 1977; Zakaria 1988). Men are rational while women are emotional. The dichotomy of rationality and emotionality is the theoretical foundation of several Muslim ideologues such as Nuri and Motahari. The latter, for instance, argues that the findings of the modern age all testify to the fact that women's actions are dominated by their emotion. He buttresses his argument with examples of female behavior in everyday life within both Islamic and Western societies (Motahari 1978b: 167–90). Men are physically stronger than women, have a passion for physical activities, and are adventurous and aggressive. Men are superior to women in science and logic, but "in literature, painting or other fields which are dependent upon elegant taste and talent women are no less than men" (175). Being emotional and sentimental, women are desperately in need of love and, unlike most men, it is affection they search for in a relationship, not lust. They are capricious and get easily excited. Mohammad Javâd Bâhonar agrees with Motahari's concept of different but complementary roles for men and women. He argues women's brains are smaller than men's and that sections of the brain related to emotions and reason are more developed in women and men respectively (Bahonar n.d.: 11–12).

We remember that the female protagonist of Mostafavi's book objected to men and women studying the same subject. What women need to learn, she suggested, was not physics and geometry. They should know about running an effective household, taking care of their husband, nurturing their children. Though other Islamists did not necessarily share this view, they did acknowledge the possible dangers education had for women. Education could easily open the door to a corrupt society and take women away from the righteous path Islam designed for them. Zamani offers an example of how education could be detrimental to women's health—both morally and physically. "Those girls who seek a husband by writing letters will develop a habit and even after they marry. They will keep old letters or even write new ones to keep prospective future husbands for a rainy day. They might be throwing themselves into the bosom of death" (Zamani 1970: 181).

We can now understand why when women do break these social and "biological" barriers, their achievement receives no acknowledgement. We note further two important characteristics of the religious texts regarding women. First, even though written to inform women, the texts enter into dialogues primarily with men, both as the public audience and as intellectuals who have addressed women's issues. If women's argumentation is taken into consideration, the purpose is either its vilification or its presentation as a case in point (see, for example, Qorbani n.d.: 80–109). A next characteristic is the condescending tone of much of the religious literature. Since women are incapable of understanding the severity of the contemporary social and political maladies, they should be reminded that though what they read may not appeal to their taste initially, they should bear with the author and realize the veracity of his arguments (Qorbani n.d.: 9–11). Undiscerning women are so mesmerized with the Western propaganda that they are ready to not only abandon their Islamic identity, but also defy the laws of nature and vie for equal rights with men (19).

The dichotomy of rationality/emotionality has practical consequences. If the laws of nature ascribe certain characteristics to the sexes, the division of labor in society as well as within the family cannot be oblivious toward these differences. Bâhonar (n.d.), for example, describes the family as a microcosm of society requiring a corresponding division of labor. Because a man's biology dictates that he provide for the family, men should head the family while women and children obey. In Motahari's view, the Koranic emphasis on *mahr* is set on the basis of the natural differences between men and women. Women compensate for their physical weakness by making it hard for men to attain them. Viewed from this angle, Motahari argues (1978b: 199–204), *mahr* is indeed a present for women rather than a price. Had the Koran considered *mahr* only in economic terms, it would have called for its abolition and, by prescribing equal inheritance, it would relieve men from the economic burden of *mahr*. Motahari also relies on biological differences to explain the Islamic requirement of a father's consent when a woman intends to be married for the first time. A young girl who confronts the possibility of a first marriage can be so overwhelmed by joy that her rational faculty may become dull. Thus, requiring the agreement of the father is a protection that Islam provides for her and should not be considered as an indication of the inferiority of her intelligence (60–61). By the same token, therefore, it is logical that men enjoy the right of divorce. After all, when a man is out of love there is no hope, whereas resumption or intensification of love can win a woman back (284).

WOMEN AND POLITICS: UPHOLDING ALLAH'S WISDOM

Though some Islamists such as Motahari accept women's social role and approve of their involvement in politics, others such as Yahyâ Nuri, Khomeini, and Nâser Makârem Shirâzi oppose women's participation in public life. Nuri argues that society needs to allocate responsibility to its members in accordance with their capabilities. In that sense, he writes, society resembles the human organism—"Hands cannot be sent for a walk and eyes cannot be responsible for hearing." In human society, too, sensitive governmental and judicial positions should be filled with "knowledgeable, able, willful and adamant men" who can avoid nepotism and take the nation's fate seriously (Nuri 1964: 260). Besides, women themselves do not show interest in politics because in their eyes, "politics is like mathematics: dry, lifeless, and dull" (261). This line of work, obviously, does not fit women's sensitive and delicate nature. Even in the West, where women have had equal access to education, millions of women have appeared in various fields of arts and sciences, but they are completely absent in the sphere of politics.

Women's enfranchisement, as mentioned before, drew hostile reaction from the clergy. Several ayatollahs residing in Qom, including Khomeini,[15] issued a communiqué in condemnation of the enfranchisement (reprinted in Rowhani 1981: 296–302). They state that the decision regarding women's voting was illegal. The reason, they point out, is that Iran's Constitution prohibits the adoption of any law which is contradictory to Islamic precepts (297). Therefore, the Constitution did not grant women voting power. Having the national interest in mind, the Constitution also denied such power to a number of other groups.[16] Then why should only the status of women change? Surely, argue the Islamists, those who claim women should have the right to elect officials and be elected to various offices are not going to put a minor in charge of the military; why then is the same consideration not made on the subject of women? At a time when our society is riven by serious social and economic predicaments, "the government, instead of searching for a solution, diverts its attention and the concern of the people toward issues regarding women's participation in the electoral process, women's rights, or the inclusion of half of Iran's population into social life and similar illusive matters which have no consequence but calamity, corruption and prostitution" (300).

The clerical reaction apparently met with some resistance. To appease the public, the Nehzat-e Âzâdy-e Iran (The Liberation Movement of Iran), whose founding members included Mehdi Bazargan and Ayatollah Tâleqâni, issued a statement, arguing that the only concern of the religious community is to protect the nation against a harmful government. The religious leaders, the statement reads, do not believe that women are subhumans; they merely want to prevent the spread of corruption and promiscuity (186).

The opposition to women's political presence is based on the different-but-equal notion. According to the authors of a pamphlet on women and electoral law, recent findings of biology, psychology, and sociology aptly support the Islamic emphasis on the importance of women as mothers and managers of households (Qorbani n.d.: 21–36). Women's social involvement not only hurts the families but is also detrimental to their identity as women (35, 49). A careful scrutiny, they go on, demonstrates that women's inclusion in social life has had "catastrophic impacts" on Western societies. At a personal level, the results have included the spread of venereal diseases, increased mental illness, alcoholism, and drug addiction, and the rise in the rate of suicide among women (110–122). At a social level, the consequences of women's employment and political participation have been even more devastating. Children have been deprived of maternal care; women's life cycles (as mothers and wives, of course) have been regulated by the demands of their jobs which in turn have created social imbalance; the number of illegitimate children has increased; youth have become disinterested in marriage; the crime rate has ascended; and, most important of all, the divorce rate has skyrocketed (123–42).

Some uninformed people argue, the authors write, that women's presence in politics is compatible with the teachings of Islam. To support this, they even cite a verse from the Koran as an example that the holy book recognizes such participation. The authors look askance at such practices since, first, these people do not have the authority to interpret the Book (35, 54–55); and furthermore, they completely misconstrue and misrepresent the verse. The verse in question is from the sura *She Who Is Tested* and reads as follows:

Prophet, if believing women come to you and pledge themselves to serve no other god besides Allah, to commit neither theft, nor adultery, nor childmurder, to utter no monstrous falsehoods of their own invention, and to disobey you in nothing just or reasonable, accept their allegiance and implore Allah to forgive them. (Koran 1988: 268)

The authors subsequently mention that the above verse is about women pledging themselves to believe in Islam and obey its laws and teachings. Their pledge (*bay'at*) differs from those made with men which entail social and political implications; the two should not be confused. Insofar as legislating is concerned, the Islamists bring to the reader's attention, one should not forget that Allah is the only authority who can make and unmake laws, but He has endowed Islamic religious authorities with the responsibility of interpreting given circumstances and introducing practical guidelines which should not at any rate contradict the divine laws (Qorbani n.d.: 59–60). Just because Islam prohibits women's partaking of politics, they assure the reader, there is no reason to conclude that Islam regards them as incomplete beings. Men, too, are considered unprepared for raising children and performing the duties that nature has bestowed upon women (79).

SAVING WOMEN FROM THE ENEMY WITHOUT

The present analysis has so far concentrated on Islamists' reaction to internal changes. But our study will be incomplete if we overlook the fact that one important reason for the religious preoccupation with women is that women constitute the last bastion of the Muslim man's resistance against the non-Muslim West. Many Islamists and religious authorities regard any demand for sexual equality as an indication of succumbing to Western values. This accusation has historically imposed serious limitations on the women's movement not only in Iran, but also in other parts of the Middle East. Leila Ahmed identifies this predicament of the Muslim woman as an important factor in her resistance to modernity and women's liberation:

For the Islamic woman . . . there is a whole further dimension to the pressures that bear down on her urging her to silence her criticism, remain loyal, reconcile herself to even find virtue in the central formulation of her culture that normally she would rebel against: the pressure that comes into being as a result of the relationship in which Islamic society now stands in relation with the West. (Ahmed 1982: 162)

In effect, the religious writings from the seventies, of which the most outstanding representatives are those of Ali Shariati, abandon the crude and simplistic biological determinism of the earlier ideologues and instead emphasize the nationalist and anti-imperialist aspect of the issue. The fear of Western infiltration, however, was present even earlier and even preceded the writings of figures like Motahari. Thus, the female body becomes the point of enemies' infiltration. Islam's internal enemy now carries the external foe inside her. To completely destroy Islamic resistance against colonialism and imperialism, the West sheds crocodile tears for Muslim women and encourages them to demand equality with men. Women (and some men) are intoxicated by such propaganda and in their imitation of the West, they establish Western-style women's societies every day (Nuri 1964: 285). Thus, it is incumbent upon devoted Muslims to instruct the public about the harms of adopting these values.

Western feminists, according to their Muslim critics, base their demands on a wrong presupposition. They seek identity with men while claiming to seek equality. Identity of the sexes, as we saw earlier, is contrary to the laws of nature. Besides, by acknowledging equality and rejecting sameness and uniformity, Islam has extended equal, but dissimilar, rights to women and men. That makes any demand for a radical change in women's status invalid. Admittedly, the argument continues, there is always room for improvement. Yet the point is that any attempt at improving the status of women should coincide with their natural gifts as mothers and housewives. As Nuri puts it, "If we are to teach women arts and crafts, is it not the best to teach them the art of knitting, and sewing? Isn't this kind of art more useful for them than to learn music, dancing, and other corrupting 'arts'?" (54).

Indeed, according to Motahari, the women's movement in the West acted too hastily to pay attention to the scientific foundation of the male/female relationship. As a consequence, the women's rights movement had paradoxical outcomes. On the one hand, it "succeeded in meliorating some of the miseries in women's lives, assuring them several rights, and opening many doors to them." On the other, "it generated even bigger problems and more serious agonies" (Motahari 1978b: 185). The Western women's liberation movement was a tactic deployed by capitalists in order to do away with the moral codes and loosen family relationships. In pre-capitalist times, women enjoyed the economic support of their husbands. A close (and closed) family circle prevented women's exploitation as cheap labor power (xx, 132). In his own way, then, Motahari shares the nostalgia of many Europeans and Americans for the classical family of the West (Goode 1984; Coontz 1992).

Motahari was not the only Iranian Muslim ideologue who disparaged the Western notion of sexual equality. Others, including Ali Shariati, criticized the West for promoting a false notion of womanhood and condemned the imperialist intention behind the penetration of these ideas into underdeveloped countries. Shariati's attack on "cultural imperialism," however, had an additional target, that is, the traditional or "false" Islam.

According to Shariati, underdeveloped nations have eventually to bear the influence of modernization. Therefore a rejection of modernity by traditionalists and fanatic religious leaders (akhoondhay-e qeshri) is not worthy of support. Yet, he is cautious about the negative effects of unfettered Westernization. Through "real Shiism," Shariati hopes, Shiite societies like Iran will effectively combine modern technology and science with their religious and cultural heritage. This combination should lead Muslims to the "classless divine society" (see Akhavi 1983).

Shiism, Shariati believes, has been diverted from its right path through different historical events and has become apolitical, nonpartisan, ineffective, and indeed reactionary. The most pivotal turning point in the history of Shiism came in the seventeenth century when, under the Safavid, Shiism became the state religion. That event neutralized the role of the clergy by devoting their energy exclusively to theology and remaining aloof from politics. The result, he concludes, was the isolation of the clerical community from day-to-day social life (Shariati 1980).

The primary focus of Shariati's analysis of women is the Western exploitation of Third World societies through cultural imperialism. As the center of family life, woman is the perfect target for imperialists:

She is used to change the form of society. She is used to destroy the highest values of the traditional societies. She is used to change ethics. She is used to change a traditional, spiritual, ethical or religious society for the sake of an empty, absurd, consuming society. She is used to transform art that had been the theophany of the divine spirit of humanity. She is changed into an instrument for sexuality in order to change the type humanity. (Shariati n.d.-a: 102)

"Sexuality replaces love" and woman, no longer the source of inspiration, transforms into a sexual image. She becomes the mean for the adaptation of the values of a consumer society. Here, Shariati's analysis, in addition to sharing important themes with other Iranian Muslim ideologues, resembles Frantz Fanon's ideas. According to Fanon, the French could control Algeria only through the manipulation of Algerian women. Fanon's analysis is devoid of any notion of patriarchy and considers the source of the problem to exist in the unequal relationship between the West and the Third World. One presupposition of this analysis is that Third World women had an ideal, egalitarian status in the pre-imperialist invasion era—a position which finds no supporting evidence in either history or Shariati's addendum.

Shariati treats the question of women in two parts. In the first section he analyzes the plight of the middle-class Iranian woman who, in rejecting "false Islam," had become a victim of cultural imperialism, which turned her into a "consumerist animal." This served two imperialist interests. First, it has reduced her to a "one-dimensional" entity with nothing to offer but her sexuality. Her main function is to promote the Western mass-produced goods. Therefore, unknowingly, she serves imperialism. As a "Western doll," she diverts minds from politics and preoccupies working people and intellectuals with superficial concerns (100–102). To facilitate its pillage of the Third World, the West has to first void us of any notion of our own self. "Once empty-headed with an impotent spirit, crippled and without content, we must become exactly like garbage cans which are filled with dirty and useless things and then are emptied" (104).

Woman is the first to be hypnotized by the "new civilization." She is not prepared to resist the temptation of modernity because outdated traditions exploit her and confine her to a degrading life. She is denied basic human rights and never is given the opportunity to develop her abilities. Her being is reduced to a "breeding machine" and her function is nothing more than that of a "washing machine." Thus, he argues, what paves the way for the West's easy success is the traditional, "false Islam."

The creation of superstitions and the spreading of ignorant backward beliefs of family traditions, the inherited faulty system of order along with servitude, the tradition of "father power" in the community . . . all weave themselves together like a spider's web. And it is this very web which impoverishes the woman. She becomes known as "someone who is behind the curtain." All of this occurs in the name of Islam, in the name of religion, in the name of tradition. (109)

In this way, Shariati complains, women are swindled out of all the rights that Islam granted them. Again in the tradition of Fanon, Shariati argues that Muslim Iranians are responsible if Reza Shah became the champion of women's liberation while his real intention was to divert our minds from thinking about real freedom and to turn our society into a market for imperialist production.

The outcome of the interplay of the external and internal factor was a dilemma before the Muslim woman. On the one hand, refuting the "new civilization" and pledging allegiance to the traditional life would cost her rights as a human being. On the other, rejecting her tradition and past, she would become trapped in consumerism.

Thus, he concludes, traditional limitations are hazardous to both women and society. Not only do women become an easy prey of imperialist aggression, but they are also rendered unable to perform their social duties. How can an illiterate and superstitious woman raise educated children to serve Islam and society?

MOBILIZING WOMEN FOR ALLAH . . . AND PATRIARCHY

Shariati's suggestion is to disregard both the traditional and the imperialist options. Neither a close-minded traditional woman nor her Westernized "identityless" sister can respond to the needs of our society at this time in history. The only woman who can contribute to our victory is one who creates her identity based on the history, culture, and religion of a society which owes its spirit to Islam.

Women in Islamic societies must not only be changed from being consumers of goods exported from Europe and America but they must also become active participants within their households. They must learn to relate according to today and tomorrow's generations. They must change the form of society. They must have an effect upon ethics, values, literature and art. They must have a deep revolutionary effect upon everything. They should be put to work upon this way. . . . Women become obliged to change internal and external conditions because the past conditions for women today are no longer practical or sufficient. (120)

The model to be emulated by liberated Muslim women, Shariati believes, is Fatima, the prophet's younger daughter and the wife of Ali (see Hermansen 1983). Fatima, rebelling when the caliphs usurped Ali's right to succeed the prophet, symbolizes militancy against injustice. "Fatima is the woman that Islam wants a woman to be. The prophet paints her visage himself. He melted her and made her pure in the fire of difficulties, poverty, resistance, deep understanding and the wonder of humanity" (Shariati n.d.-a: 224).

She owns a strong sense of commitment to society:

Fatima was not an unaware house dweller. She had learned how to walk in the midst of struggle, how to speak in the teaching of the faith. She spent childhood in the cradle of the storm of the (Islamic) movement and was tempered in the crucible of politics. She is a Moslem woman: a woman not prevented from social responsibility by the requirement of moral chastity. (Shariati n.d.-a: 168)

Fatima led a simple life and shared the poverty of her husband. But above all she was a wife and a mother—mother of the martyr Hussein and "mother of Mohammad." Close relationship to the prophet as his companion and caretaker in difficult times won her the title *umm al-nabi* (mother of the Prophet). Here Shariati includes the role of sacrificing woman into his "multidimensional" picture of the feminine ideal:

She is a symbol in all the various dimensions of being a woman. The symbol of a daughter when facing her father. The symbol of a wife when facing her husband. The symbol of a mother when facing her children. The symbol of a responsible, fighting woman when facing her time and the fate of her society. (225)

An important element of Islam's treatment of women is missing in Shariati's analysis, namely the treatment of women in the Koran and its discriminatory laws. How is the "modern," "progressive," and "true" Islam to deal with important practical issues like polygamy, divorce, and inheritance? On these issues, he could not reject the traditionalists' approaches since they were based on the explicit dictums of Islam. In fact, in *Woman in Mohammad's Eye and Heart*, Shariati writes that he sees no need to discuss women's right in Islam since Muslim theologians and scholars such as Motahari and Hassan Sadr had already written a great deal on that subject (Shariati n.d.-c: 4).

Shariati's concept of women's gullible and naive nature and their role and position is indeed a "modernized" version of what Muslim clergy have preached before him. His discussion of the infiltration of the West into the Third World through the female body rests on assumptions he shares with the clergy, namely, that women lack discerning ability and that, as Nuri puts it, "the downfall of woman is the collapse of the family and the death of the family is the demise of the society" (Nuri 1964: 92).

In Shariati's opinion, too, women's role is a supportive one. If they undertake an active role, it is only after fulfilling their primary duties as daughters, wives, and mothers. Even then, their personality should be molded by a great man, as the Prophet molded his daughter's. Thus, in a passage about the injustices of modern society to women, lamenting the loss of the great feminine qualities and values, he writes:

Women are no longer creatures who excite the imagination nor speakers of pure feelings. Neither are they the beloveds of the great lovers, nor do they have sacred roots. They are no longer spoken of in terms of mother, companion, center of inspiration and mirror of life nor are they faithful. Rather, as an economic product, women are bought and sold according to the positive-negative qualities of their sexual attractions. (Shariati n.d.-a: 100–101)

Interestingly, in Shariati's writings, love appears merely in its metaphysical form. His passionate passages reflect mystical love that always consumes the lover, but is never consummated (see Rahnema 1998: ch. 11). Real women appear as detractors from "worthy" spiritual, intellectual, or political preoccupations, and often in denigrating terms.

Some of Shariati's followers addressed issues about women in contemporary Iranian society after his death. Zahra Rahnavard (n.d.) in her book, *The Dawn of the Muslim Woman*, concurs with Shariati about contemporary Iranian women as having become sex objects and attempts to concretize the practical implications.

She defends the injunction "Woman should obey her husband and she should not go out of the house without his permission" by arguing that as long as women suffer from lack of consciousness such injunctions are necessary and good (22). With regard to the notorious verse 34 of the Koran's sura on women, Rahnavard attempts to play with words to defend its content but in the end gives in to the most significant part of the verse. She interprets "the beating of disobedient women" as "not referring to disobedience toward the husband but to society," with the "beating" as punishment administered not by the husband but by Muslim authorities. She interprets "some are superior to others" not to mean that men are superior to women, but to mean that there is mutual superiority between men and women; men by being providers are superior to women and women by being mothers are superior to men (77–80). Finally, she redeems the phrase "men are the managers of the affairs of women" as based on the biological constitution of men and women. "That is," Rahnavard contends, "only natural. It is also very beautiful. It is both just and logical" (81). Rahnavard supports this argument with the assumption that "worth" and "rights" are two different issues. Men and women may not have similar rights due to their different social functions (which in turn stem from their different physiology), but in the eyes of Islam both have the same value. Thus she denies domination in the family and the division of labor according to gender as its basis. The implications of Rahnavard's position are serious. Because women's roles are not economic, participation in production is not a step toward emancipation. Participation in political parties substitutes for playing a role in economic production as a means of liberating women, while not interfering with their role as mothers.

RECAPITULATION

In this chapter I discussed the reaction of the Islamists to the refashioning of patriarchy in pre-revolutionary Iran. At the heart of this reaction, I argued, is the symbolic characteristic of gender and family. Mediated through the media, the changes of the sixties were gauged in a global context. The Islamists saw Iranian society on the same path as Western societies. The refashioning of patriarchy then became significant for both its immediate effect and future ramifications.

From that vantage point, women simultaneously embodied two archenemies of Islam: the infidel without and the chaos within. Islamists argued that saving Islam from its internal enemy meant rescuing women from women. To accomplish this, Islamists suggested, women should live in an environment that protected them from men's deception—a task for which Islam was uniquely qualified. Restoring the power and rights of the patriarch in the family would create a harmonious, happy family that would nurture women's best qualities. Women would learn to be productive members of society by bringing tranquillity into the domestic life and instilling appropriate values in the new generation.

When the locus of control over women shifts away from the family, rational mankind can no longer supervise the development of emotional womankind. In search of self-expression and independence, women overlook family concerns and moral guidelines. But far from liberating them, this tendency makes them prey to men's sexual advances. In or out of public life, a Muslim woman's hejâb becomes her most effective weapon in warding off men. Hejâb conceals the woman from men's view and gives sex its proper field, the matrimonial bed.

A major point of contestation between the Islamists and the Pahlavi regime was the enfranchisement of women. To Islamists, the Pahlavi regime's intention was to subvert the natural rational-emotional dichotomy. Women are drawn to politics as yet another way to mimic the West. The colonialist West targets the heart of Muslim societies by directing its propaganda at the heart of the Iranian family: the woman. Women are offered a phony vision of liberation. According to this vision, following the Western lifestyle and fashion is the ultimate preoccupation of a woman. Women, then, are reduced to mere sex objects, empty-headed dolls who can implement colonialism's hidden agenda. The external enemy of Islam, in other words, hires Islam's internal enemy. Muslims should fight this ploy by resorting to authentic role models such as Fatima.

Things fall apart; the center cannot hold.

I quoted Yeats at the beginning of this chapter to communicate a sense of doom expressed by Islamists in pre-revolutionary Iran. Though many believed that the Shah's Iran was moving rapidly toward a fatal collapse, not all—even among Islamist critics of the Pahlavi regime—concurred in the specifics of the Islamists' gender analyses. Indeed, much of the simplistic arguments by authors like Mostafavi and Zamâni were dismissed summarily as old-fashioned or "too idiotic" to be taken seriously. Yet it was this very stratum that gained a leading role in the 1979 revolution. And it was the gender analyses of this stratum that shaped the post-revolutionary gender relations and conflicts. What caused such a marginal view to assume a hegemonic role? An immediate response is that, save for the extremities, the Islamist vision reflected the fabric of the Iranian ethos. But beyond this Weberian account of culture as internalized beliefs and value systems, we need to understand how the cultural politics of the pre-revolutionary days shaped the context of individuals' actions. How did other participants in the revolution, particularly the Left and progressive women, contextualize shifting gender boundaries and norms that made them vulnerable to the assault of patriarchy on women's rights? The following chapters will address this concern. Chapter 5 discusses the impact of the rise of the IRI on gender relations, while chapter 6 analyzes the Left's initial reaction and resistance to Islamists' plans.

NOTES

1. The vacuum of power following Reza Shah's abdication in 1941 gave a breathing space to progressive political activism. In 1943, the women's branch of the communist Tudeh Party was established and called "all Iranian women, regardless of their nationality, strata, class, religious or ideological conviction to unite under the banner of this Organization to fight for and defend just rights" (DOIW 1984a). Tashkilât-e Zanân-e Iran (The Organization of Iranian Women) published

a monthly journal called *Bidâry-e Mâ (Our Awakening)*, advocating women's employment and economic and legal rights for workingwomen. Hezb-e Zanân (Women's Party) was also established in 1944. The goals of the Women's Party included improving the living condition of women, economic independence for women, and education for women. Jam'iyat-e Zanân (Women's League) was also founded in 1942 to improve the legal condition of women. In 1945, the short-lived autonomous governments of Azerbaijan and Kurdistan for the first time approved of enfranchisement for women (Abrahamian 1982: 408). Before being banned in 1949, the Tudeh Party also introduced a bill to the Iranian Majlis that called for improvement in women's condition and voting rights for them. In 1952, some 100,000 women signed a petition to demand improvement in their political and economic status. The petition was sent to the Prime Minister Mossadiq, majlis, senate, and the United Nations. High-ranking clergy rejected women's franchise and called it anti-Islamic. For details about these and other organizations, see Bamdad (1977) and Sanasarian (1982).

2. For more on this, see Shahidian (1995: 118–19).

3. The exception was the Mojahedin who advocated militant overthrow of the government.

4. A similar dilemma confronted Muslim thinkers in other countries. On the debate over Islam, modern science, and sociocultural change, see Rahman (1982) and Tibi (1991).

5. This is a collection of lectures originally delivered in 1966.

6. Also see Motahari (1978a; 1987a).

7. "Westoxication," "Occidentosis," and "Euromania" are suggested translations for Al-e Ahmad's *Qarbzadegi* which literally means "Weststruck." See Al-e Ahmad (1982) and Hanson (1983).

8. For an excellent summary of Islamists' views on men, see Zakaria (1988).

9. For an example, see Khomeini's 1979 lecture on the occasion of Fatima's birthday (1982: 17).

10. Consider, also, that less than a month after the establishment of the Islamic Republic, on the eve of International Women's Day, Khomeini asked women to appear in public wearing the veil.

11. I have not seen any research on whether this decree was actually implemented after the revolution. Several attorneys have informed me, however, that they have never seen a case argued based on Khomeini's decree about the illegality of divorces after the passage of the Family Protection Law.

12. Shariati's (and Mojahedin's) emphasis on a classless society is not shared by all Islamist authors.

13. For valuable discussions of virginity, see Vieille (1978), Mernissi (1982), and Bouhdiba (1998).

14. The ambivalence of Iranian women toward sex is visible in the push-and-pull forces present in Forough Farrokhzad's early poetry. Nawal El Saadawi (e.g., 1981) paints a similar picture of Arab women.

15. The others were ayatollahs Morteza Langeroudi, Ahmad Zanjâni, Mohammad Hossein Tabâtabâ'i, Mohammad Yazdi, Mohammad Reza Golpaygani, Mohammad Kâzem Shari'atmadâri, Hâshem al-Amali, and Morteza Hâeri.

16. The Electoral Law, Article 10, states: "Those deprived of the right to vote consist of all females, minors and those under guardians; fraudulent bankrupts, beggars, and those who earn their living in a disreputable way; murderers, thieves and other criminals punished under Islamic law."

4

Gender in Revolution:
"Shrouding Freedom"

No sin should be committed in Islamic ministries. Naked women must not come to Islamic ministries. They [should be permitted to] go, but veiled.

Merely 24 days after the downfall of the Pahlavi state, on the eve of International Women's Day (8 March 1979), the Ayatollah made the initial stipulation about gender relations in the Islamic state. In his address to *tullâb* (students of Islamic education centers who would later join the ranks of the religious authorities), Khomeini chastised the government and different ministries for not following Islamic teachings. One criticism directly concerned women for not wearing the veil (*Kayhan* 7 March 1978: 3). Immediately, women responded to this attack on their most basic human rights by staging sit-ins and street demonstrations (for an account of those events, see Millett 1982). Veiled and unveiled women opposed mandatory veiling, calling it "the shroud of freedom." They cried: "We did not have a revolution to go backward." The newcomers retreated temporarily, but they were too adamant about their gender ideology to accept a total defeat. From the outset, the officials of the Islamic Republic of Iran (IRI) clearly delineated that women might participate in a revolution, but their first duty was to be good wives and mothers. The next few months witnessed a series of attacks and counter-attacks between the IRI and women and other progressive forces, contestation that set the mode for their relationship ever since. Women's resistance to the policies of the Islamic state has been a constant in the post-revolutionary years—now high and strong, now curbed and contained, but never dissipated completely.

The IRI justified its Islamization policies with the argument that the revolution was *Islamic*, that *Muslim veiled women* revolted against the Shah to make the veil and the purity and chastity that accompany it the order of their lives. Pictorial representations of women in revolution emphasized this aspect. Yet these images overstated the presence of veiled women, effectively excluding non-veiled secular women from the representation of the revolution. To this date, the veiled crowd is iconographic of women's role in the revolutionary process. In ensuing debates, many based their analyses on the erroneous assumption that even leftist women wore the veil as a symbol of anti-Shah solidarity.[1]

Islamists never enjoyed an unchallenged monopoly over the masses in revolt. In effect, Khomeini and other leaders of the Islamic movement had to make empty promises to overshadow their invidious future plans. And if they managed to gain a leading position in the revolution, it was in part because these false promises created an illusion of democratic adherence. In retrospect, many Iranians acknowledge the mistake of not recognizing the limits of those promises. At the time, however, the vision of the future was too mixed with hopes and dreams to reflect such cautions.

Yet one thing is undeniable. The *Islamic* revolution was based on a social vision that was not terribly popular among the modern middle class. What kept many revolutionary critics of the Islamists quiet in those days was their nationalist and, we must add, socialist inspirations, not their dedication to Islam. This rift was most evident with respect to gender. The secular, non-veiled participants of the revolution had no clear agenda for gender relations. They hoped that the change would bring democracy and freedom, that the revolution would create a more egalitarian environment—even that it would curb some of the moral anarchy of the Pahlavi Iran by ameliorating social and cultural disorganization (*nâbesâmâni*). None of these desires, of course, were articulated and clear. But, as the immediate and non-compromising reaction to the veil decree indicated, an Islamic revival of the private patriarchy was not a viable alternative for these women.

In this chapter, I will concentrate on women's mobilization in the revolution and their initial encounter with the IRI. I will argue that though secular women did not share the religious concern about the pre-revolutionary gender crisis, the gender ideology of the Pahlavi state equally lacked legitimacy in their eyes. But secular women did not rally around gender-specific demands; instead they placed their faith on revolution as a savior, as a guarantee that all problems would be solved after the removal of the Shah. Yet even the Islamists had to recast their approach to women in politics both to attract women believers and to ideologically accommodate their participation in an Islamic revolution.

THE ATTRACTION OF THE REVOLUTION

The refashioning of patriarchy during the sixties and seventies undoubtedly affected gender relations and created some free space for women in both private and public spheres. So, when women chanted against the Shah, many observers were taken by surprise (e.g., Afkhami 1984). Were women opposing the changes? Were they more "comfortable" with their traditional roles? Were women reacting to "rapid modernization"? Undoubtedly, these reflect the concerns of some women's antipathy toward the Shah. We should recall Deniz Kandiyoti's observation (see chapter 1) that at times of patriarchal crisis, some women join men in calling for a halt to the tide of change. The changing structure of patriarchy threatened the material *and* ideological interests of some women—women who reclaimed their status by marching for an Islamic state.

I will discuss the reaction of these women in the next section. Here, however, I would like to emphasize another dynamic behind the mobilization of women in the revolution. I believe what enticed women (and men) to question, if not challenge, the changing gender relations of the Pahlavi era reflects more on how the change was perceived than on its content.

Hegemonic leadership cannot be based on coercive domination alone. As Gramsci has suggested, hegemony and consensus must co-exist in order for a state to enjoy legitimacy in the eye of its subordinates. Such leadership requires intellectual and moral consent from a vast segment of the population (Buci-Glucksmann 1982). Gramsci suggests that the state—that is, political society—controls the coercive aspect of political domination, whereas civil society enables the ruling class to exercise its control through noncoercive means. As such, then, though civil society cannot be viewed as immune from the control of the ruling groups, it becomes the site of all the popular democratic struggles of different social groups (Bobbio 1979; Simon 1982).

Under the Pahlavis' reign, the role of civil society was minimized. Intolerant of any independent expression of will, the state went to a great length highlighting its presence in every societal domain. Such a line of action had serious implications for gender politics. I consider two tightly connected factors of considerable significance in this regard. First, the weakness of civil society obfuscated the nature of the reforms and limited their scope. Second, by placing itself at the center of social life, the Pahlavi state made it impossible to distinguish between the politically motivated policymaking (in other words, Realpolitik) and broad sociocultural changes. Working together, these factors contributed to a censure of the Pahlavis' gender politics, a crisis in the hegemony of the state's gender policies.

The dictatorship both delimited and concealed overt power struggles. The Shah could circumvent all social, political, and legal norms, declaring an act, or even a tendency, legal or illegal according to his discretion.[2] The origin of social reforms as an outcome of the struggle of various social groups was mystified. They seemed spun from the capricious will of a ruler. Numerous examples can be supplied from Iran's contemporary history. One source, for instance, comments as follows on the emancipation of Iranian women:

Women's emancipation dawned on January 7, 1935, with a royal proclamation by Reza Shah the Great unveiling the Iranian women. Soon, women were able to obtain jobs in government and commercial offices, work side by side with the men, go to the university, and engage in a number of professions which had been closed to them until then. . . . It was only natural that the White Revolution [a series of social reforms which included the land reform], launched on January 26, 1963, should also pay attention to the status of women in the modern Iranian society. Point 4 of the White Revolution concerned elections and called for an amendment of the election law. The new law gave women full franchise rights. Women were given the right to vote and to be elected to the Parliament as well as to local councils and other elected bodies. (*Iran Almanac* 1970: 528)

The passage not only does not mention the suppression of all grassroots women's organizations under the two Pahlavi monarchs, it also omits decades of struggle by Iranian women to abolish the veil and gain enfranchisement: the right to vote *was given* to women by the Shah (for further discussion, see Shahidian 1995).

Thus, women's ties with their history were severely damaged, depriving women of an important source of social and political knowledge. Reforms, or any kind of policymaking for that matter, appeared divorced from the social pressures at bottom. That explains why even when reforms improved women's lives, the public remained unconvinced that an authoritarian government would—or indeed could—actually do anything to their benefit.

We need to emphasize, however, that one reason for this reluctance was the limited scope of the reforms. Consider the example of the increase of the minimum age at marriage in Iran. Research on the effects of the introduction of this reform concluded that legislation played "a minor role in setting the actual age at marriage" (Momeni 1972: 551). Since the introduction of the law coincided with no relevant economic, social, and cultural changes that strengthened the practice of early marriage, the laws remained relatively ineffective (also see Saney 1974).

The Pahlavis were resistant to radical social transformations, a tendency that severely paralyzed the transition from private to public patriarchy. The refashioning of patriarchy under the Pahlavis limited the clerical influence on some aspects of family law or revised certain aspects of the shari'ah vis-à-vis women and family. But it never undermined the shari'ah completely. This equivocal relationship was doubtless influenced by the societal balance of power. When the government was powerful and had a tight grip on sociopolitical affairs, it tended to take more than it gave. When conditions were less favorable, however, the government acceded to the demands of the religious community (Hudson 1980: especially 16–18). As Mahnaz Afkhami, the Minister of Women's Affairs under the Shah, points out,

One phase of legal action always involved convincing the Monarch—whose national role was the essence and symbol of patriarchy. Since he was regularly briefed by the Queen and Princess Ashraf . . . constantly exposed to international opinion and attitudes and possessed by a vision of Iran as a "progressive" nation, it would sometimes suffice to demonstrate to him the importance of the proposal to national development. On issues which were in apparent conflict with the text of the Koran, he took a very rigid stance. (Afkhami 1984: 333)

The Pahlavi state constantly pledged allegiance to the precepts of Islam. Religious rituals were on the whole observed. Though intent on reviving the pre-Islamic Iran to legitimize kingship as an integral part of the Iranian culture, the Pahlavis paid lip service to the Islamic cultural heritage. After the mid-seventies, the regime went so far as openly criticizing the West and calling for a rejection of both East and West in favor of an indigenous value system.[3] Some ideologues, such as Ehsan Naraghi, aired a series of TV interviews chastising the "alienation of the West" (*qorbat-e qarb*) much in the tradition of conservative, religious writers like Al-e Ahmad and Ali Shariati (Naraghi 1974; 1976a; 1976b; 1977). Needless to say, the religious hierarchy also returned the favor, either through outright support of the regime (e.g., Nesârizâdeh 1966) or by its crusade against Marxism.[4] The flirtation between the state and religious circles partially explains the reluctance of the clergy—with the exception of Khomeini—to call for the downfall of the Pahlavi regime until the very end.

This political culture was key in women's attraction to the anti-Shah struggle and shaped the gender politics of the 1979 revolution. Changes in gender relations were viewed as merely window dressing for political propaganda. The scope and implications of the development of public patriarchy were not assessed objectively. That in the Shah's Iran "neither men nor women were free" (Khomeini 1982: 25), that one could not talk about "women's rights" in a tyrannical system, was an argument that we often heard, believed, and made. A polemic displaced sound social analysis. At the same time, the clerical rhetoric during the revolution was construed as exclusively anti-Shah, its sociocultural implications overlooked. Consider this—one instance among many—comment by Khomeini in an interview with an Iranian female reporter shortly before the downfall of the Shah's government:

Progress means human values, it means women's significance in the country, not going to movie theaters or dances. Those are the kind of progress that Mohammad Reza dreamed up for you, that pushed you back in time. We must compensate for that. You are free to do all the right things, free to go to college. . . . The whole nation is free in that respect. But if they are to do things against the nation or that conflict with morality, we will prevent that. And that is the sign of progress and being progressive. (19)

Many participants of the revolution heard only in this comment that the Shah's claim to be progressive was false, that the anarchy of the Shah's Iran must come to an end, that the interest of the nation should be protected. But Khomeini's concerns about the public presence of women struck at the cultural politics of daily life. Women going to movie theaters meant that they were neglecting their natural duties; discos signaled ubiquitous corruption and moral anarchy. At this point, he no longer merely opposed the Shah; he countered what women had achieved through decades of struggle. Ignoring that distinction was easy at the time. Changes in gender relations were severed from women's social struggle; these were regarded as royal donations (as the state propaganda promoted). Thus, contradicting the state meant opposing the "royal donation," *not women's achievement.* The state was everywhere and everywhere people recognized the state; nothing the government had done enjoyed legitimacy. That the Pahlavis located the state at the center of all social life was indeed the Achilles heel of their reforms in the domain of gender.

Yet more in Khomeini's statement was overlooked. He said: "You are free to do all the right things, free to go to college. . . . The whole nation is free in that respect. But if they are to do things against the nation or that conflict with morality, we will prevent that." His qualifiers—"all the *right* things" or "things against the nation or that conflict with morality"—escaped our notice. Why? First, because of the attraction of the anti-Shah rhetoric. Second, and more significantly, because the sociocultural implications of the changing gender relations were rarely discussed in prerevolutionary days. Perhaps fear of persecution and censorship discouraged overt discussions. But, again, the fear that a recognition of social change might become a credential for the Shah, strengthening the regime's position against its critics, was quite strong (e.g., Nategh 1967: 16).[5] Thus, such concepts as "morality," "purity," and "appropriate behavior" were not scrutinized and contested. As the Shah's regime promoted corruption and anarchy, the opposition represented moral order. Exactly what that "moral order" entailed was neither clear nor of concern. Women who demonstrated against the Pahlavi regime agreed upon two points: that women were equal to but dissimilar from men; that Western values were "a corruptive menace to be avoided" (Sanasarian 1986: 214).

The 1962 opposition to the land reform and women's enfranchisement was also enigmatic. To many, the idea that the clergy-led June 1962 demonstrations were for reactionary reasons—especially as far as women's rights were concerned—was unacceptable. This was in part due to the lack of adequate historical information, as the documents and narratives of the June demonstrations were suppressed. But it was also partly due to the popular misconception that Khomeini's opposition to the Shah somehow absolved him of the antiquated ideas about women. The movement opposed the Shah, and that was all that mattered. Incidental matters could be altered later.

Consequently, the women present in anti-Shah demonstrations did not find the message of religious authorities strongly at odds with those of their own. To be sure, many regarded the clergy's proclamations as too rigid and troglodytic—some even demonstrated their objections—yet most did not consider such extremism insidious enough to endanger the unity of the "revolutionary camp."

WOMEN IN REVOLUTION

Women's participation in the 1979 revolution was greatly affected by social origin. Rural women took little part; at the most, their involvement was supportive, and even then ambivalent.[6] Mary Hegland, for instance, reports that when trading women in the village of Aliabad finally decided to join the protesting crowd, many drew the line at marching, deemed an inappropriate form of feminine behavior (Hegland 1986; Hoogland 1980–1981).

The bulk of the female participants of the revolution came from urban migrant families and the traditional and modern middle classes. Of these, the majority was either from working-class and migrant families or from the traditional or modern middle classes. As discussed earlier, landless peasants who migrated to Tehran mainly settled in the slums and formed an underemployed proletariat. Tehran's shantytown became the locus of much anti-government protest and generated the first waves of a storm which put an end to the long-lasting monarchical rule in Iran (see Hooglund 1980). Migrant women played a significant role in the resistance of the slum-dwellers to the governments' recurrent attempts to remove them from their homes, in late 1977 and in 1978. According to one source,

In a particularly harsh fight with the officers of Teheran Municipality in August 1978, 200 men and women of a settlement known as Shahbaz-i Junubi fought the invaders for five hours. The squatters' efforts were, however, to no avail, as their 50 shacks were leveled by bulldozers. About 13 of the squatters were injured also, some seriously enough to require hospitalization. (Bayat 1987: 87)

The traditional middle class considered Islam their savior. Their adherence to Islam shows their loyalty to their class interests—or those of their male relatives—and to their own demands qua women. Many of these women, especially their leading members, are educated and had knowingly chosen Islam, mainly due to their age-old familiarity with it. Islam served them on many occasions as a weapon in their life-and-death struggle with external and internal enemies. The clerical establishment and the bazaari merchants always enjoyed a mutually supportive relationship.[7] The two also could communicate with little barrier because the leading ayatollahs came predominantly from well-to-do bazaari families. (Rank-and-file *âk-hoonds*, or preachers, came from lower classes.) As the main and most powerful traditional segment of the Iranian population, the bazaaris relied on Islam to safeguard them against the evils of atheism and modernity. During the seventies, when the penetration of state control into the bazaar upset the merchants, the religious establishment responded favorably to their grievances. Though, as Graham (1979: 222) correctly mentions, this resentment was insufficient to goad the bazaari merchants into nationwide anti-regime campaigns, the increasing anti-Shah sentiment among the clergy encouraged them to organize and finance the pandemonium.

After decades of humiliation as "regressive" and traditional, through Islam they would own an opportunity to dominate. Islam would allow these women to dismiss the "sinful" and "promiscuous" life of the "Westernized doll-women." Under the Shah's dispensation, younger women were especially prone to confusion. As a university student or an office employee, she had to lead a dual life. Often, she carried her traditional life to the edge of the other one—wearing the châdor to the vicinity of school or office, at which point she would take it off, fold it, put it in her bag so that she could once again wear it on her way back home. But her Islam was more than a necessary practice. She was trying to rescue what she considered femininity. Her gender identity was tied to the primacy of her domestic role. A good woman was supposed to have limited contact with members of the opposite sex. When the time came, she would marry a good man who would take care of her and their family. Her domain of control would predominantly concern the private sphere. Regardless of her own strength, she had the privilege of a man's protection—his success would give the family status and honor. Her behavior would protect family honor.

The refashioning of patriarchy under the Shah had rendered the traditional bargain and its accompanying female gender identity obsolete; Islam enabled traditional middle-class women to revive it, to "do gender" (West and Zimmerman 1987) as she was prepared for and guaranteed her interest. Islam's emphasis on the sanctity of the family, they believed, would restore women's virtue and their dignity in the society.[8] So, for them, Islam was indeed a messiah. It should be added that as Anne Betteridge (1980) argues in her study of *rowzeh* (religious gathering), these Iranian women adapted Islamic rituals so that those rituals would meet with their own lifestyle and responsibilities.

Shariati's teaching appealed particularly to the bazaari youths who were the first generation of their families entering higher education or, for that matter, finishing high school. They were going through a transitory period: college education opened up new horizons (in terms of both social status and ideology) while they could not make a rupture with the past. Shariati's version of Islam provided them with a worldview that combined old and new, tradition and modernity, Islam and Western social sciences. The militant People's Mujahedin Organization of Iran (PMOI) was also an attractive alternative among this group.

The professional women of the modern middle class were another actively present group in the revolution. As main beneficiaries of the Pahlavi reforms, their objective in the revolution was not to bring Islam to power. On the contrary, as James Bill comments, the professional middle class (what he identifies as "the intelligentsia") "has very decidedly discarded old values and value systems" (Bill 1972: 61). Nevertheless, as discussed above, they found both the limitations of these reforms and the chauvinistic culture promoted by the government objectionable. They were nurses, doctors, lawyers, authors, teachers, and students who first and foremost had political grievances against the regime. Their demands as women were secondary to their exigencies as oppressed Iranians.

Finding legal and organized methods of politics closed, urban professional middle-class women channeled their energies and talents into new ways of political involvement. Among university and college students, militancy manifested itself in the form of numerous strikes and demonstrations (Halliday 1979: 217–21; Keddie 1981: 235–37; Nategh 1982). The emergence of two clandestine guerrilla organizations—The People's Mojahedin Organization of Iran in 1965 and the Organization of Iranian People's Fedaii Guerrillas in 1971 (OIPFG)—provided a new opportunity for women to express their dissent and carry out important military attacks on the regime. PMOI adopted an Islamic ideology mixed with certain arguments of Marxist political economy and epistemology (see Abrahamian 1989). OIPFG adapted Marxist-Leninist tenets, without Islamic trappings (Abrahamian 1982: 483–89; Halliday 1979: 235–48; Jazani 1980: Introduction; Shahidian 1994; Zabih 1986).

Determining the exact number of women who participated in secret guerrilla organizations is impossible due to the secrecy surrounding this form of political activism (for details, see Shahidian 1997a). According to Abrahamian (1982: 480), of the 341 guerrillas killed in opposition to the Pahlavi government, 39 were women. Housewives (14) and college students (13) headed the casualty list. Of the remaining twelve, nine were schoolteachers, two were doctors and one was an office employee. The majority of dead female guerrillas were from the Fedaiin.

All in all, secular Marxist organizations attracted more women than the religious ones. This could be explained by the fact that armed struggle started in the early seventies, the years following the reforms and the oil-boom. Though Marxist organizations claimed to represent the interest of the working class and peasantry, the bulk of their membership was drawn from colleges, urban intellectual circles, and professional centers—the loci of educated women. Marxists' secular ideas were more attractive to these women than the Islamic ideology. As Abrahamian observed, "although the Mojahedin made major inroads among the college-educated children of the

traditional middle class, it met with less success among the two other major
sectors of the intelligentsia—the older generation of professionals, and the
college-educated youth from modern, middle-class homes" (Abrahamian
1989: 230–31). The same could be argued about the followers of Ali Shariati. The still-dominant Islamic aspect of their doctrine had less attraction
for the educated and modern women.

Other Islamic groups that relied on a more orthodox Islam attracted no
women to their activities. In fact, Muslim activists on college campuses
often resorted to violence and harassment of women and non-Islamist student activists. Islamist student activists report the existence of a *gorouh-e
zarbat*, a hit squad of about 40 people, active on the campus of the University of Tehran from spring 1975 to the revolution. The squad warned,
harassed, and physically attacked students who did not adhere to the Islamist code of decency, that is, students who wore revealing dress or had
amorous relationships. "We decided not to hit girls, but beat up the boys
severely," narrates a member of the *gorouh-e zarbat* in a recent interview
with 'Emâdudin Bâqi (2000: 234). Another activist relates a snowball attack against "licentious" female students on a snowy day in winter 1976
(248). A third one recalls participating in an attack against a first-year
female student "who dressed very badly and walked coquettishly," hitting
her on the head with an egg and rolled-up papers (248–49). In the fall of
1977, Islamist students attacked the women's dormitory on the campus of
the University of Tehran, set their bus afire and issued a threatening communiqué, giving the following ultimatum to women:

Do not come to the men's cafeteria, do not enter the men's campus under any
circumstances—even for the purpose of obtaining food, do not use the men's bus
under any condition and exert pressure on the authorities of your campus to provide you a dining hall and a bus. If you fail to comply, your life may be in jeopardy.
(Quoted in Nategh 1982: 30)[9]

The icon of women in revolution, as I mentioned at the beginning of this
chapter, is the veiled crowd. Within Iranian political circles, the assumption
is frequently made that women, even secular and leftists, participated in
the revolution wearing the veil. My review of pictures of and documentaries
about the revolution does not support this assumption. Nor does my interview with exiled Iranian leftists. If anything, the situation was quite to
the contrary. Leftist women were distinct with the famous trousers and
long shirts. One woman recalled her experience during the days of the
revolution:

At first little distinctions were made among different participants in street demonstrations. Everybody mingled, but leftist women did not wear the veil or the scarf.
Veiled women distributed scarves among them. Leftist women, on the other hand,
tried to politicize the chants and orient them more toward the objectives of the

anti-Shah struggle rather than allegiance to Islam or to Khomeini, or promoting the veil. (Personal correspondence, 14 June 1997)

Though often unspoken, the differences in objectives were evident. The leftists and other secularists critiquing patriarchy were incidental, but their comments were overall directed at the oppression of women; they did so in order to fight the discriminations of private and public patriarchy. The critique of the Islamists, however, aimed at the opposite direction. They criticized the new image of women because it posed a threat to the traditional form of men's power over women. They criticized the emergence of public patriarchy because it denied men's *exclusive* rights over women. Thus, when traditional Muslim women, dressed in long, black veils, came to the streets and demonstrated against the Shah, they were not simply using the veil as a unifying anti-Shah symbol. They were putting forward a specific definition of womanhood, sexuality, and male/female relationship delineated so clearly in the writings of, among others, Motahari and Shariati.

CULTURAL ACCOMMODATION OF WOMEN IN POLITICS

We recall that the clergy was quite opposed to women's presence in the public sphere. Indeed, Khomeini urged his followers to express their disapproval of and hatred (*tanaffor*) for equal rights (Khomeini 1982: 14). He considered the franchise for women contradictory to the shari'ah (13) and conscription for women tantamount to sending them to brothels (14). Such an assessment of women's social and political role could not easily accommodate their mass participation in the revolution.

We also recall that Islamists like Shariati realized the obsolescence of clerical doctrine in this regard. Using Islamic figures like Fatima and Zeynab, these authors promoted an ideal type of Muslim woman who not only accomplished all her traditional duties, but was also mindful of her social responsibility. If women's participation in politics could not be avoided, it should be utilized in favor of Islam. As the revolution approached, the clergy embraced this rhetoric instead of the earlier rejection of women's participation in politics. The new discourse not only accommodated women's presence in the revolution, but also their continued involvement in post-revolutionary politics. Women should play their role in bringing Islam to power. And in the protective bosom of an Islamic government, there is little concern about corruption due to women's social presence.

Thus, instead of condemning women's presence in society and calling for their return to their "proper and natural" confinement, Khomeini promised female anti-Shah protesters equality in the Islamic regime. He appealed to them for active participation in the movement. "Shiism not only does not exclude women from social life, but it elevates them to a platform where they belong" Khomeini said in an interview with a German newspaper (Khomeini 1982: 18). In an interview with Amnesty International, on November 10, 1978, the Ayatollah said: "According to Islam, women have a sensitive role in constructing an Islamic society. Islam raises the status of women in society so that they might regain their human dignity, not be objectified. They can assume responsibilities" (Khomeini 1981: 20).

Motahari, too, commented on the qualitative changes in women's social role in contemporary Iran. His ideas on this issue are best expressed in an unfinished postscript to his book, *The Problem of Hejâb*, written after the revolution and published posthumously (Motahari 1979a).

In the course of history, Motahari writes, women have performed a pivotal "indirect creative role" by giving birth to men, nurturing them, and being a source of inspiration for them. Women owe their "indirect creative role" to their "special sexual morality, i.e., shame, chastity, virtue and the female inaccessibility." Whenever women do not honor morality they end up not fulfilling this "historical role."

So, Motahari continues, it seems as if there is a contradiction in the two roles: women have either to perform an "indirect role and stay behind the scene" and cherish their feminine values; or become directly involved with social life at the expense of their natural worth as women. But an alternative has been actualized by the Muslim Iranian women. During the Iranian revolution, although the Iranian Muslim woman participated in the making of history, she did not relinquish her female responsibilities. "She did not abandon her shame, chastity, and the necessary cover. She remained inaccessible, and maintained her grandeur and glory. She did not dishonor herself like the Western woman or the woman of the Pahlavi era."

Motahari divides women's participation in history into three different periods. In the first stage, woman played a negative historical role. She was nothing but an "object" out of reach, confined to the "internal family life." If we refer to our own history of the last half a century, Motahari writes, that is exactly the kind of women we find. They existed merely as "adored precious objects." (Clearly, the women Motahari refers to are from the traditional middle class, the bazaaris, since the women of other classes and strata did play a direct role in society.)

In the second stage, woman deserted the home. She "became a man's partner in the realm of science, art, [and] politics. However, she lost her value and price by completely abandoning her own circle (*madâr*), putting aside her appurtenance (*harim*), making herself accessible to men in public places, cabarets, discos and on street corners, announcing her presence and willingness everywhere." At this stage, "a woman was a person, but a person without any value. . . . She gained her direct role in the making of history but lost her indirect role which is no less [important and valuable] than the direct one." When a woman loses her indirect role, she "destroys not only herself but also the man." "Such was the path of the 'Pahlavi-style' woman that constituted a large segment of Iranian women for about forty years."[10]

Motahari never finished the manuscript but it can be inferred that he contends the third period—which he calls "masculine-feminization of history"—to be Iran of the post-Islamic Revolution where women can effectively participate in politics without abandoning their natural duties.

The People's Mojahedin Organization of Iran (PMOI) embodied new visions of women in politics by combining the new interpretation of Islam with armed struggle. In this way, to borrow Shariati's metaphors, they mixed the Islamic "message" with the "blood" of martyrdom. The Mojahedin's concentration, however, was basically on the fight against the Pahlavi dictatorship and the cause of women did not receive the same theoretical consideration in their writings that it did from the rest of the religious community. The participation of women in the Organization, as mentioned before, was marginal. It was only after the revolution that massive numbers of young women, captivated by the Islamic fervor, but appalled by the atrocities of the Islamic regime, joined the Mojahedin.

The Mojahedin did not comment on the status of women in Iran or Islam prior to the revolution. Since shortly after the revolution, they have published a series of essays called *The Woman in the Path of Liberation* in their official paper *Mojahed*, also published independently as a pamphlet (PMOI 1980).[11] The pamphlet begins with a condemnation of attributing women's oppression to natural orders. Islam, Mojahedin argue, adopts a sophisticated outlook in which neither economic nor cultural issues are overlooked. In Islamic ideology, women are not denigrated as sex objects. The Mojahedin's discussion focuses on women's status under capitalism in both developed and underdeveloped countries. Under capitalism, women not only have to shoulder the burden of office and factory work as providers of cheap labor power, but they must also do household chores. Furthermore, by making family the locus of consumption, capitalism limits women's role to that of motherhood (43). In underdeveloped countries, we are faced with an additional aspect of capitalist expansionism. Imperialism not only economically exploits the Third World—or in a terminology which the Mojahedin borrowed from the left, turns nations into dependent capitalist societies—but also subjects these nations to "cultural metamorphosis" (48). Thus, all the negative characteristics of the capitalist treatment of women are present in the Third World as well as a new component, that is, the humiliation which the native women experience in comparison to the Western woman. Mojahedin's argument fails to provide women with anything that has not already been their lot under patriarchal systems. The only difference is that capitalism and what the Mojahedin call the "reactionary Islam" produce ignorant mothers but the Mojahedin's Islam, educated ones.

PATRIARCHAL TRIAD

Less than a month after the downfall of the Shah, some three weeks before the formal establishment of the Islamic Republic of Iran, Khomeini launched the first major attack on women's rights. On the eve of International Women's Day, in his address to students of Islamic education centers, Khomeini demanded that women should observe the Islamic dress code. After only a few days, continuous demonstrations and sit-ins forced him to recant. Ayatollah Tâleqâni stated in a press conference that what Khomeini said regarding hejâb was merely "advice of the sort a father gives to his children" (*Kayhan* 11 March 1978: 3). The retreat, however, was tactical. Other anti-women measures continued. The Family Protection Law was repealed. The new laws based divorce, custody of the children, and the taking of a second wife all upon the husbands' wishes instead of depending on the court's decision. Women were denied eligibility for certain occupations such as judge or attorney. Ayatollah Shariatmadâri, quite influential at the time, expresses a sentiment common among many new leaders:

Judgment is not an easy job. There are certain qualifications for a judge and we believe this is not an appropriate job for women since they are not qualified enough. . . . One day a lawyer came to me and said: "We have some women judges. I have usually to view some corpses. In one case, a woman judge had to go and see them. When she did, she screamed and fainted." Consider this simple example and see if having women as judges would work. If a woman judge has to daily view several dead people and faints every time and needs a doctor, what will happen then? Women are very sensitive and this job does not suit their nature. (Quoted in Fashkhami 1979: 3–4)

Mehdi Bazargan, the Prime Minister of the Provisional Government of the IRI, was quoted in *Le Monde* (1979): "talking of absolute equality of sexes is impossible. Nature did not want it either for the human race or for plants and animals." As Nashat (1983; 1980) remarks, such an argument has its roots in believing in the "fact" that men are superior to women in intellectual ability and self-control. According to Muslim leaders women are emotional, sensitive, and lacking in intellectual discernment. "It is more appropriate for women," says Ayatollah Nuri, "to leave politics to their husbands and to busy themselves with the work for which they are best suited" (quoted in Nashat 1980: 181). What are women "best suited" for? According to Mehdi Bazargan, "The first right of a woman is to have a

husband and to be a mother. Nobody can deprive a woman of these rights"
(*Le Monde* 1979).

I discussed in the previous chapter a sense of urgency echoed in many
pre-revolutionary religious writings. In response to that urgency, rescuing
man- and womanhood from external and internal attacks was a mandate
of the new state. A union was formed among patriarchy, Islam, and the
state to reinstate the ideal gender through a revival of male power. This
patriarchal triad was to return "order" to family and society, an "order"
in which gender would be constructed on binary oppositions and hierarchic
division of characteristics and role; sexual division of labor would be complementary; moral, and preferably Muslim, men and women would reproduce the ideal family on which the Islamic society is founded.

Islam, state, and patriarchy thusly form a patriarchal triad whose objective is to uphold order by reinstating the traditional patriarchal bargain.
Though there has always been some degree of cooperation among these
elements in contemporary Iran, the establishment of an Islamic state affords
patriarchy the added oomph of sacred blessing. Private patriarchy can re-
invigorate its ailing structure, have increased representation in the state,
and enjoy the immutable divine approval. At the same time, hierarchical
order in the family predisposes the public for other hierarchical relationships in society. When a hierarchy of roles and power is assumed "natural"—however masked in the benign language of family relations—class,
ethnic, and political hierarchies gain more legitimacy. In the new Islamic
state, that assisted legitimacy is particularly helpful, since in the new political order, the state rules over people, and both are overshadowed by the
imposing *Rahbar*, the religious leader, the *valy-e faqih*. When dissention in
the realm of gender is defeated, when the polity is in the hand of the clergy,
Islam can feel more secure. Moreover, with the clergy occupying key positions in society and polity, not only is Islam rescued, but also the men of
God regain their lost privileges of running the shari'ah courts. The earthly
distractions—be it the "naked woman" or the critical educated mind—can
be parried to the benefit of Allah.

RESCUING WOMEN AND MEN, IN THE SERVICE OF ALLAH

Under the rule of the patriarchal triad, women become more than ever
vulnerable. Having just seized state power, the Islamists indeed had a well-
planned program to restructure society along Islamic principles. Women
were the first to bear the attack of the Islamic state. The IRI would restore
the traditional relationships of power and return to the family its poignant
role as the locus of legitimate procreation of faithful Muslims. All that was
denied Allah and the divine-designed order would be restored. Article 2 of
the Constitution of the IRI specifies that the IRI is a system based on belief

in *one* Islamic god—"There is no god but Allah"—His exclusive sovereignty and lawmaking, and the submission of all to His command. "Absolute sovereignty over the world and man belongs to God, and it is He who has made man master of his own social destiny" (Article 56).

To achieve the ideal divine society, Article 3 specifies, among other needs, that of "the creation of a favorable environment for the growth of moral virtues based on faith and piety and the struggle against all forms of vice and corruption." Human beings, on their own, will undoubtedly fail to achieve such a state. Only Islam can guide people through the Koran to achieve that state. Khomeini frequently refers to Islam, to the doctrine (*maktab*), to the Koran, as human-makers (*ensânsâz*). Women are the agency for making human beings—both physiologically and morally. "Women raise courageous men in their bosom. The Koran makes human beings. Women, too, make human beings. If brave and human-maker women are taken away from a nation, that nation will be defeated and destroyed" (Khomeini 1981: 19).

The "undeniable right of women to be mothers" is militantly guarded in the Preamble of the Constitution, under the heading entitled "Women and the Constitution."

The family is the cornerstone of society and the primary institution for the growth and improvement of the individual; consensus and ideological belief in the principle that the formation of family is fundamental for the future development of the individual is one of the main aims of the Islamic government. According to this line of thinking regarding the family, women will no longer be regarded as mere objects in the service of consumerism; but, while being restored to the worthwhile and responsible task of motherhood, they will be primarily responsible for the raising of committed individuals.

Under the Pahlavis, women's right to motherhood was denied. As Khomeini put it:

There was so much propaganda that perhaps even mothers believed it themselves. Under the influence of those words, they sent their beloved children to daycare centers,[12] kept them away from their bosoms. There, children received satanic rearing (*tarbiyat-e sheytâni*). We are responsible to produce human beings. Only human beings can prevent corruption. (Khomeini 1982: 73)

Both men and women were in effect paralyzed in pre-revolutionary Iran. Women were objectified (*shey'i*) through colonialist plots implemented by the Pahlavi kings (Khomeini 1981: 132–33). Their men were not alert to intervene. Women's obsession with superficial Westernized lifestyle made them bad mothers. Male and female children were not raised properly. When children are separated from mothers, they develop numerous psychological problems and complexes—the root cause of a horde of social problems (Khomeini 1982: 72).

The Islamic state, then, should usurp men's supervisory role. Men, feeble poor excuses for ideal Muslim men, are to be expropriated by the ultimate Islamic state and its supreme leader. It is from the status position of the leader of the Islamic state that Khomeini reminds women of their duty: "You women are obligated (*mokallaf*) to make human beings. You are obligated to rear refined (*mohazzab*) individuals for your country" (Khomeini 1981: 138). "From Islam's perspective, women have a sensitive role in constructing an Islamic society. Islam raises the status of women in society so that they might regain their human dignity, not be objectified, and can assume responsibilities" (20).

The ideal Muslim can be raised only in the bosom[13] of the ideal Muslim mother, in the ideal Muslim family. Islam is mindful of all these aspects of a woman's life:

Islam deals with issues of your marriage even before you prepare to marry. Unlike the anarchic lifestyle of animals, Islam wants the fruit of your marriage to be a healthy human being.

Before marriage, there are laws in Islam stipulating whom she should choose for a mate, whom he should choose as a wife. Characteristics of the man, characteristics of the woman. These are stipulated in Islam. In no other government can you find specifications about the man, about the woman, about the time of marriage, what kind of relationship should exist between the couple after they get married, what kind of life they should have. (125)

A first step is to purify women from the influences of the West. A true Muslim woman cannot be an "accomplice to CIA and SAVAK" (13). Until, under the leadership of the clergy, we liberate ourselves from the West, true victory is not achieved (26–36). A Muslim woman will put all other women to shame: "Other women, those who wanted to show off with their corrupt makeup and expensive dresses in our society, among our women are condemned and ashamed" (128).

Pivotal to the efforts of the enemies of Islam, is to sow disbelief in our hearts about the real meaning of Islam. Those who do not believe suffer from "the reality . . . beclouded before them, it is covered and concealed."

They are pushed away from absolute light, from guidance, independence, nationality, and Islamic identity (*islamiyat*) and led to darkness. We have now lost ourselves, and until we find our missing parts, you will not become independent. Search for them. Search for the East (29).

As long as we define freedom by a Western standard, nothing will change. Thanks to the *âkhoonds*, turbaned preachers, things are kept at bay.

They cry out that there is no freedom. What has happened that there is no freedom? The *âkhoonds* do not let women and men mingle at the beach together. These *âkhoonds* do not let that happen. That our youths go to the bars and gambling houses and sink in corruption there. They do not let our radio and television show [*sic*] naked women and that cataclysmic, shameful condition [of the Pahlavis' time] to preoccupy our youths with. This is an imported freedom from the West, a colonialist freedom . . . so that the youths of a country become oblivious to their future. (29)

Central to this new identity is hejâb. "Islamic women are not dolls. Islamic women ought to appear in public veiled, not made up" (124). Prior to the victory, hejâb was only a choice of the Islamist women. In January of 1978, some three weeks before the February Uprising that put an end to the monarchy, Khomeini said in an interview with the Arabic *Al-Safir*: "Based on their Islamic upbringing, Muslim women have chosen the châdor as their cover. In the future, women will be free to decide about this themselves; we will only forbid distasteful dresses" (Khomeini 1982: 41).

After the Uprising, the tone has changed. What used to be a *choice for Muslim women* in a corrupt state has become a must for *all women* in an Islamic state: "Women must not come naked to Islamic ministries . . ." (41). The air of Islam was all over the place and, save for the corrupted ones, whoever breathed that air would become Muslim. And in Islam, the individual is nothing; it is the divine law that rules. In an Islamic state, *all* are subject to the Islamic law:

In Islam what rules is the divine law. The Prophet himself acted in this manner. We, too, are obligated to act the same way. In Islam, the law rules. The individual has no rule, even if that individual is the Prophet. The individual is not important. In Islam the law is important. Everybody is subjected to the law and the law is God's. It is based on the Koran, based on the intention of the Prophet. We are all his followers. (Khomeini 1981: 54)

Hejâb will give women personality. It will prevent them from regression to the pre-revolutionary time:

The danger we feel is that women might be attracted again to that corruption. What does Islamic hejâb mean? Islamic hejâb means cover for dignity, cover for character. That is not made by me or someone else. This is the direct order (*nass-e sarih*) of the Koran. What the Koran has specified neither we can deviate from nor the women who believe in this grand divine book. (133)

Safeguarding is not easy. Not only the Islamic government, but also every single individual must be in a position to condemn sin and promote goodness. Article 8 of the Constitution encourages all Muslims to enjoin the good and forbid the evil. *Amr beh ma'ruf va nahy az monkar* is an

Islamic dictum: "The true believers, both men and women, are friends to each other. They enjoin what is just and forbid what is evil" (Koran 1988: 328). Not just the state apparatus, but millions of watchful eyes control the woman. She is, after all, too doltish to understand the services Islam offers her. Yet, the more she is distrusted, the more she resists.

Distrust and resistance have set the undertone for gender politics in the Islamic Republic of Iran since its inception, leading to what I call *gender agony in a dual society*. I shall probe this issue in *Women in Iran: Emerging Voices in the Women's Movement*.

CITIZENS, BUT NOT QUITE SO

Upon coming to power, the Islamic state has undertaken the construction of new gender relations based on its ideological principles. Women and men are defined in accordance with the IRI's ideology that aims to create an Islamic community of believers, the ummat. In this communalist vision, individuality is reprehensible because it inspires idolatry. Led by an imam, the ummat is characterized by its members' oneness of thought *(towhid-e fekri)*. Aberration is not tolerated since only the leader knows what is best (see Rose 1983). Years before the revolution, Shariati commented on this subject: "The members of an ummat—from whatever family, society, or race they might be—think in one way, have a similar faith and are dedicated to carrying society to perfection—and not happiness and prosperity *(sa'âdat)*—under one social leadership" (Shariati n.d.-c: 520).

Article 2 of the Constitution stipulates the IRI's foundational principles as belief in the Islamic Allah and revelation, and Article 12 identifies the Twelver Ja'fari school of Islam as the official religion of Iran. These constitutive principles define the Islamic ummat and set the living conditions of Iran's inhabitants. The Islamic state plays the role of a benevolent father that "guides" its children to the "right" Islamic path. As Ayatollah Motahari expresses, an Islamic society cannot remain indifferent to the wrong choices of its members. Those who deviate from the right path have to either reconsider or be removed (Motahari n.d.-c: 222–28). Islamist ideologues have frequently repudiated "democracy" as a Western political philosophy that is incompatible with an Islamic system that is based on the wisdom of Allah, not mortal beings. Ayatollah Mesbâh Yazdi (1993) explains this duality: "If we believe that God's laws must govern people, there will be no room for democracy since it means whatever people want. If Islam means what God desires, then democracy is rendered meaningless."

This outlook jeopardizes Iranians' status as citizens by denying their individuality and individual rights (as I will discuss below, especially in chapter 6). The normative role of Islam predefines manhood and womanhood and denies both any right to autonomy (see chapter 6). The effects of Islamization on women's rights are even more severe. Nowhere in the Constitution of the Islamic Republic are women relegated the status of a second-class citizen, but the Constitution necessitates the compatibility of every law with *Islamic standards*. Article 4 reads:

All civil, penal, financial, economic, administrative, cultural, military, political, and other laws and regulations must be based on Islamic criteria. This principle applies absolutely and generally to all articles of the Constitution as well as to all other laws and regulations, and the *fuqaha'* of the Guardian Council are judges in this matter.

So, every discussion of "women's rights" in the IRI must be understood in its religious context. As "citizens," women can vote and be elected to some offices. Yet the Islamic articulation of their "rights" prevents them from becoming judges or the "supreme religious leader," the *valy-e faqih*. To women are attributed characteristics that, though not explicitly distinguished as deficiencies, deny women basic socio-political rights. To bear witness, two women should be present to be equal to the testimony of one man. Women are eligible as character witnesses *only if* they are married, while all men can perform that function provided that, of course, they know the individual in question. In the case of retribution, women are valued less than men (see Kar 1993b). Section 6 of Article 976 of the Civil Code grants Iranian citizenship to any woman of foreign nationality who marries an Iranian citizen. But, according to Article 1059 of the Civil Code, a woman marrying a non-Iranian is treated on the basis of the laws of her husband's country of citizenship (see chapter 7).

The IRI has thus subjugated women's rights to religious interests—a trend associated with the rise of religious fundamentalism and the convergence of the state and religious advocacy for patriarchy throughout the Middle East (Joseph 1996). Women's rights as citizens are defined in the context of their "worthwhile and responsible task of motherhood." The primacy of women's domestic role has affected their presence in social, economic, and political spheres.

THE AWAKENING

The initial reactions of both Islamists and secularists to these events and opinions were mixed with denial and disbelief. Although women and the Left shared some common assumptions with the Islamists' analysis of the "woman question" under the Pahlavis, they did not concur with the specifics of the clerical agenda for a reorganization of Iranian society. The result was an ambiguous association. The religious faction had to conceal its specific demands while the progressive faction denied or dismissed them. Before seizing power, the religious leadership rarely stressed hejâb or any other discriminatory measure. Even when directly asked about women's future in politics, Khomeini dismissed the issue as speculative, something that only a new government could answer. "Now," he said, "is no time for these issues" (Khomeini 1982: 18). If anything, Khomeini consistently emphasized the importance of women's participation in the future Iran. Even after the revolution, after Khomeini's decree on compulsory veiling, Islamists like Taleqani refused to acknowledge that as an ordinance. Women demonstrators were permitted to enter the Office of the Prime Minister of the Provisional Government where they found Amir-Entezam, the spokesman of the government, receptive to their complaints (Soroush 1979a; Afshar 1983: 86).

Eslam Kâzemiyeh (1979), who later became a key figure in composing the laws of censorship, in a commentary in the daily *Kayhan* wrote that he had no intention of siding against his "modernist *(motejaded)* sisters" who refuse to wear the veil. Indeed, "as a firm believer in women's rights," he considered it his responsibility to voice his dissenting opinion whenever someone abrogated their rights. However, he contended, there was no reason to be alarmed. "The divisive propaganda about women's rights" originated around the discussions concerning the fate of the Family Protection Law. Kâzemiyeh found it bewildering that anybody would even show the slightest concern; after all, "when a nation revolts against a regime and calls for the annihilation of its every aspect, it means that people want the abrogation of that regime's every fundamental institution and law. The Family Protection Law was a small portion of the Shah's laws and should be annulled along with the rest." The question, he stressed, was not to veil or not; it was to avoid corruption and Western influences.

Mojahedin discouraged women from opposing mandatory hejâb lest it would "provide opportunities and pretexts for conspiracy and agitation by the counterrevolution." As a "revolutionary foundation of Islam," they argued,

hejâb is indeed nothing but a social effort in order to observe and protect the morality of society which is without doubt one of the necessities of society's material and spiritual development; and we are sure that our revolutionary sisters and mothers, as they have so far proved in practice, also have observed this necessity and will continue to do so. (PMOI 1979)

Though recognizing the importance of hejâb as an important component of the struggle against imperialist culture, the Mojahedin rejected its "compulsory imposition" as an " irrational and unacceptable act." The heavy burden of the imperialist culture, they continued, cannot be eliminated all at once and without a long-term and gradual process.

The secular opposition and women activists had criticized women's social status from a viewpoint not too different from that of the religious opposition: the Shah intended to turn women into dolls. Yet, as the Islamic regime moved to implement its policies, many women realized the essential difference between their demands and those of the religious leadership. Their initial reaction was astonishment. One woman found it amazing that though women fought shoulder-to-shoulder with men, the new regime refused to accept women in the Revolutionary Council (Soroush 1979b). On another occasion, a college student protested against the sex segregation of sport under the new regime. She started her letter to the daily *Âyandegân* by stating: "It is hard to believe; yet it is real." "I don't believe and I don't want to do so," she wrote, "that we have regressed instead of moving forward." She pleaded to one of her former professors who, as the Chair of the Tehran-e Javân Stâdium (Tehran's Stadium for the Youth), participated in the making of the new regulations, and reminded him that the "women's volleyball team only played volleyball and was only concerned with the game." There was no sign of any corruption, any wrongdoing. "You claim that in the Islamic Republic women can even become presidents; then what does it mean to separate them from the rest of the society with a wall?" (*Âyandegân* 1979) The denial continued even after the hizbullah attacked women's demonstrations. Many reacted by denying that the assailants *were* the Muslim warriors. Homa Nategh said: "Those who have troubled us in the streets today were not our Muslim militant brothers and sisters. They were the lackeys of the old regime and supporters of the [Pahlavi regime's] Constitution and monarchy" (Nategh 1979).

It *was* indeed hard to believe—yet it *was* real.

Women's post-revolutionary demonstrations were, on the whole, defensive ones. In the absence of an autonomous women's movement, gender relations in women's social and political vision continued to be obscured. The Left was preoccupied with maintaining the revolutionary unity and thwarting possible counterrevolutionary offensives (see the following chapter). Women socially asserted themselves *as women* only *after* the rights given to them were in jeopardy. And the women who turned to the Left for an alternative were discouraged from addressing gender politics.

RECAPITULATION

In this chapter I analyzed the cultural politics of gender that shaped the events of the revolutionary days. I argued that because of the Pahlavi state's monopoly of political expression, changes in gender relations were severed from women's social struggle. Thus, opposing developments in gender relations became synonymous with opposing the Shah. This political culture created a prism through which anti-Shah activists observed their environment and interpreted sociopolitical doctrine. Through this prism, the Islamists' opposition to the refashioning of patriarchy was misconstrued as anti-Shah, progressive, and revolutionary. The anti-women pretext was lost in translation.

The majority of women who participated in the revolution came from traditional or modern middle-class urban families. Both because of social class background and gender identity, some women from traditional middle-class families considered Islam a desirable alternative. The shifting patriarchal character toward public patriarchy made the lifestyle and home-maker role of traditional Muslim women obsolete. Honoring traditional family, Islam revived the gender identity of these women.

The professional women of the modern middle class also strove for revolutionary changes. The history of their political activism predates the 1979 revolution. In the most recent past, they were active in clandestine political and guerrilla warfare against the Shah. These women participated in the revolution to fight against discrimination and social injustice. Yet the political demand of overthrowing the Shah overshadowed their concerns about the discriminatory practices of public patriarchy, especially for its commodification of female sexuality. These concerns echoed some similarities with the Islamists' critique of the changes in gender relations. What the Islamists opted for, however, was to restore the prerogatives men enjoyed under private patriarchy and the obligations women undertook according to the traditional patriarchal bargain.

Islamists were originally opposed to women's presence in social and political activities. Indeed, that was a main grievance in the June 1962 movement against the reforms proposed by the Shah. Eventually, they realized that women's presence is an undeniable aspect of Iran's social reality. Islamists' strategy then changed. Instead of barring women from politics, they summoned women to take part in bringing Islam to power. The ideas of Shariati and the Mojahedin organization, as well as the reinterpretations of such clerical figures as Motahari, provided a cultural accommodation for Muslim women's participation in revolutionary upheavals. The new Muslim woman participated in history-making without renouncing her responsibilities as a woman.

Upon coming to power, Islamists embarked on an elaborate program of reconstructing private property. Family laws that partially favored women were repealed. Polygyny became lawful. Divorce became a man's prerogative. The veil became mandatory. Women were barred from certain occupations like judgeship. These measures were based on a conviction of women's emotionality and lack of intellectual discernment.

The newly established IRI set about protecting the "undeniable right of women to be mothers." Mothering, as I will discuss in chapters 6 and 7, is deemed women's quintessential characteristic. Rearing good children, especially refined sons, for the Islamic state is women's divine responsibility. No other tasks she might assume should contradict this grand destiny. The women of the Pahlavi era were ill-equipped to perform this role. The Islamic government should reconstruct the ideal woman. Motherhood should regain its due respect so that women can find satisfaction in performing their sacred duty. Under the Pahlavis, men, too, were ineffective in their supervisory role. The Islamic state thus usurped men's supervisory role, establishing itself as the ultimate male, under the leadership of the *velâyat-e faqih*—the rule of the jurist.

A first step is to purify women from the influences of the West. Hejâb plays a pivotal role here, and the Islamic state ought to safeguard itself against the evils of "naked women." Women resist, and the Islamists attribute this to the sabotage of Islam's enemies. Women should be repeatedly reminded of the significance of Islamic laws, and constantly admonished for undermining Islam. Such an involved task can be accomplished only if all members of society are deputized to control one another. Muslims are required to enjoin the good and forbid the evil. Coercion becomes central to the Islamization of gender relations (see chapter 6). Resistance and distrust mark gender politics under the IRI.

With the 1979 revolution, the women's movement lived through an important stage of its life. The radicalism that swept the entire society, directly followed by the threat of a theocratic government, pushed the demands of the movement beyond those that could be proposed and fulfilled in the framework of the royal reforms. The terms of the movement were transcending women's demand for basic human rights, which were under attack by the new regime, and aiming to eradicate patriarchy at its source. The enemy was fully armed. To survive the storm of reaction, women had to develop a movement independent both in its organizational form and in its ideological content. This alternative, however, did not exist at the time. The Left had a strong presence in the opposition and did not favor an autonomous women's movement. In the next chapter, I will discuss the cultural politics of gender among the Iranian Left.

NOTES

1. After the establishment of the new regime, however, female activists felt pressure from their organizations to observe the increasing public conservatism. The dominant understanding among the Left was that activism in traditional neighborhoods where unveiled women were perceived to be "corrupt" required activists to mind their appearance, even wear scarves. Wearing the hejâb, at least before it became mandatory, among the Left was a function of political expediency. Some activists were critical of this compromise, but the consensus was that insistence on hejâb deflected attention from "important issues." For further discussion, see Shahidian (1997a).

2. For a discussion of this kind of political rule, see Huntington (1966).

3. Homa Nategh, interview by Zia Sedghi, 1 Apr. 1984, audiotape 2, Harvard University Iranian Oral History Project.

4. A good example is Nâser Makârem Shirâzi's attack on Marxism in his *Filsoofnamâhâ (Pseudo-Philosophers)*. The book was published after the coup of 1953 and won the Royal Award.

5. As I explain in the next chapter, the reluctance to address gender also stemmed from the conviction of many secular and leftist intellectuals that gender— or, in the parlance of the Left, the "woman question"—was not a real *political* problem to which one needed to pay much attention.

6. For a discussion of the rural participation in the revolution, see Kazemi and Abrahamian (1978) and Eskandari (1984).

7. In the Tobacco Boycott of 1891–92, for instance, alliance with the clergy secured the bazaari merchants' interest and succeeded in the cancellation of the tobacco concession to the British Regie Company. Another incident of the co-operation of the two is related to the coup of 1953 when the bazaaris, under the aegis of the religious establishment, financed pro-Shah demonstrations against Mossadiq's elected government. So, one should bear in mind that the bazaaris' opposition to the ruling power, like that of the clergy, was not a sustained one; depending upon the circumstances, the bazaari changed its approach toward the dominant political circle. For a discussion of the relationship between the clergy and the bazaari merchants, see Ghandchi-Tehrani (1982).

8. For a comparative study of the appeal of fundamentalism for women, see Hélie-Lucas (1993) and Afary (1997: especially 99ff).

9. Originally published in *Majmou'eh-ye Asnâd va E'lâmiyeh-hâye Row-hânyoun-e Mobârez (A Collection of Documents and Communiqués of the Militant Clergy)*, Paris: September–October 1977.

10. Motahari's periods of Iranian women's history need clarification. The essay was written after the downfall of the Pahlavi regime. The Pahlavis ruled Iran for over half a century. But he divides women's history into two parts: a forty-year period of "Pahlavi-style woman" and a ten-year period of what perhaps could be called the emergence of the "Muslim woman." The implication is that the preparatory work for the Islamic revolution has been under way for some ten years.

11. After the summer of 1981, the Mojahedin have been forced into exile. Since then, they have turned into a cult. My assessment of gender ideology in Iranian politics does not include the Mojahedin in the post-revolutionary era because addressing that requires detailed information about their organizational culture and practices not available to me. Their practices in this period include—to name but a few: adhering to the hejâb, creating a personality cult which revolves around their leader Massoud Rajavi, and using women as symbols of men's alliance. As to the personality cult, there are two outstanding examples. When the Mojahedin entered a coalition with the former President Banisadr and formed the National Council of Resistance, Rajavi married his daughter. Later, when the coalition fell apart, Rajavi divorced her. Later, a couple in the higher echelon of the organizational hierarchy had a divorce so that the woman could remarry Rajavi in order to form a sexually mixed leadership under his shadow. For a favorable interpretation of the Mojahedin's gender policies, see Shoaee (1987).

12. Khomeini uses the word *parvareshgâh*, which means orphanage.

13. Khomeini frequently refers to "a mother's skirt" (*dâman-e mâdar*). A close equivalent for this Persian expression is "a mother's bosom."

5

Gender Ambivalence: "Cultural Imperialism" and Representative Revolutionism

I'm a woman
A woman who from the start has crossed fields step by step
with her comrade and brother
A woman who has reared the powerful muscle of the worker
and the strong hands of a peasant.
I'm a worker myself
I'm a peasant myself
I'm a woman
My statue is the image of pain
and my body is the expression of spite.
How shameful it is that
I'm told the pain of my hunger is my imagination and
the nakedness of my body just an illusion.

I'm a woman
A woman who can't be found anywhere
in your brutal culture.
A woman whose heart is full of infected wounds
A woman whose eyes reflect the red bullets of freedom, and
whose hands are molded for holding a gun!

These verses from Marziyeh Ahmadi Oskoo'i's poem "Eftekhâr" (Honor) sum up the Iranian Left's assessment about women's issues in Iran—or the "woman question," *mas'aleh-ye zanân,* in the Left's terminology (n.d.).[1]

Ahmadi Oskoo'i posits women against the "brutal culture" of the ruling regime. The woman in her poem is not just a woman; she is a *toiling woman*. She is a woman who rears powerful workers and peasants. She is herself a laborer whose strength is smashed by the cogwheel, with skin mirroring the desert sun. She is herself a peasant from the small hamlets of the North who brings dawn to dusk in the tea fields. She is a tribal woman, giving birth to her child in the mountains, or mourning the loss of her sheep in the fields. Nothing about male domination shapes her life. There is no indication that she lives in a family, except her matter-of-fact statement at the beginning of the poem: "I'm a mother. / A sister. / A wife." Not even a cursory reference to Engels' proletariat, who in his family life acts like a bourgeois and exploits his proletarian wife. There is no mention of university students or professionals. The brief, indirect presence of middle- or upper-class women merely points up the contrast to the toiling woman: *they* are women with white hands, delicate figure, soft skin, and perfumed hair.

The toiling woman has every reason to participate in a popular revolution, none to raise any fuss about sexism.

That perhaps explains why one finds little about women in pre-revolutionary leftist literature. Even Engels' *The Origin of Private Property, Family, and the State* was mainly read for its implications on the formation of class and state. The Marxian theses about the decline of matriarchy and the rise of patriarchy as by-products of class relations were highlighted. Leftist assessments of Iran's social condition after the reforms of the 1960s mostly focused on the land reform. They contained nothing specifically about women's franchise. Women's right to vote was, of course, implicitly accepted. The peripheral concern with gender emerges only in relation to capitalist development, or more specifically, a *dependent capitalist development*. And the analysis is fairly straightforward: Capitalism exploits; dependent capitalism is not deep and far-reaching; dependent capitalism is not genuine because it is consumerist; remnants of feudalism still persist; women are abused by either the consumer culture or outdated cultural beliefs.

After the 1979 revolution, the Iranian Left has often and rightly been criticized for its indifference to the multifaceted character of women's oppression. (Afshar 1983; Alaolmolki 1987; Moghissi 1994; Sanasarian 1983; Tabari and Yeganeh 1982; Yeganeh 1982) Dominated by male activists, it reduced the oppression of women to a simple "problem of superstructure" which would disappear in a socialist Iran, and adopted an ambivalent attitude toward feminist militancy. This attitude was manifested clearly during the first few years of the Islamic Republic when tens of thousands of women filled the streets of Tehran in opposition to the regime's incursion upon their rights.

In this chapter I will address the ambivalent gender politics of the Iranian Left. I will argue that to understand this issue, one must locate the leftist movement within a complicated historical and political development in both national and international contexts. Nationally, the emergence of public patriarchy raised new questions to which the Iranian Left was unable to provide satisfactory answers. Internationally, the legacy of socialist revolutions around the world prevented the Left from addressing the "woman question" as *gender, ethnic,* and *social class* problems. One of my main concerns here is to move beyond the customary explanation of the failure of the Iranian Left resulting from its underlying religious mentality. I would like instead to limn how the culture of the Iranian Left and the Left's cultural politics shaped the role of the leftist movement in the gender struggle of the Iranian revolution.

PARADIGMATIC CRISIS: FROM WOMEN'S RIGHTS TO WOMEN'S LIBERATION

Despite disappointing policies during the revolution of 1979, the earlier generations of the Iranian Left had better records with regard to women's rights. The support and advocacy of sexual equality by the Iranian Left dates back to the early days of the twentieth century when *Iran-e Nou* (The New Iran), a social-democratic paper, took up the cause of women's liberation (Nategh 1983, 1980). Later, following the First Congress of the Communist Party of Iran in 1920, Jam'iyat-e Peyk-e Sa'âdat-e Nesvân (Messenger of the Prosperity of Women) was established in the northern city of Rasht. Several progressive women of the Province of Gilan joined the organization which established night classes, schools, and libraries for women, published a journal called *Peyk-e Sa'âdat,* and for the first time celebrated International Women's Day. Theoreticians of the Iranian communist movement, such as Avetis Mika'iliân (Sultânzâdeh) (n.d.) and Taqi Arâni (1983) also supported the women's movement.

In 1943, the Tudeh Party established the Tashkilât-e Zanân-e Iran (The Organization of Iranian Women) (Abrahamian 1982: 335ff). *Bidâry-e Mâ* (Our Awakening), the monthly journal of the Tashkilât, demanded radical transformations in the laws governing the rights of women in the family and at the workplace. In 1945, the short-lived autonomous governments of Azerbaijan and Kurdistan for the first time approved enfranchisement for women (408). The Tudeh Party and other communist organizations played an important role in mobilizing women during the pre-coup years before the Party was banned in 1949. The Tudeh Party also introduced a bill in the Iranian Majlis that called for improvement in women's status and voting rights for them. Three years later, under the premiership of Mohammad Mossadiq, the bill came to a vote, but because of the firm opposition of the clergy and other conservatives, it was rejected.

In the revolution of 1979, the militant Left assumed a passive attitude toward women's causes. When women opposed mandatory veiling in

March 1979, the popular Organization of Iranian People's Fedaiin Gueril-
las (OIPFG) did not call for a protest, though many of its members and
supporters demonstrated as individuals. When women's demonstrations
were attacked by supporters of the Islamic regime, *Kar* (Labor), the official
paper of the Fedaiin, condemned the attack and called for the punishment
of the "reactionaries and counter-revolutionaries who one day attack political organizations and the next day assault women" (OIPFG 1979d: 1).
But the organization's support of women's activism remained weak even
when women activists appealed for its support by marching toward the
Fedaii Headquarters on International Women's Day. Two years later, Fedaiin admitted their mistake, but did not change their policies (OIPFG
1979b: 1).

Notwithstanding their minimal participation in the March 1979 demonstrations, leftist organizations vehemently condemned the Bill of Retribution (*Lâyeheh-ye qesâs*), passed in 1980, and particularly its treatment
of women. According to the fifth article of this bill, "if a Muslim man
willfully murders a Muslim woman, he will be sentenced to *qesas* [retali-
ation] but the woman's guardian must pay the murderer one half of a man's
blood-money before he receives *qesas*" (IRI 1982). In addition, leftist organizations have been a source of information about the working class,
peasants and tribal women and women of national minorities, and have
sought to protect their rights.[2] Even the Tudeh Party, which supported the
Islamic regime, documented the hardships of workingwomen, as issues of
Jahân-e Zanân (Women's World), a publication of the Democratic Organization of Iranian Women, show. Critics of the Left, however, concerned
mainly with middle-class women, overlook these contributions.

The Left's ambivalence may be ascribed partly to its predominance of
males, but that explanation alone will not suffice, if only because the Iranian Left is not monolithic. Some partisans, like the Tudeh, took the oath
of allegiance to Khomeini and argued that "never before in the history of
Iran have we seen a person who has valued women in as fitting a way as
Imam Khomeini" (Maryam Firuz as quoted in Tabari and Yeganeh 1982:
139). Yet others, like the Organization for Struggle in the Path of the Emancipation of the Working Class, known as the Peykâr (Struggle), the Communist Unity, and the Fedaiin condemned any cooperation with the Islamic
regime. Ideologically, too, there have been differences within the Left.
While some could not fathom the severity of mandatory hejâb, others like
the Socialist Workers' Party argued that "women should have control of
their bodies" and demanded the legalization of abortion (quoted in Tabari
and Yeganeh 1982: 133).

What, then, accounts for the change in the Left's attitude vis-à-vis the
"woman question"? Historical changes play an undeniable role. The favorable stance toward women's concerns effected by the earlier generation
in part reflects Iran's sociopolitical situation at the time. Fighting against

internal reaction was deemed inseparable from fighting for women's rights, prior to the land reform. Most leftist and nationalist activists agreed with progressive women that the degrading condition of women was due to outdated traditions. They insisted on women's right to receive an education, universal franchise, and the freedom to choose their own outfit (Abrahamian 1982: 335–36). Advocates argued that no one could expect women to be conscientious wives and mothers unless they first received a better education. Thus, the left could incorporate these demands into its agenda without reformulating its ideology on feminist principles. Those demands aimed to limit the power of the patriarch and re-map gender boundaries to relieve women from the confines of private patriarchy. As such, they coincided with the objectives of the progressive movement. The coincidence of modernization and enhancement of women's rights inspired the earlier generations of the Left to endorse the women's rights movement.

But at the time of the 1979 revolution, many of the objectives of the women's rights movements during the early-to-mid-twentieth century were accomplished. New concerns could no longer be addressed solely in the context of women's *rights*. Women's exclusion from the public domain was no longer the only problem to address. Instead, for example, issues of sex segregation in the job market and the persistence of traditional sex-segregated education had to be addressed as well. The complex changes in sexual morality could not be duly reflected only in the objectification of women's bodies in consumer capitalism. Combating violence against women, both in private and in public domains, was not possible while adhering to the "sanctity of family relations," or to "women's noble status in our society." Any discussion of rape, incest, or other forms of sexual abuse or harassment required first an admission that these problems *did* result from male domination, not just from "outdated feudalist residues" or "decadent dependent capitalism." It required discussions about women's control over their bodies and sexualities, intergenerational control within the family, sexual and moral codes, and changing worlds and demands of the youth.

The Left's reluctance to address these issues certainly reflects many leftists' personal biases and values. More significantly, however, the theoretical paradigm of the Left did not offer any answer to many of these challenges. It instead posited them as insignificant secondary issues. The theoretical foundation of the Left in twentieth-century Iran has rested solely on politico-economic analyses. The leftist movement articulated its *raison d'être* and objectives in the context of politico-economic crises. That is why, for instance, the post-1960 developments in Iran are exclusively analyzed from the vantage point of political economy, or why the debate about the nascent IRI in the early 1980s revolved overwhelmingly around its class nature—is the IRI a capitalist state? Does it espouse a dependent capitalist system with a religious pretense? What the Left considered "problems of superstructure" (e.g., culture or the "woman question") were addressed only as anomic consequences of a decaying politico-economic system. Such an approach may succeed in reminding us that by any other name, ours is still a capitalist world in which the political economy of class relations prevails. Yet, limiting social movements to mere expressions of economic crisis hides the complexity of the very social relations it aims to unravel.

Social processes of capitalism and public patriarchy politicized issues that the Left customarily categorized as culture, that is, nonpolitical, in essence. The politico-economic crisis paradigm could not accommodate the politicization of non-political demands. This deficiency is evident in the Left's approach to issues of women, the youth, or the students. That is why the Left could not launch a widespread movement to counter the hegemonic culture despite the fact that many have approached it and sought in it the leading role out of traditionalism. In the analysis of the Left after the reforms of the sixties, imperialism substituted the internal reaction—especially in the domain of culture. This is a crucial rupture from the orientation of the earlier secular Iranian intellectuals who found the changes in the West inspirational. In recent decades, however, this attitude has changed and for the secular, Leftist Iranian intelligentsia, the West in its entirety stood for decadence and corruption.

Attributing the consequences of the refashioning of patriarchy to cultural imperialism, the Left did not recognize the contradiction between residual and emergent cultures (in Raymond Williams' terms [see chapter 1]) and value systems. The heyday of the Left's attraction for the youth did not come till the upsurge of the revolution. Since then, many have joined the Left in accord with the revolutionary fervor. Besides, due to the dominant sentiment of the time, the mobilization revolved mainly around political issues. Issues pertinent to the lives of these activists played a marginal role—they were baits to politicize young men and women.

BETWEEN MARXISM AND ISLAM?

Some aspects of the Left's approach toward gender suggest serious similarities with Islamic interpretations. Indeed, the similarity is often overstated within Iranian circles. The Left is crudely shrugged away as "just a different form of Islamism when it comes to women, sexuality, and morality." Yet the problem is not so simple. Though the persisting echo of conservative morality among the Iranian Left is undeniable, one cannot ignore the differences. After all, the women and men who participated in the leftist movement became attracted to it at least in part because of its distinctions from Islam. One post-revolutionary woman activist commented in an interview with me on the sharp contrast between hers and the IRI's understanding of male-female relationship:

We had a very close relationship with all of our relatives. Every weekend we would all get together. We would go on picnics or to the pool during the summer, all of us, boys and girls. Now they were telling us that it was sinful to be in each other's company! How backward! Yes, only the Islamic Republic separated us from each other. (See Shahidian 1997: 37)

In the absence of a feminist awareness, however, this realization stemmed from a reaction toward the restrictive policies of the Islamic regime, rather than emerging from demand for radical structural changes in the patriarchal foundation of society.

Much of the Left's analyses of gender clearly transcend the limits of religious social criticism. While in pre-revolutionary days analyses of gender relations were predominantly concerned with either praising the Pahlavi state or portraying Islam as liberating, Marxist authors presented the "woman question" in the context of a sociohistorical theory of evolution. While Islamic discourse emphasized social progress as man-made and considered a peripheral role for women, Marxists discussed women's role in the making of history (Navâbakhsh n.d.: especially 54–62). Some undertook serious studies of women's participation in the Constitutional movement and the formation of the women's movement (see various works by Nategh. Also see Nâhid 1981). Furthermore, unlike Islamic discourse, which regarded moral values as universal and ahistorical, Marxist interpretations pointed out the sociohistorical character of morality and the role played by religion in the development of patriarchy. Afshârnyâ, for instance, wrote:

It is vitally important to analyze the relationship between male and female not from the angle of ethics, morality, or honor (nâmus)—which are themselves products of certain socioeconomic relationships . . . —but on the basis of historical and economic concepts and categories. This is the only way which enables us to understand why things are the way they are, and why they should change—whether we like it or not. (1978)

He was also one of the first scholars to point out the role of housework and mothering in the persistence and reproduction of class and sexual oppressions (142, 144–45).

Navâbakhsh's Woman in History is particularly relevant to my point here because of its publication date. Though the date of publication is not specified, based on the date of the author's references, it is evident that the book was published sometime between 1976 and the revolution. Navâbakhsh rejects Islamists' interpretation of sexual inequality. Motahari's view, he contends, is based on the different-but-equal assumption. This assumption he dismisses for "there is no room for equality" in this doctrine (n.d.: 7). "Those who adhere to the different-but-equal doctrine in effect intend to present women's subordination and men's supremacy as a natu-ral, ahistorical and unchangeable phenomenon" (7). The doctrine rests on a biologically determinist view. To those who adhere to this theorem, "women's interval disability (*natavany-e motenaveb*), caused by menstru-ation, pregnancy, and lactation, means women's natural weakness and in-feriority" (7). One must of course take issue with Navâbakhsh's reference to menstruation, pregnancy, and lactation as "women's interval weakness," yet the door is cracked open to escape the confinement of biological deter-minism. This is evident, again, in Navâbakhsh's critique of Hassan Sadr, (1940) for believing that women and men have different tasks in familial and social lives because "women lack the necessary growth and maturity" to be equal to men (172).

Restrictions of theory, however, never allowed these contributions to fully flourish. While Marxist social theorists emphasized women's role in human development, their analyses of the decline in women's status and the formation of patriarchy fell short of discussing the patriarchal control of female sexuality. While they underlined women's role in primitive reli-gions and recognized patriarchy as the cause of women's low status in organized religions, they overlooked menstrual taboos, female genital mu-tilation, or foot-binding (Âryânpour 1951: 71–74; Navâbakhsh n.d.: 79–91). While they pointed out the need for women's economic independence, they denounced the women's autonomous movement as the "hue and cry of women's liberation" (Afshârnyâ 1978: 143). Moreover, since the orga-nized Left was convinced of the accuracy of its theory and practice, the ideas of Marxist scholars exerted little impact on the Left. In effect, the rank and file of the leftist movement has studied these texts only after the defeat of the Left.[3]

Authors have to constantly calculate the possible reactions of their read-ers and safeguard themselves against them. Navâbakhsh, for example, cites anthropological studies about the permissive sexual attitude of early soci-eties. But the author is quick to disavow any responsibility for "wrong" conclusions:

To avoid any possible misunderstanding, it is important to add that chastity, purity, and premarital abstinence are necessary and essential for the exaltation and health of youth. And the only ideal form of marriage which could be based upon accept-able contemporary morality is the marriage between a man and a woman. Today, uncontrolled and promiscuous relationships will lead to ominous results. (Navâ-bakhsh n.d.: 45)

What encumbers the analyses of Marxists like Navâbakhsh, Afshârnya, and Âryânpour is not religious convictions, but a populist notion of rev-olution that aimed to maintain the unity of all anti-Shah forces. Not reli-gion, but an analysis of gender that is reduced to its class component. Not religion, but a political imperative not to affront "the people." If anything, the Left's concerns with the needs of working mothers, and with economic independence as key in ensuring women's rights clearly undermined the Islamists' objective of restrengthening private patriarchy. Problematic as the similarities between the Left's and the Islamists' analyses of gender relations under the Pahlavis were, it is misleading to equate the two.

HISTORY AND POLITICS IN THE LEFT'S VISION OF GENDER POLITICS

One crucial factor to understand in the Left's approach to women's struggle—or much of the Left's politics for that matter—is the circumstances surrounding its emergence during the revolution. As suppression in the Shah's Iran increased, many leftist intellectuals saw guerrilla action as the only way to victory (Halliday 1979: 211–48). The government did not take its armed adversaries lightly, and joining the movement as a professional revolutionary meant on the average six months to live (see Mirsepassi-Ashtiani and Moghadam 1991). Most guerrillas had little interest in theoretical considerations, especially beyond what Marxist orthodoxy approved. One survivor of the first generation of Fedaii guerrillas related a telling incident to me in an interview in Canada. One day in the early seventies in the Qezel Qal'eh Prison, he was approached by an admiring university student who asked him to clarify the movement's social, political, economic and cultural analyses of the Iranian society. "Confused about what he meant," the guerrilla recalled, "I excused myself by saying that I had to go to visit someone and told him that we would resume our conversation soon. I ran immediately to a cellmate and asked him: 'What is an analysis? And what are our social, political, economic and cultural analyses of the Iranian society?' And don't forget that we were more knowledgeable than many others."

The Left faced the approaching revolution in a weakened condition: most of its leaders had been either executed or killed. The rank-and-file were young and inexperienced with little theoretical knowledge. New leaders, having spent much of their lives in prison, were also uninformed. Though many student activists in Europe and the United States, who had had a better opportunity to familiarize themselves with various political debates, returned to Iran after the revolution, they were looked down upon as "armchair intellectuals" out of touch with the realities of the Iranian society.

After the rise of the IRI to power, the Left's gender politics was a derivative of its overall politics toward the new regime. The most conciliatory toward the denial of women's rights were the Tudeh Party and the Majority Fedaiin. Hoping for a share of power, these organizations collaborated with the clerical government (see Moghadam 1987). The Fedaiin's treatment of the women's movement immediately after the revolution reflected their in-

ternal disputes over the Islamic government. Before the split in the organization in the summer of 1980 into the pro-government "Majority"
(aksariyat) and the oppositional "Minority" (aqaliyat), contradictory policies were adopted by the organization. Their ambiguous absence-presence
tactic in women's demonstrations on International Women's Day in 1979
is a case in point. Though they did not participate in the events as Fedaii
supporters, they did so as concerned individuals—and some, along with
others, formed a wall around demonstrators to protect them from the attack of the hizbullah. To compensate for this ambivalence, the Minority
Fedaiin published a special issue of Kar in March 1981. Save for that issue,
however, the Minority Fedaiin never again addressed issues related to gender and the revolutionary movement.

The Tudeh Party and its women's branch continued their support of the
Islamic regime and the Imam's Line until 1983 when the regime arrested
party leaders and cadres. The arrests, according to the party officials,
marked the government's turn to the right. The Democratic Organization
adopted a similar position, and after some five years of collaboration with
the ruling clergy began to complain about their mistreatment of women:
"The right wing Islamic Republic is trampling over the constitutional law
for which people sacrificed their lives, through their special civil courts that
are based on the 'Islamic Laws,' and this has turned into ashes all the hopes
that Iranian women cherished" (DOIW 1984b: 3).

The zigzag of the Iranian Left toward the women's movement, of course,
is not uncommon among the Left worldwide. The relationship between
feminism and socialism—in both the theoretical and practical realms—has
been marked with difficulty and "unhappiness" (Hartmann 1981). Feminists have criticized leftists for their lack of attention to sexual domination,
and many socialists, in turn, have looked at women's liberation movements
as a bourgeois deviation or, worse yet, a conspiracy against the workers'
struggle. Nineteenth-century social democratic movements in Europe had
constant conflicts among feminist-socialist advocates of women's rights like
Clara Zetkin, and "proletarian anti-feminism" among workers and communists (Boxer and Quataert 1978; Evans 1976; Quataert 1979; Thönnessen 1976). Eventually, guided by the theoretical insights of a number
of socialist leaders such as Bebel, Engels, and Zetkin, socialist parties of
the First and Second Internationals came to realize the just cause of the
women's movement and to accept autonomous women organizations. The
Third International, or the Comintern, though it initially claimed to liberate
women "not only on paper, but in reality, in actual fact" (quoted in Waters
1989: 30),[4] treated the inequality of women as a secondary consideration.
Focusing on production and labor conflict, the Comintern paid attention
only to women's exploitation by capitalists to the extent that "by the end
of the 1920s, any special emphasis on women's social subordination in
communist propaganda or campaigning came to be regarded as a capitu-

lation to bourgeois feminism" (51). Leftist women activists lost their organizational autonomy and had to work under the supervision of their national communist party. The hegemony that the Communist Party of the Soviet Union—which occupied a leading role in the Comintern—and the Comintern exercised on a great portion of the communist movement worldwide left a long-lasting effect on the Left's relationship with the women's movement. In China, the Communist Party first supported the feminist movement, indicting the Confucian moral code, female chastity, and traditional marriage and family structure, and advocating women's education and economic independence (Gilmartin 1989: 83–97). But this was tempered after their accession to power (Johnson 1983: 215–33; Stacey 1983: 158–94).

In 1980s Iran, the ambivalence of socialism toward feminism wielded substantial power. To fathom this strength, we need to consider the relationship of the Left and the classical Marxist texts. The ideas of Bebel, Engels, Zetkin, and Kollontai made original contributions to the analysis of women's oppression, but for the Iranian Left these "classical thinkers" were authoritative figures whose ideas were beyond challenge and modification. This problem was augmented by ignorance of the history of socialist movements. State censorship was partly responsible, but so was the inclusive "party version" of the history of labor movements around the world: Zetkin rectified the reformist approach of the Second International, Lenin corrected her; Kollontai suffered from bourgeois sexual morality, Lenin criticized her, and so on. Thus, for instance, one of Kollontai's radical visions—that *a successful revolution had to affect women's daily life, their daily social relation* (Mullaney 1983: 72)—about socialist revolution was lost in her modification through Lenin. Tensions between the feminists and socialists remained virtually unknown to the Iranian Left. Discussion of contemporary movements, too, was for the most part limited to the official party line; alternative interpretations were viewed with suspicion. Since these official versions usually omitted women's criticisms, even when women's participation in the liberation movements were discussed, they served to buttress the Left's position regarding the primacy of national/class struggle over women's emancipation. The Iranian Left's narrow assessment of the situation in Afghanistan is a case in point. The controversy over the events in this neighboring country focused more on the Soviet Union's foreign policy; for instance, did the Soviets go to Afghanistan to practice socialist solidarity or for social-imperialist gains? Should their action be supported?

In some societies, feminist movements affected the sensitivity of the Left toward feminism. In Nicaragua, for instance, an important element in the Sandinistas' openness to women's demands was the spread of feminism in Latin American countries like Mexico, Peru, and Brazil (Molyneux 1985: 236). The Iranian revolutionary movement had no such influence.

There was, of course, the successful regional socialist revolution in the People's Democratic Republic of Yemen. But, as Aisha Mohsen, a member of the General Union of Yemeni Women expressed, the Yemenis revolution held the conventional belief that "women should not make it their most important aim to oppose men because in capitalist countries men are also oppressed" (quoted in Molyneux 1979: 17). In any event, Iranian and Yemeni women had little in common. Chief among the reforms in the status of Yemeni women were free marriage, the abolition of child marriage, the abolition of polygamy, the reduction of bride-price, the recognition of both spouses as the sources of family income, the abrogation of men's power to divorce through unilateral repudiation, and the alteration of custody rights (Molyneux 1985). These reforms had all already been introduced under the Shah.

National and international history and politics are thus constitutive elements of the Iranian Left's perspective on gender issues. Though the Left's approach to the "woman question" appears simple, it is nevertheless filtered through a myriad of considerations and influences. The women's movement, as Melucci (1996a: 137) points out, is the product of a complex set of relationships involving manifest struggle; demands for access to, and pressure on, the political market; absence or presence of mobilization; processes of self-reflection; and the development of new collective forms of behavior. The women's movement in Iran, too, reflects a similar complexity. Accordingly, the Iranian Left's response to gender politics should be seen in the context of this complexity.

SEXUAL INEQUALITY AS A CULTURAL CRISIS

As I mentioned earlier, the dominant leftist paradigm of social analysis revolved around politico-economic crisis. This tendency was reinforced in discussions about gender because class inequalities gravely limited the changes brought about by the refashioning of patriarchy. Social and economic inequalities rendered reforms meaningless for the majority of the female population. The Family Protection Law is a good example. The right to divorce or the requirement of having the first wife's consent before marrying again cannot accomplish much for women who do not have economic independence, are illiterate, and are at their husbands' mercy for survival.

Central to the Iranian Left's analysis of sexual inequality was the notion of class. Class society oppressed women, though the oppression took a different form in each class. "The exploitation (estesmâr) of the women of toiling classes is in no way comparable to the injustices (setam) inflicted upon bourgeois and petit-bourgeois women. Indeed, peasant or working-women are exploited exactly like the men of their classes and at the same time have to endure extremely harsh pressures from their husbands" (CIS-NU n.d.: 27).[5] With the increasing influence of imperialism in Iran, the analysis continued, women were absorbed into the labor force as providers of cheap labor power. Although labor laws existed to promise equal pay for equal work, they were nothing but hollow gestures. In reality, work-ingwomen were paid several times less than what their male colleagues earned. Women's entry into the labor market, therefore, "does not increase family income; it merely increases the capitalists' benefits." In addition to economic exploitation, male chauvinism "manifested" itself in the domi-nant culture, which in Iran—"a dependent capitalist society"—was the im-perialist culture with "traditional and antediluvian ideas of feudal culture" with its concomitant religious mentality (28, 47, and 48).

From the Leftist point of view, problems of culture, including sexual domination, would gradually resolve by the formation of the new socio-economic order. Socialism would construct a proper culture. To fully un-derstand this approach, one should consider that an overwhelming majority of the Iranian Left had learned Marxism through outdated textbooks. Of particular interest were Stalin's pamphlet *Dialectical and Historical Mate-rialism* (published in 1938), Georges Politzer's *The Elementary Principles of Philosophy* (published in France in the early 1930s), and Maurice Corn-forth's three-volume *Dialectical Materialism: An Introduction* (published in the mid-1950s). Cornforth, for instance, formulated the relationship be-tween base and superstructure in the following manner:

The upheaval in the economic sphere, in the basic social relations, brings an up-heaval also throughout the whole sphere of ideas and institutions. The old is over-come by the new. . . . With this the entire content of social consciousness is eventually changed. With the discussion of old relations of production, ideas which were formed on that basis become at first outmoded and reactionary, and in the end irrelevant and absurd. (1971: 105)

Culture in this traditional Marxist analysis is understood as a product of the underlying material conditions which reflects the dominant socio-economic formation. Every mode of production relies on compatibility be-tween the forces of production and the relations of production in order to survive. Therefore, development in the mode of production leads to a change in the culture. In other words, culture is a product of objective laws which exist independently from human will. This analysis has been criti-cized in recent decades (see chapter 1). Gramsci's notion of hegemony dis-closed culture as entrenched in a society's consciousness, instead of considering it the imposition of a cluster of values and beliefs in the interest of the ruling class. Williams' distinction between residual and emergent cultures also shed some light upon the complex processes of social trans-formation. The dominant culture could entertain either alternative, de-pending on the dominant short- and long-term interests.

In Iran, the challenge facing the leftist opposition was to establish a link between its own ideal, proletarian culture and the dominant, residual, and emergent cultures. Considering the dominant culture as decadent led the Left to reject even aspects of the emergent culture that were incorporated into the dominant culture but could still contribute to the formation of the Left's ideal "free and democratic Iran." It could not identify with the residual culture as it saw religion and other "remnants of feudalism" to be incompatible with its socialist ideals. On the other hand, many of its own values such as sexual morality and the primacy of collective over individual were deeply rooted in the residual culture. Consequently, the Left developed an implicit love-hate relationship with the residual culture, which resulted in ambivalence and ambiguities in its politics.

To maintain the unity of "all anti-imperialist and anti-Shah forces," the Iranian Left also shied away from discussing topics like sexuality, which concerned youth and especially college students from whose ranks the Left frequently recruited. It is apparent that by adopting a conservative approach toward dominant beliefs, the Left has alienated a major portion of the population, and since some 55% of the Iranian population was twenty or younger (60% in rural and 40% in urban areas), that was a lot of people. This conservatism also reflected the Left's orientation toward the youth as a group whose energy could be useful only if directly tied to the revolutionary movement of the toiling masses. As Bizhan Jazani, a founding member of the Fedaiin, put it: "Young intellectuals are not aware of the important role of the toiling masses in the realization of the revolution and forget that the youth can only be the detonator of the revolutionary dynamite and not its full explosive power" (Safa'i-Farahani n.d.: 54).[6]

Cultural criticism—or "cultural work" (kâr-e farhangi), in the Left's jargon—did not mean what Williams called easing the emergence of new "experiences, meanings and values." Instead it was identified with criticisms of government policies regarding art and culture, renunciation of conspicuous consumption, and a rejection of apolitical intellectuals. The aim was to instill revolutionary sentiment in the youth and students in order to attract them to political activity.[7] A major component of this task was to discredit cultural imperialism.

The Left never clearly defined what "imperialist culture" and "cultural imperialism" were, but translations of Franz Fanon and Aimé Césaire had their effect. To colonize African societies successfully, Césaire and Fanon believed, the colonial powers had rejected the native cultural heritage. Subsequently, many natives came to define themselves in the same terms as their oppressors did. In other words, as Fanon put it, they wore a white mask over their black skin. To defeat colonialism, therefore, it was essential for native Africans to take back their stolen heritage.[8] Since Iran never formally became a colony, contributions to this theory by Iranian Marxist scholars, and critics like Manouchehr Hezarkhani (1973; 1977) who translated Fanon, Césaire and other anti-colonialists into Persian, Samad Behrangi (1984), Khosrow Golesorkhi (n.d.), and Saʿid Soltanpour (n.d.) emphasized education, mass culture, and art. Later, the domain included most aspects of cultural life, including male-female relationships. To guarantee its dominance, imperialism "exported" a decadent and corrupt culture to dependent societies, heavily based on fashion, commercial art, and lax sexual morality. The function of the "imported culture" was to displace young people's energy and distract them with matters that had no bearing on the nation's politico-economic conditions.

This cultural imperialist theory was a shift from the previous generation who emphasized the evils of domestic reactionary forces. Women's oppression was now attributed to world imperialism and its internal allies—the Shah's state apparatus and the comprador bourgeoisie—rather than to the social, economic, political, and cultural conditions of Iranian society itself. This style of thinking replaced patriarchal oppression with consumerism and imperialist manipulation. Discussion of women's social status concentrated on issues like obsession with cosmetics and fashion and the influence of Western culture.

The very idea of an "imperialist culture" is of course an oversimplification, based on a mechanical understanding of the relationship between culture and relations of production. It treats culture as a thing, not as a process. It assumes a homogeneous reflection of the substructure called "the imperialist culture." The dominant capitalist class, according to this understanding, can unilaterally create a culture.

This theory hid the changes in the status of women under the Pahlavis by analyzing these as Pahlavi conspiracy. As a statement by the Minority faction of Fedaiin put it,

[The] toiling women of our homeland are well aware that the liberation promised by . . . supporters of the bourgeoisie, these lackeys of imperialism and the anti-people regime of the Shah, is nothing but the freedom to exploit more, and the liberty to sell the luxury imperialist goods at the expense of plundering the toilers; it is nothing but spreading the penetration of degenerate imperialist culture. Their defense of women's liberation means defending prostitution, drug addiction, setting up houses of lust and a thousand other manifestations of capitalist culture. (OIPFG 1982a: 129)

The Left's version of cultural imperialism blurred the dividing line between the Marxists and the religious opposition to the Shah. It is important to emphasize again, however, that the Iranian Left never adapted an Islamic approach to cultural imperialism, especially one developed by Shariati. But the similarity of the two discourses disarmed the Left in its confrontation with the Islamic opposition. The Left's analysis of cultural imperialism was concerned with the eradication of social and economic inequalities; it was never an invitation for, as Shariati put it, a "return to ourselves" (see Hanson 1983). Indeed, in the early seventies, one leader of the leftist movement expressed this idea as follows:

We have no animosity toward Western culture. Nor do we consider Western technology to be an enemy for us and our culture. We are against the West's exploitative
relations, against the monstrous capitalism of the West which has kept our nation
in poverty and backwardness. (Safa'i-Farahani n.d.: 41)

When authors like Jalal Al-e Ahmad and Ali Shariati enjoyed popularity for their anti-Shah activities, some Marxists did criticize their ideas. Homa Nategh (1975), in her *Az Mâst keh bar Mâst (Nobody Else to Blame But Ourselves)* criticized the historical roots of such approaches. Mohammad Bagher Momeni on several occasions analyzed the ideas of Shariati and Al-e Ahmad and considered them to be "some three hundred years" behind contemporary civilization (e.g., Momeni 1977: 62–66). Ali Akbar Akbari (1977) devoted a book to the criticism of Shariati's views. Founding members of the guerrilla movement, too, were critical of Al-e Ahmad's theoretical orientation (Hamid Momeni 1979; Pooyân 1979). One should also mention the long conversation between the sociologist Ehsan Naraghi, who believed that the East had to search for its own roots and find the future in its past in light of the West's enslavement by technology, and the Marxist poet and philosopher, Esmail Khoi (Naraghi and Khoi 1977).

According to the Left's argument, any reform in the condition of women must *either* have benefited the Shah *or* women, but not both. Women could not have benefited from these reforms, leftists contended, because their purpose was to create a facade of progressiveness for the Pahlavis. This idea was reflected in an article by an Iranian leftist published in an international radical journal:

Following in his father's footsteps, the last Shah attempted to force women into
"emancipation" by imposing other changes from above. But, these new measures,
while progressive on paper, were for the most part not transformed into reality.
Although some archaic laws were changed, others were not. Most women were
unaffected by these laws. (Az 1981: 25)

"Thus," the article continued, "women's 'emancipation' as defined by the Pahlavi dynasty served its own needs, not those of women" (26).

The leftist view of cultural imperialism had one assumption in common with the Islamists: women were considered to be more prone to deceit; they could be used to deceive men and especially male revolutionaries (see Shahidian 1993: 48–49). Consequently, women's demonstrations in post-revolutionary Iran were deemed to serve imperialism to undermine the revolution. In Chile, the Left argued, the ploy proved effective, and therefore the imperialist powers had targeted Iranian women to implement a similar tactic. In fact, as a proof of their argument, the Fedaiin translated and published Michele Mattelart's (1975) article, "Chile: The Feminine Side of the Coup or When Bourgeois Women Take to the Streets." Yet the Chilean analogy (not Mattelart's discussion) overlooked that the Chilean right succeeded in organizing women primarily because when the Popular Unity government was in power, no party in the socialist-communist coalition addressed women's issues and took any measures to win their political support (Chinchilla 1977: 89). Capitalizing on this failure,

the same bourgeoisie that waited until 1949 ungraciously to accord its women the right to vote (they had been petitioning for it since 1898) and that never favored their requests in the matter of civil rights, suddenly hurried to expand the woman's traditional roles. Obviously the bourgeoisie could no longer sit by and allow the female to limit herself to an existence as the passive mother, spouse, and the lady of the house who traditionally assured the reproduction of the key values of the system. The bourgeoisie now required that she become active, that she organize, that she mobilize herself for the defense of "democracy," of which she was about to become the living symbol. (Mattelart 1975: 289)

When the mission was accomplished, the military regime asked women to go back to their traditional roles of mothers and wives.

Many leftists understood the imposition of the veil in post-revolutionary Iran as deploying a wrong method of struggle against imperialism. The pro-government Majority faction of the Fedaiin complained that

from our 17-month political experience with the Islamic Republic, we know that it invariably attempts to deal with social problems in isolation from the socio-economic factors at the root. This perversity has resulted in the imposition on the people and society of its own ideals and preferences, a policy that has inevitably led to the inflation of secondary issues and to ignoring the fundamental demands and needs of people . . . preparing the ground for the friends and spies of American imperialism. (OIPFG 1982b: 136)

The Majority's policy of avoiding conflicts with the regime can in part explain the conciliatory tone of the text. But even the radical opposition to the regime did not formulate its criticism any differently. Another reason for the Left's attitude was its puritanical concept of sexuality. Since women were socialized to be sexually passive and to deny their desires, sexuality was equated with men's pleasure. While the feminist critique of sexuality has aimed at its reconstruction on a non-patriarchal basis—that is, one that acknowledges and responds to female sexuality—the Iranian Left based its criticism of the objectification of sex on a tacit *denial* of female sexuality. That assumption led the Left to see no distinction between patriarchal manipulation of sexuality and women's self-assertiveness.

The roots of this attitude should be sought in the sexual morality of the

Iranian culture which, profoundly influenced by Islamic values, advocates chastity and purity as primary attributes of womanhood (see Azari 1983a). In the last decade of the Pahlavi rule, the prominent form of political activism was armed struggle, which required strict discipline with no room for idiosyncratic considerations. That condition augmented the sentiment generally dominant among revolutionaries which found, to quote Hobsbawm, "personal libertarianism a nuisance" (1970: 40). This has been a problem common to most guerrilla movements. Byanyima (1992), for instance, recalls how the National Resistance Movement in Uganda had to establish separate camps for each sex to maintain discipline and to respond to the shortages of supplies for birth control, prenatal care, and venereal disease.

The Left also overlooked the slowly emerging new female identity. Growing consumerism and the increasing use of cosmetics and luxury items among women were often seen as proofs of the undesirable direction of social change in Iran. As one source put it,

Constantly exposed to decadent Western culture never having fought for their rights, absorbed mainly into the service sector, and utilized as decorative objects, many [middle-class women] became mere consumers of luxury goods. If the traditional religious woman had to hide her body from the public and be the obedient slave of her father and then of her husband, the "new woman" had to ornament her body in order to please both the public and her man. The determining factor in the actions and reactions of both categories of women was the pleasure and will of men. In neither case were their bodies or their minds their own. (Az 1981: 25)

As the author acknowledged, the use of ornament was not a practice unknown to the Iranian society. So the significance it gained in the Left's criticism of the Pahlavi state should be primarily attributed to two factors. First, it was detested because it was imperialist-made and therefore an example of cultural imperialism. More importantly, however, it was identified with an assertive woman who was demanding an increasing share of the public world. The public woman was a sign of a capitalist transformation of patriarchal control over women's life. This rearrangement of sexual norms not only threatened the interest of Iranian males—including those with leftist inclinations—but also presented a puzzle for which the Left did not have a sufficient answer. As Ong (1987: 179–93) demonstrates in her study of change among factory women in Malaysia, claiming new sex roles to be detrimental to moral values is a reaction to the challenge this represents to the control exercised by groups who resist or are at least ambivalent to social changes.

THE IMPERIALIST TRAP: SEXUALITY, INDIVIDUALITY, AND FAMILY

One aspect of the change in patriarchal structure, I discussed earlier, was the emergence of new sexualities. Sexual interaction was slowly but surely moving beyond matrimonial sex. Secularization and commercialization of sex intensified the reflexive character of both the human body and sexual desire. On a par with the tradition of modernity, the self became an ongoing project, constantly shaped and reshaped as individuals contemplated emerging social relations and their resultant limitations and opportunities. Popular magazines and sophisticated literature alike reflected reflexivity of the modern self. Self-help books by authors like Dale Carnegie and treatises on love and marriage, such as marriage manuals, Bertrand Russell's writings on education and marriage, or Erich Fromm's *The Art of Loving*, attracted intellectual curiosity among educated youth. The Left regarded these projects as preoccupation with insignificant mundane problems.

While the Left recognized that the endeavor of human beings focused primarily on relieving the burdens of the body and mind—equal access to social and political resources, solving the problems of hunger, lack of proper clothing, shelter, health care, etc.—the body itself was absent from the Left's discussion. The body was merely the vessel of the mind, something that the mind inhabited. And the body was prioritized—its basest aspect, sexuality. One reason why the imposition of the veil appeared inconsequential to the Left was that it was a bodily matter. Similar injustices not of corporal origin inflicted upon women's rights (witnessing, inheriting, the law of retribution) were opposed. The veil merely affected the body; inequality between male and female witnesses was detrimental to women's human dignity. The body was also a sign of individuality, a trap of individualism devised by the consumer culture. Revolutionaries were to be above such mundane matters.

From this vantage point, it was difficult to recognize that nonpolitical demands became politicized. The crisis here was not of politico-economic nature, but one caused by developing and anticipating social relations. It concerned cultural codes, not confrontation with the political order. The Left avoided cultural matters to safeguard its radicalism—overlooking that radicalism was not in the issues, but in their articulation.

In the Left's analysis, advocacy of free sex was castigated as a "bourgeois deviation" (CIS-NU n.d.: 5–6). Bizhan Jazani, a leading theoretician of the Fedaiin, criticized "promiscuous" intellectuals and those who, in the tradition of the *lumpenproletariate*, use foul language, and referred to them as "lumpenintellectuals" (Jazani n.d.: 188). In the dominant prerevolutionary mentality of the Left, as I have discussed elsewhere (Shahidian 1996), love and sexuality were deemed antithetical to revolutionary activism. The Pahlavi propaganda presented activists as a threat to the morality of society by showing, for example, films of contraceptives found in activists' safe-houses where unmarried men and women lived together. To ward off this accusation, revolutionaries presented a counter-image of themselves as serious, modest, devoted activists whose love for the masses left no room for carnal love. To be sure, this ideal type of asexual and desexed revolutionary did reflect traditional and Islamic sexual morality; but at stake was also upholding an ideal image of militants beyond the temptations of bourgeois morality. One activist related to me that a leading activist did not agree to have regular meetings with a female sympathizer at Tehran Polytechnic, arguing that were he to be seen with a woman, activists would think their meetings were amorous rendezvous' and would doubt his commitment to politics.

For die-hard revolutionaries, marriage signaled the adoption of a routine lifestyle and preoccupation with daily family matters. As such, though marriage was not condemned, it was deemed a threat to revolutionary commitment. Love detracted attention from politics at a time when there was "no time for kisses and amorous lyrics," as Siavosh Kasraii's then-popular poem "Gâlyâ" expressed. Reza Baraheni's (1982) *What Happened after the Marriage* (written in 1974) promotes this dangerous side of love, where a wife becomes the only obstacle that a heroic man, who had withstood the harshest tortures, could not survive.

This mentality was modified in post-revolutionary days. The popularization of revolutionism brought "ordinary" individuals (as opposed to the heroic few of yesteryear) into political activism. Yet even then, leftist organizations tried to promote marriages that accommodated and strengthened political commitments. Some even argued for a "proletarian love and marriage" based on common political analyses and advocacies. The Peykâr organization issued an internal guideline on how members and supporters should choose their mates. Supporters of the Fedaiin translated a collection of short articles by Lenin, Alfred Uci, an Albanian author, and an article from the Chinese *Renmin Ribao (People's Daily)* on the subject of family and socialism. The introduction stated the purpose of compiling the pamphlet to be raising an "awareness of the illness and corruption of class societies and to spread genuine proletarian culture." In this way, the movement could not only better educate men and women revolutionaries, but also assist women in "contributing their share in society's transformation to socialism" (ISA-US n.d.: 2).

Defending the sanctity of the family also became a recurring theme. The introduction to a pamphlet published by the Supporters of the Peykâr expressed concerns with the slanderous propaganda by the Islamic regime regarding lack of morality among the Left and their intention of dissolving the family (Supporters of Peykâr 1979: 3). The introduction argued that Engels, in his *Origin*, made a correlation between marriage and three stages of human progress and demonstrated that group marriage was a savagery and cannot be attributed to progressive communism. Furthermore, although capitalism introduced the monogamous relationship, it also promoted adultery and prostitution. True monogamy then for the first time in history would find a chance to develop fully only after the abolition of private property (4).[9] The article also condemned "the so-called leftists and Marxists who use Marxism as an excuse for their licentious and promiscuous life" and, quoting Lenin, warned them that such a lifestyle was bourgeois and corrupt (5). Tudeh publications demonstrated a similar approach. After the falling-out between the Tudeh Party and the Islamic regime, the party published a supplement to its organ, *Mardom (People)*, in response to a Friday sermon by Hashemi Rafsanjani on 15 June 1984. Marxism, Rafsanjani contended, had no respect for family values and sought to destroy the foundation of that institution. The supplement emphasized that contrary to Rafsanjani's contention, "the founders of Marxism-Leninism considered the family to be of great importance" (Tudeh Party of Iran 1984: 3).

Marx and Engels expressed two different attitudes toward the family. One position condemned the destruction of family life under capitalism and argued against the *capitalist* family; the other called for the destruction of *family* as such and its replacement by higher forms of human ties (see Landes 1989). What is noteworthy, however, is that the Iranian Left did not acknowledge this second attitude for several reasons. First, the Marxist education of many Iranian leftists was through Soviet Marxism, which a few years after the 1917 revolution became quite adamant in its pro-family stance. Second, and more importantly, leftists' upbringing was in a culture that regarded the institution of the family as a "natural" given. Thus, even those who question the "naturalness" of the family refrained from voicing their opinion, lest it downgrade Marxism in the eyes of the public and the Left's unwillingness to discuss sensitive topics.

Another practical consequence of the Left's approach to gender was the desexing of female activists, clearly visible in the baggy clothes and absence of cosmetics among female revolutionary activists. Female activists learned quite early in their political life that in order to be taken seriously by their male comrades, they *had to* have a *zâher-e sâdeh*, modest appearance. For some, though, this appearance was not just adherence to an unspoken code of revolutionary conduct; rather, it represented progressive politics. As one activist commented, "similar to the hippies in the West, we were rebelling against the dominant culture, against our parents' lifestyle, against the capitalist system. So in that respect we were influenced by the progressive movements of the sixties" (telephone interview, June 1993). Furthermore, working in poor neighborhoods required activists to both comply with dominant dress styles in such areas and be mindful of any act that might separate them from the poor, especially any action that hinted at class differences.

The desexed revolutionary woman was a leftist prototype, an alternative to the sexually exploited woman of the Pahlavi era. Qodsi Qâzinour (1979), for instance, clearly expressed this ideal in a commentary on the imposition of the veil. She rejected policies like mandatory veiling as simplistic and regarded them as futile attempts to solve the woman question. With or without a scarf, she argued, a woman-doll *(zan-e 'arousaki)* will remain the same. "If by hejâb is meant modesty, then why not do something fundamental? Why not teach women to dress simply—a baggy pair of pants, a long and loose blouse with hair tied behind the back with a rubber band." That way, the woman question would no longer be pertinent and women would not have to rely on their womanhood:

Then womanhood will no longer be so problematic, the borders of a woman's freedom will not be a problem anymore, her hejâb will not be a problem. Instead, she will be a human being armed with knowledge. If she seeks knowledge, if she seeks awareness, then being a woman will not be her tool anymore.

Both the Left and religious right considered self-assertion as a manifestation of decadent bourgeois culture. For Islam, the foundation of this belief was the denial of human individuality before a god who viewed any diversion of its believers' attention as a sign of idolatry. The Islamic critique of liberalism culminates in the individual's loss of identity in the community, which then becomes the basis of a "monotheistic society," a community of believers with no individual identity. Dissimilarities disappear because there is no difference of ideas and lifestyles—"one can breathe the oxygen of Islam everywhere" (Shariati 1977: 23).

Marxists have also criticized the individualist capitalist ethos and proposed collectivity as an alternative. Marx and Engels have argued that individualization is a historical process (Lukes 1984; Tucker 1980). Humankind "originally appears as a *generic being, a tribal being, a herd animal...*" (Marx 1980: 96). The emergence of free labor power and the formation of the working class under capitalist systems of production provided the historical foundation for the destruction of the herd and establishment of human individuality. However, while capitalism for the first time realized the right of the individual beings, it did not liberate humankind from class relations. As long as class society exists, social relationship is not the free association of individual persons; it is rather the association of classes (Marx and Engels 1976: 80). In this respect, communism is supposed to overcome the shortcomings of both individualism and communalism. By destroying class distinctions, communism will give complete individuality to people and will consequently create a society of "united individuals" and not an animal herd (81).

According to the Iranian Left, capitalism advocated individual rights as a justification for private property, but socialists should stress the rights of all members of society. This argument was originally intended to protect people against exploitation. However, since the Left's reading of Marx and Engels made no distinction between individuality *(fardiyat)* and individualism *(fardgera'i)*, it ended up downplaying individual rights. The Iranian Left rejected many features of capitalism as examples of decadent capitalist culture. Individuality—misconstrued as individualism—was consequently jettisoned as the decadence of the capitalist West, antithetical to commitment to the collective (especially the family) and the revered values of modesty and "purity;" that is, being uninterested in non-marital sex. Society should be protected against the "deviations" of the individuals. In addition to these cultural factors, the disdain for individualism also reflected an awareness of the dangers of political involvement in Iran; struggle under police persecution required strict discipline, especially for guerrilla groups. These exigencies, however, were elevated to the level of ideological principles that shaped not just activism, but also worldviews.

REPRESENTATIVE REVOLUTIONISM: MOBILIZING WOMEN

Though the Left recognized sexual oppression, it did not acknowledge the need for an autonomous women's movement. Leftists considered it hypocritical to emphasize women's rights when neither sex had any freedom. Fedaiin admitted that there was significant discrimination between the sexes "in the dark years of dictatorship" and that equal rights of men and women had to be achieved, but did not acknowledge the possibility of a woman's movement since "freedom is a humanitarian goal which is not determined by sex."

Dividing the society into two parts—men and women—to make the cultural struggle a main issue, or to place women in opposition to men is a dramatic deviation from the main path. . . . Women's liberation is possible only through class emancipation and women's participation in the struggle. . . . To make false agitation among women is a conspiracy and is a policy adopted by reactionaries and imperialists to dissipate our people's struggling forces. What distinguishes men and women is not their appearance but their class status and their advocacy to the revolution. (OIPFG 1979e: 6)

Since only socialism could liberate women, any hope for sexual equality under capitalism was nothing but an illusion. The bourgeoisie's intention was merely to exploit women's labor (CIS-NU n.d.: 100–101). Some admitted that women's involvement in capitalist production "guarantees women's independence to some extent," but they were quick to add that "that is not tantamount to achieving liberation" (OIPFG 1979e: 6).

Many years before the revolution, women partook in leftist politics by joining the guerrilla movement (see Shahidian 1997). They received the same military training as the men and participated in guerrilla attacks. The revolution encouraged this participation, because it was supposed to challenge society's stereotypes of sex roles. This goal was not achieved completely. The experience of revolutionary movements in Vietnam and Palestine—two movements that inspired the Iranian Left—have shown that revering dedicated women soldiers of the revolution does not necessarily diminish men's sexual stereotypes. Commenting on women's political participation in the Palestinian movement, Orayb Aref Najjar distinguishes between "change in the role of women" and "change in their status within the general population" (1992: 157), and concurs that liberation movements "do not necessarily ensure equal rights and opportunities, nor do they restructure asymmetrical gender relations" (Peteet 1986: 23).

Though involvement in Iran's underground politics made women independent and assertive, it did not inspire them to advocate women's rights. These women participated in the revolutionary movement as representative of other women: sexism was the problem of "toiling women." Discriminations and injustices that these revolutionary women experienced were deemed, by comparison, insignificant and less pressing (Shahidian 1997: 34–38). Female revolutionaries concentrated on problems concerning workingwomen and the travesties of the bourgeois women's lifestyle (see, for instance, Ahmadi Oskoo'i n.d.). Guerrilla women remained "symbols" of revolutionary women who though admired, had little relevance for the woman who was busy changing diapers and preparing meals and outraged by the exploitation of her sexuality in everyday life. Despite the concern with workingwomen, the Left never fully conceptualized women's role in the economy. Therefore, they did not take women's militancy even in the workplace seriously. For instance, in the five issues of *Nabard-e Khalq (People's Struggle)*, which the Fedaiin published prior to the revolution, there is only one extensive report on women's involvement in the class struggle (OIPFG 1974). During the revolutionary period (March 1978–March 1979), out of some ninety statements and leaflets published by Fedaiin, only one, issued on International Women's Day, addressed women (OIPFG 1979f: 235). The political priorities of the Left also influenced its approach toward the woman question. Leftists who supported the Islamic regime tended to emphasize the limitations imposed on women less than did the dissident Left.[10]

The Tudeh Party called Khomeini the most dedicated supporter of women's rights and before the arrest of Tudeh activists and subsequent outlawing of the party by the regime in 1983, criticisms of the regime's

policies regarding women were rare.[11] Accounts were limited to the hardships of peasant or working-class women. *Jahan-e Zanan*, a Tudeh-
affiliated women's magazine, printed recipes and sewing advice. One could
argue that these were issues relevant to the daily lives of millions of women
and by paying attention to them, the party responded to real needs of these
women and tried to reduce their burdens. Yet, it cannot be denied that
such treatment of "women's daily concerns," without addressing patriarchal relations, would serve to perpetuate them.

The Democratic Organization of Iranian Women, the women's branch
of the Tudeh Party, approved of the regime's policies regarding women,
believing that the 1979 revolution drastically changed women's role in society. The revolution, "desperately in need of women's fighting power in
the battleground" (DOIW 1980: 12), encouraged women to wage a struggle both as members of the society and as women. Following the revolution,
according to the Democratic Organization, women had the right to participate in politics and to make decisions. Since the revolution was the protector of women's rights, guarding it—or "the social front of the women's
movement"—had to be women's main goal.

To be sure, the Democratic Organization admitted, "there were shortcomings regarding the position of women and their struggle" (DOIW 1982:
6). The problems, however, were not indigenous to the Islamic Republic;
they were rather caused by saboteurs and enemies of the revolution. "The
sensitive question of women is one of the areas where counterrevolutionary
and bigoted elements have pinned their hopes for weakening the revolution" (7–8). Therefore, minor flaws could in no way affect women's adherence to Khomeini's leadership:

At this time of grand confrontations when classes are polarized and in the light of
the [anti-imperialist] struggle and the enmity of the United States imperialism, when
the ideas of political groups, parties and organizations find their clear manifestation—many people want to use women's oppression as an excuse and mobilize
women against the real path of the revolution and give secondary importance to
what is presently of major and principal importance. [This is accomplished through]
the use of shortcomings, ambiguousness, and lack of the necessary clarity in the
laws which makes some articles of the Constitution subject to interpretation.
(DOIW 1980: 13)

The Democratic Organization's Program of Action proposed the "abrogation of all laws injurious to the respectable status of women and mothers." It also called for women's right to elect and be elected to all offices,
and for their increasing participation in public and private institutions "especially those which are directly related to sanitation and education"
(DOIW n.d.: 9). The program criticized unfair family laws that, by cate-
gorizing women as irrational, condemned them to a life of slavery. These

by and large uneducated women had to shoulder the responsibilities of organizing the family budget, managing the household, and attending to the needs of their husbands and children. "It is surprising that many women, in spite of all barriers and limitations and through heroic sacrifices, have accomplished these tasks very well and have succeeded in raising children who make all of humanity proud." In the revolutionary Iran, the program contended, new laws needed be promulgated which would clear women's path for betterment (9–10).

The program also advocated traditional socialist demands for advancing women's role in production and education, and legal provisions for working mothers, women farmers and carpet weavers. It also demanded the eradication of prostitution and criticized methods implemented by the Islamic regime (such as burning down Tehran's red light district and public humiliation of "deviant" women), since "corruption and prostitution are the products of poverty" (12) and could be removed only by eliminating economic and social inequalities.

Other groups also tackled the question of how women should be mobilized and participate in the revolution. The consensus was that the women's movement had a dual function: it prevented the spread of "bourgeois feminism," on the one hand, and mobilized women to join the struggle for proletarian emancipation on the other. The Peykâr organization distinguished three different arguments concerning the "toiling women's movement" among the Left. According to the first argument, any action to organize toiling women should be postponed until the days after the establishment of the popular democratic republic.[12] The Peykâr found this approach incompatible with the interests of the revolutionary movement and proposed that mobilizing toiling women would provide the revolutionary movement with a chance to educate the masses and prepare them for the socialist revolution.

The second argument, the Peykâr comments, accepted the need to organize toiling women in theory, but did not take any practical step toward mobilizing women: "We should allocate only as much energy to this task as we can afford" (Peykar 1981a: 19). The third argument rejected the need for any practical step to mobilize women. This approach, according to the Peykâr, was incapable of understanding the complexities of the "double oppression of women" in class societies (19). The Peykâr then quoted the oft-mentioned conversation between Lenin and Clara Zetkin to support its own point of view regarding the necessity of addressing toiling women's issues through special channels. But who were the "toiling women" and how could communists mobilize them?

The Peykâr identified three groups of women who should be mobilized: (1) women involved in production, such as workers and peasants; (2) women in social services, such as professional women and teachers; and (3) women of national minorities involved in the struggle against the Islamic regime. Historically, the Left had a problematic relationship with housewives. The Comintern viewed them with suspicion. Many communist women's organizations worked diligently among housewives and encouraged them to join cooperatives, fight inflation, and support their husbands' strikes. But they also believed that "unless properly supervised, [they were] a liability, capable of infecting the movement with their petty bourgeois mentality and of sapping the militancy of their husbands" (Waters 1989: 40). The Peykâr, too, argued that even if they were from working-class families, housewives were unlikely to join the struggle.[13]

Because of their social position as housewives these women are unable to understand the contradiction between their class and the hostile ruling class. The reason is that exploitation in a working-class family occurs indirectly and through a man. . . . That is why they do not do anything to find a solution [and join] the struggle and fight against their class enemy. Not only that, they grow inimical toward anything that disrupts their monotonous and meager life. (Peykâr 1981b: 23)

The Peykâr organization proposed that "democratic organizations" were responsible for the mobilization of women. Nonetheless, the article went on, democracy was a class category. Thus it is only reasonable to assume that democratic organizations can be "truly democratic" only when they work under the hegemonic leadership of the working class and aim at "the annihilation of imperialist domination and the establishment of the popular democratic republic" (24). Neither of the examples of the women's organizations that the Peykâr offered—the Association of the Mothers of Martyrs and the Association of Widows—were to struggle for women's rights. They were women's organizations only insofar as the sex of their members was concerned. Although in the context of a popular women's movement such organizations can play an important role in mobilizing women (see Jetter, Orleck, and Taylor 1997; Holst-Warhaft 2000), they nevertheless cannot substitute for organizations that lead assaults on the patriarchal structure.

The experience of other social movements suggests a similar conclusion. In Palestine where the movement relies extensively on informal women-centered networks, women have shown an active commitment to their national cause. Such an engagement which overlooks women's need as women, however, mutes women's concerns and "deflects" their feminist consciousness (Najjar 1992; Peteet 1986: 23–24). A more successful case is that of Brazil. Though Brazilian women commenced their activities by working alongside women's neighborhood associations, feminist groups succeeded in representing themselves only *after* they entered the political arena with demands which affected their roles as women in production and reproduction (Sarti 1989).

The Peykâr's further requirement for democratic women's organizations

is their covert direction by the vanguard political organization, or the communist party. The rank and file can choose their individual leaders only
after the vanguard party had secured its leadership in a women's organization. To guarantee the dominance of the vanguard organization, the Peykâr requires all women cadres to join women's organizations. The Peykâr
concludes by restating its goal for the women's movement:

The democratic organization which we have in mind is one that does not becloud
class contradictions, but will rather make the uncompromising army of the proletariat ever more united by organizing toiling women around the democratic goals
of the proletariat. According to this principle, any organization which seeks to
organize toiling women around slogans such as "women's general issues" and
"women's common grievances" and to obfuscate existing contradictions among
antagonistic classes, and consequently cause a class compromise; or seek to advocate that securing women's denied rights, which requires proletarian leadership and
can be achieved only in a socialist society, can indeed be accomplished in a capitalist
society—will be considered a deviationist organization and shall have no function
but to misguide and waste women's fighting spirit and shall betray them and serve
the bourgeoisie. (Peykâr 1981b: 24)[14]

This hierarchical organizational design is rooted in the orthodox communist notion of the relationship between the party and the masses.[15] Lenin
and Stalin saw this relationship as similar to the "transmission belts" and
the "directing force." "The levers or transmission belts," wrote Stalin, "are
those very mass organizations of the proletariat without the aid of which
the dictatorship [of the proletariat] cannot be realized. The directing force
is the advanced detachment of the proletariat, its vanguard, which is the
main guiding force of the dictatorship of the proletariat" (Stalin 1954: 34).
This "democratic centralism" was supposed to ease a flow of information
and decision from bottom to top and vice versa. In practice, however, democratic centralism—especially in repressive states and under the harsh conditions of underground politics—has worked predominantly from the top
down. As the examples of Mozambique and West Bengal show, such organizational design means that women's causes would be subsumed under
party and/or state priorities (Kruks and Wisner 1989). In the case of Iran,
the fact that numerous "democratic women's organizations" of the Left
could not reach a unifying understanding in the face of a misogynist Islamic
state because of the ideological differences among their "mother organizations" reaffirms this point.

Like the Peykar, the Fedaiin also condemned the violation of women's
rights by the new regime but discouraged agitation around "secondary"
issues, though as discussed earlier, the Fedaiin's policies regarding the
women's movement wavered due to factionalism. To compensate for this
ambivalence, the Minority Fedaiin published a special issue of *Kar* in
March 1981. One article reviewed women's contribution to the revolution-

ary process that led to the downfall of the Pahlavi regime. The article admired women's militant opposition to the discriminatory measures introduced by the new Islamic system. The article then pointed out "a particular problem" in the Iranian women's movement: the apathy of working-class women toward the Islamic Republic regime's assault on women's rights.

Working-class women, due to the lack of the most basic necessities—such as adequate food and water or housing because of inflation, etc.—are keenly aware of the economic inequalities which have led to spontaneous protests and actions on various occasions. These women, however, are insensitive and pay no attention to negation of women's democratic rights, though they are the primary victims of such anti-democratic measures. (OIPFG 1979b: 1)

The first wave of reaction to the imposition of the veil was strong. Anti-hejâb demonstrations in 1979 were mainly by middle-class women and, though some "bourgeois elements among women attempted to divert the movement," progressive women's organizations managed to stop the diversion. These events proved that "the formation of . . . democratic organizations was a necessary step in mobilizing the large masses of women, as well as shaping and guiding their political struggles" (5). This need, however, was never fulfilled. In the months following the anti-hejâb demonstrations,

not only did most of the progressive forces fail to mobilize women for democratic participation, but also most of them functioned within the framework of political organizations as sympathizers of the main vanguard groups. As a result, many women's organizations that had been formed following the February Uprising were not able to survive. (5)

This condition provided a good opportunity for the new regime to gradually implement its discriminatory policies. Resistance to the regime's subsequent discriminatory measures, according to the Fedaiin, was not as successful as the reaction to Khomeini's mandatory veiling order of 1979. "Lack of attention paid by the communist movement as a whole to the question of the woman's position and her oppression in the society" should be held partially responsible for this failure. Nonetheless, the article remarked, lack of social and political awareness of most women regarding the severe implications of these measures prevented women's mobilization on a mass scale.

Many women, for historical reasons, did not appreciate the social implications of the laws which would take away their rights to professions or would encourage them to return to household duties only; they did not realize that the renunciation of women's rights to divorce and the reinstitution of men's freedom to practice polygamy and "sigheh" [temporary marriage] would have immense destructive effects, and would in the end imply nothing short of the outright denial of women as human beings. This lack of awareness resulted in the absence of any uniform opposition. (5)

The article concluded by emphasizing the need for "organized and disciplined" democratic and independent women's organizations to mobilize working-class women and to stand up resolutely against the discriminatory policies of the Islamic regime.

After the special issue of *Kar* on women, the Fedaiin did not publish anything substantial about women; the few articles that did appear concentrated on exposing the Islamic government's discriminatory policies. Now and then the usual statements were issued: women suffer from double oppression; they should resist the regime's reactionary policies; women can attain real freedom only in a socialist society. The Fedaiin did not establish a women's branch, but—without openly admitting an organizational link—pro-Fedaiin women got together with other leftist women to form a woman's organization Ettehâd-e Melly-e Zanân (National Unity of Women) in March 1979 (Moghissi 1994; Matin 1999). The National Unity declared willingness to cooperate with any progressive "individuals, independent nationalist groups and all revolutionary minorities, irrespective of their ideological and religious beliefs" (NUW 1982: 204), and announced:

We do not consider our emancipation separate from the emancipation of the toiling classes, and therefore consider the establishment of a direct link with deprived classes, investigation of their working conditions and the health and welfare of workingwomen, as our primary task and responsibility. Also, the promotion of cultural and political consciousness of the working classes is one of our essential programmes. (205)

The activities of the National Unity were deeply affected by the balance of power inside the Fedaii Organization. Before the split in the Fedaiin, the National Unity avoided any confrontation with the Islamic regime. Its activities included publishing critical articles about women's status and governmental policies, translating and publishing classical Marxist literature on women and some writings of the Western Marxist feminists. It was the National Unity's policy not to participate in any demonstration; individual members were encouraged to participate but without revealing their membership. After the Fedaiin split, the National Unity policies also underwent radical changes. Even so, the National Unity remained a reactive organization, and most of its proposals and demands were introduced "as and when the context and necessity arose, such as the demand for equality of rights in family matters, which came as part of the condemnation of the government's abolition of the Family Protection Law of 1976" (206). The National Unity's radicalism attracted women from other groups, but the pro-Fedaiin women continued their dominance within it. With the rising political repression after the summer of 1981, the organization ceased to exist. In short, the National Unity activists were situated between a male-dominated Left and "bourgeois feminism." This has been a common experience for women in organizations that are ideologically and/or organizationally affiliated with the Left. As Ellen DuBois concluded in the case of women suffragists and the social-democratic movement in nineteenth century Germany, "the balance they struck [was] always fragile and often upset, between these two political forces that determined their political environment" (1991: 30)—and, one should add, determined their survival.

Fedaiins also established two women's committees in the southeastern province of Sistan and Baluchestan.[16] The first one dates back to 1980. The committee was established primarily to provide a front for women activists. "Since Baluchi women's presence in public has historically been minimal, Baluchi families did not permit their daughters to participate in leftist groups, but they were more accepting of women's organizations." The committee was based in Zahedan, an important urban center of the province. Though it ceased to function after the suppression of 1981, committeewomen developed a long-lasting bond. As one former member of this committee expressed: "A strong feeling of sisterhood still exists among these women and they go through the trouble of finding each other and reestablish broken ties even in exile." The second committee (1984–85) "existed more on paper." Fedaii women who left their hometowns to seek refuge in the Province of Sistan and Baluchestan, where Fedaiin continued to be active, formed it. This time, too, the women's committee helped activists to cope with the police and organizational disputes. It published statements to honor March Eighth (Supporters of OIPFG: Sistan and Baluchestan 1985; 1984a; 1984b) and a pamphlet on Iranian Baluchi women, which claimed that the Islamic Republic had taken "the meager rights" women had acquired toward the end of the Pahlavi era (Supporters of OIPFG: Sistan and Baluchestan 1984a: 14). The Baluchi Women's Committee disappeared owing to disputes and the Islamic Republic's pressure.

RECAPITULATION

From the outset of their activism, Iranian socialists have addressed women's rights and issues affecting their social status by supporting women's demands for suffrage, education, participation in the labor force and equal rights within the family. In the 1978–79 revolution, too, the contribution of the Left to the struggle against the discriminatory policies of the Islamic regime is undeniable, though its record on this matter is far from ideal. Leftist organizations, for instance, adamantly opposed the Bill of Retribution and severely criticized restrictions on women's access to work and education. They also upheld the rights of many working-class women by their active involvement in factories and working class neighborhoods. Their concern with the rights of national minorities provided recognition and support for Turkaman, Kurdish, and Baluchi women. These practical and theoretical undertakings reject the suggestion of an overlap between the Left's and the Islamists' agendas in the realm of gender.

Yet, the Left's sexual politics proved insufficient as women's conflict with Iranian patriarchy sharpened, and fighting for women's rights came to mean harsher and more complicated confrontations with the structure of male domination. Censorship, suppression, the harsh conditions of fighting against ruthless and dictatorial regimes, male domination, and culture have contributed to the failure of the Left to adopt a more gender-conscious theory and practice. Nonetheless, it is important to examine the theoretical orientation of the Left to understand the roots of its ambivalence toward the women's movement.

For the earlier generation of Iranian communists, the modernization model of women in revolution-accommodated fighting against internal reaction was deemed inseparable from fighting for women's rights. The development of public patriarchy shifted the emphasis of the women's movement from rights to liberation, from allotting women a greater share of the public domain to recognizing women's autonomy. The politico-economic paradigm of the Left, however, could not accommodate the politicization of unconventional political demands.

The Left's analysis of women's oppression primarily focused on two points. The first was women's exploitation in the context of a capitalist system, and the second focused on the imperialist manipulation of sexuality through cultural imperialism. Though the Left acknowledged the role of traditionalism in the reproduction of sexual inequality, its populist program, which emphasized the importance of unity in the anti-Shah struggle, curbed its criticism of traditional and religious beliefs about sexuality and sex roles. Furthermore, considering women's oppression to be a problem of the "superstructure" which socialism would solve, the Left did not recognize the need for an independent struggle against both the material and cultural bases of women's oppression. Therefore, women's oppression was seen as a secondary problem, which led to the dissolution of a feminist agenda in socialist priorities.

After the revolution, women's rights were overshadowed by the anti-imperialist struggle. The Left first denied the importance of anti-women measures of the new government. Following the spread of the women's movement, women's organizations with overt or covert ties to leftist groups were formed. The main purpose of these organizations, however, was to promote support for their mother organizations. This shows that although participation in revolutionary movements requires a concern with freedom, equality and democracy, it does not automatically inspire a feminist consciousness. Revolutionary movements can change women's roles and improve their status insofar as they relate to national or class politics, but they fall short of eradicating sexual inequalities. To achieve that, women must organize themselves in independent organizations that target male dominance.

The suppression of oppositional forces in the IRI has been antithetical to the emergence of an autonomous women's movement in Iran. Women, nonetheless, have demonstrated their resistance in various forms. The Islamic Republic has been unable to implement its ideal gender policies. It had to concede to a dual society, one in which public compliance with moral and sexual regulations does not imply a wholehearted acceptance. The crisis of ideological legitimacy for the Islamic Republic is evident in two distinct reactions by women, one in the form of an attempted reinterpretation of Islamic doctrine on women-centered imperatives, and the other in the form of a concerted, albeit embryonic, effort to articulate gender relations on secular grounds. In the remainder of the book, I will first analyze gender politics under the IRI (chapters 6 and 7) and then discuss emerging voices in Iranian feminism and the development of the dual society in post-revolutionary Iran.

NOTES

1. English translation from *Women & Struggle in Iran*, a publication of the ISA-US. Marziyeh Ahmadi Oskoo'i was born in 1945 to a middle-class Tabrizi family. In her childhood, she worked on her father's farm, where she witnessed the impoverished life of Iranian peasantry from an early age. Marziyeh Ahmady searched many books for an answer to social inequalities. She became a Marxist while studying in Teachers' Training College. Upon graduation, she taught in Oskoo's schools for three years. After a few years, she entered the University of Tabriz. Financial difficulties, however, did not allow her to finish her education. She then joined the Literacy Corps and taught in Varâmin, near Tehran. Her involvement in a massive student strike in March 1972 sent her to prison in the summer of that same year. Shortly after being released, she joined the Fedaiin. Marziyeh Ahmady was killed in a shootout with the government forces on 6 May 1974.

2. Examples include the following: on Iranian Arab women, see Razmandegân (n.d.: 14–17); on Turkmen women, see OIPFG (1979c); and on Baluchi women, see Supporters of OIPFG: Sistân and Baluchistân (1984a).

3. It is noteworthy that the exiled Iranian Left in Europe and the U.S. has reproduced texts by authors like Navâbakhsh and Afshârnyâ in recent years. During the revolutionary period, however, these books were not included in the "study guides" compiled by various leftist organizations, nor were their ideas reflected in the writings of the organized Left.

4. This was the promise of the *Theses on the Communist Women's Movement*

formulated by the First Communist Women's Conference, held in June 1920 in Moscow.

5. This is the special women's issue of the *Nâmeh-yi Pârsi*, a quarterly published by the CIS-NU (Confederation of the Iranian Students—National Union). Although produced outside of Iran, the account can be used as a document from within the Iranian leftist movement. First, National Unity was a branch of the Confederation that actively supported the guerrilla movement. In that sense, the *Nâmeh* is the theoretical declaration of a movement which drastically affected the opposition movement. Second, the arguments made by the anonymous authors of the *Nâmeh* are based on several assumptions that are by-and-large accepted by the Iranian Left.

6. Bizhan Jazani wrote *Âncheh Yek Enqelâbi Bâyad Bedânad* (*What A Revolutionary Should Know*) in prison and smuggled it out with the assistance of Mihan, his wife. The book was published under the name of Safâ'i-Farâhâni, one of Jazani's closest comrades, and for nearly three decades it was believed to be penned by Safâ'i-Farâhâni. In a recent book about Jazani, Mihan Jazani wrote that since Bizhan wanted to conceal from the SAVAK the existence of a network connecting him to activists outside the prison, he published the book under Safâ'i-Farâhâni's name, dated a year earlier than the actual publication date of 1971. See Mihan Jazani (1999).

7. The most developed analysis of "cultural work" in the writings of leftist intellectuals is in the area of *engagé* art. See Behrangi (1984), Golesorkhi (n.d.), and Soltanpour (n.d.).

8. For a review of the definitions and impacts of cultural imperialism, see Roberts and Marsh (1974: 77–98).

9. For Engels' classification and discussion, see Engels (1970: 209–255).

10. For an analysis of similar concerns between reformist and revolutionary approaches to women's rights, see Lise Vogel (1983: 101–103).

11. A similar orientation can be observed in the evaluation of the Iranian revolution by the Communist Party of the Soviet Union. See Agaev (1988).

12. "Popular democratic republic" referred to a stage in the revolutionary struggle of the working class in underdeveloped countries in which the primary goal was not to establish a socialist system, but a "popular democratic republic" under the leadership of the proletariat in alliance with the peasantry and the lower stratum of the petit-bourgeoisie.

13. Haideh Moghissi writes: "Very often, when [leftists] write about the sufferings of women under Islamic rule, women are referred to as 'our mothers,' 'our wives' or 'our daughters' and not as women" (1993: 163). Moghissi does not specify to which leftist organization she is referring, nor does she cite a source for her claim. I have not come across any example of addressing women other than as "women," "militant women," or "toiling women" in my review of the literature.

14. Using long jargonistic sentences is a stylistic trait of the Iranian Left. Statements should say everything and cover all bases at all times. The organization should secure itself against every conceivable attack. A primary purpose of writing, therefore, becomes to state one's position and to inform others of their "deviations."

15. Comintern suggested the same relationship between women's organizations and the party. See Waters (1989: especially 46–50).

16. The information presented here is based on my interviews with Fedaii women.

6

Patriarchy Blessed: Gender Teleology and Violence

Who is woman? A creature with free will, intelligence, and awareness whom God created to shoulder half the human mission and to embark upon the journey toward Allah. In this universe, women will selflessly and sincerely submit their lives to the ordinance of creation and the symphony of life. Men define their relationship with this mind-boggling factory only in terms of pleasure and ordering a product called generation.

Central to the woman's symphonic performance in Fatemeh 'Alâ'i Rahmâni's narrative (1992: 17) is the recurring note of familial harmony and procreation—divine tasks bestowed upon woman as the signs of her "authenticity and superiority" (18). To her chagrin, however, 'Alâ'i Rahmani notices that men's material privileges often seduce women to abandon their divine tasks only to mimic manliness. This temptation bears no fruit:

You women must realize with certainty that the ultimate losers of standing on a par with men are *you*, by losing your real glory and allowing irrational men to consider you inferior and diminutive. One irredeemable injury has been that looking for glory in quantities, both sexes overlook the utmost significance of qualities. Since a family is smaller than a society, it is devalued beyond belief. (18)

Such oblivion toward divine designs in an Islamic state is unacceptable, but understandable. Anti-Islamic colonialists have tried hard to create such diversions long before the Islamic revolution. Pre-revolutionary changes lured women in the name of freedom away from the family and Allah to the brutal world of immorality. Though the supreme ruler of the universe, Allah leaves His subjects "free." But this freedom is indeed a test: He wants us to prove that we use our intelligence to discern the correct path to our destiny. Blinded by Pahlavi extravagance, pre-revolutionary men and women failed that test. Only the determination of a group of God-fearing people has saved Iranians—with the advent of the Islamic Republic, "the devil has been ousted, the angel has descended."[1]

The Islamic state rights the wrong by bringing men and women to serve Allah, their creator and owner. His objective is to create a harmonious life for His creatures in this world and beyond. A peaceful family, a miniature society in which all members play their proper notes, is the building block of this symphonic orchestra. Mending the injured family revitalizes society. The shifting locus from private to public patriarchy prior to the revolution denied, Islamists felt, women their proper roles as wives and mothers by pushing them into the labor force. It also limited rights granted men by God. To create an Islamic society, these mechanisms needed reversal. The Islamic state quickly attended to directing women and men to act out their holy duties. The patriarchal triad—a union of Islam, state, and patriarchy—safeguards the sanctity of family and relocates men and women to their proper divine orbits. Keeping Allah's subjects in line calls for policing the "sexual instinct." Like a concerned father, the Islamic state protects women and men from potential self-incurred sins by controlling personal and social spaces. The grand task of reintroducing Allah's plans to society would undoubtedly evoke enemy sabotage and the resistance of the deceived and the infidels.

In the divine order, individuals come to life gendered and sexed. They are manufactured to perform a particular task. This blessed system has two quintessential characteristics. First, individuals in the Islamic regime are *Muslim beings*, not citizens. I discussed in chapter 4 the inherently contradictory womanhood in post-revolutionary Iran: though the woman of the IRI enjoys franchise, she is fundamentally a deficient being, equal to half a man. I will here argue further that a teleological gender identity denies the individuality of men and women, leaving them little room as autonomous actors. In this heavenly arrangement of life, one may be entitled to many Islamic rights, but only as an Islamic being. Nonbelievers become included only after accepting Islamic perimeters.

Coercion, secondly, permeates this Islamic divine order. Constitutionally recognizing men as heads of household offers them considerable latitude in treating "their women." But gender violence under the IRI goes far beyond the private. The IRI considers gender relations as society's weakest link, most susceptible to enemy infiltration. Policing gender and sexuality is inseparable from post-revolutionary social restructuring. The IRI implements divine will through public policies, and by controlling the most mundane aspects of the quotidian. But far from indicating victory, coercion signifies the persisting defiance of a subjected populace, particularly women.

The subsequent chapters address the cultural politics of gender under the Islamists' rule. Chapter 6 delineates Islamist gender ideology that in pursuit of harmony imposes metaphysical objectives on corporeal bodies. Though the IRI has made significant inroads into women's rights, it has faced considerable resistance. This and the following chapters explore the dynamics of strengthening men's role in family and society and returning the locus of patriarchal domination from public to private.

A NOTE ON READING IDEOLOGY AND LAW

Gender relations in the IRI are contentious and volatile. It is difficult to identify a singular explanation of "Islamic gender ideology." Throughout Islamic history, authors' interpretations of "women in Islam" have been influenced as much by Koranic axioms and hadith narratives as by authors' own sociohistorical specificities. In 1961, Ayatollah Khomeini reacted vehemently to women's enfranchisement. Yet in 1979, the Ayatollah finally recognized women's political role and solicited their vote for establishing an Islamic government. In both cases, his ideas were based on Islamic principles—different times, however, made conflicting interpretations possible. In recent years, Muslim reformists have similarly attempted to revise Islamic discourse in response to internal societal changes, political exigencies, and international opinion.

Thus, one must read Islamists' gender ideologies and the IRI's laws not as reflections of "Iranians' popular beliefs," but as delineating parameters of *Islamists' aspirations* and gender policies in post-revolutionary Iran. These articulations may reflect some social norms, but even among Islamists it is hard to find total conformity. The legal implications of *nafaqeh* and *tamkin* threaten all women, yet many families do not engage in these practices.

Islamists came to power following decades of refashioning patriarchy that afforded women greater freedom and mobility and curbed men's power within the family. The IRI has sought to reinforce male dominance within the family, reinstate men's prerogatives compromised under the Pahlavis, and define women primarily in their private roles of wife and mother. Women's social role in pre-revolutionary Iran has made it impossible to send them back into the home. Though successful in passing legislation that limit women's options, Islamists have been forced to accept women's limited public presence, so long as it did not interfere with familial duties.

Resistance has forced the regime to modify policies in some areas. In education, for instance, the IRI had to revise its initial banning of numerous majors for women. In employment, the regime had to compromise women's exclusion from judgeship to accept them into this position—in a limited capacity, of course. Though opposition to men's unilateral right to divorce has effected slight revisions in family law, it has, nonetheless, made it mandatory that marriage contracts list stipulations under which a woman could initiate divorce. In many areas officials have been forced to justify their praxis through reinterpretations that acknowledged discriminations and pledged change. In the quotidian, a *dual society* has emerged that observes Islamic rules, but lives differently.

Gender relations in post-revolutionary Iran must be understood in this conflictual relationship between conservative clergy who opt to reinforce men's power and confine women to domestic roles, and women and men who fight to safeguard and expand their rights. To this complexity one must also add the IRI's factional differences. While conservatives propose strict gender relations, reformists realize the incompatibility of such interpretations with contemporary life. Women have played an essential role in this conflict, as the 1997 presidential election testifies.

Despite these vicissitudes, the Islamic interpretation of gender cannot be overlooked. Just as ideology and law cannot be read as a substitute for daily lives, it is equally mistaken to understand daily life severed from the ideology. The power of ideology must not be overlooked, *especially when ideology is in power*. Religious imperatives constitute a fundamental concern of all Islamists—conservatives and reformists alike. Several common threads—for example, women's familial roles, natural bases of sex roles, and the assumption that women need protection—link diverse articulations. To accomplish these aims, conservatives propose seclusion; reformers, a "safe," regulated social space for women. Though women have resisted attacks on their rights, the IRI coerces many Islamic ideals.

THE TELEOLOGY OF GENDER

Key to understanding Islamist gender ideology is a systematic, goal-oriented universe. God is the creator, lawmaker, and judge. He has predefined a perfect order. To be Muslim, to surrender (as the word suggests) to Allah, means to understand one's part in that universe and to live accordingly. Men and women have distinct responsibilities, corresponding to their nature. They do not make manhood and womanhood; they strive toward these already-made identities. Gender is not made—it is teleological.

Creation, writes Ayatollah Javâdi Âmoli, is the "manifestation (*jelveh*) of the creator in different creatures" (1993: 19).[2] No doubt, he writes, Allah manifests His "glory" (*jalal*) and "beauty" (*jamal*) in myriad ways, yet "since God's glory is hidden in His beauty and His beauty in His glory, whatever manifests divine excellence also possesses its beauty" and vice versa (21). That God's characteristics simultaneously exist in every phenomenon without necessarily being immediately visible requires us to scratch the surface to uncover infallible divine wisdom. Good and evil, just and unjust, are rendered meaningful only in the context of their preordained destinies. What may appear negative may serve grand functions.

In family life, some tasks might appear taxing or evil (*shar*), "yet these have in their kernel many good (*Kheir*) consequences for family stability and for the preservation of its sanctity" (22). Apparent injustice toward women is just that—*merely appearance*; in *reality* God never mistreats His subjects. Ayatollah Hosseini Tehrani succinctly formulates this idea. He writes that in this universe, "the rights of no creature are ignored" (1997: 30) because justice is the nature (*zât*) of God. Every thing in this universe receives a fair share based on its "intrinsic and instinctual needs" (31). Thus, limitations on women must be viewed not as an injustice, "but according them their full and complete rights" (32). It is not that women were initially entitled to certain rights and then Islam limited their rights. Prohibitions on women's roles mean recognizing what God has considered just. Critics of Islam are wrong because they do not realize what women's rights are. It is a woman's right not to undertake "difficult and backbreaking tasks"; so regulations concerning women's employment merely uphold what God bestows upon women. "Hejâb and covering the body from lustful eyes is a woman's primal right. Being naked and on display is not her right to be compromised by God as a result of ordering her to wear the veil and stay home" (32–33). The words of Malekeh Yazdi, Chair of the Women's Bureau of the Judicial Branch, make perfect sense: "in many cases, if the law does not grant women certain rights, it is indeed a favor to women since we consider [our] laws emanating from the sacred Shar,' " which, as the divine law, cannot be but fair (*Akhbâr* 6 November 1996).

A Muslim woman garners "Islamic ideas, outlooks, and temperaments" (Ommi 1987: 10). She conceives life as an "interconnected, dynamic, and goal-oriented system." She recognizes her function in forming a couple and accordingly defines her identity. "The axis of her movement is her sex; the authenticity of her movement lies in its humanity; and the destination of her movement is divinity" (10). Thus, the identification of a Muslim woman as a female is an imposition she must endure only to achieve her humanity on a godly assigned route. Were something to divert her from that path, asserts Mahboobeh Ommi, she would sacrifice her sexual rights with no qualms. In a corrupt society, woman is barred from reaching her godly potentials. In that case, a Muslim woman guards her sacred duty first and foremost, overlooking what appears beneficial to her *qua* woman:

Woman is not safe in such a society. She is certain that her public presence will damage her human values. Thus, she prefers to stay at home. In her isolation, she becomes neither an inventor, nor a historian, nor a craftsperson. To quench her thirsty spirit, she becomes a mystic, a poet, a religious scholar (*faqih*) . . . She turns to fields compatible with the necessities of time and social constraints. (43)

Sexual justice ought to be defined on the basis of the roles of an "authentic" womanhood, that is, roles God has considered for women in this world. When we realize that mothering is women's prime duty, things fall into their proper place. Consider, for instance, prohibitions imposed on women's religious duties during menstruation. It may appear degrading that menses bar woman from prayers. But situating that edict in its proper context reveals its fairness. A fetus receives nutrition from the pregnant woman's blood. "This blood must be kept at a standard level"; what is not needed is disposed of. "Obviously certain impurities occur during this process, and it is not appropriate for an [impure] person to appear before God and converse with Him" ('Alâ'i Rahmâni 1992: 89). Therefore, the endowment of women with mothering *and* the regulation of women's prayer during menstruation—a consequence of their divine role—are compatible. That attunement makes the restrictions just. If women do not reproduce the race, God's various plans for human beings will not actualize. At the same time, as a pivotal column of life, prayer must be performed under strict rules. Prayer is significant, but reproduction is vital: what is "important" is sacrificed to achieve what is "more important" (89).

The objective of this sacrifice and other (gendered) practices is the creation of an Islamic ummat (umma), or community, which secures believers' prosperity on earth and in the hereafter (see, e.g., Khamenehii's remarks in *Zan-e Rouz* 11 June 1994: 4). Ummat is not synonymous with society, for the former is a purposive community of believers, opting to create an *Islamic* system with little tolerance for aberration (for more on ummat, see Paret 1987). The *valy-e faqih*, the jurist guardian of the community, supervises the implementation of Allah's rules. The jurist is the brain and heart of society, the ultimate arbiter between healthy and harmful, good and evil. A pyramid of authorities—Allah, Islam, the Prophet, the imams, and the *valy* via the Islamic state—set the limits; the ummat follows.[3]

In Iran, where the government is Islamic, the criterion for every thing is Shar,' the divine law. Any action that is pleasing to God is valuable; any deed that contradicts God's command is anti-value (*zedd-e arzesh*). In the Islamic moral system, knowledge about God, the Prophet, and the resurrection are at the top of the value pyramid; any other valuable deed, expression, or idea lies underneath. In Shiite doctrine, the jurist guardian is the knowledgeable, sagacious, and source of values. (*Ettella'at* 22 December 1998)

All efforts of the Islamic community are directed toward a single goal. The ummat,[4] in other words, lacks the heterogeneity of society as well as the freedom that—at least in theory—society members enjoy.[5] Idiosyncrasies are acceptable only in the context of the individuals' journey toward the godly designated goal. The "authentic" believer plays his or her function in a teleological gender construct.

Not only are individuals predefined within the ummat, but they also shoulder the grave responsibility of upholding Allah's grand design. As all acts must be directed toward one objective, a single wrongful act could mislead the entire community. Actors do not lead individualized lives; they are responsible for the well-being of the entire society. As Zahra Mostafavi puts it, "One young person can lead the entire nation to prosperity or destruction—that is quite obvious. And authorities must enlighten our youths so that they will not be influenced by corruption" (*Ettella'at* 14 December 1992).

This project denies citizens basic rights by rejecting their individuality and requiring that they define themselves in and through fixed identities. This Islamic arrangement does not allow room for dissent. Strictly speaking, there are no "nonbelievers" among Muslims—there are "good" and "bad" Muslims, but not "ex-Muslims" or "nonbelievers." No one of Muslim descent can claim to be a nonbeliever. Confessions of conversion will be punished severely. At best, "bad Muslims" are tolerated, *if* they do not break the laws.[6]

Until the collective conviction necessary for an ummat is reached, the Islamic regime can at least create a society in which the norm is Islamic and everything else the exception. The divine gender plan of Islamism does not enjoin believers alone—the persistent monitoring and policing of gender and sexuality imposes that plan on all society members. The "bad Muslims" and non-Muslims not sharing this ambition must oblige. This creates major concerns especially for the treatment of "bad Muslim," Zoroastrian, Jewish, Christian, and Bahaii[7] women. "Others" are tolerated only as long as they obey the rules, making coercion central to this scheme, engendering politics and politicizing gender. Biology becomes destiny, a sacred, inviolable destiny.

HOW DO GENDERS LOOK?

Individuals accomplish their gender, West and Zimmerman (1987) inform us, through organizing their activities "to reflect or express gender." We are not gendered once and for all, but must perpetually maintain our identities by "doing gender," publicly appearing as belonging to the right gender. In post-revolutionary Iran, gender expression has become a gauge of conviction, a testimony to the person's loyalty to Islamic fundamentals. In other words, public appearance discloses political determinants of individuals' self-expression. The IRI came to power as a government of the oppressed, the *mostaz'afin*. Inexpensive khaki and green army pants, often worn with army jackets, represented oneness with the downtrodden, while expensive and fashionable clothes were looked down upon, deemed to indicate wealth and Western influence. As a symbol of Western decadence, jeans were prohibited in schools. Class scare (see chapter 1) and ideological correctness were thereby used to suppress dissension. When women demonstrated against the mandatory veil, they were branded monarchists. Clean-shaven men, wearing suits and ties, were suspected of counter-revolution.

Class relationship in the IRI has gradually changed, however. Many among the clergy have accumulated wealth and gained access to luxuries previously unavailable to them. Also, a group of Islamist technocrats have emerged who—thanks to the political and economic resources presently at their disposal—can indulge themselves in a Western lifestyle while maintaining an Islamic appearance. Symbols of a wealthy lifestyle such as high-class restaurants, exclusive clubs (e.g., the Presidential Club—Bâshgâh-e Riyâsat-e Jomhuri), health spas, ski resorts, and brand-name clothes are all acceptable now *provided that an Islamic appearance is maintained*; for example, gatherings are sex-segregated, or fasting and prayers are observed. This is not to say, of course, that "Islamic morality" rules at all levels or in every aspect of life. Iranian society is in fact flooded with rumors about "immoral conduct" among the clergy and government officials. On occasions, rumors are substantiated and prosecuted, or used against factional rivals.[8]

Gender identities have found rigid models, which the people are policed to emulate in private and public. Regulating the presentation of the self—as in rules against "decadent and obscene dress" (*qânun-e albaseh-ye mobtazal*)—Islamic authorities explicitly define the parameters of gender appearances. The law prohibits a range of gender-inappropriate behaviors (e.g., long hair for men, "unladylike" comportment for women) and deviant clothes (including see-through, short scarves that do not completely cover hair and neck, non-matching socks, fluorescent colors, anklets, sunglasses, symbols like bunny and victory, and foreign flags). Though there is no specific punishment for men who violate "chastity and public morality," the IRI's Penal Law stipulates that women who do not adhere to the dress code, could be fined *and* imprisoned from 10 days to two months (Center for Women's Participation 1999: 112). According to a 1996 report, in addition to being fined, offenders could be punished by imprisonment of up to 12 months and by 14 lashes (see *Resâlat* 14 February 1996 and 22 February 1996).

Khomeini instructs that women must modify their behavior to suit the Islamic Republic (quoted in Mohammadiniâ 1992: 162). An honorable woman is so solemn that she discourages male strangers. Her monotonous speech does not arouse men (174). She wears long pants since "pants are the most covering" and protective of her modesty. The cut and color of her dress must not stimulate the eye. Her walk ought not to draw attention. Hence, high heels are ruled out because of their "exciting sound." A Muslim woman need not only take care of how she looks, "while walking, [she] must be mindful of how she looks at others. She is to avoid casting sinful glances. Though in her house, in interactions with her husband and children, she should be jovial and warm, outside she must avoid any demeaning and suspicious behavior" (178).

Asadullah Mohammadiniâ cites a narrative attributed to Imam Ali that obligated "Muslims not to wear thin, see-through clothes, for whoever has thin clothes also has weak and thin convictions" (117). "An unveiled woman demonstrates that she is hollow and has no faith in the resurrection day. Had she believed, she would have covered herself" (118). A woman who does not wear the veil is not a true Muslim because she imitates non-Muslims.

A true Muslim is one whose name, visage, clothes, demeanor, eating manners, sleeping habits, house design and furniture, etiquette, talking, laughing—in sum, her culture and social manners—follow the tradition of the Prophet and the innocent imams, not somebody who looks and dresses like infidels (koffâr). (118)

Barnstein observes that "gender play really worries many religious leaders" (1998: 113). In the Islamic state, individuals *ought to* belong to the "right gender" and have the "right gender interaction." Yet, even under IRI restrictions, gender offers individuals a continuum of accepted expressions of identities. Hierarchy of gender identities accords male Islamists a prominent share of power. Gender and politics become intertwined: correct politics creates correct gender and correct gender increases one's chances in the social and political arenas (see, e.g., Habibi 1989).

The male clergy, of course, occupy the top of the pyramid, but even the most devout Muslim cannot claim this status unless properly trained. It is, however, possible to be a close second. A man of this tier is a devout Muslim, well-versed in his beliefs, and politically faithful. He is a "family man": a dutiful son and a fair head of the household. He avoids non-relative females, but if contact is unavoidable, he will avert his "pure eyes." His gender markers are not merely internal: he must also have the right look. He is bearded or has stubble, appears sullen, and wears silver jewelry, especially silver rings with carnelian and turquoise gems (gold jewelry in direct contact with skin is prohibited in Islam; but agate and turquoise are coveted). Neckties are unacceptable, because they symbolize Westernization. He wears dark suits and completely buttoned up white shirts. His shirt is tucked into his pants if worn with a coat; without a jacket, however, he wears his shirt over the pants to conceal his pelvis and buttocks. Tight clothes must be avoided, for they accentuate the body and attract attention (Haddad ʿÂdel 1995: 64). Proper Islamic dress must fade the person in public, among the Islamic ummat. The use of any distinguishing dress is frowned upon as lebâs-e shohrat, the clothes of fame.

The picture of the ideal hizbullah man has undergone some modification in recent years. Post-revolutionary social class development has modified the appearance of the ideal male gender. So, one may find clean-shaven men among the IRI statesmen, but the tie is still unacceptable in the hizbullah wardrobe. Contrary to yesteryears when drabness signified devotion, some Islamists now try to emphasize their distance from rigid measures of the past by adopting new styles of clothes. Until recently, election propaganda posters demonstrated bearded men in army dress. Now, however, photos show clean-shaven candidates in suit and ties. Rank-and-file hizbullah may not be as prim and proper, but they emulate the elite as much as possible.

The lower we go down the pyramid, the less rigid the prescribed look, but the more vulnerable to coercive control. This elasticity is caused by the fierce contestation over the ideal gender (see chapter 1). As the IRI employs all means to regulate the quotidian on Islamist grounds, nonbelievers negotiate gender boundaries. Anything that could express distance from Islamism is so used—wearing a tie or a mustache, being clean-shaven, body language. Among the nonbelieving public, especially young males, virtually every "masculine" or "feminine" look is possible *as long as it is accepted as manly somewhere, be it Iran or a Western country.* For the IRI, the tolerable minimum varies from time to time, depending on a variety of factors, including the political atmosphere of the country. Crackdowns on "deviants" typically escalate when the state encounters economic or political crises. This is, then, a dangerous territory, open to haphazard persecution and terror by the moral police. The inhabitants of this hinterland live at the margin of Islamic society. To minimize their persecution, they must quickly maneuver in and out of the accepted gender boundaries.

Many non-hizbullah men find their notch on the gender hierarchy somewhere in between the hizbullah man and the acceptable minimum. The closer one is to the ideal gender appearance, the more accepted he becomes. Facial hair is negotiable; nonbelievers indeed often avoid the full beard. Color finds a wider range of acceptability, though bold colors like red and "non-masculine" pink and orange must be avoided. Neckties are acceptable in some settings, but generally not favored. "Trustworthy" men in this intermediary level can create a safe zone for transgressions by hizbullah men. They can, for example, offer the Islamist alcoholic beverages or other "decadent Western luxuries" in private get-togethers or during business transactions. Each overlooks the other's transgression. The devout ignores his host's punishable offense and the host overlooks the guest's hypocrisy. Intermediary men may also prove helpful when the hizbullah invades deviants' territory. Through bribe or connection, these men may arrange the release of a "deviant" friend or relative from the IRI's moral jails.

Just as men are supposed to participate in the rituals of their gender, women are also expected to portray the proper Muslim femininity. The ideal hizbullah woman is a dutiful daughter-wife-mother who may or may not work outside the house. She may or may not seek her husband's permission on domestic affairs, but always makes sure that she would garner his approval. A guardian of family tradition and honor, she is veiled. She, too, is conversant in her creed and a faithful participant in female religious events. Though her prime concern is her family, she knows that defending Islam may claim her men. Heartbreaking though it is, sacrificing her men for Islam is a supreme duty.

An edict by Khomeini stipulates that a woman "must avoid any dress that excites" (Vahidi 1994: 37). A hizbullah woman attends carefully to her veil. She wears a black châdor over a *maqna'eh*, a black scarf completely covering her hair and concealing her chin and, at times, even mouth. According to Zahrâ Shojâ'i, hejâb is a prerequisite for a woman's entering society (*Zan-e Rouz* 18 December 1993: 19). With or without *maqna'eh*, she reveals only a tiny portion of her face. No makeup for a hizbullah woman, though in the privacy of her home, she should beautify herself for her husband. Minimal use of jewelry, especially gold, is acceptable, but it should not be worn in excess. "A woman must refrain from displaying her ornaments for male strangers as much as possible and absolutely not let her jewelry be exposed for others to see" (Beheshti 1985a: 40). Khamenehii urges her to avoid "life's allurements" like fashion, cosmetics, and consumerism (*Zan-e Rouz* 18 December 1993: 8). "Covering head and chest with ornaments," he states, "and making fashion one's idol is a shame for the revolutionary Muslim women of Iran" (*Jomhury-e Islami* 18 January 1989).

Women of the bazaar merchant class stand closest in their appearance to the ideal modern hizbullah woman. Though adhering to the hejâb regulations, they may wear colorful dresses under the chador. The expensive fabric and shining jewelry attest to their financial privilege. These women are joined by those from Islamist technocrat families who abide by the Islamic regulations of daily life, but have incorporated luxuries of a modernized upper-class life. They abide by the hejâb, but use the latest Western fashion. Western makeup—damned by Islamists women and men a few short years ago—has become quite popular for this group of Islamists. Western furniture and appliances are displayed at lavish, sex-segregated, religious, or non-religious gatherings. Activities heretofore deemed decadent, such as attending music classes, English institutes, skiing, and horseback riding, are now popular.

Next to these and the hizbullah women, nonbelievers (that is, "bad Muslims") must abide by coverture laws, but they can negotiate color and fashion. The "multiaccentuality" of symbols, the capacity of symbols to contain divergent social meanings and interests (Vološinov 1973: 23), allows for modification of the use and meaning of hejâb. Instead of *maqna'eh*, they wear a scarf and do not cover their hair completely—but they must quickly cover all their hair should the religious police or hizbullah approach.

Hejâb regulations are quite strict in small cities, particularly during holidays and vacation times in tourist areas by the Caspian Sea. Women from central small towns cover themselves much more conservatively than women from northern small towns. This could stem from the popularity of conservative attitudes, especially in such religious cities as Qom and Kashan, or from the fear of punishment in small urban areas with little anonymity. Even when these women do not cherish Islamic teachings, they are less likely to defy them openly because the pressure is high and traditions are more strongly enforced on women. The dress code enforcement is less stringent in villages, since women have their traditional clothes, which are more colorful. But, compared with the past, going to public places and to the bazaar, women tend to cover themselves in black chador instead of bright colors.

In large cities, hejâb regulations may not be as strictly enforced as in small towns, though here, too, variations exist. Cities like Tehran, Isfahan, and Shiraz are more relaxed, perhaps in part due to hosting foreign tourists. The people in the holy city of Mashad, on the other hand, dress more conservatively, though that city equally attracts international visitors. There are also variations in different areas of a city. Lower class neighborhoods observe the hejâb more closely, often out of conviction, while upper-class neighborhoods show looser interpretations of the dress code. In large urban areas, women can wear a long, loose, dark manteau over pants and thick, dark stockings in place of chador (Shirazi-Mahajan 1995). Makeup is tolerated if not too strong. Yet to enter most governmental offices, women must comply with the more restrictive dress codes. The government's tolerance level depends upon the politico-economic situation. Usually, women are the first targets of a clampdown on individual liberties at critical times.

Women's location on the gender pyramid of the Islamic Republic is not always clear-cut. Collectively, they have a smaller share of power and own fewer rights than men. At the same time, however, Islamist women, especially those with political connections, enjoy some privileges in relation to non-Islamist men. This control of course varies, depending on one's economic and political resources.

Puberty marks a transition from "girlhood" to "womanhood." *Jashn-e taklif* or *jashn-e 'ebâdat* celebrates young girls reaching the age of obligatory prayer and observance of religious rituals. This ceremony venerates "girls' " embarkation on their journey to womanhood. Before puberty, girls are *expected* to observe religious rituals and act along proper gender lines. Observing hejâb is a de facto must; but, away from prying pious eyes, parents can indulge their daughters' preference for unveiling in public, or even allow them to play with male playmates. After puberty, however, that is, around the age of 9, gender norms become exceedingly difficult to break. *Jashn-e taklif* is an invented tradition, initially popular particularly among upper classes and in metropolitan cities. Gradually, it spread to other parts of Iran. According to a recent report, 2,500 primary school students participated in a citywide ceremony in Bojnord, a mid-size town in northeastern Iran (*Sobh-e Khânevâdeh* 17 December 1998). Though primary schools often organize this event, well-to-do families may also have private ceremonies. In fact, though Islamists welcome this rite of passage as a mechanism of religious socialization, some raise concern about it becoming an opportunity for the rich to display their wealth. According to a *Zan-e Rouz* commentary (26 January 1991), this practice helps the upper classes maintain a devout public image, but in a fashion that does not require too much sacrifice. "Since authentic and true religion is too cumbersome, these people innovate a mixture of religion and luxury, creating something appealing to their class taste" (19).

Boys go through a similar ritual, though in high school and in their teen years (in Islam, boys reach puberty at a later age than girls). Thus, whereas for little girls, encouraged by both their families and religious education teachers, *jashn-e 'ebâdat* is an exciting event, 15–18-year-old high school boys have a higher tendency to treat it as a mere formality.

The Islamization of societal fabric has meant severe encroachments upon the quotidian. Always "acting and looking Islamic" has made every aspect of people's lives subject to Islamists' intrusion. According to the Koran (sura *The Greeks*, v. 30), "Allah's creation cannot be changed" (1988: 194). Khomeini states in *Towzihul Masâ'el (The Explanations for Problems)* that men and women must avoid wearing each other's clothes (n.d.: 137, Problem # 846). So, for instance, if a pair of sandals is made specifically for females, men must not use them (Vahidi 1994: 36).

Though hermaphroditism as a medical complication requiring treatment is acceptable, transvestitism is intolerable.[9] In 1997, after President Khatami's election, the Ministry of Culture and Islamic Guidance released a film entitled *Snowman* after several years of being banned. The male protagonist presents himself as a female to a woman in need of refuge. Under the impression that her host is female, the woman does not follow regulations pertaining to proper interaction between members of the two sexes (which would prohibit them from living under the same roof to begin with). Outraged believers attacked movie theaters in several towns. Hossein Allah-Karam, the leader of the Iranian Islamists, stated in a lecture at Gilan University (winter 1998) that the hizbullah objected both to a woman being with a fake-woman and to a man dressed as woman—things "prohibited in Islam."[10]

Reports of persecution of men appearing other than "manly" confirm that the IRI is particularly concerned about a "heterosexual look." A letter in *Homan* (a journal published abroad by the Group to Defend the Rights of Iranian Gays and Lesbians) narrates the detainment of a young man by *dâyereh-ye monkarât* (the Bureau of Prohibition) because he "looked and acted" homosexual. After a long night of intimidation, insult, harassment, and inquiry, a physician finally examined him. "You are a male," the doctor told him, "your only problem is your voice. But that is all right, too. It is normal" (Anonymous 1998: 39). He was released, but for two weeks "imprisoned" himself in the house and for two months wore nothing but allowable clothes.

This, however, does not mean that the lines of gender divide are impassable. Cross-gender appearance is possible, but it marks the deformation—if not the demotion—of the male. In a system wherein female sexuality is deemed dangerous, feminine-looking males can *act* as women, accomplishing something that only women can do but are not allowed to. Young feminine-looking men play female roles in shows and plays, but women are not allowed to act the same role in such brightly colored clothes and make-up as their male impersonators wear. These men, in other words, transgress gender boundaries; they become harmless make-believe women who can compromise gender propriety because they cannot accomplish what they pretend to be capable of: to be sexy and alluring. Or, they can act unmanly to portray the socially denigrated *evâkhahar* (sissy). The objective is to make the audience laugh, not to entertain revisionist gender.

In the immediate post-revolution days, anybody at any time anywhere could become subject to harassment and public humiliation. These violations later became more "systematic," though never illegal. Thus, even under the most "relaxed" conditions, people are vulnerable to the state's implementation of moral codes. More striking still is the fact that the Islamization project permeates every domain of life. Something so seemingly simple and personal as a name is subject to restriction. To name their newborn, parents must choose from an approved list. Naming purportedly shapes one's personality; naming one's son after a ruthless historical figure, for instance, could make him hard-hearted (see a report in *Qods* 1 November 1997: 5). The daily *Zan* (12 December 1998: 11) reports about the agonies of Turkmen parents who, in addition to the limitations of name choices, bear the burden of ethnic discrimination, for no Turkmen names are included on the master list. In a not-so-atypical instance, the parents of a boy named ShahRouz realized that their son's report card is issued to one Mohammad. Wondering to whom the report card belonged, they contacted school authorities and were told that since their son's name had the prefix "Shah," his name was changed into something religiously more "rewarding." Name-change for peace of mind—whose?

SACRED BIOLOGY

Gender, sex, and sexuality are circularly connected in the Islamist doctrine. None is rendered meaningful without the others. We arrive in this world fully sexed, fully gendered—we simply have to live out our sex and gender in suitable manners. Sexuality not only makes reproduction possible, but also becomes a means for sexed bodies to "properly" act out gender roles. Mirroring their creator's glory and beauty, human beings are soul *and* body responsible for implementing His will. Spiritual qualities are reflected in our corporeal bodies. As God's chosen creature, for instance, the sacred attributes of the Prophet affect his descendents' physiological makeup for times on end. For example, Sayyedeh women (female descendents of Mohammad) become menopausal at the age of 60; ordinary women at the age of 50 (Khomeini n.d.: 390). Differences of this sort reveal to the Islamists that our corpus is more than decomposable flesh; it is a heavenly body, the medium through which our spirituality—or lack thereof—discloses itself.

Islamist texts frequently refer to the detrimental effects of illicit thought and conduct. Effeminate and homosexual men, writes Kâzemi Khalkhâli, come from fathers who, while copulating with their wives, fantasize about other women (1991: 238). Fornicators particularly cause severe damage to society because illegitimate children are spiritually deformed and carry the sin of their "parents" (118). Children of fornication in the West, for instance, have become "murderers, criminals, deviants, hippies," and bomb makers (Isfahâni n.d.: 4).

Devotion to Islam plays a focal role here. An apostate becomes *harâm* to his or her mate. If a woman deserts Islam, her marriage to a Muslim becomes annulled if they have not already consummated the relationship. If a menopausal woman disavows her belief, her marriage is annulled, irrespective of the couple's sexual history. If a man turns renegade, his marriage is annulled (Khomeini n.d.: 390–91).

Conception, pregnancy, and delivery must all be Islamic in order for a woman to be a true servant of Islam. As an Islamist physician puts it: "Only a hypocrite or infidel (*kâfar*) woman, or a woman whose husband is not happy with her, suffers the heaviness of her stomach and will eventually deliver a child prone to become an enemy of Islam" (Pâknezhâd 1991: 138).

Sex and reproduction are at the mercy of shari'ah. Just as heteromarital sexuality is rewarded, deviation is punished. "Sin and corruption negatively affect the body and cause early death," writes Mohammadiniâ (1992: 156–57). Proof? Sinners killed by AIDS; the rampant spread of epidemics in the United States; and music band members growing deaf (157–58).

Yet one need not transgress that far to damn the body. Consider, for instance, the predicament of women's beauty. Since divine agenda charges humans with the task of forming happy families, women's inclination to beautify themselves for their husbands is congruent with their nature (*fetrat*). Even before marriage, if they take care of their physical appearance (within acceptable limits, of course) *with the objective of finding a husband*, their action still coincides with their nature. But, before or after marriage, if they use their beauty to attract strangers, they betray their nature and, along with their oglers, will pay for that treason. As physician Pâknezhâd comments: "The impressions she leaves on lustful eyes will exchange information with every cell of both parties, even with their chromosomes. That is a kind of signaling to the cells of the [next] generation originated by somebody other than the legitimate father" (1991: 86).

This kind of "evidence," to the Islamist, proves that Islam's teachings coincide with the laws of nature. What modern medicine "accepts with certainty has already been mentioned in Islam 14 centuries ago" (140). Any Islamic law has a justification in nature. Unveiling, for instance, is deemed injurious because, in addition to its many social and moral damages, it harms women *physically*. Short skirts, for instance, cause thighs to grow fat to survive the cold weather (Pâknezhâd 1989; 1990). Pâknezhâd also attributes cystitis, excessive vaginal secretion, breathing problems, and influenza to short and tight dresses.

We belong to Allah, body and soul, and must follow His wisdom in our every act. "Behold the semen you discharge," the Koran guides (sura "That Which is Coming," v. 58), "did you create it, or We?" (Koran 1988: 111) Marriage is the only proper context for discharging and receiving semen. Yet marriage is not solely for sexual gratification. All animals engage in sexual intercourse, but as the superior species, human beings ought to search for something in marriage to transcend "natural desire" (Khamenehii 1992). The Koran, of course, states that women are men's fields; it also bids men to till their fields as they please (1988: 356). But procreation is not the only purpose of marriage; otherwise, the couple could easily separate after contributing to the continuation of the human race (Sâdeqi Ardestâni 1989b).

The uniqueness of marriage lies in securing goodness and prosperity for both family and society. As a microcosm of society, family life shapes social relationships. Human societies, Javâdi Âmoli contends, must ensure the inner beauty of their members, something regulations alone cannot effect. Family—the source of kindness in society—performs this function. Mothers play a crucial role:

The most important cause of kindness and sacrifice is the manifestation of the mother's spirit among family members. For, though—in accordance with "men have authority over women"—the father is in charge of administrative and executive duties in the miniature society of family, the foundation of the family rests upon kindness and connectedness. Mothers create [kindness and unity] by giving birth to siblings. (Javâdi Âmoli 1993: 31)

At the heart of motherhood's many functions, Javâdi Âmoli considers an Islamic edict—*saleh-ye rahem*, a familial interdependency and support system. *Saleh* means bond and affinity; *rahem*, womb. As family relationships are formed through the womb, mothering becomes a pillar of societal bond. "Individuals raised in authentic religious families, who can truly understand *saleh-ye rahem* and membership ties, will not engage in corruption upon entering their society" (32). Pure mothers' milk nourishes such children both physically and spiritually, according to Hojjatulislam Sâdeqi Ardestâni (1989b). From a long chain of narratives attributed to the Prophet and various imams, Sâdeqi Ardestâni concludes that the woman who nurses the newborn—the mother or the nanny—ought to be of good moral and physical standing. Devout, kind, well-mannered, healthy, and beautiful women transmit high qualities to children (16. See also Sâdeqi Ardestâni 1989a). Mothers' sinful *acts and thoughts* adversely affect their milk: "Women who sin destroy their lives with lust and impure unhealthy thoughts. These qualities undoubtedly transfer disorder and impurities to the child through the milk" (44).[11]

Nursing a child is then not a simple act of caring for the newborn—it is a religious performance. In a seminar on Nourishing Children with Mother's Milk (1 August 1995), the then-President Rafsanjani expressed in a message that because of Islam's concern with children's physical and moral development "in a stable and lasting religious mold," the Islamic government must introduce measures to secure "this undeniable right of children." Increasing the practice of breast-feeding "protects the Islamic revolution's investments for tomorrow" (*Zan-e Rouz* 13 August 1995: 27). The Law of Protecting Feeding with Mother's Milk afforded women 4 months of maternal leave and required the government to provide facilities for working mothers who nurse their children (Center for Women's Participation 1999: 183–88).

TILLING THE SEXUAL FIELD

How individuals tend to their carnal and moral needs affects their success in implementing Allah's grand plan. Sex, gender, and sexuality must create a balanced world in which men and women perform their nature. Just as transmitting desirable qualities to children—through good milk, for instance—is a prime parental duty, so too is making the right baby. Sex and procreation must not be rushed. A farm must be tended to harvest the best crop; the sexual field, too, must be fallow—that behooves sexual hygiene (Mahmoodi 1981: 101).

Intercourse cannot "just happen"; it requires special care. Khomeini outlines the dos and don'ts of a sexual encounter, as they fall under the Islamic categories of *mostahabbât* (recommended, favored) and *makruhât* (reprehensible) acts (quoted in Ma'sumi 1998: 146–49). First and foremost, ecstasy must not divert attention from Allah. The couple must undergo ablution (*vozu*) to cleanse themselves as though they are preparing for prayer. They must embark on their journey of intimacy by reciting "In the name of Allah, the compassionate, the merciful" in order to ward off Satan and demonstrate allegiance to God. Then follows a prayer, asking Him for a healthy child. Since the sexual act leads to impurity (see Bouhdiba 1998), sacred items must be distanced from the passionate embrace. The couple cannot make love facing either toward or away from the Mecca; and they must remove any ornament on which the name of God or His words are inscribed. Only one partner can be fully nude. There are, in addition, a host of other conditions that make intercourse excellent: foreplay, love-making in a private area, or when she is eager to have sex. Lovemaking in certain places or under certain conditions is deemed reprehensible: on the eve of some Islamic holidays; on a ship; in open air; right after a meal; standing; under a fruit-bearing tree; on a rooftop; at the time of solar and lunar eclipses. But sex is recommended on the first night of the month of Ramadan; in the evening, Monday through Friday; at noon on Thursdays; and on Friday afternoon.

'Abbasali Mahmoodi (1981) stipulates certain conditions for a healthy sexual encounter. First, the man must be pure in body and thought. He must not desire his woman solely out of lust, but for fulfilling the divine duty of reproduction (101). Moreover, sexual intercourse must ultimately strengthen marital unity and create a quiet environment for children.

A man must prefer his wife's friendship and kindness to his own sexual instinct and avoid forcing her into sexual relationship. Otherwise, they will both be harmed by that intercourse. And should a child be conceived, society will also suffer. Therefore, in intercourse, more than any other situation, one ought to mind the cooperation and mercy that must govern family life. (101)

The woman, no doubt, ought also to be pure. Mahmoodi reminds the reader of verse 222 of the sura *Cow*: "They ask you about menstruation. Say: 'It is an indisposition. Keep aloof from women during their menstrual periods and do not touch them until they are clean again. Then have intercourse with them as Allah enjoined you . . .' " (Koran 1988: 355–56).

In order for her body to be receptive to his seeds, the woman should enjoy sexual relationship. The husband is instructed to engage in foreplay and "to play with her breasts and other erogenous zones" to assist her in reaching orgasm (Kâzemi Khalkhâli 1991: 265). Men are advised to give their spouses ample time for sexual gratification (Sâdeqi Ardestâni 1988). Officials attempt to familiarize young couples with the basic methods of birth control when the couples take a blood test before marriage. In some centers, a video is shown for the couple. A clergyman gently recommends that the man should treat his bride kindly and fulfill her sexual desires. The couple will also be provided with a guidebook.

Finally, to ensure healthy babies, it is imperative that intercourse occurs with the expressed intent of "sowing and harvesting good seeds" (Mahmoodi 1981: 101). Without concern for procreation, the partners are not investing good deeds for the Judgment Day, as the Koran instructs them.

Yet not all sexual relationships end in pregnancy. Are those sinful conducts? Mahmoodi responds that since marital sex averts the couple from sins and strengthens their family, even fruitless intercourse fulfills a divine function. Sex may not result in procreation, but it is gratifying and prevents the partners from lusting after others (104).

Sexual pleasure, in other words, is good *if* it coincides with Allah's master plan for reproducing humans in a happy, sin-proof family. Heteromarital intercourse—"marital relationship"—is thus defined as the only appropriate sexuality in which the man has virtually unlimited claims on a woman's sexuality: "Women are your fields: go, then, into your fields as you please" (Koran 1988: 356). While a woman is entitled to sexual intercourse once every four months, she is mandated to be sexually available for her husband. As Khomeini puts it: "A woman must surrender to her husband for any pleasure" (Khomeini n.d.: 386). Even if he is excessive, she must serve at least to a reasonable point. Beyond that, if satisfying his needs does not harm her, she has to be responsive, according to Ayatollah Fâzel Lankarâni (quoted in Maʿsumi 1998: 87). In effect, her refusal can deprive her of his financial support (*Zan-e Rouz* 16 July 1994: 4). Khomeini declares that a woman must avoid anything that may make her husband sexually uninterested. If he desires that she clean herself up and put on makeup, she must oblige him (quoted in Maʿsumi 1998: 88–89). She has to be a good cook, but cannot smell as if she has spent all her day in the kitchen.

Tamkin, a woman's duty to her husband, in its general sense, means cohabitation. According to the IRI's Civil Law, a woman is obliged to live under her husband's roof, unless she has been granted the authority to choose otherwise at the time of signing the marriage contract. She is also required to have his verbal consent for leaving the house. Even when a woman has secured the right to leave the house at will in her marriage contract, if she leaves the house after an argument with her husband, she will be treated just like other women who have not asked for such authority. In the specific sense, *tamkin* requires the wife surrender when he desires intimacy (Kar 1996). *Noshooz* is a woman's refusal to *tamkin* in either sense of the term. A woman is *nâshezeh* if she does not *tamkin*, leaves the house without his permission, or does not make herself sexually appealing for him (Khomeini, as quoted in Maʿsumi 1998: 90). *Noshooz* is punishable: a man can refuse to provide for a disobedient, uncompromising *nâshezeh* wife (92). To be sure, a man, too, will be *nâshez* if he does not pay his wife's *nafaqeh*. But, the only recourse at her disposal is to advise or to sue him. Khomeini was asked if a woman had the right to ignore (*qahr*) or beat her husband. His response was unquestionably negative (95).

Women have opposed this blatant subjugation to men's pleasure. But Islamists have not changed their position—it is men's God-given right and with God one cannot quarrel. Instead, some clerics have offered "alternative" explanations for *tamkin* and *noshooz* to make them less appalling. According to Ayatollah Mohammad Bojnourdi, for instance, *noshooz* does not mean *any* refusal of sexual pleasure by the wife. If she, for a reasonable excuse, does not want to have sex—just as he may not desire sex in some instances—that is quite acceptable. *Noshooz* applies to situations when "the woman has no problem, is able to have sex, but refuses sexual relationship out of stubbornness or just to irk the husband" (*Hoquq-e Zanan* no. 3, June-July 1998: 8). In this case, the man can advise his wife, refuse to sleep in the same bed, or beat her.[12]

That women are sexual is accepted, but it is equally regarded as axiomatic that "sexual instinct" remains dormant in "good women" until marriage. Women are supposed to have two contradictory and mutually exclusive sexual selves: one, uninhibited and pleasing; the other, demure, practically nonexistent. The sexual and asexual woman lives in one, but when the sexual is present, namely, when in bed with her husband, the asexual partner should depart. Conversely, women should show no sign of sexuality before marriage or in public. Sadeqi Ardestani (1988) quotes two narratives from the Prophet and Imam Sadeq that clearly explicate a woman's sexual responsibilities. The Prophet purportedly said: "The best women are those chaste and ready for copulation, who guard themselves from strangers but approach their husbands with utmost excitement, readiness, and joy."

The hadith from Imam Sadeq is equally emphatic about the dos and don'ts of women's sexuality: "The best women among you are those who when alone with their husband, pull aside the curtain of shame and with complete readiness gratify him, but at the end, wear the clothes of shame to protect themselves from strangers."

Men are also categorized as having two sexual personae—as honorable, expressing sexuality only within approved contexts; or lecherous, for whom *every woman* is sexual prey. Like women, men could easily become victims of temptations, and exactly because of this inherent male vulnerability, women must cover themselves.

The duality of sexual selves creates a hierarchy that also works as a control mechanism. "Good" women can coordinate both their sexual and asexual dimensions. They become "honorable," respected by the community, and a desirable prospective bride for other honorable families. "Bad" women bring disgrace to their families by failing to bring to the fore their asexual self in relation to forbidden men. Similarly, "respectable" men avoid contact with non-relative females as much as possible and seek gratification only in relationship with their lawful mate(s). Honorable men and women "look out" for instances of indiscretion and slippage by others. They guard innocent women from the guile of lascivious men. Ultimately, this role is played by the Islamic state as the quintessentially benevolent father of the ummat.

Gender and sexual socialization are essential to the construction of sexuality. In popular magazines, women are encouraged in advice columns to marry, discouraged from initiating a relationship, and reproved for premarital sex. In an issue of *Zan-e Rouz* (8 June 1985), for instance, a 26-year-old woman is advised that she should seriously "consider marrying a suitable man" (52). Another woman who suffers depression is guided similarly: "If you cannot continue your education, you should get married. Maybe that would resolve your worries" (53). Yet a woman must refrain from any initiation: "If he really wants you, he will ask your family's permission to marry you" (52). Indeed, when a woman actually offers a man the marriage option, the counselor of *Payâm-e Zan* (no. 46, December 1995: 73) warns him: "Regarding the girl who has been in telephone communication with you for a while, attracted you little by little, told her family about you, and then suggested marriage to you . . . you should treat this person and her family with utmost caution." A *Zan-e Rouz* reader is chided for her unruly behavior. What she did goes unspecified; possibly she wrote love letters, but the relationship failed and she grew concerned about her reputation:

Dear Sister, your behavior was inappropriate from the outset. How can you so disregard yourself and muddy your name everywhere? This action is not suitable for a Muslim woman. We recommend that you put a halt to such inappropriate actions at once. Mend your behavior and make such missteps a thing of the past. You can gently ask him to return them to you. If he refuses, you can file a complaint. (*Zan-e Rouz* 8 June 1985: 52)

Acknowledgement of explicit sexual relation evokes even harsher scolding: "Premarital sexual relationship does not befit the dignity, chastity, and purity of Muslim Iranian women. Be concerned about your future and avoid these relationships" (54). Advice of this sort is frequent:

You are on the verge of straying from the right path. At this period of puberty, you really do not know what is going on in your life. Before it is too late, change your behavior, otherwise, you will lament your clean past. If he is really interested in you, he must marry you and that can take place only through your family. You may marry a suitable man. Do not forget that this kind of behavior does not have a good ending. May God guide you. (*Zan-e Rouz* 3 August 1985: 41)

The striking commonality of these admonitions is their ominous prediction of the future: the woman is warned not to ruin herself for future marriage opportunities. Instead of talking to the woman, the paternalistic voice terrorizes her and teaches passivity in establishing relations with a man. She has little, if any, room as a moral actor with the right to decide—rightly or wrongly—and face the consequences. No doubt, teenagers should benefit from the guidance of concerned parents and friends, but addressing them as clueless youths differs much from discussing right and wrong with autonomous individuals. Not only are teenage women thought unable to judge: in accordance with the shari'ah, unless in exceptional situations, all women are required to have paternal permission for their first marriage.

Restricting sex to the marital bed creates strict moral codes and calls for extreme personal and state control over sexuality. Islamist ideologues expend energy delineating the whos, whens, wheres, and whys of sexual gratification. Religious police patrolling public places are to ensure that only legally related men and women interact. Any deviation is tantamount to evil and anarchy. *Zena*, voluntary sex outside marriage, is punishable by death. This preoccupation with (re)confining sex to the private is congruent with the Islamist plan to reshape society from the Pahlavi "whorehouse" to a "pure" house of faith, love, and fidelity.

The policing of sexuality in the IRI makes the marital bed the sole legitimate outlet for sexual relationship. For that reason, young people are encouraged to marry sooner, rather than later. As Ayatollah Hâeri Shirâzi clarifies, those who suggest that the age of marriage be raised from mid-teens to 30 or 40, "either pay no attention to the realities of their time and place, that they live in an Islamic society, or belittle the influence of sexual instinct on human beings" (*Zan-e Rouz* 23 November 1991: 6). Late marriage purportedly causes social ill, especially when it leads to permanent bachelor- or spinsterhood (*Iran* 27 July 2000).

Parents are advised to encourage children to marry soon after puberty (Fazlullâh 1998; Kâzemi Khalkhâli 1991: 109–18). Early marriage is favored since it creates a legitimate outlet for sexual enjoyment. (The legal age for marriage was reduced to 16 for females and 18 for males. According to the 1996 census (Iran Statistical Center 1999: 84), mean age at first marriage for men is 25.6 and for women, 22.4. In the fall of 2000, the Majlis passed a law to make marriage before the age of 15 for girls and 18 for boys contingent upon the court's approval.) Most Islamist authors, however, recognize that in contemporary society, high unemployment and skyrocketing inflation seldom make early marriage a viable alternative. Thus, former President Hashemi Rafsanjani encouraged youth to use temporary marriage (*mot'ah* or *siqeh*) as a safe, sanctioned zone for interaction, rather than succumb to the anarchy of Western-style dating.[13]

"Premature" sexual awakening—that is, before marriage—leads to anguish and moral degeneracy (Safari 1999c: 36–38). Parents must be careful so that teenagers are not preoccupied with sex (see, e.g., Qaffâri Marân 1994; Keyhânniâ 1997). Parents must encourage children to participate in collective sports or other such activities "so that they are not by themselves and not absorbed in their genitals" (Kâzemi Khalkhâli 1991: 111). Teachers and physicians must advise youth about healthy and appropriate sexuality.

Male physicians must especially explain the harms of masturbation for boys and make them aware of the dangerous consequences of this seemingly pleasurable practice. Medical doctors and mental health specialists believe that masturbation not only physically weakens boys, but also causes mental disorder. (114)

Young women must be warned about the perils of losing their virginity: dishonored girls bear unwanted, illegitimate children. The fear of being examined for virginity is great among the new generation, knowing that the nightmare portrayed in Rasool Sadr-e-ʿÂmeli's movie *A Girl with Sneakers* could easily come true for them. In this movie, a schoolgirl, arrested for being with her boyfriend in a park, is taken to the medical examiner's office to determine her virginity.

Being alone, especially in the case of adolescents, breeds evil: young boys and girls will wander off into the forbidden land and will consequently seek sexual gratification outside the heteromarital confine. Masturbation is deemed a "grand sin" (*gonâh-e kabireh*), a "despicable act" that "makes anyone with the tiniest faith in God shiver" (*Payâm-e Zan* no. 72, March 1998: 72). Imam Ali reportedly hit on the hands of an offender so harshly that it caused swelling (*Payâm-e Zan* no. 55, October 1996: 70). Though no physical punishment is spelled out for masturbation, Islamic sexual socialization instills tremendous guilt and shame on doers. Responding to a female reader, the counselor of *Payâm-e Zan* (no. 83, February 1999: 85) writes:

You have made a mistake and committed a grand sin. But praise the God that you came to your senses soon. . . . Now that after such a grand sin, you are so sorry that the flames of repentance are consuming you and anxiety is burning your flesh and soul, you have taken a good step toward repentance. God willing, your pain can open for you the doors to God's mercy. He likes young people's contrition more than old folks' prayer. Take refuge in God. You pay for your sin with your unbearable pain. There is yet hope that, as the Prophet said, your hours of suffering would make up for your hours of sin. Do not give up on God's mercy. Since you have shown remorse, do not humiliate yourself any more. Do not despair.

Readers are warned that masturbation can cause several physical and mental problems, including genital infections, disfiguration of genitalia, rupturing of the hymen, mental anguish, dereliction of religious duties, and disinclination toward "legitimate" marital sex (see e.g., *Payâm-e Zan* no. 52, July 1996: 85).

Terrorized and confused, readers like a 20-year-old woman painfully express internalized guilt:

It has been five years since I have fallen prey to the contemptible act of masturbation; I have had no luck stopping myself. I have learned recently that this act is sinful. Now I feel desperate and guilty. I am scared that I might have developed some sexual problems. I am ashamed to see a doctor. For this reason I keep rejecting my suitors for no reason. . . . For a long time now I have not done anything useful. I have no goal. Whatever I do—be it studying or artwork—I abandon in mid-course. Guilt and despair do not leave me alone. I feel I have infections; without consulting a doctor, I have started taking antibiotic. I am failing in my studies. In junior high and high school, I was the best student in memorization of the Koran. But I have forgotten most of it now. . . . My family thinks I am a calm girl who will imminently finish memorizing the Koran and will pass the national college entrance examination. They do not know that I have not even finished my high school yet, that I am so immersed in abomination that I am ashamed to get near the Koran. I wish I would die and become free from this condition. (*Payâm-e Zan* no. 60, March 1997: 50)

Preoccupation with art, reading religious books, especially the Koran, and diligence in religious duties are introduced as remedies for masturbation.

This restrictive ideology has thus created tension for many men and women. Marriage counselor Asqar Keyhânniâ writes in his *Youths and Marriage* that "even the most pious young men" have expressed to him that, on seeing a woman, they are forced to combat feelings of consuming "desire." " 'Subsequently,' they tell me, 'we feel both guilty for having such feelings toward a stranger and helplessly frustrated from suppressing sexual desire' " (Keyhânniâ 1998: 16).

A study about university students' views regarding marriage, presented to the Seminar on Youths and Marriage, Fall 1991, found that while over 83% of students interviewed believed marriage of utmost importance, only 24.6% thought themselves "fully ready" for marriage. Lack of financial resources, particularly for men, ranked highest (62%) among "barriers for marriage." Related barriers included lack of housing (44%) or of other life necessities (34%). Nearly half the students doubted ever finding a suitable mate. Over 53% believed that sexual gratification made marriage important—of these, an unspecified majority is male (*Zan-e Rouz* 23 November 1991: 6).[14]

The study confirms some expected trends. Economic hardships deprive the young from the only legal opportunity for sexual pleasure. That a majority of respondents considered sexual gratification "the most important objective of marriage" raises concern about the realism in young Iranians' perceptions about marriage. This can especially lead to difficulties in a society where divorce is still stigmatized. A report by the State Organization for Personal Status Registration (Sazeman-e Sabt-e Ahval) for the first six months of the Iranian calendar year 1375 (from 21 March to 22 September 1996) reveals a marriage rate of 12% compared to a divorce rate of 17% (reported in *Zan-e Rouz*, quoted in *Avaye Zan* no. 28: 27).

The high portion of interviewees who considered finance a deterrent to marriage indicates the failure of the Islamist agenda to make marriage a

sacred duty, rather than a secular concern. Some 93% of the students interviewed believed that the government must provide financial aid for those
who otherwise could not marry (6). Such recommendations, however, are
impractical to Ayatollah Hâeri—when such assistance cannot be afforded
for populated families, how can we expect it to be available to the young?
He narrates a hadith from a Shiite imam who refused to take "every thing
in the world in exchange for a day spent with his wife." Our imam believed,
Hâeri states, "that 'life without a spouse is a sin and I am not willing to
barter the whole world for one single sin.' " Marriage, to Hâeri, is a function of faith, not of material life:

The more intense a man's faith, the greater his need for a wife . . . Those who
believe it is possible to control the need for a wife with heightened religiosity ought
to remember that this is not an ugly, shameful feeling. Those closer to God experience this feeling more. (6)

The detrimental consequences of making marriage the most urgent concern of every youth are not solely in their limiting of sexual satisfaction to
one legal form. The emphasis on marriage, and marriage at the first opportune moment, reveals an increasing closure of alternatives in women's
lives. The decrease of women's age at the time of the first marriage is
disconcerting. In the year 1370 (March 1991–March 1992), 2.2% of girls
between 10 and 14 years of age had been married. Sociologist Zhâleh Shâditalab reports that since 1976, "and especially in recent years," the number
of married girls in this age category has "considerably increased." Though
marriage for young boys has also risen, this trend is nowhere comparable
to that among young girls. Of every 15 married girls in this age group,
according to Shâditalab, one is a widow—an indication of the age gap
between these wives and their husbands. Shâditalab cites research conducted by the State Organization for Personal Status Registration covering
a sample of 50,000 mothers. Of these, nearly a quarter married for the first
time before 15. Reviewing the statistics, she concludes that "nearly 50%
of all Iranian women marry before the age of 19" (Shâditalab 1995: 9).

Punishment of practices that jeopardize the sanctity of the family constitutes a pivotal component of regulating sexuality. Zena (adultery) receives a stiff punishment. According to sura Light, v. 2: "The adulterer and
the adulteress shall each be given a hundred lashes" (Koran 1988: 214). If
zena is mohsana, the parties are sentenced to death by stoning. Mohsana
adultery occurs between adults of sound mind who have experienced legitimate sexual intercourse in a marital relationship. Yet men's prerogative
is evident even in the case of zena. La'ân or execration in the IRI Civil Law
(Article 1052) allows a man to accuse his wife of adultery when he has no
proof. He has to swear four times that she sinned, and once that he is
telling the truth. The wife can renounce his accusation four times and swear

that she is being truthful. The judge will subsequently pronounce the couple divorced. They can never remarry each other. Only the husband can execrate his wife; the wife cannot. And though his claim is rejected, the accuser is not subject to the penalty of unfounded accusation (*qazf*).

Deviation from the "healthy" heteromarital sexuality is denounced. Though temporary marriage for the sole purpose of sexual pleasure in exchange for remuneration is legal, sexual liaisons without religious sanction are not. Such relationships signify lax morality and defective personality. A delicate issue both socially and politically, there is no systematic research about prostitution in the Islamic Republic. Scattered reports, however, surface every now and then. The daily *Iran* (26 July 2000) reports, for example, that in 1378 (March 1999–March 2000), 350 women were treated at the rehabilitation centers for "harmed women" in a northern Tehran district. This number reportedly indicates an increase from the previous year. (*Iran* reveals neither the name of the source nor data for previous years.) At any rate, prostitution has a visible presence in people's daily lives. In Tehran, for instance, prostitutes conspicuously queue in motorways and other known areas. Many people tell stories of men being approached by women for sexual transactions, mostly attributing these incidents to poor economy.

In the Islamic state, a "deviant woman," that is, one who engages in illegitimate sexual relationship, holds a precarious position. On the one hand, she is pitied as a victim of social ills; on the other, whether she turns to selling sex because of a dysfunctional family life, deception, or economic needs, she leads a "pathological" life and must be cured. She is at once "socially harmed" (*âsibdideh-ye ejtemâ'i*) and "socially deviant" (*monharef-e ejtemâ'i*). The medical language of the discussion reflects not only the influence of a strong positivist trend in the Iranian sociopolitical discourse, but also an Islamic conviction that there is a natural, normal, and healthy sexuality compared to which all other sexualities are unnatural and sick.

IRI policies refer to two groups of "socially deviant women" (Center for Women's Participation 1999: 260–68). *Dokhtarân va zanân-e dar ma'raz-e âsib-e ejtemâ'i-e hâd* are the highly-at-risk girls and women who run away from their families, have no guardian or visible means of support, or the savvy (*derâyat*) to manage their lives on their own. The category of *zanân-e âsibdideh-ye ejtemâ'i (vizheh)*, the Socially Harmed Women (Special), includes those who engage in prostitution, or "women who do not adhere to moral and social values and engage in illegitimate sex, though accrue no income in this way" (261). In both cases, the intention is that, after due punishment, conditions are created for these women to return to "a healthy life" through reestablishing familial bonds, education, employment, and marriage.

Emphasis on the institution of heterosexuality leaves no room for homosexuality. The punishment for sodomy is death for "both the active and passive persons" (IRI Penal Law, Articles 109–26). If one partner is not of legal age, "the doer" will be killed and "the passive one" will be subject to 74 lashes. Should both parties be below legal age, their punishment will be 74 lashes. If the sexual contact between two males is limited to touching the thighs and buttocks, the men will receive 100 lashes. If this behavior is repeated four times, the penalty is death. Yet if a non-Muslim man touches a Muslim man for sexual pleasure, he will be sentenced to death after the first incident. Lesbianism (*mosâheqeh*) is punished with 100 lashes; its fourth repetition invokes death (Articles 127–34).

It is noteworthy, however, that as in other Middle Eastern societies, "homosexuality" in Iran refers predominantly to *levât* or *hamjensbâzi*—both terms meaning sexual liaison between two men. *Levât* is believed to be widely practiced with young men or children, especially in rural Iran. Such sexual contacts do not constitute "homosexual identity" as they duplicate conventional male/active and female/passive roles.

"Homosexuality" refers specifically to passive homosexual behavior, which is considered particularly objectionable, because it turns God's creation topsy-turvy, and threatens the God-given harmony between men and women, which is reflected in the social role pattern. A man who plays the active, penetrator role in a homosexual act behaves like a man, and is therefore not considered "homosexual." Passive homosexual behavior, however, implies being penetrated like a woman, and is considered to be extremely scandalous and humiliating for a man, because it is feminine behavior. (Schild 1992: 185)

Thus, so long as no emotional ties grow between the men, their relationship is considered merely *hamjensbâzi*, "playing" with someone of the same sex, not *hamjensgerâ'i*, being homosexual. A man could therefore be married and have sexual relations with other men without casting any doubt on his heterosexuality.

Though punishment for homosexual acts is theoretically harsh, Islam has largely ignored homosexual relations. Comparable to the "Don't ask, don't tell" policy in the U.S. military, there is a "will not to know" among Muslims (Murray 1997a). This is in part because homosexuality is an alternative outlet for sexual gratification when lawful conjugal sex is not possible. Then, too, practical complications inhibit implementing the law. According to the rules of penal procedure, four trustworthy Muslim men must testify that they have seen the arraigned engage in sodomy, or the culprit must confess four times. Since there is a severe punishment for unproven accusation, individuals rarely risk reporting suspected same-sex conduct. As Schild correctly observes, "in practice it is only public transgression of Islamic morals that is condemned, and therefore Islamic law stresses the role of eyewitnesses to an offense (1992: 183). All these strictures, to be sure, do not preclude the possibility of harassment for suspected homosexuals, or accusation of homosexuality to discredit foes. There are also recorded incidents of punishment, as in the case of Mehdi Barâzandeh who in November 1995 was stoned to death after a court found him guilty of adultery and homosexuality. In addition, Iranian refugee groups in Europe and North America have reported cases of harassing gays and lesbians.

Detecting a homosexual couple in public is rather difficult since public shows of affection, for instance, holding hands and kissing on the cheeks, is customary among friends. In fact, under the guise of normalcy of interaction among members of the same sex, homosexuals can live together as housemates without arousing much suspicion, provided that they maintain the appearance of sleeping in separate beds. Male homosexuals seem to have a more difficult time living together: landlords are not too eager to rent to single men. Dâneshju Park in central Tehran is known as a meeting place for gay men. Ja'far Bulhâri, the chairman of Tehran's Psychiatric Institute, has disclosed the existence of an underground self-help movement for transsexuals and transgenders among Iranian youth of 16–30 years old (*NimRouz*, 2 February 2000). Whether homosexuality has actually increased or not, people talk about the "frequency" of homosexual liaisons as compensatory—albeit to many, deviant—sex in a strict and segregated system. The media occasionally report news about homosexuals and warn youngsters about the "immorality" of homosexuality. *Râh-e Zendegi* of 6 December 1998 (10–11) comments on the story of a 17-year-old girl. Her father is a successful businessman. Her mother has a BA in business, but has been a housewife all her life. But suddenly she decides to enter into a business partnership with her husband. That takes her out of the house and leaves the young narrator in charge of her two siblings. Little by little, differences in business strategies cause quarrels between her parents. The unhappy family environment is compounded by the mother's total immersion in her business. She does not notice the growing alienation between herself and her teenage daughter. To compensate for her loneliness, the narrator spends her time with school friends. She is particularly attracted to one and with her, she enters the "forbidden realm" of a liaison. Her mother is still of no help, and had it not been for the guidance of another schoolmate, she might have "eternally sunk into the abyss of bad friends" (11). She is no longer with that friend, yet she feels lethargic, depressed, and uninterested and disoriented in life.

I am so tired. Recently, my mother takes every opportunity to discuss marriage with me. Without asking my opinion, she accepts suitors' requests for visits. She does not know how disgusted I am with men and how much I despise marriage. . . . Everybody says that I am an unkind, selfish girl, but nobody wants to understand the reasons for my behavior and help me. (11)

These depictions, however, say nothing about the violence that the institution of heterosexuality perpetrates on individuals, not only by perpetuating patriarchal gender relations, but also by exposing vulnerable individuals to the sexual impositions of those with power. There are cases of trafficking in young boys, though like female prostitution, its existence is either denied or jettisoned as a rarity. Residents of Tehran report that Karimkhân-e Zand Street is a popular place after sunset for picking up boys. Young—and often destitute—boys line up for older men who arrive in their cars, blink at the boys, make an offer, and take them away. An Aid Agency worker in Mashhad wrote to me (August 2000) about the sexual abuse of some young Afghan refugee boys in schools on their way to immigrating to Iran: "When a family does not have enough money to pay for all its members, the smugglers keep one member with themselves in areas near the eastern Iranian border. The rest of the family has to collect the required money to save their son or occasionally their daughter. Many of these children are molested while kept for ransom." Former Iranian prisoners of war also tell horrifying stories of Iranian hizbullah men's abuse of younger captives in Iraqi prison camps (see, for example, NimRouz 13 May 2000).

A CROWDED FAMILY: SIGN OF A POWERFUL UMMAT

When population control policies were first introduced in Iran in the late 1960s, the clerical community opposed them as a colonialist ploy to reduce the number of Muslims. Following the 1979 victory, Islamists held firmly onto their conviction that behind family planning proposals, a colonialist conspiracy was at work. Contraceptives became rare and expensive. Many IRI leaders regarded a large population as a symbol of Islam's strength, not to mention a source of future soldiers for a warring Islamic state. Encouraging early marriage as a weapon against immorality also contributed to the population increase—Iran's population growth rate rose to more than 7% in the early 1980s. Iran's population, which was about 39,250,000 in 1980, neared 60 million by 1990 (UNESCO 1998).

After Ayatollah Khomeini's death, IRI statesmen finally approved of population control policies (see Aghajanian 1994b; Hoodfar and Assadpour 2000). Ayatollah Khamenehii issued edicts allowing contraception and sterilization, including tubal ligation for women and vasectomy for men. The population control initiatives aim to limit family size to four children. The 1993 Family and Population Planning Law does not allow such provisions as maternal leave or subsidized use of daycare facilities at the workplace after the fourth child (Center for Women's Participation 1999: 241–42). The Iranian population growth rate dropped to 1.5% in 1996 (Iran Statistical Center 1999). Still, with half of Iran's 70 million people under 20 years of age, a baby boom would not be a surprise. A report in the daily

Hamshahri (27 and 28 July 1998) warns that the nation's population is rising due to service deficiencies or lack of a deeply shared belief in population control among the IRI decision-makers. The report estimates some 60% of all births after the fourth child are unwanted.

Unless medically required, abortion is illegal and the woman, her husband, and the operating physician will be punished. A fetus is deemed alive—with *rouh* or spirit—after two months. Part of the punishment for abortion is the payment of *diyeh*, the monetary compensation for the lost child, in accordance with the law of retribution. Within the first eight weeks there is no difference in the diyeh for an aborted fetus. But as soon as the fetus becomes alive, gender differences come into effect: a female requires only half the diyeh of a male fetus, just as a grownup female requires half of the blood money of a man (Center for Women's Participation 1999: 109).

Though sanctioned by the Leader himself, the decision in favor of population control has not been unanimous by any means. Partisans on both sides base their arguments on Islamic interpretations of gender. According to opponents, birth control deprives men and women of their basic "right" to reproduce. But the repercussions of population control go far beyond a couple's life, they contend. The ultimate harm is inflicted upon the Islamic society. Muslims grow weak as their numbers decrease and the institution of the family dissipates in their society. The argument against population control proceeds along three basic lines.[15] First, verses from the Koran are cited advocating population increase. In the sura *Counsel*, v. 11, for instance, we read: "Creator of the heavens and the earth, He has given you wives from among yourselves to multiply you, and cattle male and female" (Koran 1988: 155). The second line concerns God's responsiveness to the needs of His creature. According to the sura *Houd*, v. 6: "There is no creature on the earth whose sustenance is not provided by Allah. He knows its dwelling and its resting-place" (133). And finally, in verse 31 of the sura *The Night Journey*, Allah unequivocally condemns infanticide: "You shall not kill your children for fear of want. We will provide for them and for you. To kill them is a great sin" (235–36).

Supporters of population control counter that uncontrolled population growth, especially under an Islamic state, jeopardizes the institution which reproduction is supposed to protect—that is, the family—and hurts the very heart of that institution—the mother. Nâhid Shid, for example, opines that too many children cause poverty (1995: 46–48). In large families, living expenses become unbearable; young mothers suffer from a multitude of health problems; malnutrition persists; and parents cannot attend to their children's needs. But in a small family, everybody is happy. Educated women marry later in their lives and have smaller families. So, these women are in an advantageous position from the start. Women in small families also have more opportunities for personal growth. They can maintain their financial independence and thereby contribute to the family's finances. This contribution enhances women's status within the family. They become decision-makers in family and society, eventually acting as "what the late Imam [Khomeini] envisioned for women: 'the origin of all good whose goodness would eradicate poverty for future generations' " (48).

Ayatollah Hosseini Tehrani (1994) argues against population control, holding that since fruitfulness is an essential gender characteristic for both males and females, pregnancy prevention jeopardizes individuals' gender identities. Reflecting on tubal ligation, Hosseini Tehrani writes:

Women who tie their tubes indeed destroy, ruin, and corrupt the most significant organ of their existence—it is their ornament. A woman's uterus is one of her organs, like her eyes, hands, feet, and heart. Even more importantly, the uterus is such a vital organ that its survival and health guarantee her existence and femininity; but its destruction and illness ruin her femininity. (47)

Since gender is politicized, nothing happens to an individual without having political implications. Thus, population policies cannot be correctly understood unless the hostility of the West toward Islam is taken into consideration. The political dimension of population control, states Hosseini Tehrani, has become more crucial than ever after the Islamic Revolution. Muslims asserted their identity by staging a revolution that allowed them to be true to themselves. The enemies of Islam want to fight back by stripping Muslims of their regained identity:

The enemies of Islam [opt to] eradicate you . . . tie women's life-giving tubes and make brave (*rashid*) and strong men, unmen (*nâmard*) and sterile (*akhteh*). Because, after the revolt of the courageous Muslim people against impiety, after our people's courageous and resourceful fights, [our enemies] want to eradicate us from the roots. . . . These birth control pills, using instruments in women's uteruses, tying women's tubes, depriving men of their manhood, causing them uncountable complications such as neurological diseases, blood circulation problems, heart attacks, mental disorders, and the flood of cancers—the impact of these measures is no less severe than the destruction caused by missiles. (Hosseini Tehrani 1994: 4, 5)

Iran can easily accommodate 200 million people, asserts Hosseini Tehrani; asserting that the need for planned parenthood is nothing but a lie that intends to "kill, defeat, and destroy the family" (6).

As usual, God's rights on earth must be preserved. Do we not all belong to Allah? How can we then decide about what truly belongs to Him? Hosseini Tehrani reminds us that no hardship justifies a premature death, not even the fear of a torturous death in the hands of the enemy.[16] Urologist Nâser Simforush similarly opposes tying tubes because "protecting human life is ordained by God and fulfilling this duty is made obligatory by the shari'ah" (*Jomhury-e Islami* 19 November 1992).

A two-part article about colonialist plans under the disguise of population control (*Jomhury-e Islami* 14 and 15 November 1993) stipulates the
principle objectives of "atheistic demography" in advocating population
control: strengthening atheism and impiety; spreading individualism; weakening public morality; and undermining fundamental societal values. Why,
then, so much propaganda promoting population control in an *Islamic*
society? Hosseini Tehrani's answer is clear: to secure the enemies' political
control over Muslims (1994: 87). Islam's enemies accomplish this by "pulling women to the market and wasting their lives" (89). Unfortunately, he
laments, authorities of the Islamic state silence Muslim opponents of population control and offer the tribunal only to the advocates (65). He falls
short of making specific accusations, or identifying what forces in what
part of the Islamic state have colluded with the enemies in the post-
Khomeini era. But he is quite sure that population control is one component of the conspiracy to promote "corruption, prostitution, and the
destruction of this society's divine and revolutionary values" (124).

Population control also affects individual women and men. Pregnancy
prevention first and foremost harms the woman, since "a woman's health
is guaranteed by giving births and nursing" (Hosseini Tehrani 1994: 228).
Mothering will not prevent a woman from education. Nor would having
too many children become a financial burden. Quite the contrary, "a
woman's very presence, her marriage [and pregnancy] will become a source
of prosperity. More marriages in a society increases prosperity; more children will enlarge human capital and God's blessing" (337). So, unless her
life is at stake, a woman must not sterilize herself even if her husband
allows her: he has no right here, first, because her body belongs to Allah,
and second, what if he divorces his wife or dies, and she decides to remarry?
Who gives her present husband the right to compromise the right of her
future husband (320)?

Hojjatulislam Ahmad Sâdeqi Ardestâni argues in favor of family planning, in a series of *Zan-e Rouz* articles devoted to the perils of uncontrolled
population growth, published in October and November of 1991. He concurs with opponents that, overall, Islam favors reproduction and population increase among Muslims. He cites Mohammad's command to his
followers: "Bring children into this world, because the plentitude of my
people in the Judgment Day will make me feel prouder than do people of
other faiths" (quoted in Sadeqi Ardestani 1991a: 10). Thus, comments Sâdeqi Ardestâni, we are all proud that Muslims are outnumbering Christians
around the world (10). But, he says, this pride must not lead us to closing
our eyes to real problems of hunger, poverty, and meager facilities Muslims
suffer so frequently.

In the Islamic Republic of Iran, he writes, population explosion bars the
implementation of fundamental Islamic policies. Islam mandates all believers to learn; yet due to overpopulation, many Iranians are deprived of ed-

ucation. Islam wishes health and prosperity for believers. But natural resources in the country are rapidly depleting; a vast portion of the population is concentrated in less than 16% of the land; medical standards fall woefully beneath the World Health Organization standards; and unemployment, housing shortage, and food shortage constantly threaten Iranians (Sâdeqi Ardestâni 1991a).

Before the revolution, Sâdeqi Ardestâni reminds the reader, critics of population reduction underlined the colonialist conspiracy to weaken Muslims. Now, however, Muslim leaders are in charge and protect their people. So, we must devise new methods of dealing with population issues (Sâdeqi Ardestâni 1991b).

Nothing compromises our belief in the sanctity of marriage and procreation. Indeed, "we consider the best women to be those who are not barren and can bear many children . . . Barrenness is a defect (naqiseh), and lack (kambud) for a woman" (Sâdeqi Ardestâni 1991b: 13). Yet having "too many" children is not necessarily good. The Koran (e.g., sura Cow, v. 249) teaches us that "Many a small band has, by Allah's grace, vanquished a mighty army." What good is having too many people when we are unable to meet their basic needs (Sâdeqi Ardestâni 1991b: 13, 58)?

Neither does support of birth control jeopardize Islamic convictions, according to Sâdeqi Ardestâni. Indeed, Muslims can, as always, look to Islam for guidance. Islam holds that all children are entitled to being nursed by their mothers. Nursing is a natural birth control mechanism. If a woman nurses her newborn for two years, each child's birth would be separated from the next by about three years. The best age for a woman to reproduce is between 20 and 35; that means that recommending families limit the number of their children to four is quite logical (Sâdeqi Ardestâni 1991b: 59).

Sâdeqi Ardestâni maintains that the most common form of birth control is 'azl, or coitus interruptus, but he disapproves of this method as "the worst method of pregnancy prevention." Coitus interruptus is unnatural and "undoubtedly harms the couple both physically and psychologically. . . . It deprives the woman of a right, harms her, [and] . . . interferes with her pleasure" (Sâdeqi Ardestâni 1991c: 14). Sâdeqi Ardestâni falls short of recommending a specific contraceptive method; he limits himself to emphasizing that Khomeini declared acceptable any method that did not permanently sterilize, and did not kill the baby. But the author considers it every couple's duty to learn and use the most effective and compatible contraception, just as it is the responsibility of the Islamic state to take the population issue more seriously (15). Immediately after declaring a couple's "ethical and social" responsibility, the author cites a hadith from Mohammad that declares men accountable for what happens in their families: "A man is the overseer and guardian (sarparast va negahbân) of his family members; he will be questioned and punished for them." This assertion is not elaborated upon.

Opponents and adherents of population control share several fundamental assumptions. For both, virility is a masculine attribute that must be guarded, just as fertility is feminine and ought not to be jeopardized. Both groups concur that a woman's body belongs first to God, and then to her husband. So, any birth control measure that may lead to a sinful act in the eyes of Allah is prohibited. Since no man other than her husband should look at a woman's vagina, contraceptives that require a (male) physician seeing or touching a woman's genitalia are not acceptable (Ma'sumi 1998: 131). The husband's unilateral sexual possession becomes abundantly clear in edicts concerning birth control. Under no circumstances can a man's entitlement to sexual service be denied. Massoud Ma'sumi has asked five grand Ayatollahs if a woman can prevent pregnancy without her husband's permission.[17] With one exception, the respondents discourage such an action, unless pregnancy puts her health in serious jeopardy. But even the dissenting Ayatollah has no doubt that a woman's use of contraception must not prevent her from *tamkin* to her husband, that is, obligation to provide him sexual pleasure (130). Anything that jeopardizes her husband's sexual rights is prohibited. She may use birth control pills, but cannot deny her husband entry, force her husband to withdraw, make herself permanently sterile, or use an intrauterine device since it requires that a strange man see her vagina (131). If a woman causes her husband's withdrawal without his consent, she must pay diyeh, the blood money, for the fetus, as specified in the IRI's Penal Law. Khomeini calls forced coitus interruptus a *harâm* (unlawful and punishable) act if done by the wife. But if, contrary to his wife's wishes, the husband withdraws prior to ejaculation, his act is merely *makruh* (reprehensible)—even that, of course, only if she is a "good wife," that is, does not have a sharp tongue, nurses her baby, and is not sterile (132).[18] Pregnancy prevention, grand Ayatollahs concur, does not require both parties' consent; the husband's decision is enough, though it is preferable if he also has her consent (132). According to IRI laws, a woman can use temporary birth control methods (e.g., an intrauterine device) without her husband's consent, but permanent contraceptives (e.g., tubal ligation) require his written permission. A man does not need his wife's permission for using any form of contraception (Kar 1999b: 348).

HEJÂB, "THE FIRST HOME"

In light of Islamist conceptions of gender, sex, and sexuality, we can see why preventing "public nudity," that is, unveiled women in public, numbered high on the wish list of the IRI architects. Veiling is a sensitive sphere where divinity and polity intersect. The veil conceals women from public eyes and symbolizes selfless women of the Islamic state. Thus Ashraf Gerâmizâdegân relates "the culture of hejâb" to women's "self-sacrifice" (1996: 62). In this regard, the veil is best understood in the broad context of modesty in dress, applicable equally to men and women. Both sexes must avoid competing with Allah for attention. All fascination must be exclusively with Allah—everyone else must fade to the background in the Islamic ummat. Detracting attention from individuals ensures that energy is invested in God's work. Those inimical to Islam dissipate Muslims by presenting them a false path of indulgence in earthly pleasures.

Qolâmali Haddâd ʿÂdel addresses the significance of hejâb for an Islamic society in a short pamphlet called *The Culture of Nakedness and the Cultural Nakedness.*[19] Haddâd ʿÂdel argues that a society's culture determines its dress style (1995: 7). He compares the dress philosophy in post-Renaissance Europe and non-Western societies. A cursory comparison, he holds, demonstrates that Western clothes are tight and short, whereas Eastern clothes are long and loose. Haddâd ʿÂdel attributes this difference to divergent notions of humankind. In the post-Renaissance era, humanity has been defined exclusively as a material being. "For more than four centuries, God has left mainstream social life, exiled to the church. . . . In Western civilization, no fundamental difference pertains between human beings and animals" (27). In a materialistic world, with no prospect of a life hereafter, Western man or woman seeks maximum pleasure. This one-dimensional, pleasure-seeking individual has been promoted by the capitalist pursuit of profit, science—"especially Freudianism" that deems sexuality the central force of life—and such philosophical orientations as existentialism that "exclusively stress human freedom" (37). Western humanity, to Haddâd ʿÂdel, is reduced to the flesh (32). Clothes, then, have become "a second layer of skin," a window to display the body (40).

Islamic culture, conversely, regards human beings as quintessentially moral (38–39). Sexuality, though a basic human instinct, must be tamed. This Islamic philosophy of humankind as simultaneously moral and susceptible to sexual temptations explains the difference between Islamic and Western fashion:

A Muslim wears clothes not to present the body, but to conceal it. For a Muslim, clothes constitute a sacred, inviolable space (*harim*), walls of a bastion that secure the body from incursions and maintain its nobility. Dress is not a second layer of skin; it is the first home. A Muslim does not consider decorating and offering the body for sale a sign of perfection. Instead of selling the body to others, a Muslim offers his or her soul to God. (40)

Anything that accentuates a person's presence is prohibited. According to an edict by Khomeini, what is perceived as ornamental in public opinion must not be displayed before strangers (Vahidi 1994: 19). What "the public" does not find alluring can be left alone. The relentless preoccupation with covering the female flesh is more a reaction to *what is deemed sexual* than to the flesh itself. Thus, for instance, a woman wearing makeup and a colorful dress, but fully covered, can appear more enticing than a farming or working-class mother nursing her child in a public space. One could also note the impact of social class in the construction of the "deviant woman." To the rank-and-file hizbullah, predominantly from traditional middle and lower classes, the familiar mother breastfeeding is deemed natural, whereas the "Westernized" woman appears exotic, alluring, and dangerous.

Hejâb plays an essential role in God's design. The attraction between the sexes transcends the sexual domain: humanity must be reproduced in a happy family. Ayatollah Javâdi Âmoli addresses hejâb from this vantage point. According to the Koran, peaceful life is the family's prime objective. "Responsibility to create tranquillity is bestowed upon woman ... Mankind is attracted to her kindness" (Javadi Amoli 1993: 38). Hejâb guarantees a comfortable family life by preventing strangers' transgressions, including nullifying the attractiveness of women.

Linking mundane to eternal, profane to sacred, veiling derives from divine law. Woman's role in the universe accords her honor, transcending that conferred by human law (41–42). Had it been but a this-worldly matter, a woman might have chosen to go unveiled:

Hejâb is a divine right (*haqq*) ... A woman's honor is not hers; nor her husband's; nor her brothers'; nor her children's. Even if all these people are willing to relinquish this obligation, the Koran will not forego that. For a woman's honor, her reputation is Allah's right. The pure (*sobhân*) God has created womankind with the capital [*sic*] of emotion so that she could teach kindness. ... If a society forgets this lesson of kindness and follows instinct and lust, it will become corrupted like the West. Thus, no one has the right to say that I do not mind going unveiled ... A woman's chastity is Allah's right ... All family members, all members of the society, and especially the woman herself must be faithful guardians of what God has lent them. (425)

It is noteworthy that instead of *qanun*, the law, Javâdi Âmoli uses *haqq* and *hoquq* that connote double meanings of laws and rights. Hejâb, then, is not merely a God-designed regulation; it is *His* privilege to command from women. And in the laws of the Islamic state, hejâb is not an imposition (*ejbâr*); it is a necessity (*elzâm*). Women are not *forced* to wear the veil so long as they avoid spaces or situations that necessitate compliance with the Islamic dress code. Hejâb is not an external imposition; it is a woman's right which, fortunately, she enjoys in the Islamic government. One aspect of male domination has been to deprive her of this proper coverture. In the words of then-President Khamenehii: "Today's woman is oppressed, and one dimension of her oppression is that with deceptive propaganda, she is goaded to appear without coverture in public, degrading her to an object of pleasure" (*Zan-e Rouz* 4 February 1989: 4).

Mandatory hejâb emerged through stages. Some ministries, such as the Ministry of Education, had introduced hejâb for some time before the veil became mandatory in all aspects of public life. At the beginning of the 1980–81 academic year, school personnel were required to wear the hejâb. The next year, all government offices were obligated to wear the veil. As one woman wrote to me, "rules for hejâb at the workplace are different from the traffic regulations that you might disregard, pay the fine and break again every now and then." All private businesses are required to post notices that women's failure to abide by the dress regulation will cost them services. But the signs, too, underwent a metamorphosis. Whereas in the early 1980s stores put up signs to refuse "*bihejâb*" or veilless women, in later years they would not even welcome "*badhejâb*" women (see below for *bihejâbi* and *badhejâbi*). When hejâb was first introduced, women on the street were fined and imprisoned. But women at work had been threatened in advance. Any woman seeking a job, or interested in keeping hers, must observe the dress code—gender boundaries may be negotiated *outside* the workplace.

The strict imposition of hejâb, even in such exclusively female spaces as women's educational institutions, indicates the IRI's intent to make hejâb a constitutive element of womanhood. Regulations about hejâb and women's comportment are quite specific. One memorandum issued by the Ministry of Education in the summer of 1995 stipulates the following for junior high and high school female students:

1. Students must not wear bright and "repulsive" (*zanandeh*) colors;
2. Students are prohibited from thin and lace stockings, even under long pants;
3. Students are prohibited from wearing high heels or brightly colored shoes;
4. Students are prohibited from wearing name brand clothes, luxury and decorative ornaments;
5. Female students must obey Islamic morality and hejâb outside the school environment and on the way home.[20]

The punishment for transgression is designed to guarantee future compliance. A woman who worked as a vice principal of female primary and junior high schools explains this point in an interview with me (Fall 2000):

Having a mirror, a comb, or any cosmetics is grounds for punishment. The severity of the punishment depends on the repetition of the behavior. For a primary schoolgirl, we will summon her parents that same day. A junior high and high school girl will be suspended immediately. We call her parents and ask them to accompany their daughter to school the next day. We will admonish her in that meeting and have her sign a promissory note that she will not bring these items with her. If she does it again, we will write her a suspension for one week, though we don't really carry this through. We ask her parents to bring her back the next day, sign the promissory note, and ask for forgiveness. After that, we allow her to go back to class. Sometimes, if the girl is too frightened, she may sign the statement immediately; in this case, we won't suspend her, nor would we call her parents.

Regulations—or their implementations—have become more relaxed in recent years, but they are still in existence. The Tehran Bureau of Education announced in July 2000 that elementary school students are now allowed to wear "happy, bright colors," in place of the traditional black (*Bahâr* 19 July 2000). According to the Bureau's directive, the new policy "is to brighten the mood and raise hope among students, and preserve their psychological health." "Happy, bright colors" include light blue, beige, pink, light green, and yellow. But the Bureau is quick to exclude "loud and gaudy" (*tond va zanandeh*) colors or dress cuts that are "beneath the dignity of an educational environment." The Bureau's Advisor on Women's Issues explained that the coverture project (*tarh-e estetâr*) compelling students to be veiled and use only drab dark colors forced "unnecessary veiling" in girls' schools and deprived youngsters of a natural tendency to present themselves to classmates. The new rules, however, are limited to elementary students in Tehran. It is also noteworthy that "appearing" before classmates (*zâher shodan*) and "presenting oneself" (*khodnamâ'i*) to them is still only allowed within acceptable limits.[21]

Indeed the impact of hejâb on female students of all ages is serious. But to fully understand this problem, one must consider not just the coverture, but hejâb in the general sense of separating male and female spaces. Though surrounded by walls of up to two meters high, schoolyards are not deemed appropriate for exercising because neighbors may see females in motion (the problem of *eshrâf*). Female students are left on the average with five square centimeters in which to exercise (*Iran* 5 October 2000). A recent study of female students in 16 provinces has revealed 22 physical abnormalities that result from lack of movement (*Âftâb* 8 October 2000). Women's sports like cycling, even in closely supervised public areas, are restricted to reserved sections. According to a UNICEF study,

Horseback riding and swimming pose even more serious problems because of the need for special clothing, which is close fitting or revealing. Although there are separate areas at the seaside where women are allowed to swim in bathing suits, the excessive policing of some areas makes some women construe it as harassment, discouraging them from making full use of the facility. Private swimming pools are expensive and out of the reach of common Iranian women. Public swimming pools are few and inadequate. Moreover, the time allocated for girls' swimming, as compared to that for boys, also limit the access of girls to these facilities. (UNICEF 1998: 68)

This does not mean that male students are in an envious situation. But, as the reporter of the daily *Iran* notes, all the factors that confine women in other spheres of life accentuate their limited access to sports. For one thing, at least male students do not have to deal with the problem of peeping neighbors.

But why are only women restricted in their appearance? To Islamists, the reason must be sought in the compatibility of shari'ah with nature. Women care about concealment more than men must because men respond more to visual stimulation, a point to which "scientific studies" about male and female differences attest (Haddâd 'Âdel 1995: 63). And why must women wear the hejâb even when performing daily prayer in solitude? Why be veiled when only Allah—certainly no stranger to His creatures—is present? Vahidi explains that we have no way of knowing all the logic behind Allah's edicts. But, he opines, perhaps veiling is the consummate manner whereby women can present themselves to God. Besides, praying veiled is "the best practice for wearing the hejâb, for a woman who five times a day covers herself even in the absence of strangers, will undoubtedly do a better job of covering when around strangers" (1994: 18).

Many Islamists vie for a more inclusive covering for women. Châdor, the enveloping black cloth, is routinely promoted as *hejâb-e bartar*, a form of hejâb superior to the acceptable minimum of a headscarf and a long manteau. In the words of Khamenehii, "châdor is not the exclusive form of hejâb, but it is the best form and our national emblem" (*Zan-e Rouz* 4 January 1992: 1). Despite the choice implicit in this remark, individual Islamists could require the châdor in their sphere of influence. According to *Resâlat* (28 December 1994), for instance, Qolâmreza Mesbâhi, Khamenehii's representative in the Islamic Âzâd University system, made the châdor an entrance prerequisite in several city branches such as Arâk, Torbat-e-Heydariyeh, and Roodhen. Even women working in the university administration were forced to comply, though women professors refused. In 1994, wearing the châdor was compulsory in 80 of 120 branches of the Azad University. (On compulsory châdor in the University system, see the daily *Zan* 29 and 30 November 1998.)

Châdor *is* an Iranian invention, predating the advent of Islam. Yet the Islamists' promotion of chador as a national symbol ignores that in pre-Islamic Iran women of nobility customarily wore it to distinguish them. Lower-class women's participation in the labor force was not conducive to the physical restrictions of chador. Châdor, then, had a function completely different from the Islamic hejâb. In post-Islamic Iran, chador was gradually reinterpreted in Islamic terms and assigned the function of the veil (Ravandi 1977: 658).

Châdor proper has been debated, but the *veil* is an Islamic institution of patriarchal control beyond question. Any criticism is summarily condemned as a Western conspiracy. Khamenehii stipulates that "no discussion about women's coverture can be inspired by the propaganda invasion of the West" (*Zan-e Rouz* 4 January 1992: 1). The veil is a must if women want to cross over their feminine boundary. As Khamenehii exhorts:

In an Islamic system, women should possess political savvy; know the art of house-keeping and taking care of the husband; and symbolize chastity, purity, and inaccessibility in social, political, scientific, and service domains. They must beware that hejâb is a precondition, for without the veil, women will not enjoy the opportunity to accomplish all that. (*Zan-e Rouz* 18 December 1993: 8)

And an Islamic state must guard its subjects—first and foremost, women.

GUARDING WOMEN IN PRIVATE AND PUBLIC

Sin is the sword of Damocles in the world according to Islamists, hiding in every corner, able to sneak upon the unsuspecting. Evil can appear in many forms: grand sociopolitical entities, bad friends, misdirected youthful energy, or even minute, seemingly insignificant phenomena such as clothes and makeup, all can disguise evil. And who more than women could be susceptible to satanic deception? Women lack a suspecting nature, a detriment especially in these trying days when Muslims are hard at work building an ideal society on the ruins of a corrupt system. The Islamic state monitors its subjects' private and social lives to protect them from self-incurring harms. In the words of Majlis representative Assadullâh Bayât, "the Islamic state is the guardian and head (*sarparast*) of Islamic society and particularly its women" (*Zan-e Rouz* 1 June 1985: 6).

For many, the state must ideally guard women in the private walls of their homes, a vision compatible with Khomeini's rejection of the Shah during the early sixties. Such *exclusionist-protectivism* preferred to bar women from social life because they "enjoyed the right" to be protected by their men and a paternal republic. The IRI Constitution's exclusionist-protectivist approach defined women as mothers. As Haleh Esfandiari observes, concern over the sanctity of the family by the Assembly of Experts (*Majlis-e Khebregân*) was caused by considerations of "keeping women in the home, restricting the participation of women in the workforce and, more generally, maintaining the separation of the sexes in society" (1994: 67). (The Assembly of Experts was an elected 73-member body, with one woman representative, that drafted the IRI Constitution between August and November 1979.) This policy was also compatible with the Islamist agenda of restrengthening private patriarchy. To return the locus of sexual domination to the private domain necessitated guarding women in both senses of the term: keeping them from public harm *and* preventing their possible indiscretions.

But this policy required that women stay home and be provided for by men, something that never completely materialized. Women's increased public presence due to pre-revolutionary structural changes made seclusion impossible. Besides, in light of women's crucial role in the revolution and Islamists leaders' recognition of their participation, asking women to leave the public *exclusively* to men did not seem viable. Recall that even in pre-revolutionary Iran, prevalent Islamic theories (e.g., by Shariati or the Mojahedin) endorsed an active political role for women. Also, women's staunch insurgency against excluding them from judgeship, or changing their work status to part-time, demonstrated that suggesting total domestication was politically asinine. Furthermore, the exclusionist-protectivist policy very quickly proved impractical. Dual income families and often multiple jobs for each partner have become a necessity in the crisis-ridden post-revolutionary economy. Besides, absent sufficient institutional supports for families with no male breadwinner, widows, divorced women, war widows, and wives of POWs and MIAs have to work to survive.

These realities made Islamists resort instead to a segregationist-protectivist policy. The former approach, of course, was never completely abandoned, but that *Islamists and some clergymen* have supported it is conveniently glossed over. Such "extremism" is attributed by IRI authorities to greedy people or "suspicious and misled groups who do not really believe in Imam [Khomeini], and the Imam's line" (Hojjatulislam Rowhani, quoted in *Zan-e Rouz* 5 September 1987: 11). The segregationist policy shares with exclusionism the fundamental assumption that women must be guarded. After failing to privatize their appropriation, IRI leadership conceded that women could enter the public domain so long as they were firmly grounded in the private sphere—where "men have authority over women." As Hojjatulislam Hâsheminezhâd explains:

There is much emphasis in beloved Islam that women should appear in public less and that there is no need for them to be in everybody's sight, since naturally many problems arise from that. Our veiled believing women are priceless jewels, even more priceless than jewels. We must protect (*hefz*) them. Even if they work in offices, they must be placed in a more secure environment where they are safe. (*Zan-e Rouz* 19 January 1997)

In public, the Islamic state protects women from the dangers of mixed company. This requires a two-pronged plan: creating a "safe" space for women *and* socializing women to accept the necessity of protection. Representative Nafiseh Fayyâzbakhsh, in one of her addresses to the Majlis, articulates the need for a protected female space:

Islam has always encouraged women's social and political presence while clearly emphasizing adherence to complete chastity, shame, and hejâb for women. It is desirable that our officials, in the path of guiding to goodness and prohibiting from evil, make serious considerations about segregating women's and men's spaces. (*Iran Times* 21 January 1993)

Windows in girls' schools are painted with dark colors to prevent on-lookers' prying eyes; most, if not all, public places have been segregated—buses, schools, university classrooms, stairways, beaches, movie theaters, queues, mosques, parent-teacher associations, libraries . . . even the Majlis (see *Zanân* no. 41, March 1998: 5). Police forces designated to safeguard "public morality" blanket the streets on behalf of female safety.

The second component of a successful segregationist-protectivism involves persuading women of their need for protection, even in the safety of an Islamic society. Advice columns and stories chronicle pitiful tales of those who stray from the "right path." Yet where men are warned to shun dishonest business partners, women are lectured on losing their modesty and virtue. Family magazines are deluged with such titles as "The Deceived," "The Abyss," "Repentance," "Sorrow," and "Warning." These exposés warn women about the destructiveness of temptation, the imminence of corruption, and the significant role of sincere guardians or guides. In "The Whirlpool" (Gerdâb), for example, we read about Mahdiyeh, a pious girl from a small town who, on entering college, moves to a city considerably larger than her hometown and shares a house with another female student. Bahâreh "was oblivious to matters of faith, which made her suffer from self-doubt and mental anguish." But as Bahâreh's friends frequent their house, Mahdiyeh undergoes a metamorphosis. She becomes preoccupied with her look, pays little attention to faith and education. Fortunately, however, her mother intervenes by removing her from that house. Though initially angered, Mahdiyeh eventually learns to appreciate her mother's wisdom. "Had my mother left me on my own, today I would have lost all that is valued in a woman" (*Majalleh-ye Khânevâdeh* March-April 1997: 28).[22]

The election of Khatami raised hopes among many women that the impetus for their protection would be relaxed. Chaotic fissures have emerged from Islamists' factional fights in recent years. Consequently, women have found a more relaxed control that allows diversity of color or moderate hejâb. But hopes have also vanished. In spring 1998, conservative Majlis representatives—perhaps in retaliation for the women's support of Khatami (Ebadi 1999: 37)—introduced two bills to the Majlis. One would segregate hospital care. The other sought to amend the laws regarding journalism by forbidding women's pictures on magazine covers, and curtailing discussions of women's rights outside the shari'ah. The latter bill passed easily, despite women's opposition (see, e.g., the protest letter of 402 authors in *Hoquq-e Zanân* no. 3, June-July 1998: 38–39). Only the section on photography was slightly revised.[23] The second bill requiring hospitals to fully segregate all health services raised concerns among many observers over limiting women's access to care. (See, e.g., *Zanân* no. 43, May-June 1998: 15–23; *Hoquq-e Zanân* no. 3, June-July 1998: 20–21; and *Zan-e Rouz* 13 June 1998: 8–9.) While the Guardian Council favored passage, it nevertheless stopped implementation as law.

The introduction of the Plans to Further Promote the Culture of Chastity is another example of the persistence of limitations. Maryam Khazʿali, director of the Women's Cultural and Social Council, comments that the Chastity Plan aims to promote the use of chador among women (*Jomhury-e Islami* 17 August 1998). The Chastity Plan is part of a broad attempt to further sex segregation in society. The daily *Resâlat* (5 August 1998) reports about this objective, highlighting the creation of a safer educational environment for women:

In order to make favorable conditions for the growth of female students' talents and to encourage them to wear the chador more frequently and conventionally, the Ministry of Education has commenced a plan to build exclusive schools for girls throughout the country. These schools are constructed in a way that has no way for anybody to look in. After entering the school, students can be wearing their regular clothes and study without any concern. Only when they are about to leave the school should they put their hejâb back on.

Despite its proposed objective of "serving women," protectionism has deprived them of many services. According to the director of the Tehran City Buses, for instance, the segregation policy has been neither successful by the government criteria nor convenient to passengers (*Zan-e Rouz* 21 January 1989: 9). Segregation of medical care—actions which go beyond those stipulated in the 1998 law that awaits implementation—limits women's access to many medical services.

Fear of punishment for offering aid to an exclusively female clientele (i.e., women unaccompanied by a male guardian, or women in unlawful mixed company) has made many institutions reluctant to serve women. The writer of a letter to *Zan-e Rouz* (19 October 1985: 44) planned on traveling from Tehran to Isfahan with a female friend. They contacted different hotels, but as soon as managers realized that two women were traveling without a male guardian, they refused to make reservations. These women were told that a directive from the Organization of Tourism forbade hotels renting rooms to women. "If a woman has to spend a night or two out of town, don't restrictions like this, albeit originally intended to protect a woman, deprive her of security and peace of mind? Should women who do not have the opportunity of being accompanied by a man, be deprived of traveling forever?" According to another report (*Zanân* no. 18, June-July 1994: 46–50), some 400 taxi drivers were fined within a short few months for seating non-related male and female passengers together. Subsequently, many taxi drivers refused female passengers or charged them extra to compensate for the male passengers that they had to forego.

Protectionism has also meant increased violence. Implementing Islamic moral codes has been intertwined with injury. Islamist ideologues knew, for example, that women would resist mandatory hejâb. They were also aware that they would not succeed in winning a consensus: "We will not forget . . . that in every society, there are people who cannot be dissuaded from their paths with logic and reasoning. With them, we cannot talk but in the language of coercion" (Haddâd ʿÂdel 1995: 57). This message was delivered to women much earlier—during the March 1979 demonstrations, hizbullah men gave them the options of yâ rusary yâ tusary, either a scarf over the head, or a beating on the head.

VIOLENCE UNDER THE STATE'S HOLY BOOTS

Despite the IRI's self-proclaimed role as women's guardian, women have been quite vulnerable in private and public. Violence against women persists, stemming from structural inequities between sexes and predating the IRI (Ezazi 1999). But the advent of the Islamic regime has exacerbated women's vulnerability in family relationships. Their exposed position results from specific Islamic laws that treat women as lesser human beings. Men's power in divorce and custody, for instance, limits women's freedom to leave abusive relationships. That men head the household (Article 1105 of the Civil Law) justifies spousal abuse, "jeopardizing thousands of women due to men's use of instruments of power and violence against women" (Hoquq-e Zanân no. 2, May-June 1998: 27). This stipulation, as discussed earlier, is based on a Koranic verse affording men "authority" over women and instructing the use of force in response to a wife's disobedience or noshooz.[24]

Ayatollah Ahmad Beheshti's treatises on "Marriage in Islam," published in Zan-e Rouz, dictates that a husband's fair supervision predicates a happy marital life. Beheshti (1985b) instructs the husband that qeyrat—a combination of jealousy, protectiveness, and sense of honor, usually demonstrated by a man toward "his" women—is commendable; even so, men ought to perform it in moderation. "A man must not ignore perilous consequences, but should also avoid excessive probing and suspicion" (40). Male authority makes the husband ultimately responsible for his wife's morality. "If a woman does not know an edict concerning women and her husband fails to teach her, the man is guilty" (40). This superiority becomes particularly manifest if she disobeys him. Then, he must not only exercise his "authority" as a man, but also perform his ultimate role as her guide. Beheshti's narrative is self-explanatory: "If the woman disobeys, it is up to the man to chastise her and break her into obedience. According to the

Koran man has authority over woman. . . . That means he must make her (*vâdârad*) grow and do good deeds and protect her from deviation" (41).

Beheshti then repeats the Koran's three-step "remedy" for wives' insubordination—advising, refusing sex, and beating. But he recalls the Prophet's dicta, "do not beat her unless the beating does not injure; do not leave her unless inside the house."

To be sure, not all theologians nowadays draw the gender line so clearly in the familial battleground. Yet that such prescriptions appear in the pages of a women's magazine indicates that Beheshti's ideas are not too alien to the Islamist familial relationship. Other authors may avoid such extremism, but the principle of a man's authority in the home is not denied. According to those close to Khomeini, the Ayatollah's role in the family exemplified a man's subdued but undeniable authority within the family. Farideh Mostafavi, Khomeini's daughter, recalls that her father "was never strict" in treating his wife, though her mother "was obligated to avoid sin." Mrs. Khomeini, on her part, "was quite concerned not to take any step contradictory to the Imam's wish and consent" (Mostafavi 1992: 24). And the Imam was indeed quite concerned about women behaving properly. Even as a guest during his exile to Turkey in the mid-1960s, he was incensed that his Turkish hostess and her 12-year-old daughter appeared before him unveiled (see Moin 1999: 132–33).

No (re)articulation of Islamic family relations has refuted the axiomatic male position within the family; revisionists have merely proposed *modification*. Islamists have, for example, presented as one ideal a benevolent man who is a boss, an economic manager, yet not a tyrant. He is punishing and charitable at once, because, to quote Hojjatulislam Hasheminezhad, "forgiveness by a powerful person, a superior, is beautiful" (*Zan-e Rouz* 19 January 1997). A powerful man does not haphazardly limit his wife's activities, but, to protect his family, may forbid her from doing something or going somewhere (Ayatollah Bojnourdi in an interview with *Zan-e Rouz* 18 December 1993: 17).

We recall the Koran's suggested three steps to control a defiant wife. Bojnourdi suggests redefining "beating" since, he holds, it is a mistaken understanding that the Koran would actually condone wife battery. In Islam, he says, we only have chastisement, *ta'zir*, while beating is a vengeful act. And *ta'zir* must be implemented only by proper authorities. If one cannot persuade his wife to comply, he must go to court to determine her guilt and physically or financially chastise (*Hoquq-e Zanân* no. 3, June-July 1998: 9).

Islamist ideologues thusly locate violence outside Islam, and those who commit family violence are believed to violate Islam out of sheer ignorance (*Hoquq-e Zanân* no. 3, June-July 1998: 7). But under the Islamic Republic, where the state sanctions religious laws fundamentally injurious to women, attributing male violence to the misguided behavior of some men conceals

the systematic character of male violence. Severing male violence from politics and culture obscures the fact that under the IRI's patriarchal triad,
male violence might be regulated but won't disappear. The construction
that "not men, but only proper authorities can 'chastise' women" does not
hold sway. No provision states that only a "proper" governmental or religious authority must "chastise" women. Besides, even if we construe *ta'zir*
as chastisement and not violence, there is no reason that "non-torturous
chastisement" and "torturous treatments of women" cannot coexist. What
is the difference between beating someone and using force, physical or otherwise, to chastise? Does it matter if one's husband batters her, or that a
court does so on his behalf? The term "chastise" conceals the horrendous
nature of what males are licensed to do—beat their wives—and depoliti-
cizes male violence. Is it any less violent if the court physically punishes,
admonishes, or fines her for refusing sex to her husband? Such a relationship is violent at its core. However *noshooz* is defined, and whoever owns
the proper authority to "chastise" a wife, neither his privilege nor the cul-
pability of her "offense" is questioned. True, the wife is also entitled to
sexual satisfaction by her husband, but her right hardly compares to the
man's prerogative. After 4 months of refusal from her husband, she can
ask for a divorce, whereas his pressure must be relieved within a few short
days.

Though family violence is recognized, little is known about its extent
(Abbas-Gholizadeh 1995–1996b: 141). No statistics exist on the subject.
Deemed a private matter, it is rarely discussed outside the family. When
violence against women is acknowledged, like in a three-part interview in
the daily *Iran* (29–31 July 2000), violence is treated as occurring in public,
by "some [men] with abnormalities" (*Iran* 30 July 2000). The IRI Civil
Code says little about family violence. Marital rape is unrecognized; incest
treated as aberration (though if proven, harshly punished). IRI rhetoric
admonishes against marital violence and reminds the public that, in the
words of Khamenehii, "Islam despises a man who acts unjustly toward his
wife and daughter, and the Prophet considered a man ugly if he physically
mistreated a woman" (*Zan-e Rouz* 18 June 1994: 4).

Policing gender and sexuality has proven integral to the IRI's coercive
policies. And, as elsewhere, due to their presumed role in crafting a healthy
society, women have borne the brunt of this coercion. As Mehrangiz Kar
sums up:

Iranian law not only provides ample excuses for violence against women, but is
also written in such a way it can easily work against women in the implementation
process. The lawmaker offers vague and equivocal definitions for many offenses
that pertain to honor (*nâmus*) or public morality. Clarifications of these ambiguities
are contingent upon religious criteria that can only augment the confusion. (Kar
1999a: 56)

Segregation has made aspects of living "easier" for some women. According to a *Zan-e Rouz* report, for instance, some express content with the segregation of city buses because of the "comfort" afforded them (14 January 1988). "Ease" and "comfort" are of course vague concepts, in need of specification. These could simply mean the comfort of less crowded queues, or less obtrusive contacts with men. Even so, the IRI's measures fall considerably short of ensuring safety. Transgressors might receive stiff penalties if caught, but much goes on without police intervention. Consider a bike rider groping a woman in an alley darkened by a blackout, or a man masturbating in a public place. There is no shortage of verbal assault either, and the alleged decrease in sexual slurs masks the reality of coercion. Verbal harassment merely intimates the systematic physical and visual as well as verbal brutality inflicted upon women. Observers complain about the frequency of drivers honking at female pedestrians, an act known as *autozani* (*Iran* 30 July 2000).

Undoubtedly, some transgressions go unpunished in all societies. The point here is to emphasize not only the deficiencies of the Islamists' protectivism, but also how this vision leaves women vulnerable. A case in point is rape. The punishment for rape is the death penalty, but women are extremely vulnerable in a rape case. The main proof in a rape claim is eyewitness—to provide that witness is the claimant's responsibility. The medical examiners' testimony does not suffice by itself. Thus, attorneys advise women not to pursue a case unless there is a high probability of conviction; if a woman cannot prove rape, she can be found guilty of *qazf*, that is, unfounded accusation, punishable by 80 lashes. Besides, the danger also exists that the rapist would claim that they had engaged in a consensual sexual liaison. If the woman is unable to disprove him, she can be punished for zena along with her rapist (see Kar 2000: 155).

Since they are presumed to be in need of protection, women's defiance of Islamic restrictions is answered by attempts to return them to the "right path." Such efforts, however, have been insulting and intrusive, even violent on most occasions. To demonstrate his interest in reforming her, a male hizbullah might well spit on the ground upon seeing a woman whose hejâb is less than perfect. The sight of the Ansâr-e Hizbullah ("assistants of the hizbullah") rouses fear in the public. Each dreadful instance is founded on male "authority over women," on men "hav[ing] a status above women" (Koran 1988: 356), on men's entitlement to their "fields," on men's ability to define women in culture, politics, and society. Women become vulnerable when men can negotiate *amongst themselves* the limits of male authority. Women become vulnerable, as the line separating the "respectable" from the damned is easily crossed with slippage of a scarf or boldness of lipstick.

Islamic society is a goal-oriented system, in which every measure must be taken to prevent any hindrance to its drive toward perfection. Khomeini's instruction regarding the "36-million-people SAVAK"—that is, each individual spying on others—was a step toward that goal. The religious basis of this pervasive intrusion and control is the edict "bid unto good and reject the reprehensible" (*amr beh ma'ruf va nahy az monkar*). This injunction obligates all Muslims to enjoin right behavior in their fellows and deter them from wrong and "immoral" conduct. (For a discussion of this Islamic edict, see Williams 1962: 125–32.) In the Islamic state, this edict, stipulated in Article 8 of the IRI Constitution, operates as a control mechanism. According to Mirsalim, then Minister of Culture and Islamic Guidance, "the day that we fail to implement this grand mission in our Islamic society, we are doomed. . . . If we adopt optimistic policies toward unlawful acts, we embark on a downhill course to destruction." Habibzâdeh, a faculty member at the Tarbiyat-e Modarres University, argues that due to the importance of this enjoinment as "a facet of Islam's social defense," any possible legal complications stemming from the execution of this edict must be dismissed as "justifiable offense" (*Zan-e Rouz* 6 August 1994: 4).

Compliance with Islamic norms—or at least convincing others that one does comply—is a prerequisite for employment and educational opportunities. Until the early 1990s, for instance, before college entrance was granted, authorities canvassed the neighborhood to gather information about the candidate's moral standing and dedication to Islam. Coercion could be mild or strong, physical or symbolic, violent or "peaceful"—it is nonetheless extensively present, making the populace vulnerable. Any behavior could be defined as unlawful at any juncture. One could at any moment face an accusation. The police are omnipresent; but anyone can bid others to abide by "moral principles."

The state punishes violently. We recall that homosexual liaisons can bring a death sentence, adultery 74 lashes or stoning to death. Stoning is a regimented public event. The victim is buried from the waist down in a ditch and the public, including members of the revolutionary guards, Basij activists (members of the Organization for the Mobilization [*Basij*] of the Oppressed), and hizbullah militants, stone the "sinner"—stones must be neither too large to murder immediately nor too small to spare the victim, who must suffer the grave implications of a moral offense. One does not simply do wrong, but becomes "the source of corruption" (*jorsoomeh-ye fesâd*); does not merely defy the state, but "causes corruption on earth" (*efesâd-e fel arz*) and launches a "war against God" (*mohârebeh bâ khodâ*). Punishments, consequently, often involve degradation. People are publicly lashed, hanged, or have hands amputated. These injuries, however, are not violent and torturous in the eyes of Islamic authorities—in Islam, it is held, there is no violent punishment, no torture, only *ta'zir*, chastisement.

Whatever the authorities wish to name it, violent coercion has played a vital role in the construction of the Islamic state (see, e.g., Shahidian 1999), a role so widespread as to have caused much frustration throughout society. Victims of *political violence* include all ages, but *this* ubiquitous terror is also gendered. Female political prisoners, for instance, report of gender-specific forms of violence like rape and knifing breasts. Virgin activists sentenced to death were "married" to their executioner because Islam does not approve of the execution of virgin women. Imprisoned pregnant activists had to give birth in prisons, even raise their newborns in jails. On 22 February 1994, Homa Darabi, a pediatrician dismissed from an academic post for failing to adhere to the Islamic dress code, immolated herself in protest—one of many women who have chosen this solution under the Islamists' rule. At a spring 1998 Majlis session, speaking in support of an act that criminalizes non-shari'ah-based discussions of women's rights, Representative Marzieh Vahid Dastjerdi quoted excerpts from articles by Mehrangiz Kar and Shirin Ebadi (two prominent women attorneys working for women's rights), and issued a stern warning to her colleagues and the two lawyers: "If you [members of the Majlis] do not pass this bill, we will take care of them [women activists] ourselves." Veteran activist Parvaneh Eskandari Forouhar was murdered along with her husband Darioush Forouhar on 21 November 1998; prior to that date, numerous other female activists were likewise executed. Laypersons and intelligentsia alike have voiced concerns regarding brutal constraint, lack of tolerance (Mokhtârî 1998), and the pressures of prohibitions and controls (Keyhânniâ 1998: 15).

State monitoring of appearance has been vital in constructing Islamic gender. This notorious mechanism has been frequently denounced for enforcing the dress code, but the objectives of this policy are indeed broader and focus on constructing gender. Gender *appearance*, not just dress, is regulated; for example, people wearing jeans, sunglasses, men with long hair, and women with improper hejâb are rounded up. Such monitoring not only enforces the dress code but also symbolizes the dominance of the Islamic state. To be sure, hejâblessness (*bihejâbi*) is impossible under the IRI. But *badhejâbi* (inadequate hejâb) and hejâblessness refer to "improper dress," such as not pulling the scarf all the way down to cover the hair, wearing bright colors or (heavy) makeup. (For detail, see, Shirazi-Mahajan 1995.) Hejâb, IRI authorities frequently remind the public, is the *flag* of Muslim womanhood.

Legal ambiguity about "proper hejâb" creates space to negotiate proper behavior, but also makes women vulnerable. What is acceptable one day might be outlawed the next. Indeed, the IRI often utilizes this uncertainty, especially during politico-economic crises. In the spring of 1985, for instance, after a heavy loss of Iranian troops, enforcement of hejâb was so severe that the police, in search of violators, even checked waiting rooms of medical and dental clinics.

Within one week in April of 1987, 165 women in Tehran's fourteenth district were lashed and sentenced to up to 25 months imprisonment (*Zan-e Rouz* 1987). In 1989, the Social Council of the Tehran Province, pursuant to a decision of the Security Council regarding the need for decisive action, announced regulations subjecting bad veilers to 74 lashes and, if the disheveled were a government employee, dismissal from her job (*Zan-e Rouz* 22 April 1989: 4). The existence of "sick women" in the Islamic Republic, according to Marziyeh Dabbâq, a female representative in the Iranian parliament, calls for such tough measures:

In my opinion, we will always have some sick women in our society who should be treated. We should hold classes for them, advise them, and explain the philosophy of hejâb for them. I believe, however, that ten years after the Islamic Revolution, considering all the talks, lectures, and education through the media, we can expect our women to have understood the purpose of hejâb. In the past eight months, during which I have been in charge of women's prisons in the Province of Tehran and have been in constant contact with the prisoners—particularly those who have been arrested for moral reasons—it has become clear to me that some women are fundamentally opposed (*'enâd dârand*) to the Islamic Republic. We have no other choice but to turn them away from their wrong path and direct them to a correct and healthy path . . . by means of coercion and implementing some laws and guidelines. However, I consider these women's fathers and husbands even more at fault for allowing their daughters or wives to appear like this [i.e., mal-veiled and improper] in public. (*Zan-e Rouz* 1989)

Years later, the same complaint was echoed in *Zan-e Rouz* (18 January 1997), a pro-government women's magazine:

Is there a worse insult than a woman with heavy makeup, dyed and made-up hair, chewing gum, walking in public, laughing hysterically with her friend and wearing the châdor at the same time? And as soon as she opens her mouth, she refers to châdor as "that damned thing" or "that horrible thing"—isn't this an offensive and degrading treatment of the châdor?

After President Khatami's election, dress code enforcement has become looser and less systematic—but the regulations do exist and can be enforced at any time security forces decide.

Hizbullah zealots "autonomously" aiding the police are particularly effective at terrorizing the public into compliance. But the hizbullah does indeed enjoy governmental sanction. According to a 1989 report about a Security Council meeting, for instance, the Committees of the Islamic Revolution were instructed to "act expeditiously and resolutely" against bad-veiling and, "utilizing the divine power of the hizbullah, deal with this anti-Islamic phenomenon and those who practice it" (*Etella'at* 12 April 1989).

An exposé in *Zan-e Rouz* about one such incident reports of "anarchy" in a Tehran square. The hizbullah crowd savagely assaulted women for violating the dress code and cut men's long hair and jeans. The Revolutionary Guards took no action against them though the militants failed to obtain permission to "demonstrate." According to the Deputy Director of the Revolutionary Committees, they "neither condoned nor condemned the demonstration" (6).

A hizbullah woman justified their action:

We, the hizbullah ummat, families of martyrs and prisoners of war, relatives of the missing and the militants [of the war], are present here. So far, we have only talked; this is our last talk with *monâfeqin* [hypocrites] and hejâbless women. We all know that not having hejâb in our country does not mean only not wearing the veil: it is a political issue. We demand the Minister of the Interior and other dignified authorities to approach this problem with firmness. Our militant youth fight and we, Zeynab-followers of the time[25] and our children's mothers, are gathered here to deliver our children's message to authorities. We will not allow this behavior to persist in our society. As a member of a martyr's family, I tell you that as long as these actions are not completely weeded out of our society, we will come to the street every day and shout so strongly that we shake the world. We tell authorities to continue with the war with determination until injustice is uprooted in the world. We also say that unless something is done within the next few days, we shall be determined in our response. We shall not allow hejâbless women to appear in public and make a mockery of us. We tell hejâbless women that the problem is not that they do not wear the veil, but that they do not cover themselves properly. This anarchy must come to an end. We will not allow them to look like that in public. In schools, universities, or offices, we will deal with this dross, these U.S. puppets. We'll erase them from the face of the earth. (*Zan-e Rouz* 27 April 1985: 7)

Many among the public, however, rejected the mob's action. They believe that one's dress is a personal choice—hejâb, they say, is something between a woman and her God, not between her and a group of vigilantes (54). Yet public opinion does not concern the hizbullah. They are "Zeynab-followers of the time," determined to accomplish a historical mission. And if the government, albeit an Islamic one, fails to do its duty, they will take matters into their own hands.

Slogans in these rallies—popular ones appearing everywhere in the Islamic Republic—reveal men's role in "managing their women": "A woman's hejâblessness shows her husband's lack of honor." These slogans also confirm the link connecting enforcement of proper gender appearance and private and public violence: "Hejâbless, death to you; have shame of martyrs' blood"; "Boutique-owner, this is your last warning"; "We are followers of the Koran, we don't want any posers."

Interestingly, that report, entitled "Is the Use of Cold Weapons the Only Way to Fight Corruption and Veillessness?" does not question the equation of veillessness with corruption. Nor does it deny the need to launch a war against hejâbless women—it merely criticizes a certain kind of war. The report begins by juxtaposing one "manifestation of ignorance and savagery" to another—the demonstrating mob *and* hejâbless women, youngsters with long hair wearing jeans "who, knowingly or not, are manipulated for the colonialist aspirations of internal and foreign enemies" (6). The commentary emphasizes the state's role in guiding the "pure sentiment of the ever-present people" (i.e., the protesting Islamists) toward the proper ways of "correcting the deviants."

The problem, however, is that as long as there are predefined genders, "proper" and "improper" gender appearance, and sacred and sacrilegious sexualities, the battle persists. The emphasis on "guidance" might afford the Islamic state a gentler face, but does not resolve a crucial problem that necessitates policing gender: those who simply fail or refuse to see the light even after years of kind Islamic advice. What is the Islamic state to do, as a *Zan-e Rouz* reader expresses, with those who "use bad-veiling as an opportunity for following an anarchic lifestyle, opposing the revolution, and devaluing revolutionary values?" Could one envision any alternative to "armed forces and legal authorities intervening in a reasonable manner to protect society from anarchy" (5 May 1990: 52)? The contention that women need a moral guardian, as we have already discussed, is shared among Islamist ideologues. "Men are superior to women," we recall, and as long as women's moral autonomy goes unrecognized, coercion along "the path of righteousness and health" remains inevitable.

RECAPITULATION

In this chapter I have discussed Islamist gender ideology, emphasizing the intertwining of gender teleology and violence in this view. I have argued that a systematic, purposive universe is central to an Islamist analysis of gender. This teleological system assigns men and women distinct but complementary roles. Sex, gender, and sexuality are circularly connected in the Islamist doctrine. Sexed corporeal bodies house spiritual qualities that are acted out through gender roles and transmitted from one generation to the next. Pious parents are essential to the health of society. Procreation creates familial—and consequently social—bonds through the mother's womb. Besides, moral characteristics are transmitted at the time of conception and through childrearing, both physically (via gestation and breast-feeding) and intellectually (via socialization and role modeling). Sexuality, then, contributes to the creation of a harmonious world. Adhering to sexual hygiene is important for both partners not only because it leads to the creation of healthy individuals, but also because it protects society against men's and women's wandering off to the sinful territory of non- or extramarital sex. Modesty in dress, especially women's hejâb, secures society against chaos and individuals against self-incurred harmful thoughts and deeds.

The Islamic state's mission has been to create an ideal Islamic society wherein women and men can accomplish their holy duties. As the family is a microcosm of society, reviving the family is tantamount to revitalizing society. An ideal Islamic world directs women and men to act out their holy duties. The patriarchal triad in the Islamic regime has sanctified men's role as head of household and women's, as wife and mother.

In post-revolutionary Iran, gender identities have found rigid models and the population is policed to emulate these models in private and public. Proper gender appearance—how Muslim men and women ought to look—is important for the IRI because the form and content of an Islamic society must possess an Islamic character. Besides, monitoring gender appearance facilitates policing gender interaction and sexual rapport. Regulations concerning dress and appearance tediously stipulate how men and women should appear and behave. Though these statutes are modified in real life, their existence legitimates a system of control that could be implemented or ignored at the state's discretion. Ideal gender comportment also creates a pyramid that places devout men on top and others underneath. Women have a precarious status in this pyramid: collectively, they receive less power and rights than men, but Islamist women, especially those with political pull, can wield considerable influence in relation to non-Islamist men.

The IRI's sexual politics pushes women to the margin, or to certain "feminine fields." Political and economic exigencies have led Islamists to modify their initial plan of excluding women from the public. Instead, a segregationist-protectivist policy has been implemented whereby women maintain a public presence, but increasingly in female-exclusive spaces. By regulating appearance, movement, and deeds, the state claims to "guard" women both in secluded private spheres and segregated public environs.

The objective of the Islamist project is the creation of an Islamic ummat or community, with the *valy-e faqih*, the supreme religious leader, presiding over it. In the homogenous system of the Islamic ummat, all actions must have the approval of the shari'ah. With or without *valy-e faqih*, an Islamic system is one of guardianship from top to bottom with little tolerance for aberration. This arrangement, I have argued, strips individuals from their rights as citizens both by placing them in a pre-established path and by subjugating them to the unrestrained power of the theologian leader. Reliance on the bayonet has been inevitable in this system, as the history of coercion and violence under the IRI attests.

As expressed in 'Alâ'i Rahmâni's concerns that opened this chapter, the IRI's gender agenda reminds women and men of what they are created to be. The primary objective of this agenda is, then, creating conditions that accommodate their divine roles. But enthusiastic as many Islamists were, still others among both believers and nonbelievers saw in this plan a terrifying regression that only limited women's and men's lives. These people's resistance against Islamic authority has become a source of constant agony.

In the chapters that follow, I will discuss the IRI's efforts to create a society with Islamic gendered roles.

NOTES

1. A popular poster during the revolution portrayed the Shah escaping Iran and Khomeini making his triumphant entrance. The caption read: "As devil leaves, angel enters."

2. Javâdi Âmoli's *Woman in the Mirror of Glory and Beauty* (first published in 1990) is a collection of lectures delivered primarily at the Qom Theology Center (Howzeh-ye ʿElmiyeh). It is among the first attempts, as *Zan-e Rouz* (8 March 1992: 10) characterizes it, to bring women's issues to this center. To honor the holy month of Ramadan, *Zan-e Rouz* reprinted passages from the book in several issues during late-winter early-spring 1992.

3. Reformist interpretations of Islam inject a degree of looseness into this pyramid by recognizing the historicity of humans' understanding of any belief system, including Islam and the Koran. Reformist writings, however, do not question the hierarchical nature of the chain of authority. Besides, though they reject the interpretation of *valy*-as-despot—which they accuse conservatives of promoting—they fail to stipulate the valy's exact rights and responsibilities in their "humanitarian" reading of Islam. For reformist interpretations, see Hajjarian (2000: 194–204, 256–78).

4. In contemporary Islamist discourse, the term *Islamic society (jâmeʿeh-ye islami)* is also used, but this reference does not preclude the exclusivity of this sociopolitical arrangement. *Islamic society* implies that the Islamic revolution of *Iranians* brought Islam to power. Instead of separating the "Muslim community" from the rest, this phrasing turns the entire society into an Islamic community. The idea of Islam's conquest of the world through exporting the revolution clearly expands the border of the Islamic ummat beyond Iran's geography. Islamists repeatedly remind us that Islam recognizes no border, that nationalism is idolatry. The IRI's downplaying of Iranian customs—such as Norouz, the Iranian New Year celebration—aims at replacing Islam for nation. My discussion here, however, refers to the IRI's internal priorities.

5. Recent discussions about an "Islamic civil society" acknowledge diversity within the system, but the Islamic nature of the system—the Islamic Republic—is not questioned. Writings on this issue are abundant. See, for example, Bashiriyeh (1999) and Mohammadi (1997; 1999).

6. The mass execution of political prisoners in September 1988 was conducted on the basis of a simple question: "Do you pray?" Anyone who answered negatively was immediately executed.

7. Bahaiis cannot declare allegiance to their religion. They can neither live nor die as Bahaiis. For several years, Bahaiis in Tehran were buried in a cemetery called Laʿnatâbad, "the damnation place," in a lot close to the one that houses the executed dissidents of the IRI—both groups were buried in unmarked graves. In recent years, however, Bahaiis have been allowed to reconstruct their cemetery, where their deceased or executed loved ones were buried anonymously. Now, they have put

stones on the graves in a proper way with engraved names and birth and death dates. They are also allowed to bury newly deceased individuals in this cemetery in the southeast of Tehran under some conditions. Numerous accounts of the IRI's treatment of Bahaiis are made available by human rights organizations. For an eyewitness narrative on being a Bahaii in the Islamic Republic, see Roohizadegan (1993).

8. One can consider, for instance, Hojjatulislam Fallahiân, the former Minister of Intelligence, whose involvement in drugs and sex was revealed by the reporter Akbar Ganji. Hojjatulislam Fallahiân frequented the Za'farâniyeh Sauna, where he shared the favor of a 19-year-old woman with Said Emami, a high-level intelligence officer. Hojjatulislam also had a three-year affair with a stewardess who assisted him in a drug operation. The woman was killed, purportedly by Fallahiân's gang. He was a "hardliner," and a "reformist" journalist's exposure of his conduct tarnishes not only his reputation, but also his allies'. (Said Emami later married the woman. He was also implicated as a key figure behind the murder of several political activists and authors in 1998 and died a mysterious death in prison [reported as suicide].)

9. See, for example, the approving report of such surgery upon a person "who entered the hospital with the châdor and scarf and left it in pants and jacket" in *Zan-e Rouz* (19 January 1991: 18).

10. Like other gender-related events in the Islamic Republic, the reaction to the movie *Snowman* is indeed as much gendered as political. The movie gave the hizbullah a timely excuse to show their disapproval of President Khatami's policies. Other films with similar transgression of gender boundaries, but released at inopportune dates, evoked no fury. *Daughters of the Sun* is about a girl who cannot find a job—so she pretends to be a boy and finds work in a nearby village. The poster of the film shows a young woman with a well-shaved head. Similarly, in Mohsen Makhmalbaf's *The Peddler*, a man had to play the role of an old woman, so that the white hair of the old protagonist would be shown without offending public sentiment.

11. Other treatises about mother's milk are more scientific, but they all concur on the production of milk as "a secret of creation" and thus, implicitly or explicitly, equate nursing with a divine feminine task. See "Mother's Milk and Its Role in the Newborn's Development" (*Shâhed-e Bânovân* 6 December 1987: 49).

12. Bojnourdi emphasizes that only proper courts can chastise a woman. For more detail, see the section on violence below.

13. See reports in the daily *Kayhan* during the second half of December 1990.

14. The report offers no information about the objectives and methodology of the study—an omission that limits the usefulness of the research. Yet, considering that this report was presented in an official meeting, hosted by the representative of the *valy-e faqih* (the supreme religious leader, Khamenehii), one can safely assume that it enjoys the authorities' acceptance, if not their endorsement.

15. This is based on Ahmad Sâdeqi Ardestâni's discussion in *Zan-e Rouz* (26 October 1991: 10).

16. Muslim opponents of the Shah asked Khomeini (who was exiled in Iraq at the time) if they could use cyanide capsules to avoid the possibility of divulging secrets. Khomeini's answer was an unequivocal no. Unlike leftist militants, Mojahed and other Islamists never resorted to cyanide (see Davâni 1981: 238).

17. Massoud Ma'sumi (1998) has compiled the fetwas of Ayatollahs Rouhullah Khomeini, Mohammad Taqi Behjat, Javâd Tabrizi, Mohammad Fâzel Lankarâni, and Nâser Makârem Shirâzi on marital relationships. He consulted the writings of these religious leaders, especially each Ayatollah's *Towzihul Masâ'el* (The Explanations for Problems), or asked for their fetwas (*esteftâ*).

18. *Harâm* acts are punishable by Allah. *Makruh* acts, however, are only disapproved of by religious laws; they do not invoke any punishment.

19. Haddâd 'Âdel is an architect of the IRI, a leading figure during the "Cultural Revolution" and the Islamization of the educational system. Soroush Press, publishing house of The Voice and Vision of the Islamic Republic of Iran (the IRI's radio and television organization), first published his treatise in the summer of 1980. It has gone through numerous reprints since, with portions of it reprinted in high school Farsi textbooks.

20. For other examples, see *Zanân* no. 67, September 2000: 4–7.

21. For discussions on this issue, see newspapers for summer and fall of 2000, and *Zanân* no. 67, September 2000: 4–7. A reader's letter to *Iran-e Javân* (no. 161: 44) expresses the dismay of older female students by asking: "What is our share of the edict concerning colors?"

22. The philosophy of naming children, discussed earlier, comes true here: Mahdiyeh, the feminine of Mahdi, the twelfth Shiite imam, means one who has been guided; Bahâreh is a Persian name, simply meaning Spring.

23. Eventually, instead of "the instrumental use of women," the bill reads "the instrumental use of women *and men.*"

24. According to several hadiths, the revelation of this verse is related to an incident involving the daughter of an influential Arab leader and her husband. She refused to sleep with her husband and he reacted with physical abuse. She and her father took their complaint to the Prophet. Mohammad initially told her that she could retaliate. As soon as father and daughter left, however, verse 34 of the sura *"Women"* was revealed to Mohammad:

Men have authority over women because Allah has made the one superior to the other, and because they spend their wealth to maintain them. Good women are obedient. They guard their unseen parts because Allah has guarded them. As for those from whom you fear disobedience, admonish them and send them to beds apart and beat them. Then if they obey you, take no further action against them. (Koran 1988: 370)

Mohammed summoned the woman and her father back and told them that God had spoken and His words superseded Mohammad's. Beating became the husband's prerogative and the punished woman's right to retaliate (*qesâs*) was revoked. For a collection of hadiths regarding this verse, see Hosseini Tehrani (1997: especially 51–59).

25. Zeynab was the sister of Imam Hossein, the third Shiite imam. Shiite ideologues hold that after Hossein's martyrdom, Zeynab continued his mission by spreading his "message." The reference to Zeynab here echoes a popular analogy in the IRI that accords Iranian Muslim women the responsibility of protecting the message and mission of martyrs of the Islamic revolution.

7

From Mothers' Bosoms:
Patriarchy Vacillating between
Private and Public

Mr. Ali Akbar Hosseini: In employment, men have priority because God has made them women's *nowkar*, a servant to go to work and humbly offer her his legally earned money.

Mr. 'Abbâs 'Abbâsi: The man is not a servant; he is *qa'em*, the one with authority.

Ms. Emami: It was women who raised you *bozorgvaran*, as honorable great men.

The above exchange among three Majlis representatives demonstrates several characteristics of the IRI's discourses on women (quoted in *Zanân* March-April 1997: 19). The flattering language immediately strikes the reader: men are women's servants; they are honored to serve women as their economic providers. And the queen of the house, in turn, raises good children for society. At the same time, the reader cannot help but notice that underneath this flattering exchange, this wooing of women, lurks the gender politics of the Islamic Republic. As heads of households, men have primacy in employment. The shroud of flattering deception is pulled aside, not only in the specification of roles that precedes the flattery, but also in the instantaneous rejection of a fleeting cloudiness of who is in charge. "The man is not a servant," *he is the boss,* 'Abbâsi answers Hosseini unequivocally. One then hears Ms. Emâmi's voice. Precious as it is to hear a woman present in an Islamic political body, Ms. Emâmi adds nothing new. At the end of her comment, the traditional sexual division of labor

remains intact, though "the mother" is revered—again. Yet her mere presence and her contradicting Mr. 'Abbasi indicates a tension. Something must
be said to refute that Islam belittles women by making men their *boss*. She
resorts to her heavy arsenal: "It was women who raised you *bozorgvâran*,
as honorable great men." In other words, do not be so conceited, you are
a product of your mother's bosom.

The elements of this exchange are present in most Islamist treatments of
gender relations. The laudatory language, sincere as it may be in the mind
of its orator, works like a rabbit pulled from a hat in a magic show—
dazzling the public so that the trickery of the hand goes unnoticed. The
essential woman-as-mother persistently survives every attempt to subvert
conventional labor division—hence, the contradictions that women in the
Islamic state experience between their goals and the means to accomplish
them. This is patriarchy vacillating betwixt private and public; women can
no longer be confined to the private, but their presence in social life cannot
be tolerated either. As an opinion piece in the daily *Ettela'at* reads (26
December 1992):

Women's perfection is in motherhood; women were created to mother. Only then
that heaven will be under their feet, and from their embrace men will ascend to
divinity. Do we want to harm women? We want women as mothers. We want them
to emulate Fatima, who symbolizes every role expected of a woman, but whose
most amazing role is motherhood and whose most meaningful title is "the mother
of her father." Is this the Stone Age mentality? We want perfection for women,
and their perfection is in being mothers. We want women to be "exemplary mothers," not exemplary workers, not exemplary employees. Do not say these are not
contradictory, for if you really consider this issue without prejudice, you will concur
that they are.

Contrary to the assertion of the author, mothering, once a role that justified women's exclusion from public life, now bridges the private to the
public: "The prosperity and happiness of a child begins from the mother's
bosom and the prosperity of the nation comes from its good children. One
good child may bring prosperity to a nation. One good individual may save
a nation, just as one bad person may destroy a whole country" (Khomeini
1982: 70).

Mothering is the quintessential feminine role, even if she shoulders many
additional ones. Whoever she opts to be, she is first and foremost a woman-
mother. The sexual division of labor, a reflection of the grand design of
Allah's universe, cannot be subverted. Thus whoever she becomes, she
remains a woman-wife, a legal, social, and economic obligation for her
husband. That is why even when women work and are economically independent, they are subsumed under men; their contribution does not qualify them as heads of households.

In chapter 6 I argued that Islamic gender is teleological. Men and women do not determine who they are, but are assigned roles by divinity. Thus, gender politics owns two constitutive characteristics. First, men and women lose the individuality essential for citizenry. Second, coercion is ubiquitous. Gender coercion and violence, I argued, are as integral to the IRI gender policies as is devotion to Allah.

In this chapter I contend that the Islamist project has aimed to send women back to the home, but that women's resistance has made this intended revival of private patriarchy impossible. As a result, patriarchy has wavered between its private and public forms. I discern this conflict in the laws that posit in men the position of household heads, as well as in the tensional process of women's education, employment, and political participation.

PATRIARCHY BETWEEN PRIVATE AND PUBLIC

In chapter 1, I discussed Sylvia Walby's distinction between private and public patriarchy. Walby (1994) examines alterations in six patriarchal institutions in the West (the paid labor force, domestic labor, the state, sexuality, culture, and male violence). Walby detects a structural shift from private to public patriarchal relations in recent centuries. In both arrangements, sexual domination takes place in private *and* public spheres, but the primary agencies of sexual dominance and the dynamics of domination differ in the two forms. In private patriarchy, control over women is predominantly located within the family: specific men control and appropriate women's labor, sexuality, and access to culture. In public patriarchy, women engage in such roles as laborers, employees, and students, shifting the center of men's control over women to social institutions. Instead of being excluded from the labor force, politics, or culture, women are segregated within these. They are hired in certain fields with limited opportunity for upward mobility. Rather than being barred from politics and culture, they are subordinated in these areas, and subjected to double standards and objectification. Despite the officials' now-covert now-overt hesitance to eliminate violence against women, that outrage is recognized and resisted by women individually and collectively. Walby emphasizes the adaptability of patriarchy and argues that what patriarchy loses in battles over one institution, it can compensate for in others.

Earlier, I argued that in the two decades prior to the revolution, patriarchal relations underwent a transformation from private to public. Albeit limited, women's roles in the economy, culture, and politics increased. Their lives were no longer confined to the private sphere. Men's power within the family was curbed, especially in the realm of divorce and polygyny. New opportunities for interaction between the sexes inspired new sexualities, particularly among the middle- and upper-class urban youth. Slow moves toward secularization of sex have created channels for new expressions of sexuality. Though these emerging trends were not often openly verbalized, popular arts functioned as surrogate modes of expression, offering safe, impersonal spaces to express personal affections and desires. Revision in sexual beliefs and practices engenders a crisis in the implicit traditional bargain whereby "good women" who comply with the social codes of chastity earn men's respect and protection. This crisis, combined with existing sexual violence, exposed women to increased harm in domestic and social spheres.

Upon assuming power, the IRI sought to revive private patriarchy by reinforcing men's dominance within the family, reinstating male prerogatives that were compromised under the Pahlavis, and defining women primarily in their private roles of wife and mother. In the prior chapter, I discussed the Islamic regime's narrow definition of sex and gender as preordained, fixed identities that through complementarity create harmony. These sexed and gendered bodies engage in procreative heterosexual relations in the marital bed. Central to the implementation of Islamists' gender and sex ideals is coercion, and in particular violence against women.

The objective of the IRI's policies was to locate women predominantly within the private sphere, but a complete return to the past proved impossible. However limited women's participation in public life, their social role in pre-revolutionary Iran has made it impossible to send them back into the home. Remember that Khomeini's uproar about women's franchise in the 1960s was replaced by soliciting women's participation in the revolution. Islamists in post-revolutionary Iran had to similarly concede to changes that had taken root in Iran. Though more or less successful in passing legislation injurious to women, Islamists have been forced to accept women's public presence, as long as it was limited and not harmful to their familial duties. Instead of a complete return to private patriarchy, the locus of women's oppression has fluctuated under the IRI between private and public patriarchy or, more accurately, has been strengthened in both private and public.

BRINGING MEN (BACK) TO THE CENTER

Steps to restore the "natural" familial order wherein the husband exercised sovereignty and the wife-mother enjoyed the "right" to be provided for were taken immediately after the revolution. The Constitution acknowledges the man as "head" of the family. In return for his wife's submission, he is responsible for her expenses (*nafaqeh*). "At every morning," writes Khomeini, "the woman is entitled to the *nafaqeh* of that day from her husband's wealth (*mal*), but only to the amount she needs that day" (quoted in Ma'sumi 1998: 37). She can plan her budget and save some money, but she cannot ask for more than what she needs that day. She must reside in the house of his choice unless the husband grants her the right to choose their dwelling, or extenuating circumstances exist such that living together poses a potential threat to the wife's well-being.

With the repeal of the Passport Act of 1972, a woman must have her husband's written permission to travel abroad. Absent that, she must request the public prosecutor to grant permission. Until the summer of 2000, single women were not eligible to go abroad for education through governmentally approved channels that entitled them to a lower exchange rate; married women can do so *only if accompanied by their husbands* (Jalali Naeini 1995a). Traveling inside the country, a woman unaccompanied by her man must obtain the authorization of local officials to stay in a hotel. Those authorities have then the right to control her movements (Kar 1999a: 60). An administrator in the Passport Office told *Zan*'s reporter that often in times of family quarrel, the man notifies authorities that his wife is *mamnu'-ul-khoruj*, forbidden to leave the country. When a woman obtains permanent permission to travel, her passport is stamped and she can leave the country numerous times without being required to present her credentials on every occasion. Even then, however, if the couple develops disagreements, the husband can rescind his permission. "Every day several women inquire at our Office if they are forbidden to leave the country" (*Zan* 28 December 1998).

Since a woman must live under her husband's roof, she has to tag along with him when his station changes. Government offices are obligated to accept her transfer, regardless of needs. In other words, women's independence is denied and the needs of the labor force are overlooked. This has created quite a problem, especially in the teaching profession where women workers are mostly concentrated. Shortly after the start of the 1999–2000 academic year, several newspapers reported a surplus of teachers in Tehran and some other major cities (see, for instance, *Khordâd* and *Sobh-e Emrouz* 13 October 1999). According to *Khordâd*, Tehran received some 10,000 female teachers in excess of its need.

According to Article 1117 of the Civil Code, though a man cannot bar his wife from employment, he can prevent her from working if the "nature" of her profession is injurious to family honor. Maryam Khaz'ali, Head of the Women's Cultural and Social Council of the High Council of the Cultural Revolution, comments on this issue in a seminar on women's rights and the family. If a female security guard must work 24 hours consecutively, her husband has the right to order her to quit because "her job conflicts with her family and family dignity. A woman must not be away from the house for 24 hours" (*Zan-e Rouz* 1 January 1994: 47). Provided both parties agree, a woman *can* stipulate in the marriage contract her right to work. If he reneges, her only recourse is to seek a divorce. Besides, according to Article 1119, if the man reneges after marriage, her only recourse, upon proving his fault in court, is to seek a divorce. This condition

creates obvious obstacles, as demonstrated in the actual case below reported by an observer in Iran:

A woman was employed before marriage and a few years after she married. Unfortunately, she failed to stipulate the employment condition in her marriage contract. . . . Recently, her husband expressed opposition to her job, arguing that,
according to Article 1117, her working in a boys' school, where the principal and
vice-principal are male, conflicts with the well-being of the family and his and his
wife's honor. The woman agreed to transfer to a girls' school. He did not even
agree to that and forced his wife to resign. The woman took him to court. But the
court decided in his favor, reiterating that a woman's employment is contingent
upon her husband's approval, especially since in this case she did not include the
employment condition in the marriage contract. (Qâsemzâdeh 1996: 52)

Sons inherit twice as much as daughters.[1] A man inherits all his wife's
wealth, but she is entitled only to one-fourth (if he has no child) or one-
eighth (if he has children) of his moveable property and of the value of his
estate (Center for Women's Participation 1999: 30–31). This is only in
cases of permanent marriage; partners in a temporary marriage receive no
inheritance. In polygynous marriages, wives must divide among themselves
the allotted inheritance, which, according to Article 942 of the Civil Code,
can never exceed their designated fourth or eighth.

A bill which would have allowed women the same inheritance rights as
men was rejected by a large majority in the Majlis in 1998, on the ground
that it was contrary to Islamic law. The discrepancy in inheritance is justified because men are responsible for the economic provision of their families. According to Ayatollah Mohammad Khamenehii, Islam considers
"natural and social realities" in this regard (*Zan-e Rouz* 19 February 1994:
12): "When a man inherits from his father, he is told, 'this inheritance is
for you, your wife, and your children.' But when a daughter receives her
inheritance, she is not told, 'this is for you, your husband, and your children'—she is told, 'this is yours' " (56).

Since men assume the position as head of the family, their religious and
national identities govern their wives' status. A *Muslim* woman cannot
marry a non-Muslim. Even an Iranian woman's marriage to a Muslim of
foreign nationality is forbidden, save with the permission of the IRI's Ministry of the Interior (see Mehri 1998). The reason is obvious: upon matri-
mony, she gains his nationality. A man, however, can marry a non-Iranian
woman and only under special circumstances does he need official permission (e.g., as when he is a government employee working abroad). Based
on a recent decision, a Muslim man can marry a Jew or a Christian woman
or any followers of the holy book (*ahl-e ketâb*) on a temporary basis. So,
young Muslim men studying abroad can have relationships with European
or U.S. women without fearing any legal repercussions (*Iran* 27 August

2000). Offspring of a marriage between an Iranian and non-Iranian are treated on the basis of the laws of the father's homeland. Children of Iranian men and non-Iranian women automatically gain Iranian citizenship. Even if the marriage is not registered with the Iranian authority, the father's admission that the child belongs to him is sufficient ground for the child's citizenship. But the child of an Iranian woman married to a non-Iranian will be considered Iranian *only if* the marriage has the permission of, and is registered by, the Iranian authorities; the child is born in Iran; and the child spends one full year in Iran after reaching 18 years of age. This male bias of citizenship rights has caused numerous problems. Iranian men have been afforded "legal" license to abduct their children from marriage to non-Iranians (see, e.g., Amin 1998). Similarly, the citizenship rights of Iranian women married to non-Iranians, and the rights of their children, are jeopardized. (Case in point: Iranian women married to Afghan refugees. See Kar 1997: ch. 2, especially 101–5.)

Since men assume the position as head of the family, their absence makes the family *bisarparast*, guardianless. According to a recent report, there are some three million female-headed households in Iran. Of these women, 80% are illiterate, and 40% are over 61 years old (*Bahâr* 30 July 2000). A *bisarparast* family is one that has lost a father or husband, thus including only divorced or widowed women. Official statistics, in other words, do not include those whose husbands emigrate in search of employment, women who have never married, or married women whose husbands are unable or unwilling to work. According to a 1992 bill, the government must support *bisarparast* families with limited means of livelihood. "Though useful, government aid is minimal. Only a small fraction of these women actually receive financial support and there is limited attempt to empower the family" (UNICEF 1998: 58).

Changes in the Iranian legal system under the IRI, particularly the abolition of the pre-revolutionary Family Protection Law (FPL), have predominantly focused on regaining men's threatened prerogatives in marriage, divorce, and family relations. The clergy particularly objected to the FPL revisions effected in 1975, arguing that these limited men's rights in divorce and caused an increase in the divorce rate. Law professor Hossein Safâ'i sums up Islamists' concern about the FPL in the Seminar on Women's Rights and the Family, held in December 1993 at the University of Tehran: "The objective of the second FPL was to equalize women's and men's rights in divorce. That law protected women but, as some experts observe, did not protect the family. It was more a 'Women's Protection Law' than a 'Family Protection Law' " (*Zan-e Rouz* 18 December 1993: 17).

"Moral obligations" are substituted for legal protection; more accurately, legal protection is denied by invoking moral responsibilities that are eventually at men's discretion. According to the Law, marriage to a second wife without the permission of the court, or failure to record marriage or divorce, were punishable by imprisonment of six to twelve months. This law has not been explicitly repudiated, but has remained inactive. The Majlis representative Gohar-al-shary'eh Dastqeyb explains in a roundtable discussion at *Zan-e Rouz* that the law is not implemented because the punishment is not Islamic (Zan-e Rouz 1985: 10). The Koran, she holds, explicitly sets men's obligation to do justice as the precondition for having more than one wife. How can polygyny promote justice in contemporary Iran? By "marrying, say, the wife of a martyr who is left with several children who have no guardian and be a guardian for her children" (10).

Things are, of course, quite different in practice, Dastqeyb adds. The second wife is usually young and "easily tractable," or she owns considerable wealth. Both women (or all women, if he is married to more than two) are vulnerable before him; what he does might be immoral, but is not illegal. Though theoretically possible to imprison a man for discriminating among his wives, it is in practice all but impossible to prove him unfair to them. Sister Keyhâni, another participant in the roundtable discussion, interjects: "This is the naked truth of our society. And there is no punishment, no law regarding this matter at the present. What can one do? Where should one take this pain?" (11)

Islamic law does stipulate that polygynous marriages are permitted only when the man is certain of his ability to treat all his wives equally. Yet the IRI "Civil Code has designated the husband himself as the sole judge of whether he can be equally fair to two or more wives" (Pakzad 1994: 175). A woman has of course the right to object and the court might uphold her protest, but *only if she can prove him incapable of caring of two families.*

But even according to many Islamists, treating all wives fairly is difficult, if not impossible. The editor of *Zan-e Rouz* (1 January 1994: 3), for instance, criticizes lawmakers for not "designating a qualified source" to determine the fairness of men with multiple wives. "We dare say that in our society today, the fairest man is he who spends his entire life with one woman and shares with that woman his sadness and happiness."

Article 1133 of the Civil Code grants men unilateral rights to divorce: "The husband may divorce his wife whenever he wishes to do so." Under Article 1130, women may seek divorce under the conditions of 'usr va harj, that is, if living with the husband is absolutely unbearable. As Kar (1999b: 343) observes, proving 'usr va harj is extremely difficult. Men can use various ways to create doubt for the court and prolong the procedure. In most cases, the woman eventually foregoes her husband's economic obligations toward her just to buy his approval for a divorce.

In 1986 and 1992, the Majlis passed laws to amend the termination privileges accorded men (Center for Women's Participation 1999: 58–60). The amendment, however, merely changes divorce procedure without limiting men's unilateral rights. Men need not even cite a reason. If both parties agree to divorce, they may go to the notary public. If the wife objects, however, the husband must take his case to the Special Civil Tribunal. The Tribunal will attempt to reconcile the couple. Should this process fail, the Tribunal issues permission to terminate the marriage. The husband is under no obligation to follow any recommendation by either the court or involved individuals.

Upon divorce, he has to pay her *mahr* (a bridal gift stipulated in the marriage contract), her *nafaqeh* for three months and 10 days (that is, provided that she has not agreed to forego these rights to obtain a divorce). A woman may also ask to be remunerated for tasks done in her marital household *if* these were not part of her wifely duties but were undertaken at the husband's "order" (*dastur*). Proving that the claimed activities were indeed at his *dastur* falls on her shoulders. This requirement, and lack of procedure determining her labor value, make observers skeptical about women's benefits under law (see Safâ'i quoted in *Zan-e Rouz* 18 December 1993: 19). A stipulation may be made in the marriage contract to the effect that should a man divorce a woman without establishing her guilt, the court can require that he share with her up to half the wealth acquired after marriage.

Considering men's free hand in divorce, their ability to marry up to four wives, the meager divorce settlement or inheritance women receive, and in the absence of any welfare program, a housewife has no financial security in her marriage or in the absence of her husband due to divorce or death. What the IRI has offered to "protect" women amounts to the revisions in the divorce law and a stipulation that the monetary value of the *mahr* must be determined by the economic standards at the time of the divorce, not the time the marriage contract was made (Center for Women's Participation 1999: 47).

According to the Civil Code, the mother shall have custody (*hezânat*) of her son until he reaches the age of two, and of her daughter until the girl turns seven—unless, of course, she forfeits custody prior to these dates due to remarriage or insanity. From the child's birth, the father has legal guardianship and obtains custody when the mother's term expires. In the absence of the father, the paternal grandfather receives guardianship. Guardians can bequeath their guardianship, even when the mother is still alive.

Laws pertaining to marital relationships and obligations grant men a free and upper hand in many aspects of family life, including divorce and polygyny. Such patriarchal prerogatives, as discussed in chapter 6, provide a legal context for violence against women, violence that admonition alone cannot obliterate. Besides, one cannot overlook the connection between women's vulnerability under the law and the absence of women from many legal positions, including judgeships and offices of general (district) attorneys.

At the same time, however, women have persistently objected to legal discriminations since the establishment of the Islamic Republic. Virtually all magazines address laws pertaining to women's lives in family and society, not to mention women's magazines such as *Zan-e Rouz*, *Zanân*, and most recently *Hoquq-e Zanân* (women's rights) (see Ardalân 1999). Roshangaran and Women's Studies Publishing have released a series of booklets containing information about women's rights in a language accessible to the general readership. Women's battles have on numerous occasions forced IRI officials to justify their laws in conciliatory language, or even modify some statutes. Tenacious objection to women's absence in the IRI's judicial system finally created a narrow opportunity for women. A 1992 law allowed women to sit as assistant judges in courts hearing divorce cases. A limited number of women now work as prosecutors and as investigative judges who prepare cases for judgment in court, but are barred from issuing judgments (Kar 1998). In 1997, a woman was appointed judge for the first time after the establishment of the Islamic Republic. Yet overall, women's gains pale in comparison to their losses. The impacts of legal discrimination on women's laws are not limited to actual privileges and immunities enjoyed by men. Men's legal advantage also offers legitimacy to many sexist practices and beliefs, augmenting the difficulties women must overcome to enjoy a free and equal status.

PRIVATE WOMEN IN PUBLIC

Though women's domesticity has always been revered in Iran, under the IRI it has been accentuated and ruled sacrosanct. Government officials emphasize the primacy of mothering and wifehood as women's central responsibilities. Ayatollah Khomeini placed mothering above all other female duties. According to Hashemi Rafsanjani, "one of women's important tasks is housekeeping (*khânehdari*) and rearing children. Men cannot do that. It is something that creation has ascribed to women" (*Zan-e Rouz* 18 December 1993: 12). Islamist magazines warn readers that crises befall families that inadequately supervise their children. Working mothers particularly might fall short in this regard.

We recall that rights are determined by the role Allah has considered for us. Women's social rights then depend on their fundamental family roles, particularly mothering (Tabatabaie 1995–1996). "For women," said the then-President Khamenehii, "the primary issue is not being shoulder-to-shoulder with men in the house, streets, and various centers. It is rather that the capabilities endowed in the structure of her existence (*sakhtemân-e vojudi*) are not properly utilized" (*Zan-e Rouz* 4 February 1989: 4). Understanding the commitment of IRI officials to locate women primarily within the family is pivotal to analysis of gender relations in post-revolutionary Iran. Failure to understand thus would result in apologies that take hollow statements for "progressive" policies to women's issues. Nesta Ramazani exemplifies such an approach. She argues that the "pro-

gressive" approach of the Islamic state is slowed by the opposition of reactionaries. Quoting President Rafsanjani that "we are in need of a
women's labor force," and the Ayatollah Yazdi that "women enjoy the
same rights as men," Ramazani concludes that the government "faces
deeply entrenched norms and attitudes" in incorporating women into the
work force "in large numbers" (1993: 413).

Undoubtedly, "entrenched norms and attitudes" significantly limit
women's lives. But the formidable gender ideology of the Islamic state is
no less culpable in perpetuating practices and sermons antithetical to
women's rights. Ramazani's evaluation distorts the reality of the IRI's gender politics.

That is to say, woman's domesticity is central to her life in the Islamic
Republic. A woman's roles correspond with those of Fatima, the principal
feminine role model among Shiites. In a Seminar on Women's Rights and
the Family (*Zan-e Rouz* 25 December 1993: 17), Khaz'ali points out that
Fatima's highest honor came in receiving, in infancy, the title "Umm-a
Abihâ," the mother of her father. In adulthood, Fatima "presents to us the
highest form of family life" that "contains all the secrets of creation and
the events and issues yet to come." (These secrets, however, are not revealed
in Khaz'ali's interpretation.) Fatima's familial accomplishment, Khaz'ali
emphasizes, does not preclude her political capacity after the passing of the
Prophet. In defending her husband Ali, Fatima guards Islam. The common
thread of all Fatima's roles, according to Khaz'ali, is patience; "this overshadows all her other perfect traits."

The opacity of domesticity in the symbolic portrayal of a leading woman
of Shiite history becomes quite transparent in reference to other revered
women who do not enjoy the high stature of Fatima. Mrs. Sefâti, an instructor at a women's seminary school, introduces religious scholar Mrs.
Amin[2] as an exemplary woman who has it all:

God knows that when a woman is able to discern her duty, she becomes the best
housewife. She rears her children and makes the best food for her man. I offer you
the example of Mrs. Amin. You all know about the philosophical and scientific
dimensions of Mrs. Amin's work. But have you heard anything about her housekeeping skills? I heard from one close to her that she made the most delicious dishes,
the tastiest pastries. Though possessed of several servants, she managed her house
herself and also authored a treatise on the Koran. And though even more knowledgeable than her husband, she remained very humble before him. (*Zan-e Rouz* 18
December 1993: 10)

Being a housewife requires myriad tasks in and outside the home. From
cleaning and cooking to the cumbersome task of shopping in the face of
growing economic hardship; from child-care to transport to schools, supervising homework, and attending parent-teacher conferences; from main-

taining social contacts to arranging soirees—in her absence, life moves sluggishly, if at all. Much lip service is paid wives in the Islamic state, but even when their burdens are highlighted, domesticity is never questioned. "Housewives are competent managers to whom is owed the continuance of life. They see their rewards in the contented smiles of their husbands" (*Sobh-e Khânevâdeh* 13 December 1998: 1). Conferences and seminars pay homage to wives' contributions to "development"—and ignore practical implications for women's lives.

The burden of domestic responsibility sharpens for workingwomen. In the mid-1980s, of the total employed women, 62% were between 15 and 35 years old. 60% of this group was married, thus working both inside and outside the house (Kar 1994: 142). In the autumn of 1996, the Ministry of Culture and Islamic Guidance organized a conference on the Role of Housewives in Development. Addressing the conference on behalf of the Minister, Ms. Bayât stated that according to a survey of 200 married female nurses in Tehran, housework claims between 91 to 297 hours of their time every month. These women, she said, spend on average 178 monthly hours doing housework, in addition to their 140-hour workload (*Zan-e Rouz* 27 October 1996: 13).

Another study of 168 teachers—117 males and 51 females—in several cities including Tehran, Karaj, Isfahan, Âstârâ, Ahvâz, Boushehr, and Shushtar paints an even bleaker picture (Shâmbayâti 1993b). Giti Shambayati takes into consideration that most employees have to work more than one job. She measures the average working hours of male and female teachers at primary, high school, and university levels during a regular six-day workweek. In all cases, men have longer weekly working hours: 54.6 hours at the primary school level (compared to 32.8 for women); 48.9 at the high school level (compared to 39.1); and 44.7 at the university level (compared to 33.2). But, she goes on, if we consider that women workers have to spend on the average 4 hours a day on household chores, they end up working longer hours than men during the week: 57 hours at the primary school level; 63 at the high school level; and 57 at the university level. Based on the average salary of her sample, Shâmbayâti demonstrates a marked devaluation of women's labor. Male primary school teachers earn 1,506 rials per hour, while their female colleagues earn but 721 rials. The hourly earnings for male and female high school teachers are 2,217 and 1,375, respectively. These figures for university professors show a similar discrepancy—whereas male professors earn 3,956 rials per hour, female professors earn 2,042 rials.

The primacy of women's domestic role has effects that transcend the disparity in incomes. The cultural implications of this vision are even more damaging:

A man's employment gives him pride in the family, it offers him an opportunity to claim his ownership, to rectify any overlooking of his role as breadwinner or lessening of his purchasing power, to remind his family about his role as the head of the household. But a woman's employment in our society creates an artificial feeling of not paying adequate attention to the responsibilities of a wife and mother. It is considered inappropriate for an employed woman to talk about her earning, even if she spends all her money on her family. Our society does not even accept her talking in public about her job success, or what happens to her at work—that is considered a humiliation for her husband. (Shâmbayâti 1993b: 93)

Some reports about working-class women indicate that in recent years, these women have expressed the middle-class value of not working as a status symbol (see Shâhmorâdi and Moossavi 1999).

To Islamists, women's private role does not contradict their public presence. If anything, Islamist ideologues are more concerned about the harms that women's participation in public life might have on their private responsibilities. Fereshteh Baqâ'i Nâ'ini, Dean of the School of Dentistry at Shahid Beheshti University, expresses a common concern: "If women's societal participation is to be at the cost of family disputes or its dismantling, it would be worthless" (*Zan-e Rouz* 19 January 1997).

This concern is frequently voiced in discussions about family life, and particularly about working mothers. In a roundtable discussion about social problems facing women sponsored by *Zan-e Rouz*, for instance, one participant identified as Sister Razmkhâh reminds others that the Koran refers to the "main topic of parenting" immediately after pointing out that men and women are to console each other. Today, to Razmkhâh's chagrin, men and women discuss marriage without addressing parenthood. "He doesn't say I'll be this kind of a father; what kind of a mother would you be?" (*Zan-e Rouz* 1985: 53) We ought to convince our youth, she contends, that they must be good mates for each other, but that they must also be good parents. "It is not correct to teach our daughters only about being good wives, we must also teach them to be good mothers" (53). Another participant adds how Khomeini emphasized the mothering role. Imam said that, she reminisces, "a teacher's role is important, but a mother's role is even more important" (55).

Serious injuries befall families that do not provide adequate supervision for children. Working mothers could fall short in this regard, as delineated in the story of a 17-year-old girl in *Râh-e Zendegi* (6 December 1998: 10–11), relayed in the previous chapter. Due to parental neglect, she is led to the "forbidden realm" of homosexual intimacy with a classmate. Preoccupied with her business, the mother is of no help, and had it not been for the guidance of another schoolmate, the young lady might have "eternally sunk into the abyss of bad friends" (11).

The vacillation of patriarchy between private and public is evident in this portrayal of a young woman as a private being in public life. This duality corresponds with the coexistence of exclusionist and segregationist tendencies in the IRI. Women are pulled between private and public roles—private roles, to the contentment of exclusionists desiring a complete return of power to men; public roles, as segregationists are compelled to accommodate educated and skilled women. In both cases, women's "natural function" within the family is safeguarded.

EDUCATION FOR A SEGREGATED SOCIETY

The success of the IRI's segregationist-protectivist policy is contingent upon the availability of female personnel to provide services to women. The educational policies of the Islamic government have been shaped to address the needs of such a social arrangement. These policies reflect two fundamental Islamic assumptions about women, namely, the natural differences of the two sexes and women's primary role and responsibility as wives and mothers. In 1982, for instance, the Ministry of Education introduced the *Kâd* Plan (*Kâr va Dânesh*—Work and Knowledge) as a step toward national self-sufficiency. According to the *Kâd* Plan, students were to be sent to various technical centers one day a week to receive hands-on training. But, as Mr. Saʿâdat, the then–vice president of the *Kâd* Plan explains, since women's activity in society requires careful consideration of its moral implications, girl students' training was restricted to their high schools (*Zan-e Rouz* 16 March 1984: 15) and limited to such fields as hygiene, first aid, sewing, cooking, and knitting. Hooshang Zamâni, Executive Director of the Bureau of Organizational Studies of the Organization of Administrative and Employment Affairs, states in an interview with *Zan-e Rouz* (14 January 1989: 9) that it is only *natural* that technical and engineering sciences are limited to men.

Islamist gender ideology that emphasizes women's domestic role and men's duty to guard women often creates additional barriers for women's education. Mothering, the exalted female role, takes its toll on women students due to an acute shortage of daycare facilities. In many cases, women students had to choose between education and caring for children (see *Zan-e Rouz* 19 and 26 May 1990). The IRI's protectivist policy has also limited women's access to education. A reader complains in a letter to *Zan-e Rouz* (29 June 1991: 16) that authorities in the education office in her hometown do not offer adult education classes for women because they deem it inappropriate for women to go to night classes—it is not safe.

Based on recent data (UNESCO 1999), illiteracy is 30% for females 15 or over and 16.3% for males of the same age. Females aged 15 through 24 years have an 8.2% illiteracy rate, a clear indication of increased availability of education. Illiteracy for boys of the same age is 3.7%. According to a UNICEF report, 15.4% of urban women are illiterate, compared to 55.6% in rural areas (UNICEF 1998: 44).

Moderate but steady changes can be traced in both pre-college and college education. Female enrollment in primary schools increased from 38% in 1975 to 47% in 1996. Secondary enrollment rose from 36% (1975) to 46% (1996). At the tertiary level, enrollment remained between 28% in 1975 and 27% in 1990, but rose to 36% in 1996 (UNESCO 1998, 1999).

The closing of coeducational schools negatively affected women's technical education. In 1997, only 31 out of 540 technical schools (*honarestân-e fanni*) were for girls. Females lacked access to 73 agricultural schools. 949 technical classes were offered for girls, compared to 2,606 for boys. Technical classes for girls included design, sewing, childcare, graphics, and accounting, while boys learned machinery, mechanics, electronics, chemical industry, and metallurgy (Iran Statistical Center 1997).

Vast differences exist between urban and rural education (Shâditalab 1995). Educational facilities are most limited in rural areas. The higher the education level, the lower the rural access. Statistics for the 1985–86 academic year show that of the 994,203 high school students in the country, only 92,413 (9.3%) lived in rural areas. According to UNICEF, "the frequency of girls dropping out of school because of distance increases in proportion to the age of the girls" (UNICEF 1998: 44). Opportunities are unavailable for rural girls to pursue education in technical fields, agriculture, or technical or rural teachers' training programs unless they live near a city with educational facilities—something many families do not favor. But the gap between boys' and girls' education at the primary level in rural areas has narrowed since the revolution (Jahânpanâh 1997: 63). Considering shortages in rural education, the government allowed mixed primary schools (Shahidian 1990: 22).

Poor, predominantly ethnic provinces often have limited educational opportunities for females. According to the 1996 census, 79.5% of the total population six years and older were literate. Literacy rates drop considerably for ethnic provinces: for instance, Lorestan (74.9%), West Azarbaiejan (69%), Kurdistan (68.3%), and Sistan and Baluchistan (57.3%). The nationwide male literacy rate is 84.7%, compared to 74.2% for females. In all ethnic provinces, female literacy is lower than male literacy and often falls considerably below the national rate: Lorestan, 80.5% compared to 68.8%; West Azarbaiejan, 79% compared to 58.6%; Kurdistan, 78.9% compared to 57.4%; and Sistan and Baluchistan, 65.4% to 48.7% (Iran Statistical Center 1999: 587).

In higher education, the establishment of the Islamic Republic meant restrictions on access to certain areas of study for Iranian women, primarily in mathematical and technical sciences, experimental sciences, law, and management (for detail, see Shahidian 1990: 18). Restrictions in *some* fields were eased in the late 1980s and early 1990s. The Women's Cultural and

Social Council succeeded in removing some admissions barriers in engineering, medicine, and agriculture in the summer of 1989 (Center for Women's Participation 1999: 313). These limitations were finally removed in 1993, though some university fields are still not recommended to women (Kar 1999b: 213–17).

Overall, however, the percentage of women in higher education has been on the rise. In the 1986–87 academic year, women constituted 29% of all students in universities and higher education institutes. That percentage rose to over 38% for 1997–98 (Iran Statistical Center 1999: 631). In the preceding year, some 39% of students at the baccalaureate level were female, compared to almost 18% at the master's level. Women make up about one-third of doctoral students (634–35). The majority of women in higher education are enrolled in BA/S and postgraduate programs. Of 209,163 female students at higher education during the 1996–97 academic year, about 13% pursued an associate's degree, 77% a bachelor's, 2.3% a master's, and less than 7.7% a doctorate degree (Iran Statistical Center 1999: 634–35).

Medical sciences attract a high proportion of female students. In 1985–86, 85% of all women pursuing an associate's were in health care and medical-related fields. A decade later, almost one-fourth (23.5%) of all female students at the tertiary level were in medical and health related sciences (UNESCO 1998). By 1995, women constituted 58% of all medical school students (UNESCO 1999). One reason for the high level of concentration of female medical students was that caring for the sick has traditionally been a woman's task. Another explanation is the desire of families to have their children enter prestigious fields such as medicine. There is yet a third—and perhaps a more significant—factor, namely the Islamic government's segregationist policy of only female physicians and health care personnel providing medical services to women.

Female students at the university level were consistently absent from the following fields: service trades; trade, craft, and industrial programs; and transportation and communication. In 1996–97, female students had their lowest ratio in Engineering (11.7%), followed by the Law (21%). During the same academic year, all 62 students in Home Economics were women. In Fine and Applied Arts, women made up some 62% of over 1000 students. Medical and Health Related Sciences (52.1%) was followed immediately by Humanities and Theology (51.35%). Almost half of the students in Natural Sciences (47%) and Education and Teacher Training (46%) were women (UNESCO 1998).

Though a great number of Iranian rural women work on farms, they were banned from studying agrarian sciences until the late 1980s. The rationale was that after graduation, agriculture graduates would be required to go to villages, which would interfere with women's familial tasks. Only through consistent criticisms did the government revise unfair educational

policies and lift these restrictions in the late 1980s. By 1996–97, some 25%
of agriculture majors were women (UNESCO 1998). Yet to put this figure
in perspective, consider that according to 1994 data, 69% of female employment was in agriculture (United Nations 1995).

Women face considerable obstacles in continuing their higher education
abroad. According to regulations about studying abroad (Center for
Women's Participation 1999: 310), male students with a bachelor degree
or higher may be considered for studying abroad. Regulations for women
were drastically different until the summer of 2000: "Sisters applying for
scholarship to go abroad . . . must be accompanied by their husbands at
the time of being sent and during their education abroad" (*Ettella'at* 13
July 1988). In other words, if married men have priority over single men,
women were qualified if, and only if, they were married, and they had to
be accompanied by their "guardian." Under equal conditions, married men
had priority. In the Majlis, opponents and proponents of women's education abroad equally reflect Islamist gender ideology at work. Ms. Dastqeyb
opposes the restrictions on segregationist grounds: "You are well aware
that your sisters will need medical care, or a gynecologist. . . . How can
you deprive them of female doctors and make them approach male physicians?" (*Zan-e Rouz* 20 April 1985: 7) Behrouzi similarly warns her colleagues about the "corruption that ensues from women going to a male
physician," and reminds them that when Islam encourages learning among
men and women, it sets no conditions (9). 'Abd-e-khodâ'i argues for the
protection that restrictions offer women. Women's access to specialization
is not at stake here, he contends; rather, sending students to a foreign land,
a "thoroughly corrupt environment." "In some foreign universities, female
students sunbathe on campus grounds. . . . Now, no matter how pious a
woman is, she will be exposed to violation. Or in dormitories, all by herself,
without any guardian. . . . She has to travel from city to city" (8).

Movahhedi Sâvoji demonstrates more consistency in his argument: to
him, corruption awaits all non-married individuals, so the stipulation of
marriage should apply equally to men and women candidates for studying
abroad (8).

In the late summer of 2000, the Majlis passed a bill proposed by its
Committee on Education and Research to allow single women to apply for
the Ministry of Higher Education scholarship to study abroad. The committee suggested revising the law by omitting the term "only males are
qualified to attend the exams for gaining such scholarships" and by also
omitting the phrase according to which "only married women can apply
for such scholarships" (*Hayat-e No* 24 August 2000). The passage of this
law evoked the criticism of some Ayatollahs. Ayatollah Makârem Shirâzi,
for instance, in a letter to the Majlis, condemned the decision. He considers
it a law that not only does not resolve any issues, but also creates new
ones. Such provision, he believes, ignores Muslims' sensitivities regarding

the honor of women, their *namus*, by sending unprotected women to the morally corrupt West (*Hayat-e No* 2 October 2000).

What the Majlis passed, of course, had to receive various religious leaders' seal of approval. On 23 January 2001, the Security Council of the IRI rejected the bill, lest it have "problem-ridden consequences and side effects." The future of the bill is uncertain at the moment.

Gender gaps are more vivid at the teaching and administration levels. During the 1987–88 academic year, only 16.6% of the nation's college faculty were women (2,654 out of 15,950), which is disproportionate even to the low number of women college students (in the same academic year, women constituted only 29% of 204,862 attending college). Islamic policies do not support women faculty members' efforts to conduct research and keep current with recent scientific developments (see Ministry of Culture and Higher Education 1988). Traveling abroad and spending sabbaticals in foreign universities and research centers are of vital significance in this process. The policies of the Islamic regime, however, hinder the advancement of female professors. According to a study about women in Tehran's three prominent universities (University of Tehran, Shahid Beheshti University, and ʿAllâmeh Tabaâtabâʾi University), faculty members, especially women, believe that women professors are marginalized in their working environment (Shamsussâdat Zâhedi 1995). This research cites the ratio of female faculties between 9:1 (University of Tehran, perhaps the country's most prestigious institution of higher education) and 22:7 (ʿAllâmeh Tabaâtabâʾi University). Of the 93 women who responded to the survey (representing 48% of the female faculty members of the 3 universities), some 85% never received a sabbatical leave to research abroad. Ninety percent stated that they never represented their university in an official capacity. Over 70% had never held an executive position; none were offered administrative posts.

Men have dominated educational administration. As Parvâneh Fâtemi (1998: 64) points out, "a glance at the structure of the Ministry of Education reveals that the higher we go, women's role decreases, until it completely disappears at the top. All six education ministers since the revolution have been men." Administrators at national and provincial levels have been exclusively male. Fâtemi continues:

Masculinist policies of the Ministry of Education have resulted in the complete elimination of female employees. Only in secretarial positions, and recently in the computer section, women are employed, but they are kept completely isolated from other sections—a small window of 10 x 20 centimeters is used for exchanging official correspondence. Isolating even this handful of female employees in these dungeons has deprived them from decision-making, promotions, and benefits. (64)

Congruent with the IRI's segregationist policies, an important objective of the Islamic regime's educational policies has been to create sufficient skilled female personnel so that women do not have to rely on men to provide them with such services as education and health care, hence, the increase in the number of women students in educational and medical sciences. Yet, the policies of the regime in this regard have not been successful, and there are considerable shortages of labor power in these fields. Even though some 86% of all women employed are teachers, there are not yet enough female educators to create an all-female teaching faculty for girls. This poses further problems for women's education.

In health-related fields the situation is even worse. In 1974, Iran had 10,000 male and 1,041 female doctors and dentists (the population of Iran was over 30 million at the time). The situation has deteriorated since the Revolution. According to *Kayhan* (6 December 1988), "on the basis of standards laid down by the World Health Organization, Iran has a shortage of over 50,000 doctors." (Iran's population was approximately 50 million at the time.) Despite the physician shortage, there are over 13,000 unemployed doctors in Iran since financial problems do not allow the government to employ new physicians. The shortages of midwives and dentists are particularly acute in rural areas. In spite of the rapidly rising birthrate and a young female population, according to the 1988 *Kayhan* report, there was only one midwife for every 18,000 Iranian women. According to the 1997 data, 14% of all births in the IRI were deliveries by untrained birth attendants; the difference between rural and urban areas was quite remarkable: "30.4% of these births as compared to 4.7%. About one-fourth of women go through pregnancy with less than two antenatal checkups" (UNICEF 1998: 62 and 64).

Since Islamization of the educational system numbered among the top priorities of the new regime, revised textbooks were used at all levels immediately after its establishment (Mehran 1989). The new books were markedly influenced by the Islamic sex role stereotypes. Women are presented as obedient housewives, men as breadwinners and guardians of the family. Girls follow their mothers into the kitchen and boys learn from their fathers how to financially and intellectually take care of the family (see Matini 1989). According to the Institute for Cultural Studies and Research (1993), in the primary schools, specific women are mentioned by name—twice—only in the Farsi textbook for the fifth grade. For all primary school texts, male and female proper names have a ratio of 2 to 1; for specific names, the ratio rises to 267 to 1. Reference to women's names increases as grade increases. About 90% of all jobs outside the house are associated with men. As grade increases, reference to women in the job force declines—the Farsi text for fifth grade (the final year of primary schooling) contains no reference to workingwomen. These analyses are supported by the Women's Bureau of the Ministry of Education (*Zanân* March 1999: 69).

A bias toward the importance of men's preparation for social roles is evident among many IRI officials at the higher education level. According to Sorayyâ Maknoon, university professor and a member of the Women's Cultural and Social Council, "women ought to study on their own" and become knowledgeable about their Islamic rights and duties such as mothering (*Zan-e Rouz* 22 January 1990: 13, 12). "Most women are interested in technical education solely for selfish purposes (*havây-e nafs*)" (56).

And truly, if a woman wants to serve her country, she must ask herself if she goes to a university, won't she take somebody else's place? If a woman studies, for instance, mineralogy or veterinary medicine, at best, she will marry someone who is employed, but not in a village, where she could work as a veterinarian. Millions of national resources have been spent for this woman every year and she ends up sitting at home. (13, 56)

A petrochemical engineer conveys the following experience:

I remember it was the first months after I entered university. One university official told me and my three female classmates that we had made a mistake having chosen this field. His exact sentence was: "This field is not ladylike." After a while I found out why he said that. I saw that in the opinion of many people, studying and working in petrochemical fields are not for women. Of course, things were better back in the university; in the industry, our problems have been augmented. (*Zan-e Rouz* 21 December 1991: 18, 63)

That despite these convictions, women's share in education has increased attests to their resilience. Notwithstanding the absence of a favorable labor market, parents, especially among the middle classes, emphasize the importance of higher education for their children. Despite, *and because of* the high rate of unemployment, many consider education the most reliable avenue to an economically secure future. For women, a good education not only provides opportunities (although limited) for obtaining jobs, but also drastically increases one's chances of finding a husband with a higher income. A college-educated woman also enjoys higher prestige in married life. During marriage negotiations, for example, a bride's level of education is among the determining factors of her *mahr* (the bridal gift).

WORKING, AS BEFITS A WOMAN

The IRI aimed to concentrate women in the private sphere. Asserting this objective in 1979 evoked strong reaction. Since then, though women's employment has significantly declined, the government found resistance too strong to confine them to the private province. As in many other areas, in employment, too, structural changes in pre-revolutionary Iranian society (e.g., increasing female employment and education) have prohibited the implementation of many exclusionary policies. In addition, economic hardship under the IRI leaves no choice for many families other than reliance upon two incomes (and often, more than one job per partner). As long as the Islamic regime fails to meet economic demands, it has no choice but to yield. Thus the initial *exclusionist* orientation was replaced by a *segregationist* approach that accepts women in some social arenas, provided that their familial role, including husbands' agreement for wives' social presence, is not jeopardized. These considerations notwithstanding, the Islamic sexual division of labor has taken its toll on women's employment.

The IRI's employment policies channel women's economic participation into gender-appropriate fields. According to IRI Labor Policies, women work only in areas Islam deems appropriate (e.g., midwifery, medicine, teaching); deems compatible with physical and psychological capacities (e.g., laboratory sciences, electronic engineering, pharmaceutical, and social work); or in fields where gender does not affect performance (e.g., unskilled work in industries or services). The law bars women from occupations prohibited by the Islamic law or deemed harsh and physically demanding or dangerous for a woman (e.g., judgeship, firefighting). Article 10 of this law stipulates that women's work must not interfere with their familial role (See Center for Women's Participation 1999: 343–46).

Between 1976 and 1986, women's employment decreased each year by two percent (Bâqeriân 1991: 4). In 1976, women 10 years and older constituted 13.77% of the employed. According to the 1986 census, however, this share dropped to almost 9%. In 1986, there were 990,000 employed women compared to 11 million men. During this period—wrought by revolutionary changes and prolonged war—men's employment rose 2.8% (Iran Statistical Center 1988). In 1996, women comprised more than 12% of the employed 10 years and over: 11.3% in urban and 13.4% in rural areas (Iran Statistical Center 1999: 102). This decline becomes more meaningful if considered in the context of a rapidly growing population. The number of women 10 years and older in 1991 increased by 67% compared to 1976. But there was only a two percent increase in these women's employment. In 1996, the number of women over 10 years old had increased by 99% compared to 1976, but had only a 45% increase in employment. All in all, in 1976, 10.8% of women 10 years or older were employed; this number dropped to 6.6% in 1991 and 7.9% in 1996 (Malaki 1998: 16). In 1996, the percentage of female economic activities was 14.2% (Plan and Budget Organization and the United Nations 1999).

Though women have conquered some forbidden educational fields, they still suffer from a job market that overwhelmingly favors men. Job advertisements frequently specify masculinity as a requirement. That "certain jobs are degrading for women" has created an ideological justification for employers not to hire women. To IRI officials, however, this is merely managers' preferences—"the law does not say give priority to men" (*Zan-e Rouz* 29 August 1987: 52). Besides, as discussed in chapter 6, not all discriminations are "unfair" to IRI officials. The Public Relations Office of the Ministry of Culture and Higher Education writes in a letter to *Zan-e Rouz* that giving priority to men at the time of employment does not necessarily negate the capability of women graduates. After all, "the impact of higher education ought not to be gauged only in relation to employment; housekeeping and rearing children is the best context to transmit the outcome of education to society and future generations" (*Zan-e Rouz* 23 July 1988: 22).

An overwhelming majority of women's occupational opportunities are concentrated in traditional areas (Kar 1994: 143). As Majlis representative Hossein Qâzizâdeh comments, IRI policies have emphasized women's employment in educational and medical care fields (7). Representative Nâseri mentions that in order to "channel women's employment" into certain fields, married men receive monetary bonuses, but only if their wife is not employed. If she works in education or health-related fields, however, such exemption does not apply to him (47).

Ekrâm-Ja'fari, Deputy Director of the Organization of Administrative and Employment Affairs, assesses pre-revolutionary female employment policies as demonstrating "incompatibility between women's employment, their cultural and creedal characteristics, and social needs; lack of respect for women's personality in general society; false employment; and disruption of the family. Naturally, these policies underwent fundamental changes after the revolution" (7). In an Islamic state, "jobs must befit women" (47). Contrary to the Westernized policies of the past, Islamists "do not favor women's employment for its economic implications," says Majlis deputy Hojjatulislam Nâseri; female work is rather recognized as women's "social contribution" (*moshârekat-e ejtemâ'i*). Qâzizâdeh expresses this position more clearly: "We look at women's employment as a necessity, and believe that, from a social point of view, if women do not work outside of the family, if they are not formally employed, society will become lazy" (7).

Yet, Qâzizâdeh continues, many authorities fail to see the danger of increasing laziness among housewives and do not favor women's employment—"a deviant approach that dominated us after the revolution."

Whereas in pre-revolutionary times, women of all ages sought employment, in post-revolutionary Iran (1986), the percentage of women seeking employment rises between the ages of 13 and 17 to about 35%, and steadily declines to below 30% for women 18 to 22 years old. Between the ages of 22 and 32—when women are most likely to marry and have children—the percentage declines drastically to below five percent. After the age of 37, it is steadily close to zero (Iran Statistical Center 1988). Observers remark a conflict between population control policies and the declining percentage of women of childbearing age seeking employment (Baqerian 1991: 7). As Aghajanian comments, "The economic and non-economic roles of young women between the ages of 15 and 24 have changed in the decade covered by the 1986 census: the employment rate declined; the school participation rate declined; and the full-time homemaker rate increased. The same pattern of change is also evident for women 20 to 24 years old" (1994a: 50). In 1995, of the 15 million females over the age of 15, only 1.1 million (7.6%) were employed. Housewives constitute the majority of Iranian women (Sâlehpour 1998: 59).

The economically active rural female population 10 years of age and over dropped from about 17% in 1976 to almost 11% in 1996. Among men of the same age group, the economically active population also decreased from 78% in 1976 to 65% in 1996. Some 9% of urban women of the same age group were economically active in 1976 (compared to 64% among urban men); this percentage changed to 8% in 1996 (compared to 59% among men) (Iran Statistical Center, 1999 #2150: 90). These data reveal not only a considerable difference between male and female employment in rural areas, but also a substantial difference in female employment in these settings. The considerable decline in rural female employment indicates a push toward inclusion of women into unpaid family labor, thereby underreporting rural female labor. This trend is also valid for urban settings since, according to recent data, the ratio of women in unpaid family work to all women for the nation is 46.5% (Plan and Budget Organization and the United Nations 1999).

The IRI prefers skilled educated women to unskilled female laborers. "When equal employment opportunities are present," writes Mitrâ Bâqeriân, "those women who have a higher degree and scientific knowledge than men can secure a job" (1991: 8). Occupations that require unskilled or less-skilled labor are predominantly occupied by male employees. According to the 1375 (1996) census, while women make up close to 40% of the "professionals" category, they account for merely 1.15% of the plant and machine operators, assemblers, and drivers, and 4.35% of the unskilled workers (*kârgarân-e sâdeh*) (Iran Statistical Center 1999: 102). This trend is detrimental to women's employment chances, considering the discrepancies between male and female education in Iran. Poor women particularly bear the brunt of this discrimination.

Initial post-revolutionary data to some observers implied that the short-term impact of Islamic policies on skilled labor was only minimal, with female participation in the urban labor force declining from 11.2% in 1976 to 11.1% in 1982 (Moghadam 1988: 229). Besides, as Moghissi has pointed out, Moghadam refers to data for a seven-year period which includes the last three years of the Pahlavi rule. Besides, IRI data refer to a female population of six years old and over (compared to Pahlavi data for women over 10 years old) which, though it perhaps portrays a more realistic picture of female work in Iran, inflates employment data (Moghissi

1997: 84–85). The small decline to which Moghadam refers assumes more importance in light of the increase in the Iranian urban population of those over 10 years old from 11,428,000 to 23,232,600. Compared to the doubling of the urban population, women's share in the urban labor force had actually declined from 4% to 2.4%. While the overall rate of female unemployment also increased significantly from 13.1% in 1976 to 18.1% in 1983, there was an increase in the number of women employed by the state (from 87,474 in 1974 to 341,155 in 1983) (Moghadam 1988: 230). One should keep in mind, however, that following the revolution, the state took over many private business practices, and most female state employees are concentrated in areas traditionally considered feminine. Thus, the establishment of the Islamic Republic has exacerbated the limited participation by women in the already sex-segregated labor force of Iran.

For skilled employed women, the determining impact of higher educational attainment on occupational opportunities has grave consequences for their share of the decision-making process. According to one report in 1991, some 30% of all government employees held managerial positions—of these, only 3% were women (*Zan-e Rouz* 23 November 1991: 11). As Valentine Moghadam observes:

Gender gap in higher education may explain why women's participation in decision-making positions is almost insignificant in today's Iran. In 1995, there were no female cabinet ministers, and in 1994, out of 182 subministerial-level positions, women occupied only 0.5 percent. In the ministry of Labor and Social Affairs, there are seven deputy ministers, all men. There were, however, women heads of departments and one woman general director (compared with twenty-four males with that title). Similarly, at the state-owned Daroupakhsh Company in Karaj in 1994, out of twenty-six professional staff with medical degrees, five were women; and of the five with master's degrees, two were women. (Moghadam 1998: 170)

The significance of education in women's employment also leads to a somewhat more favorable situation for white-collar female workers. In 1996, women senior managers constituted 12.8% of all women employed. In the same year, 32.9% of employed women were in skilled technical and academic positions (Plan and Budget Organization and the United Nations 1999).

Iran's economy is divided into private, public, and cooperative sectors. According to the 1996 census, some 56% of employed women work in the private sector. But this percentage includes self-employed as well as unpaid family female workers, which jointly comprised 73% of women's employment in this sector. Businesswomen and female salespersons constituted 5.2% of all employed in 1996 (Plan and Budget Organization and the United Nations 1999). Women constituted 3% of employers and 7.64% of wage and salary earners. The public sector employed about 40% of all female employees; the cooperative, 0.5% (about 4.5% are unidentified) (Iran Statistical Center 1999: 103).

Women's cooperatives constitute a supposed alternative to public employment. While private employers are reluctant to hire women to, among other problems, save themselves from the harassment of the regime's policing of gender relations, women's cooperatives had all-female members. While men own a considerable portion of the capital, women's cooperatives do not require too much capital from one investor. While women may not have the financial resources necessary for running a business, women's cooperatives require minimal funds: neighborhood women can use their own sewing machine, gather at somebody's basement, and start their own production unit. This way, not only do women participate in production, their production is accounted for in national wealth (see, e.g., Khodâparast 1996).

Most significantly, however, all-woman cooperatives allow women to work without neglecting their fundamental task: mothering. "In neighborhood cooperatives," states Fâtemeh Sha'bâni, "women can maintain their native culture and outlooks while working next to their home and children, without having to travel long ways between home and workplace" (1996: 151). Thus, to create a compromise between women's demand for working in the formal sector of the economy and the sensitivities of the private patriarchy, "women's workplaces are brought inside their houses," as the Governor of East Azerbaijan Province remarks, "so that they can work while performing their roles as mothers" (quoted in Ministry of Cooperatives 1996: 28).

The cooperative sector has not received adequate attention in the IRI's economic policy, prompting the Sixth Majlis to establish a special commission to promote pro-cooperative policies (*Bahâr* 20 July 2000). Connecting women of the private patriarchy to public patriarchy through co-ops has faced even harsher challenges. By 1999, only 11% of all cooperatives were women's. Problems seem to be twofold. First, the political structure of the IRI economy restricts women's organizational efforts, just as it limits men's. Cooperatives must follow bylaws written by the Ministry of Cooperatives. Second, and perhaps more importantly, despite authorities' optimism, women still face economic hurdles, restricted capital especially. The IRI recommends that women's co-ops have only a small percentage of total capital in loans. Yet most banks refuse to comply (Khadijeh Moghadam 2000: 98).

The government is women's biggest employer. Less than one-third of all full-time, permanent government employees are women—29.16% for 1997 (Iran Statistical Center 1999: 103). In 1997, of all full-time, female government employees, some 74% worked in the Ministry of Education. These employees accounted for close to 46% of that ministry's total workforce. (Only 1.26% of women working for the government were employed by the Ministry of Culture and Higher Education—20.17% of all employed by that Ministry.) The next highest concentration of women was in the Ministry of Health and Medical Education—some 16%, or 42.55% of all employees in that office. The Ministry of Economy and Finance followed with 2.47%. The other 6.7% of female employees were scattered among other government institutions.

According to the 1996 Census (Iran Statistical Center 1999: 94), employed women are primarily concentrated in education (44.1%) and in health and social work (39.3%). Women's share of employment is quite meager in construction (less than 1%), mining (4.2%), restaurant and hotel business (3.5%), wholesale and retail trade (2.1%), and transportation (1.84%). Some 22.8% of employees in manufacturing are female. Women's presence as skilled laborers in the industrial sector has been limited. Once in the industry, women's job advancement comes with male supervisors grudgingly accepting the inevitable. In a *Zan-e Rouz* special report about the needs and roles of skilled women in the industry, the senior civil engineer at the National Petrochemical Industry states:

I had at first no problem being accepted at the site. Maybe that was due to my own personality. From day one I didn't allow anything insulting to women in the site. I never let anybody treat me as the weaker or the delicate sex. Consequently I didn't have any problems in the units. Later, however, attitudes changed gradually and the general decline for skilled women workers also affected my position. That is, I didn't succeed as men did. My male colleagues advanced much further than I did.... They don't give women the same opportunities that they offer men.... If they want to choose a supervisor, they prefer a man over a woman. (*Zan-e Rouz* 21 December 1991: 71)

There are always women, to be sure, who advance in their careers. In October 2000, for instance, for the first time in the customs history of Iran, a woman was appointed to the head of one of the most important customs ports after some 25 years of experience in the field. But, job advancement as a rule results from incidental factors, such as the institution's need or open-minded and fair supervisors, rather than from institutional guarantees. In response to a *Zan-e Rouz* reporter's inquiry "Do you feel your talents and expertise are adequately utilized?" a senior chemical engineer at Shiraz petrochemical plant says: "Not as much as possible. Of course, there are situations when, realizing the magnitude of their needs, officials are forced to do so" (77).

Interestingly, many women working as skilled laborers at industrial sites say that workers showed little resistance to accepting the authority of women engineers. "It just takes some getting used to," comments a chemical engineer. "As soon as workers get used to the presence of a woman in the factory, everything is fine" (78). Though certainly one cannot generalize this instance to the rest of society, examples of this sort indicate that decades of female education and employment have effected some change in the social attitude toward women.

Preference for skilled female labor limits wage laborers' opportunities. According to one report, in 1995, only 4.74% of all blue-collar workers were women (Mohseni 1998a: 46). The actual number of unskilled women working in the industry sector is estimated to be higher, due to informal contracting and industrial home work (Mohseni 1998b). Male workers are preferred to women, but when women workers are employed, they are mostly selected from the unmarried pool to reduce production costs such as childcare expenses. Many married women workers with children under school age, writes Maryam Mohseni (1998b), do not work in industrial units because these centers lack daycare facilities. Suri Rashvand, a workingwoman, relates information about ill-equipped daycare for the children of working-class families. During the nine hours these children spend in daycare facilities each day, they are allowed to draw one picture, having to spend the rest of the day either in silence or in sleep (Rashvand 1999: 59).

One reason for women's limited presence in the blue-collar labor force is the prohibitions of interaction between unrelated men and women. Besides, regulations regarding "special protection" for women bar hiring them in jobs involving heavy labor deemed unsuitable to "feminine nature," which further limit women's employment in industry. Women's work during the night, with the exception of medical or educational professions, is forbidden. During the war years, some employers hired women who had no economic providers. "A relatively major factory, for instance, hired only women who had no guardian or breadwinner. Of course, these women had to prove with sufficient documents that they are indeed guardianless. The Islamic Council of the factory investigated their claim before hiring" (Mohseni 1998b: 10). In post-war years, Mohseni comments, seeking higher profit through lowering production costs overshadows ideological considerations (e.g., unrelated women and men working together) in not hiring women.

High inflation and low pay force workingwomen to long hours of hard work and limited benefits. "Our hours are so long that in effect all our days are spent in the factory," says one woman worker (*Zan-e Rouz* 7 September 1985). Another voices concerns about limited and inflexible vacation time: "We have 15 vacation days that we have to take in the summer. We don't have any choice when it comes to dates. We also have five days off for the New Year celebration, but for each day off, we have to work one day during the weekend" (*Zan-e Rouz* 7 September 1985: 55). According to a recent report about female workers at several clothing production units, conditions are even worse for piecework laborers. They work at least 10 hours a day, in shops of 10 women or less, with little pay, unstable working conditions, no job security, and lack of legal protection (Shâhmorâdi and Mohseni 1998).

Though labor law considers such protections as health and retirement insurance, provisions in many cases ring hollow. Laws that are supposed to protect women work against them. Since policies provide no incentive to hire women (e.g., tax or tariff exemptions), by refusing to employ women employers increase profit margins. Another important obstacle in workingwomen's exercise of their legal rights is their lack of familiarity with the law. "Workingwomen, even the educated ones, know nothing about labor laws. We don't have any time to think about the labor law" (*Zan-e Rouz* 7 September 1985: 57).

Patriarchal biases in the law fail to recognize workingwomen as primary supporters. Though workers—male and female—pay 7% of their wages toward their retirement insurance, in the event of a woman's death, her family cannot collect retirement benefits; she is not deemed a breadwinner in the eye of the law. This, though many "workingwomen are the bread-winners of their families" (Rashvand 1999: 60).

Considering their strenuous labor and compound responsibility at home and workplace, workingwomen demand early retirement. While passage of such a bill becomes a matter of "life and death" (Mahdavi 1998: 49), IRI authorities are reluctant to recognize its need. Apparently, when Fâezeh Hashemi Rafsanjani argued with female workers that this law would prevent women from ascending to managerial levels, workers argued in response that prolonged employment might qualify white-collar women for promotion, but for blue-collar women there was little, if any, upward mobility on the job. "We cannot ask a workingwoman to forego her immediate needs for future consideration when, based on her observations of fellow-workers, she has only two or three years—or perhaps no chance—to enjoy retirement benefits" (49). After years of resistance, the IRI finally agreed in 1997 to a one-year experiment of early retirement. According to that law, workingwomen over 22 years of age, with 20 years of working experience could retire with twenty days' pay. The victory did not come easily—it is the accomplishment of years of petitioning and collective action.

For employed women, additional problems stem from domestic responsibilities. One female engineer of food technology states:

Unfortunately, women confront many problems in work and production. This is particularly acute in industrial units. For instance, daycare is not yet readily available and obviously, if the mother is not sure [about her child], her productivity declines. Another problem we face is mental and physical fatigue due to overwork. Women age faster in these units than in others and endure more physical hardship. (*Zan-e Rouz* 18 December 1993: 14)

The notion that women's primary role is in the family means that women are primarily responsible for household chores. That obligation exerts considerable pressure on women employees and curtails social and cultural leverage to challenge men's reluctance toward housework (*Zan-e Rouz* 30 November 1991). In response, IRI authorities in the autumn of 1983 offered the option of part-time employment to ease the burden of employed women—or, more accurately, to guarantee that they accomplish their primary household responsibilities. According to this plan (passed in 1985 and amended in 1997), women could reduce their working time one-fourth and accept reduced salary and benefits, contingent on employers' agreement. More recently, Zahrâ Shojâ'i, advisor to President Khatami, repeated the same solution in a meeting of educated women and woman scholars in Hamedân. Since women are responsible for domestic chores, she argues, they should not work the same long hours as men. She contends that such provisions as maternity leave and paid breaks for nursing are merely "pain relief." The real solution is "a revision of labor law considering their position, conditions, and role within the family" (*Hamshahri* 13 July 1998).

Part-time work for women has proved too costly. The condition of "employer's agreement" effectively bars some women from this option. In addition to the financial burden, women lose rights to many fringe benefits, and their promotion time—even their position—is jeopardized. Furthermore, exclusive availability to females reinforces conservative attitudes that women take employment lightly (*Zan-e Rouz* 30 November 1991: 9). Women's preoccupation with household responsibilities results in slacking off at the workplace, an indication that laws in support of employed women "had no impact but limited improvement" (*Zan-e Rouz* 22 June 1991: 6). The plan has not been an attractive option for many employees who refer to it as "much ado about nothing" (see *Zanân* March 1998: 2). According to a 1991 report, only one percent of women government employees exercised that right (*Zan-e Rouz* 22 June 1991: 7).

The future for women's employment remains grim, despite incremental gains here and there. I do not share Moghadam's assessment that "voices" throughout Iranian bureaucracy have "a new message" that favors women (Moghadam 1998: 164). I am not optimistic about "recent developments" indicating "a trend toward greater advocacy for women" (165). Moghadam's evidence of a "new trend" includes new on-the-job training programs, modifications of labor law (e.g., increase in women's leave entitlement), selection of the best woman worker of the year, and the minute increase of women's presence in politics. Yet none of these provisions is novel. IRI history is filled with "new, improved policies" that in the end amount to nothing. IRI records are filled with reverential examples of women in many positions—from the best mothers to the best beekeepers to the best farmers to the best workers. *Zanân* reports that among employees recognized for their distinguished work, only 7.1% are women

(March 1999: 67). The practical implications of this reverence, however, have remained nonexistent (see, e.g., Sherkat 1994). Similarly, welcoming the increase in the number of political women as advocates of women's rights has proved unwarranted. Remember that the notorious amendment to the law of journalism that prohibits "instrumental" use of women's pictures in magazines and criminalizes discussions of women's rights outside the boundaries of Islamic shari'ah was concocted by the women of the Cultural and Social Council.

THE POLITICAL BATTLEGROUND

Images of Islamist women in political roles are abundant in the illustrative portrayals of the Iranian revolution: women covered with the châdor protesting against the Shah, participating in demonstrations before the U.S. Embassy, or holding a gun, symbolic of determination in the war against Iraq. These representations contradict a common assumption about Muslim women's exclusion from politics. This assumption, to be sure, reflects aspects of Islamic gender politics. We recall, for instance, clerical opposition to women's franchise in the early 1960s. And a casual review of Islamist politics in pre- and post-revolutionary Iran reveals its overwhelmingly masculine characteristic. But this stereotypical assumption leaves out important developments. Changes in gender relations in the 1960s, especially in the women's franchise, set a precedent for women's entitlement to political participation such that its continued recognition under the Islamic state has become inevitable (see Saghafi 1995). Pre-revolutionary Islamist ideologues envisioned a new Muslim woman who undertook political responsibility. Female Islamist activists have been inspired by this image of a devout woman who with one hand wraps her châdor around her and with the other, holds a banner. Thus, though the IRI felt the need to contain women's political participation before, during, and after the revolution, it also realized the impossibility of a thorough exclusion of women from political life.

The patriarchy-Islam-state triad strengthened patriarchal power in the post-revolutionary era, but it also evoked unprecedented criticisms and attacks against each of its components. The Islamic government had to resort to mechanisms that simultaneously were congruent with its Islamization project and would nullify objections to discriminatory policies toward women. This quandary has shaped the Islamic state's gender politics. Gender issues have permeated cultural and political discourses. IRI officials and ideologues are compelled to defend themselves on virtually every social and political decision that affects women and the family. A common thread of all these commentaries is asserting the liberating role of Islam and the Islamic government in women's lives. A limited number of elite women appeared in visible political positions to discredit charges of discrimination and to represent "women's interests."

Though a strong social presence, and though a few hold elite positions, women have gained incrementally in politics. Islamist women—both rank-and-file members who police women's appearance and "morality" and those in higher positions—have contributed to the misogynist policies of the Islamic state. The "alternative" interpretations that these women offer on gender do not undermine the Islamic framework.[3]

This apologetic approach is not surprising because many elite women are not only ideologically dedicated to Islam, but are also close relatives of key figures in the Islamic state. They are, in other words, tied to the state with more than one thread: Farideh Mostafavy, Ayatollah Khomeini's daughter; Fâtemeh Tabâtabâ'i, Ayatollah Khomeini's daughter-in-law; Fâezeh and Fâtemeh Hashemi, former President Hashemi Rafsanjani's daughters; Maryam Khaz'ali, Ayatollah Khaz'ali's daughter; Malikeh Yazdi, Ayatollah Yazdi's daughter; Fatemeh Karrubi, Ayatollah Karrubi's wife; Goharush-sharieh Dastqeyb, Ayatollah Dastqeyb's daughter; A'zam Tâleqâni, Ayatollah Tâleqâni's daughter; 'Ateqeh Raja'i, former Prime Minister and President Raja'i's wife; Zahra Rahnavard, former Prime Minister Moussavi's wife. Even at lower levels, supporters of the regime occupy most administrative posts. "Young pro-regime women with a high school education replaced the purged professionals. . . . Many of these women, though loyal, were blatantly unqualified for their positions" (Gerami 1994: 334–35). Massoumeh Ebtekar, Khatami's vice president on environmental issues, for instance, became editor-in-chief of the English *Kayhan* in 1980, at the age of 20. These ties to the tightly knit Islamic state limit the scope of politicking that is available to Islamist women.

Despite the inclusion of token women in politics, the IRI often falls short of accommodating women as autonomous political actors. I consider two major obstacles in the IRI's espousing of a political role for women—one reflects a general tension between the IRI and free, popular political input; the other stems from the Islamic state's gender politics.

The history of the IRI, as well as its episodically emerging warring factions, has been one of violent objection to genuine popular politics. From workplace to presidential palace, every political move is monitored by the IRI ruling apparatus. The establishment of the regime meant the substitution of genuine workers' unions that flourished after the downfall of Pahlavis with *Islamic* councils, composed of pro-government and "safe" members (see Bayat 1987). Any political representation must be based on proven loyalty to the Islamic Republic and devotion to Islam: an employees' representative in an office's governance body must have the approval of an overseeing committee, just as a presidential candidate ought to obtain the blessing of a qualification-determining committee.[4] The laws of the Islamic state grant women the right to participate in professional assemblies, but in practice, women face so many obstacles in entering these institutions that many are discouraged. As a labor activist puts it in a round table discussion about women and civil society, "when a workingwoman volunteers to join the leadership of a working-class institution, one-thousand-and-one covert and overt hands appear to prevent her success" (*Farhang-e Towse'eh*, Special Issue on Women, March 1998: 22). Her colleague voices a similar concern about women's participation in workers' cooperatives:

We working women, too, have the right to elect someone to the co-op board, but in practice one person uses his influence and denies our rights. As soon as a woman volunteers to join the board, the Committee to Determine Qualifications rejects the female candidate for such reasons as not observing the Islamic hejâb or women's incapability, through threats or use of other means available inside or outside the factory. (21)

Jilâ Movahed Shariatpanâhi, a devout Muslim activist who attempted to run for the fourth parliament, disparages in an interview with *Goft-o-go* (9: 43–51) that merely two weeks after she and two colleagues announced their candidacy, the Committee to Determine Qualifications of Majlis Candidates informed them that none were qualified. They protested the decision. Movahed Shariatpanâhi's appeal was rejected, despite her long involvement in Islamist activities—she was told that committee members did not know her. But her two colleagues were eventually accepted.

Publisher Shahlâ Lâhiji narrates a similar resistance to women publishers' activities under Khatami's presidency. She who in a *Farhang-e Towse'eh* round table discussion optimistically advised the two working-class participants about legal provisions for professional activism, a short year later, "perplexed and disturbed by the chaotic cultural and political atmosphere of the country," realizes the validity of their disappointment (Lâhiji 1999: 41). The newly established "Some Women Publishers," in cooperation with several governmental and non-governmental organizations and the all-women Az-Zahra University, planned a book exhibition:

In the process of this simple exhibition, with the central theme of Promoting Reading, rocks of calamity showered us from the sky, red tape we had to face, and accusations were made against us. And eventually, all side events and discussion groups that constituted a major portion of our program were cancelled and nobody accepted responsibility for that. (42)

The second source of tension regarding women's political participation stems from Islamic gender politics. Competing Islamist interpretations invoke conflicting teachings of Islam to condone or oppose women in politics. Those readings that are supportive, for instance, quote verse 12 of sura *She Who is Tested* as a proof that the Prophet considered women's political role legitimate so as to accept their allegiance *(bey'at)*: "Prophet, if believing women come to you and pledge themselves to serve no other god besides Allah . . . accept their allegiance and implore Allah to forgive them" (The Koran 1988: 268).

Opponents similarly offer a barrage of evidence. They argue, for instance, that since, according to the Koran, men have authority over women, how can women in turn make political decisions that affect men's lives (see Hosseini Tehrani 1997: 127–27). Ayatollah Hosseini Tehrani cites a hadith from Imam Ali who instructed his soldiers not to think about their wives because doing so made warring men weak. Hosseini Tehrani then adds:

When the mere thought of women at times of war causes weakness and disruption, how can we expect national affairs and social organization to remain intact if women occupy the government and judgeship—two basic foundations of politics? Rulers and judges must be strong in their emotion, firm in their belief, and consistent in their logic. (209)

When women are not even trusted with the guardianship of their own children, how can we trust the fate of a nation in their hands? They are indeed better off doing what they are supposed to do, Hosseini Tehrani contends. Imam Ali referred to women as "basil" *(reyhâneh)*, and Hosseini Tehrani believes there is a lesson in the Imam's characterization: fragile and fragrant, a basil plant must be in a favorable environment to maintain its delicateness. "Similar [to the basil], a woman is not created strong to suffer hardship; she must stay in the garden of her family and care for her honor and virtues; she must not exceed this limit" (199).

The government's request that Muslim women participate politically *as a religious duty* legitimizes activity of a previously barred segment. But subordination of women's political role to their domestic responsibilities remains emphasized. A war widow states in an interview with *Shâhed-e Bânovân*, a magazine for war widows, that she has been involved in the war efforts for seven years. Her martyred husband, she says, condoned her participation in this holy mission, "on the condition that I would not ignore the children" (4 February 1988: 33). While his devotion is first and foremost to Allah, while he can sacrifice his family's interest to the point of martyrdom, she must make her political role subordinate to her mothering. The central message of these activists—mothering and wifehood as women's primary responsibilities—considerably diminishes the radical appearance of their activism. There is little novelty in women making a profession of telling *other women* they should make the family their primary concern, as the history of women's participation in the Nazi, Ku Klux Klan, and other rightist movements indicates (Blee 1991; Koonz 1987; Jeansonne 1996).

Islamist women's political involvement demonstrates more the inevitable—that no group can be indefinitely denied political participation—than an intention to feminize Islamist politics. Insofar as she is ineligible to serve as *valy-e faqih* (supreme religious leader), a man—whose manliness is a requirement for his post—always overshadows a woman's political life. Under the system of *velâyat-e faqih*, then, women's political participation always takes place in a paternalist context. Men also have a hold over the presidency—women's chance in becoming eligible for this office is ambiguous, for the Constitution mandates presidential candidacy "from among religious and political *rejâl*." The Arabic *rejâl* has two denotations. It means distinguished persons; but is also the plural of *rajol*, man. Hence, this statement may be read to require a male president. Some Islamists take the word in its literal sense; others favor its non-gendered connotation. According to Zahrâ Shojâ'i, former advisor to the Minister of Interior, the Assembly of Experts (*Majlis-e Khebregân*) who drafted the Constitution in 1979, intended to use the word "men"—using the ambiguous *rejâl* was a compromise they reached with Monireh Noubakht, the only female member of the Assembly (*Hamshahri* 10 June 1993). For the eighth presidential election, which will be held in spring 2001, the Iran-e Fardâ collective has nominated Farah Khosravi, arguing that *rejâl* refers to distinguished political figures, not just men (*Iran* 20 September 2000). A special supervisory committee must approve presidential nominees before they can actually run as a candidate. Sadly, however, competing interpretations could be merely academic, for something fundamentally malfunctions when a woman is elected as president but her husband's refusal to allow her to go to work affords her the choice between divorce and resignation. Even if the non-gendered definition of *rejâl* is accepted, the election of a president from amongst distinguished *rejâl* gives women a choice between definite elimination and a permanent suspension between acceptance and elimination—future interpreters could reinstate the old masculinist option.

This ambiguity is telling of a deeper conflict between entrenched beliefs about women's inadequacy—or at least serious shortcomings—in intellectualism and women's presence in politics. Despite proclaimed admiration for the partisanship of elite women in Islamic history, and despite the prominence of gender issues in political Islam, women in Islamist ideology stand on the periphery of politics. Women's politicking is predominantly *within an Islamic system*, a system supposed to protect them from the dangers of their environment. In a corrupt society, Mahboobeh Ommi writes, a Muslim woman must in the first place be concerned about protecting her sacred responsibilities. She leaves society and politics to men and diverts her attention to safe exercises such as mysticism, poetry, and religious studies (1987: 43). Muslim men clean up society and make it safe for their women's engagement. As Islam instructs, a woman's greatest jihad is taking care of her home. Omi's analysis, however, does not account for Islamist women activists in pre-revolutionary time.

The presence of women as political actors has been at best tensional, especially regarding those with agendas different from the Islamic state. Subordination of women's political role to their domestic responsibilities is recognized in all discussions. Nasrin Mosaffa (1997: 115), for instance, clarifies in her *Political Participation of Women in Iran* that women's political rights in Islam are defined in a framework that responds to women's "nature"—different-yet-equal political rights for men and women. In 1996, Tehran's Mayor appointed a woman as mayor of a Tehran district. On 7 January 1997, some 300 hizbullah women demonstrated in Tehran, denouncing *badhejâbi* (inadequate hejâb) and criticizing the appointment of that woman to mayorship—to those hizbullah women, being a mayor was a denigration of the lofty status of woman-wife and woman-mother.

It is not that women's political and familial roles are in conflict, says Mrs. Sefâti, a women's seminary instructor. "If she plans well, she can accomplish both." Obviously, however, "if she has two or three children, she is better off assuming fewer social and political responsibilities and instead taking care of her children" (*Zan-e Rouz* 22 January 1993: 16). When Massoumeh Ebtekar was assigned as Khatami's vice president, a *Zanân* reporter asked her if her husband prepared dinner "as a sign of support." She responded: "If he is forced, he might" (37: 4). The sexual division of labor might be modified, but does not fundamentally alter.

Domesticity and sexuality have functioned as grounds for curbing women's political participation, doubting their commitment, and controlling them in political arenas. Hojjatulislam Dinparvar warns against the danger of "women being abused for political purposes," emphasizing unidentified "female spies" who revealed secrets to their nations' foes (*Zan-e Rouz* 25 April 1987: 18). For many Islamists, the private realm of the family seems more suitable for women's temperament (Hosseini Tehrani 1997: 215, 219). Tâheri, a leading member of the University of Tehran's Islamic student organizations, holds that both sexes can be involved in politics, but it is "consensual" that women are not as active as men. "In this mutual agreement, women feel that they are not as protected outside the house and that men can accomplish responsibilities of outside life more effectively. This is not a historical injustice to women; it is rather a mutual agreement" (quoted in Ardalân 1998: 4).

Though Islamist women's political presence does not as a rule contradict their moral integrity or "natural responsibilities," oppositional politicking is condemned for crossing moral and social boundaries. Women who demonstrated in March 1979 against compulsory veiling were likened to whores: "Semi-naked women, dressed in black, moving like the dance of prostitutes, wearing repugnant Western perfumes, colorful jewelry, clenched their fists over the blood of martyrs to continue the rule of dissoluteness" (*Ettela'at* 6 July 1980).

Female former political prisoners stated during our interviews that to many of their jailers and inquisitors, oppositional political women were an oddity. They questioned these women's commitment to political ideals. To the Islamist wardens, they were in prison by mistake, duped into activism instead of pursuing "normal" lives. Prison authorities pitied that "young women are cooped up in a cell, instead of enjoying a calm family life." Female political prisoners considered this treatment an insult—"a ruthless form of verbal torture." Even today, outside the horrifying walls of prison, women's seriousness in (oppositional) politics is degraded. Their nonconformity is attributed to their compromised morality, not political commitment. An upper-middle-class woman whose family is well-positioned in the IRI government explains this situation as follows:

If a woman dissents, her sedition is attributed to corruption (*fesâd*), but if a man defies, his is regarded as political. "Political" is a more horrifying label, since accusations of corruption or even crime can be erased through connection or bribe, or both, but the same cannot be done with the label "political." (Private correspondence, 21 April 1997)

Preoccupation with domesticity and chastity in turn becomes a control mechanism. Parvin Ardalân, for instance, reports that Islamist student organizations avoid women's issues because many activists believe that these discussions create divisions between men and women (1998: 3). Women's virtue becomes a hostage in political battlegrounds. Mehrangiz Kar, an attorney activist for women's rights, for instance, was smeared in the monthly *Sobh* as a "corrupt woman with many faces," engaged in high-class pandering for foreign diplomats (*Sobh* 1997b). Even among competing *Islamist* factions, women's virtue is not spared. A female student told *Zanân*'s reporter that during the 1997 presidential election campaign, anti-Khatami student activists threatened to call her "father and brothers" and tell them to mind her activities and friends now that she was living in Tehran. Fearing for her reputation and family honor, she resigned (Ardalân 1998: 7).

Women's political presence is further complicated by their competition against those same ministers they revere. Questioning the wisdom of these men becomes particularly difficult for women, especially in close interpersonal relationships with fathers, brothers, or husbands. Nayereh Akhavân, who along with her husband was Majlis representative from Isfahan, rarely voted differently from her husband. In fact, when she left the Majlis to avoid voting on the 1999 budget, a surprised reporter from *Zanân* (March 1999: 72) commented that "for the first time, she made a decision independently from her husband." Fâezeh Hashemi Rafsanjani remarks in her interview with *Zanân* that when she disagrees with her father, she first tries to convince him, but if that fails, she does what he thinks is best. Her justification is illuminating: "First, because he is my father. Second, because if I am in public life, it is for him and whatever we do in society is reflected on him. He is . . . more experienced than I and is more knowledgeable in politics. . . . He can see things that I can't, is more future-oriented than I" (*Zanân* 1996: 16).

Going against the interpretation espoused by a leading ideologue is not, of course, an impossible task, since differences among the clergy always offer divergent interpretations. But, as long as patriarchy is defined as a vague "social disease" against which at least some religious authorities and true believers are immune, women's equal presence with men in politics seems redundant. This predicament curbs the sharpness of Islamist women's political demands, as the following comment by Shahlâ Habibi, President Rafsanjani's advisor on women's issues, reveals:

We believe that in an Islamic society, democracy means the rule of values. Thus, qualified individuals must hold appropriate positions irrespective of their sex. This does not mean reducing a woman's human dignity in acquiring equal posts with men. All activities by women ought to be based on considerations of their families' benefits . . . In accordance with our beliefs, we have never opted to define women's issues in limited terms of our sex. We do not consider women's issues personal and feminine at all. If, God forbid, the Majlis adopts a trend of presenting the opinion of some representative [unsympathetic to women's issues] as the Majlis' own position, wouldn't this idea strengthen in the mind of our Muslim women that women must constitute a higher number of Majlis representatives so that their concerns are better addressed? Wouldn't these women reach the conclusion that otherwise, women will not achieve their legal and Islamic rights? (*Zan-e Rouz* 26 February 1994: 9)

According to Shahlâ Habibi, increasing women's political presence ought not to be a key demand as long as there are God-fearing men who can uphold women's rights. Women's issues, she underlines, are not personal and feminine problems—they are general problems that must concern *Muslims as Muslims*, not as women or men. If Muslim politicians fail to recognize that, they run the risk of misleading Muslim women to believe that women must have more power in the political system in order to enjoy more rights. To Habibi, not only does this misconception undermine women's familial duty, but it also gives the false impression that Islamist men are not men of God, vying for justice.

The Islamic Republic has effectively mobilized women to promote its political agenda. Women are employed by various control agencies to roam the streets checking hejâb compliance. During the war, Islamist women garnered material and spiritual support. They sewed, prepared meals, collected financial assistance, and promoted the war. The Sisters' Basij Unit of the Organization for the Mobilization (Basij) of the Oppressed was established in 1980 and, according to an unofficial estimate, has over 1.8 million members, not counting its military wing (Mosaffa 1997: 130).

Women's units of the Basij offer rudimentary military training, continued education classes, and sport and cultural camps. In a 1986 communiqué, Sisters' Basij Unit expresses concern about the underutilization of womanpower in the war efforts: "Though the beloved Imam sometimes invites women to politics and prayer and the necessity of defense and jihad, asking women to be men's coaches, inspiration, and guides, do others treat women with the same due respect that the Leader of the Revolution does?" (*Zan-e Rouz* 29 November 1986: 4).

Women are not ready yet for combative tasks, the communiqué reads, but they can contribute to the war in other ways. They can protect the Islamic culture as a complement to men's militarism; mobilize women in support of the war; provide medical services; offer support-line services for those fighting in the frontline; and mentally prepare men to allow their wives and daughters' participation in defense training (52).

These efforts were indeed to use women's "sentimental connection" (to borrow Nabokov's terminology) in order to entice and emotionalize people to support the war. The uses of the sentimental connection at war times are many: *Now is the moment to protect Islam and the Islamic Republic of Iran just as one protects women. Now is the time to learn from women, young and old, who in one way or another step in to serve Islam and their country. Now that the Islamic motherland is raped, rise up and defend your honor.* The sentimental connection was vital in justifying the threat that war posed to the family, an institution that the Islamic state was to protect and strengthen. During the war, *Zan-e Rouz* featured a section called "Under the Sun of War." "Martyrs' relatives" were interviewed about their fallen men and expressed happiness that their sons or husbands had reached the noblest status of martyrdom.

In one issue, for instance, a woman identified only as the "wife of the martyr Javâd Aqazadeh" (*Zan-e Rouz* 16 June 1985) says that she married her husband at the age of 18. Her decision was based on his three-time pilgrimage to Imam Hossein's shrine in Karbalâ. She is a widow with 6 children, ranging from 3-and-a-half to 17. Upon learning about her husband's martyrdom, she turned to Allah and asked for patience. "And all of a sudden the world turned bright. My body was no longer numb. I went inside the house and prayed. Then called some relatives to arrange for the ceremonies. All the time, my only concern was that the news would make our counter-revolutionary neighbors happy" (45).

She then informed her children: "Do you remember your father always said 'May I see a day that I become pure enough that God would summon me'? God had admitted him now and we should be proud and happy" (45).

The wife of another martyr relates that "common belief" welded her to her husband. "Love of God is the supreme love and we both were in love with God and Islam. More important than anything else, I believed, marrying him would enable me to serve Islam better" (*Zan-e Rouz* 8 June 1985: 38). Nobody in the family is sad to lose a beloved, because, after all, he never belonged to anyone but Allah. That is why she thanks God that "he left behind everybody—mother, father, wife, children—and everything" to achieve martyrdom.

The martyrdom of the head of the household entails responsibilities for other family members (see Hosseini Tehrani 1994: 55). Martyrs' wives ought to raise their children to continue the mission of their fallen father. They are his and symbolize him among the living. Martyrs' wives are thus mobilized to uphold the state's objectives. One wife says:

I would like to exhort martyrs' wives that in public, in their social activities, they must behave in a manner that befits a martyr. The reason is that all eyes are watching them and their slightest slip appears grandiose in the public eye. . . . Another important issue is hejâb. These women must feel responsible for the blood of their spouse and the young martyrs of the ummat [the Islamic community] and observe the hejâb completely. (*Zan-e Rouz* 7 September 1985: 46)

Woman is absent at high levels of government. She has never been a president or minister. Only 14 out of 268 deputies of the Fifth Majlis were women (5%); this number dropped to 11 of 290 seats in the Sixth Majlis (3.8%), convened in the spring of 2000. The highest political position occupied by a woman is Vice President for Environmental Issues, a recent appointment by President Khatami—though many women expected to see several ministers in his administration. There are now 3 women presidential advisors. Under Khatami, Zahrâ Rahnavard became the first woman university president; a woman is the director of the Environmental Protection Organization. Few other women have been appointed to directorships of governmental offices.

The gap between the public's expectation of increasing women's political participation and the opportunities offered women by the IRI seems to be widening. According to the results of the Âyandeh Research Group, for instance, some 72% of voters in Tehran indicated no objection to the election of a woman to the presidency. Seventy-three percent expected to see women among President Khatami's ministers, and certainly more women in his cabinet, that is, more than the one woman presently in the cabinet (see *Zanân* 35 and 37).[5]

Women also complain of lack of responsiveness to their rights by high-level female officials. Due in part to women's demands, and perhaps partly out of their own beliefs, women politicians have been pressured at times to work for modification of laws and policies (e.g., the abolition of limitations on women's education or revisions in the divorce law). But their records have been disappointing, at best. An "open letter" published in

Salâm (quoted in *Iran Tribune* 15 January 1993) addressed to women representatives of the Majlis reads:

Honorable sister deputies, I do not know what has happened since you overcame election hardships that you have forgotten everything, to the extent that now everybody is wondering what you are doing in the Majlis. Are you aware of the dimensions of the tragic injustices that some men incur on women as heads of household, under the aegis of prerogatives that Shar‘ and customs afford men? . . . What has happened to you? Do you intend to think like men and see the Majlis only a platform for political quarrels? . . . My sisters, please explain how different it would have been if nine men were elected in your place.

More recently, Lâhiji refers to women in the executive branch as cadavers:

Let me address the few women who are in the executive branch and present at the decision-making level, yet who have performed but the role of corpses, that their actions up to now were aligned with the persisting negation of women's participation in political, economic, social, and cultural matters of this country. (Lâhiji 1999: 44)

Both women and the government have also considered women's nongovernmental organizations (NGOs). The IRI report to the Beijing conference mentions 38 such organizations. Since then, that number has risen steadily to over 90. The list of NGOs also comprises various ethnic or religious organizations, many formed prior to the revolution. These include the Armenian Women's Association, the Association of Women Friends of the Church, and the Jewish Women's Association. Women's magazines like *Zanân* and *Farzaneh* are also listed. Many concentrate on philanthropic activities, a form of social activism that extends from women's roles within the family and has a century-old history. The number of NGOs is limited compared to the total population of women and "thus cannot perform a significant role in the political participation of women" (Mosaffa 1997: 131).

Activists in Iran consider the problem with these organizations to be the central role of the Iranian government in organizing them. The overwhelming majority of these organizations, one activist writes me, "are built from the top" (4 June 1999), such that the real number of NGOs does not exceed the number of fingers on one hand (see also Jalali Naeini 2000). A few organizations, such as Some Women Publishers (Lâhiji 1999) that have maintained independence from the government, face numerous obstacles to their activities.

The Coordinating Office for Women's NGOs, a bureau within the President's Office, was set up to plan the activities of these organizations and supervise them. Activists are concerned that this Coordinating Office is a control agency of the Islamic government (see Jalali Naeini 1995b). Many NGOs are religious organizations or political groupings directly or closely related to the IRI. The Society for the Solidarity of Iranian Women, for instance, directed by Fâtemeh Hashemi (former President Hashemi's daughter), emphasizes the international representation of the IRI, the creation of networks among Islamist Iranian women abroad, and maintenance of contacts with the wives of IRI diplomats. The Society of the Women of the Islamic Republic of Iran, under the directorship of Zahrâ Mostafavi (Ayatollah Khomeini's daughter), similarly aims to promote the IRI through sponsoring candidates for the Majlis and participating in international conferences. Majlis representatives are the most prominent members of the Az-Zeynab Society that aims to promote "pure Islamic culture" among women. Nasrin Mosaffa (1997: 131) writes that several NGOs have no bylaws and maintain a corporatist relationship with the government through the Coordinating Office.

The Ministry of Interior requires adherence to a preset organizational structure in order to issue any NGO permission to be established. This also raises concern among activists, both because they need to have governmental approval to organize and because the imposed structure is too hierarchical. To avoid these restrictions, some women have recently turned to forming cooperatives (see *Hoquq-e Zanân* no. 2, April-May 1998: 42–43); it is too early to assess the outcomes of this move though early evidence is not promising.

Overall, religious and non-religious NGOs alike suffer from deficiencies that stem from their cliquish structure. Often they function as assemblies with familial or ideological ties predating their formation. Most are not "organizations" in the conventional sense of formal groups with specified objectives, which others with similar goals can join. The roots of the problem go deep into the absence of free, sustained, party-like political activism in Iranian history (Ahmady Khorasany 1998a).

Numerous stumbling blocks to women's involvement in local and national politics means that whenever women do maintain a genuine political presence, they accomplish that *despite the Islamic state*, not *as a result of* it. Though conflicts among different Islamist factions may create open spaces for women's activism—as, for instance, the recent crevices emerging from the battle between pro-Khatami reformists and pro-Khamenehii conservatives—it is women's resilience in opposing the seclusiveness of private patriarchy that has kept women's political rights integral to cultural politics. Indeed, despite all discriminations, women do find ways to exert pressure on the system and have remained key contenders in political battles. A prime example is the 1997 presidential election. The candidate most favored by the clerical leadership was Ali Akbar Nâteq Nouri, a clergy Speaker of the Parliament. His campaign promised tougher policies on gender relations. His opponent, Mohammad Khatami, promised moderation, less restrictive policies for the media, and less social control for women and youth. Khatami's promises won him an overwhelming majority (70% of all the votes), a considerable portion belonging to women and young voters.

With the passage of time, both the number of women in politics and the content of their demands have transcended the initial intention of the IRI. In state-related politics, rank-and-file members have gained experience and are claiming more prominent positions. Many women from traditional families now have a history of social and political involvement. These experiences led even many ardent Islamists to question their share in the Islamic government. Some devout women feel a tension between their active role in society and their Islamic upbringing, as a member of the Islamic Society of Amir Kabir University relates:

Since I was a kid, they gave me a doll to talk to, but they introduced the bicycle to the boy to ride in the street, taught him how to defend himself, to fight for his freedom. How can one expect someone like me to decide about women's issues and appear in decision-making positions when I enter the university? (Ardalân 1998: 3)

Political participation has created expectations among Islamist women that demand modification of the laws affecting women in family and society. I will discuss the demands of these women reformists—often referred to as "Islamic feminists"—at length in *Women in Iran: Emerging Voices in the Women's Movement*.

Beyond official politics, women's organizing efforts have led to the emergence of known and unknown leading activists with varied distance to the states. Reformist Islamist women are notable examples, as are secular and radical activists of the women's, students' or working class's movements. Also, in 1999, two percent of municipal candidates were women; 297 in urban areas and 484 in rural areas were elected (*Zanân* March 1999: 65). All candidates had to be approved as being devoted to the "Islamic system" and the Supreme Religious Leader (Khamenehii).

Women have thusly pushed the limited space of tokenism that the IRI opened for women. Though women's presence in official politics has been overall limited and constrained, pressures from below have forced the government to reposition itself vis-à-vis women. Though alterations and modifications in the law and socioeconomic policies have been too superficial to enact any long-lasting and far-reaching reform, they nonetheless attest to the fact that women are contenders the IRI cannot overlook.

RECAPITULATION

In the previous chapter I examined the Islamic treatment of gender, arguing that in this approach, gender is essentialist and teleological. In chapter 7, I discussed the implications of the Islamic analysis of gender for the IRI's social and economic policies. I argued that these policies are shaped in the context of a conflict between two agendas: one opting to exclude women from the public and revive private patriarchy, the other aspiring to afford women some public presence without compromising their domestic responsibilities in the Islamic gender ideology.

Positing different responsibilities for men and women entails different treatments under the law. With mothering and wifehood deemed women's central roles, women's public role becomes contingent upon their fulfillment of domestic responsibilities. Regarded as the sole breadwinners of the family, men gain considerable power in the family. They maintain great latitude in divorce, have custody of the children, and receive a higher portion of inheritance. In marital life, women are required to live in the dwelling of their husband's choice. Since men are head of household, women are prohibited from marrying non-Muslims, unless they convert into Islam. Women's mobility is limited by being required to have their husband's permission to travel abroad, by obstacles they face in traveling alone within the country. If husbands consider their wife's employment a threat to the well-being or the honor of the family, they can bar their wives from work. Measures of this sort reinforce men's control over women in both private and public spheres.

The emphasis on woman-as-wife and woman-as mother, especially in the face of rising unemployment, has caused an increase in the number of housewives and a decline in women's seeking employment. Though the increase in the number of housewives does not account for the various ways housewives pursue economic gains, it surely reveals a preference for women to remain "in the private sphere." The primacy of domestic roles is not undermined even for employed women, adding to the myriad problems that these women must overcome.

The IRI's educational policies reflect the Islamic assumptions about the natural differences of the sexes and women's domesticity. Based on these assumptions, for several years women were denied certain fields of study deemed unbefitting women's nature. Though opposition forced the government to lift those limitations, the labor market still accepts these skilled women only reluctantly. The IRI's educational policies aim to create female personnel for serving women in a segregated society. This emphasis has led to an increase in women's education, especially in teacher training and in medical sciences. The illiteracy rate declined, especially among the younger generations of women. But a pronounced gap exists between rural and urban areas and among provinces.

Women's overall participation in the labor force declined under the Islamic regime. The majority of Iranian women are now housewives. A marked decline in women's formal employment is in rural areas, indicating an increase in their participation in unpaid family labor. Since the Iranian labor market prefers skilled, educated women, the rural and urban female poor are inadequately prepared for competition. High inflation and low pay force workingwomen to work long hours and accept limited benefits. Laws supposed to protect women work against them because workers are inadequately educated about the laws. Besides, employers lack incentive: to lower costs and avoid labor law requirements, they refrain from hiring female workers. Conditions are more favorable for white-collar female workers. The number of women workers in this category has increased, with government employees—especially teachers—maintaining the highest share, while having a low share among the skilled laborers of the industrial sector.

In the realm of politics, I emphasized the IRI's mobilization of lower- and middle-class women into "street politics" and the use of "sentimental connection" in such efforts as gaining support for the war against Iraq. I also discussed the involvement of token women in politics, state-sponsored women's organizations, and the NGOs. I argued that women's political involvement in the Islamic Republic is tensional, not only because of the conflicting interpretations of women and politics in Islam, but also due to women's political roles tending to be ultimately contingent on their femininity. Sexuality and domesticity, I proposed, lead to restraints for women's political participation, doubt about their resolution, and control of their presence in political arenas. Nonetheless, as in education and employment, women have continued to hold ground in politics, utilizing every available mechanism to maintain social and political engagement. The mobilization of Islamist women has also led to their demands for better treatment and for a higher share of social and political resources. These attempts, however, face a serious dilemma from the outset. The IRI claims that Islam has the answer to all questions, including those related to gender. The amazing insistence that Islam is the correct alternative to everything is reflected in the slogan of "Neither Eastern nor Western; the Islamic Republic." With such persistence, gender politics becomes coercive to its core so that it can fit ideological confines. This Islamic framework limits any reformist reinterpretations. These reinterpretations, known as "Islamic feminism," I will discuss in *Women in Iran: Emerging Voices in the Women's Movement*.

NOTES

1. This is based on a Koranic edict (sura *Women*, v. 11): "A male shall inherit twice as much as a female" (Koran 1988: 367). This is the foundation of the IRI inheritance laws. See Kar (1999b: 335–37).

2. Nosrat Amin (1886–1984) was a religious scholar who authored several books in Farsi and Arabic, including a 15-volume interpretation of the Koran. For her biography, see Pouran Farrokhzad (1999: 287–88).

3. Feminists who do not share Islamist women's desire to safeguard the Islamist

state are also compelled to work within the Islamic confines, but I differentiate between the former activists who, though they may see the IRI antithetical to sexual equality, opt to gain some rights within existing relations, and the latter group of women who believe the IRI is capable of liberating women. The former has to acknowledge the actual limits in order to eventually transcend them; the latter wants to rectify mistakes to preserve the system.

4. The reformists are now proposing the political inclusion of "legal opposition," those who may be critical of the IRI, but do not aim to topple the government.

5. Nasrin Mosaffa (1997) reports a similar favorable result among women.

8

Volatile Times: Gender, Coercion, and the Possibilities of Resistance

Lit a lamp
And passed through city streets.
Our nocturnal cry
tore
the curtain of night
and slit the moon.
The horse neighed
and the leopard
cried a thousand times.

I intended to write this book in a language that could convey the tragic intensity of coercion. At the risk of presenting a monolithic Islamist discourse on gender, or a unified set of gender policies of the Islamic state, I wished to portray the centrality of coercion in the development of gender relations under the IRI. Fortunately, however, I do not seem to have succeeded. Readers can easily detect the volatility of gender in post-revolutionary Iran. Resistance and opposition are so intertwined with coercion that one cannot be depicted without revealing the other. Mahin Khadivi's poem "Nocturnal" best testifies to the inevitability of defiance in oppressive conditions (Khadivi 1999: 47). Using a metaphor so familiar to Iranian activists of all strands, the very title of the poem—*Shabaneh*—communicates struggle. *Shab*, night, images oppression in Iranian oppositional discourse. *Shabnameh*, letter of the night, refers to subversive literature distributed in night's protective darkness. *Shabaneh*, nocturnal, has encoded "rebelliousness" for a host of authors in contemporary Iranian history. When the dark clouds of oppression bar the sun, one has no choice but to light a lamp, tear the curtain of night, and cause an uproar in the tranquil jungle. Coercive gender relations under the IRI have darkened the terrain. In the midst of wretchedness, daily struggle goes on.

My goal in this book was to trace gender politics in Iran as the interplay of ideologies and sociohistorical conditions. Changes in gender relations under the Pahlavis, especially after the land reforms of the 1960s, refashioned the patriarchal system in Iran from private to public. Consequently, some women gained increasing access to the formal sectors of the economy, education, politics (with all the limitations of formal politics under the Shah), and improved legal status. Unevenly and at a snail's pace, public patriarchy aimed to shift the locus of gender control from private to public. Men maintained their position as the family patriarchs, despite some limitations on their power in divorce and polygyny. Domestic division of labor changed only moderately, with women facing the burden of both job and household tasks. Though women gained the franchise, political realms remained tightly under governmental control—independent women's organizations were replaced by the state-formed Women's Organization of Iran. Changing gender relations also modified the realm of sexuality. Public interaction of unmarried couples gained some legitimacy, especially among educated, urban families who became more accepting of dating as a prelude to marriage. Double standards persisted, nevertheless, and emergent gender relations made women more vulnerable to various forms of sexual transgression in public. Male violence against women persisted, but was unreported.

Changing gender relations were the source of a gender crisis, creating uncertainty and ambivalence in men and women about living amidst outdated beliefs and practices and emergent relations. This crisis appeared even more serious and detrimental to Shiite clerics—a sense of doom that I conveyed earlier in the book by quoting Yeats: "Things fall apart; the center cannot hold." Following the reforms of the sixties, the clergy felt more marginalized in their public roles and found changes in gender relations threatening to the Islamic family and moral system. In other words, the consequences of the changes in gender relations should be gauged not only in the actual modifications, but also in their symbolic implications. In the Islamist vision, Iran under the Pahlavis was on the same path as Western societies. Women simultaneously embodied the infidel without and the chaos within. The refashioning of patriarchy then became significant for both its immediate effect and future ramifications. In this sense, the *Islamic* revolution was an attempt to prevent the future by restoring Islam's authority and rescuing Iran from the "corruption" Islamists saw ravaging society.

Islamists sought an environment wherein women could be protected from men's deception. Reverting the patriarchal structure to the old private system would create a harmonious family that offered women the opportunity to pay their dues to society by creating a peaceful domestic life and instilling appropriate values in the new generation.

Islamists originally opposed women's enfranchisement and their political participation. But they eventually realized the inevitability of women's social presence. Muslim ideologues like Shariati, mujahedin leaders, and Motahari aimed to summon women to fight *for* Islam. The new Muslim woman participated in history-making without renouncing her responsibilities as a woman.

The Left's ideological blindness to gender was compounded by the Pahlavi state's control over political expression that prohibited the emergence of a genuine women's movement. Assessments of changes in gender relations became marred with political objectives. As the Pahlavi government presented "women's emancipation" a royal gift, criticizing—even rejecting—the changes became synonymous with political commitment among the opposition. The emergence of public patriarchy was symptomatic of increasing dependence on imperialist powers. Seeing through this prism, secular and leftist activists misconstrued the Islamists' opposition to the refashioning of patriarchy as advocating dependence and overlooked the anti-women characteristic of the Islamists' campaign.

Women, particularly urban middle-class women, actively participated in the 1979 revolution, yet women from traditional and modern middle classes pursued divergent objectives. Islamist women opted for a gender identity that accommodated their social and political involvement in the new dispensation of society and repairing of the traditional family. The professional women of the modern middle class participated in the revolution to fight against discriminations and social injustices of private and public patriarchy. Yet the overarching objective of toppling the monarchy overshadowed professional, middle-class women's concerns with equality.

Islamists' ascent to power commenced an intricate program of reconstructing private patriarchy. The Family Protection Act was repealed. Polygyny became lawful; divorce, men's prerogative. The veil became mandatory. Women faced increasing restrictions on employment. The new Constitution deemed motherhood women's "undeniable right," making mothering their focal responsibility. The newly established IRI assumed the role of women's guardian. Though officially regarded as citizens, women were legally treated as being worth less than men, raising serious concerns about their sociopolitical status. We discussed, for example, complications related to women's marriage to non-Muslims or non-Iranians. Discriminations are more pronounced among nonbeliever and non-Muslim women as they are subjected to Islamic law—a belief system that they do not share, that treats them as "the Others." The construction of the Islamic state, then, has been intertwined with systematic exclusion of non-Muslim men and women. The Islamization of society means coercing non-Islamists to conformity with Islamic rules. Compulsory hejâb symbolizes the IRI's co-ercive gender policies—and a site of women's unyielding resistance.

Though the Left resolutely opposed discriminatory measures like restrictions on women's employment or the Bill of Retribution, it failed to address sexual injustice in a comprehensive manner. Fighting against patriarchal oppression was simply not among the Left's priorities. The development of public patriarchy put the Left in the midst of several dilemmas. According to socialist visions of "women's emancipation," increased educational and employment opportunities had to be welcomed, yet these measures were evidently insufficient to "liberate" women in a capitalist system. With the rise of public patriarchy, combating overt and covert forms of patriarchal domination required a more nuanced interpretation than the Left's two-pronged analysis (the capitalist exploitation of women *and* cultural imperialist misuse of sexuality). The Left did realize the role of "traditionalism" in the reproduction of sexual inequality, but fear of alienating "the masses" prevented the Left from developing a sustained criticism of "traditional" beliefs and practices. Furthermore, as a problem of the "superstructure," sexual oppression was expected to dissolve after the defeat of capitalism. Thus leftist women, even when aware of sexual inequality, defined their goals first and foremost as fighting against class exploitation. Their representative revolutionism regarded fighting against sexual oppression significant only to the extent that it promoted class war. Many leftist organizations first downplayed the significance of the IRI's attacks on women's rights. Following the spread of the women's movement, women's organizations with overt or covert ties to leftist groups were formed. The main purpose of these organizations, however, was to promote support for their mother organizations.

As the Islamic Republic consolidated, its gender policies further unfolded in the formation of a patriarchal triad whereby Islam, patriarchy, and the Islamic state strengthen one another socially and politically. The patriarchal triad by no means connotes a unified, static set of policies. The modifications of the IRI's gender politics from exclusionist-protectivism to segregationist-protectivism, and later the support of some IRI statesmen for "Islamic feminism" indicate that the patriarchal triad can accommodate a range of gender policies. Yet, exclusionism, segregationism, and reformist women's Islamism all operate within the framework of Islam and the Islamic state. Besides, various Islamic gender relations maintain the patriarchal structure, albeit they differ in their preference for private or public patriarchy.

Islamic gender analysis presumes the world as a purposive system. Individuals' sex is predefined with assigned roles, deemed different but complementary for men and women. Sexuality plays an important role in creating a harmonious world. Intimacy enhances happiness and tranquillity in a family and, more significantly, reproduces healthy human beings. Gender teleology thusly connects sex, gender, and sexuality. The mission of the Islamic state is to create proper conditions for men and women to accomplish their holy duties. Since the family is regarded as a microcosmic society, the IRI has considered it pivotal to "strengthen the family"; that is, to emphasize the primacy of the domestic role for women and secure men's position as heads of households.

Predefined, gender identities have rigid models of private and public expression. The appearance of Muslim men and women is crucial for IRI ideologues, as an Islamic society is to have distinct characteristics. The ideal gender look and behavior also creates a gender pyramid. In this hierarchy, devout men occupy the highest position; the more removed men are from this ideal male, the lower their position. Women are allotted a precarious status: collectively, they have less power and rights than men, but *Islamist* women, especially those with political power, could wield considerable power over others, even non-Islamist men.

Coercion has been integral to the Islamic state's gender politics in several ways. The restrengthening of men's power within the family has justified family violence, and in particular spousal abuse. Furthermore, imposing Islamists' rigid conception of gender on a heterogeneous population that includes different shades of Muslims, nonbelievers, and non-Muslim has proved impossible without the use of overt force. Post-revolutionary Iran has been the scene of contentions between Islamists and the public over major issues of human rights and democratic freedom as well as such minute details as wearing sunglasses or make-up, or the interaction between men and women. The hejâb especially has turned into a battleground. Women have resisted the regime's stringent dress code, negotiating dress color and style. Though the ambiguity of Islamic law on "proper hejâb" creates possibilities for negotiating "proper gender behavior," it also puts women in a vulnerable position since the definition of "acceptable dress" could change. Especially at times of political or economic crises, the IRI has used this uncertainty to increase pressure on women as a symbol of its might.

Though the IRI's initial exclusionist protectionism aimed to keep women out of the public, politico-economic realities forced the regime to adopt a segregationist-protectivist policy. Women have maintained a public presence, but increasingly in female-exclusive spaces. The results of this policy are quite evident in female employment and educational patterns since the rise of the Islamic state. Based on the IRI's assumptions about the natural differences of the sexes, women were for several years barred from certain fields of study deemed unsuitable for women's nature and domestic role. Women's resistance eventually forced the government to eliminate those limitations, but the regime's educational policy has remained in effect: training female personnel for serving women in a segregated society. This emphasis has resulted in an increase in women's presence in certain fields such as teacher training and medical sciences.

Illiteracy is 30% for females 15 or over and 16.3% for males of the same age. Because of the increased availability of education, the illiteracy rate among females aged 15 through 24 years is 8.2%. Illiteracy for boys of the same age is 3.7%. (This data only reflects the population who can read and write Farsi. Ethnic minorities in Iran are not allowed education in their mother tongues.)

Moderate but steady changes can be traced in female education at both pre-college and college levels. Female enrollment in primary schools was 47% in 1996, compared to 38% in 1975. Secondary enrollment rose from 36% (1975) to 46% (1996). At the tertiary level, enrollment remained between 28% in 1975 and 27% in 1990, but rose to 36% in 1996. The closing of coeducational schools negatively affected women's technical and agricultural education.

Gender discrepancies are augmented in rural areas, or in poor provinces. For example, though girls and boys in rural areas have similar chances of receiving a primary education, rural girls have limited opportunities to study in technical or agricultural fields. Poor, predominantly ethnic provinces often have limited educational opportunities for females. In all ethnic provinces, female literacy is lower than male literacy and often falls considerably below the national rate.

The majority of women in higher education are enrolled in BA/S and postgraduate programs, while men constitute a higher percentage in programs offering an AA. Medical sciences attract a high proportion of women, who by the mid-1990s constituted over half of medical school enrollment. The government seeks to create sufficient skilled female healthcare staff to provide services to women.

There has been a decline in women's overall labor force participation in the IRI. In 1976, women 10 years and older constituted 13.77% of employed people. In 1986, this percentage dropped to almost nine percent. During this period—wrought by revolutionary changes and prolonged war—men's employment rose 2.8%. In 1996, women composed some 12% of the employed workers 10 years and over—11.3% in urban and 13.4% in rural areas. Women work only in areas Islam deems appropriate; deems compatible with physical and psychological capacities; or in fields where gender does not affect performance. Women's work must not interfere with their familial responsibilities.

An increase in women's participation in unpaid family labor has led to a considerable decline in women's employment in rural areas. Rural female unemployment increased from 6% in 1976 to 30% in 1986. In 1991, the unemployment rate for rural women was over 28% (compared to about 10% for men) and almost 22% for urban women (compared to nine percent for men).

In the urban economy, the more the market moves toward skilled labor, the fewer the employment opportunities for rural and urban poor women. While skilled laborers of the industrial sector have a low share of the employment, government workers, particularly teachers, maintain the highest employment rate among workingwomen.

Women's political participation in IRI politics is at best tensional, especially because sexuality and domesticity cause restraints for women's political participation and make their determination questionable. The IRI has mobilized lower- and middle-class women into "street politics," especially in using "sentimental connection" to gain support for the war against Iraq. The Islamic regime has also involved a limited number of women in formal politics, a considerable number of whom are relatives of Islamist statesmen. A number of NGOs have emerged since the 1995 Beijing conference. Most NGOs, however, are state-sponsored and activists express concern about the autonomy and freedom of action of these organizations.

But women have also gained ground in their struggle under the IRI. Despite the IRI's limitation, literacy among urban women has increased, women have remained active in the economy and politics, and women have fought for legal rights. "Iranian women have come to a self-awareness that is unique in our history," writes a feminist activist and scholar from Iran. And there is hardly any exaggeration in her statement. The issues women have raised in cultural and political fields reflect this awareness. The IRI's officials and opponents alike *have to* consider women's requests, or at least claim to do so, if they hope to be taken seriously. Every faction of the government knows the significance of women's vote and support. And women have also realized for the most part that they are a social force, though they have not designed clear ways to use this power in their favor. That is not surprising of course, since (again, in the words of the Iranian feminist quoted above) "women power/girl power is something new and forceful here–we have not experienced it before."

Women, especially urban, middle-class women, have resisted the IRI's gender policies from the outset. The Islamic government had to modify its exclusionist policy and concede to a segregationist agenda. The IRI's attempts to create a "new Muslim Iranian woman" on the basis of Islamic moral and shari'ah codes have been less than successful. The Islamist heteromarital sexuality—"chaste" women and men expressing their sexuality only within marital confines—has not become a reality. Men and women negotiate the boundaries of sanctioned sexuality. Men have access to ample resources for "licit" and "illicit" sexual relationships, through secret liaisons or available legal ways such as temporary marriage and multiple permanent marriages. Women, too, can negotiate the same boundaries, particularly in favorable conditions like having "understanding parents" who approve of their daughter having a boyfriend, or a friend who can provide them with a safe place for a rendezvous. Similarly, Islamists' emphasis on heterosexuality is compromised by the difficulties of proving a homosexual relationship and the implicit tolerance of homosexuality as "compensatory" sex.

The government employs coercive measures to Islamicize gender in public and private, to restrict male and female interactions, and to promote "Muslim womanhood" as *the* model for all Iranian women. People have to abide by these measures in public (albeit often in modified forms); yet many remain opposed to these laws and avoid them in private. Though undoubtedly the constant indoctrination has left its marks on aspects of gender relations in post-revolutionary Iran, many, especially middle class, educated, and urban women and men, comply ritualistically rather than due to earnest convictions. This duality of public and private lives demonstrates a crisis of ideological legitimacy for the Islamic Republic. The IRI's troubled gender ideology becomes evident in two reactions by women. One relates to reformist Islamist women's reinterpretations of Islamic doctrine, the trend known as "Islamic feminism." The other involves the concerted, though still embryonic, attempts to articulate gender relations on secular grounds.

"Islamist reformist women" refers to a heterogeneous group with diverse orientations and agendas. Devout Muslims work side-by-side with nonbelievers, secularists, and even atheists. These varied interests, however, converge in a conviction that Iranian women ought to articulate their demands within the dominant Islamic legal and political frameworks. Islamist reformist women propose a series of reforms to enhance women's legal protection in family and society and to increase women's share in education, employment, and politics. Yet, these reformists leave many fundamental gender issues unresolved. In exchange for better conditions for employed women, reformist women suggest a less strict traditional sexual division of labor, and encourage housewives to be content with respect for their domestic roles, rather than to challenge their imposed domesticity. Islamist reformist women focus primarily on problems affecting employed, middle-class women. Working-class women's concerns are rarely reflected in their analyses. Cultural relativism, endorsed especially by women reformers within the Islamic government, effectively leaves intact many cultural and traditional constraints affecting gender relations (e.g., individual rights, hejâb, or sexual freedom and preferences).

Continuing the discussion of gender and sex exclusively in the context of marital life, and the presumption of the heterosexual family as the building block of society, limit the variety of gender experiences and relations. Besides, remaining within the confines of the Islamic state, Islamist women reformists practically equate *Iranian* women with *Muslim* women, maintaining the subjection of nonbelievers and non-Muslims to Islamic rule. All in all, the reformist women's movement is a crisis-oriented one that does not fundamentally challenge patriarchy.

The community of believers, or the ummat, constitutes the foundation of the Islamic society. Muslim theologians are not unanimous on how to govern such a "community." While some call for extreme conformity and obedience to Islam as embodied in the Supreme Leader, others accept differences of opinion. Both approaches, however, share a fundamental belief in the sanctity of the Islamic framework. Even the reformist rhetoric of Muslim ideologues like President Khatami deems the rule of Islam beyond reproach. Diversity of interpretations, then, is true only for competing *Islamic* expositions. In either case, the Islamic ummat—a community based on the inviolability of Islam—remains foundational to Islamic society. Nonbelievers and non-Muslims are excluded from social and political control.

Iranian youth and secular activists have contested the undemocratic rule of such a community. The conflict between the values and lifestyles of the young people and Islamic rules has resulted in the emergence of "cultural crimes," the banning of acts that deviate from behavioral standards that are often only vaguely defined. The regulation of everyday activities relates to a range of behaviors that include the use of cosmetics, alcohol and drug consumption, and interactions between males and females. The tension is especially evident among the young people of middle and upper classes that benefit from familial accumulated economic and cultural capital. But the conflict is also present in lower classes. Post-revolutionary developments in some cases heightened—rather than diminished—the gap between the expectations of lower classes and Islamic alternatives. In the workplace, private life, public representation of the self, challenging gender norms and sexual values—in all these areas, ordinary men and women have demonstrated a resistance to the dominant order that goes far beyond what Islamist reformists have articulated.

Quietly but steadily, secular oppositional politics has developed through the cracks of the dual society. Despite economic, social, and political barriers, secular women activists have formed collectivities to pursue practical and theoretical objectives—celebrating International Women's Day, organizing cooperatives, campaigning for reforms in gender policies, forming informal study groups, or running small publications. These efforts have also inspired tendencies to revise leftist political culture and cultural politics. These re-readings have inspired fresh assessments of the Iranian culture, civil society, individual rights, and political priorities. This is not to suggest that these discussions have reached clear articulations; most are ongoing controversies, many in embryonic stages. There are also strong debates and differences of opinion. At the present, a major controversy among secular activists concerns the future of the Islamic Republic: some propose cautious, small steps that strengthen Khatami's position vis-à-vis his opponents, while others adhere to more radical politics that would eventually abolish the Islamic system altogether.

Bibliography

Abbas-Gholizadeh, Mahboobeh. Hameh Bâyad Râzi Bâshand: Arzyâby-e Avalin Gozâresh-e Melly-e Zanân-e JII, dar Goftogoi's bâ Khânomhâ Shahlâ Habibi va Doktor Parvin Ma'rufi ("Everybody Should Be Content: Assessment of the First National Report of the Women of the IRI, in an Interview with Mrs. Shahlâ Habibi and Dr. Parvin Ma'rufy"). *Farzaneh: Journal of Women's Studies and Research* 7 (1995–1996b):139–46.

Abrahamian, Ervand. *Iran Between Two Revolutions*. Princeton: Princeton University Press, 1982.

———. "Iran's Turbaned Revolution." *The Middle East Annual. Issues and Events*, ed. D.H. Partington. Boston: G.K. Hall, 1982.

———. *The Iranian Mujahedin*. New Haven: Yale University Press, 1989.

Acker, Joan. "Gendered Institutions: From Sex Roles to Gendered Institutions." *Contemporary Sociology* 21.5 (1992): 565–69.

Afary, Janet. "The War Against Feminism in the Name of the Almighty: Making Sense of Gender and Muslim Fundamentalism." *New Left Review* 224 (1997): 89–110.

Afkhami, Mahnaz. "Iran: A Future in the Past—The 'Pre-revolutionary Women's Movement.' " *Sisterhood Is Global*, ed. R. Morgan. New York: Anchor Books, 1984.

Afshar, Haleh. "The Legal, Social and Political Position of Women in Iran." *International Journal of the Sociology of Law* 13 (1985): 47–60.

Afshar, Soraya. "The Economic Base for the Revival of Islam in Iran." *Women of Iran: The Conflict with Fundamentalist Islam*, ed. F. Azari. London: Ithaca, 1983.

Afshârnyâ, Alireza. *Zan va Rahâ'y-e Niruhây-e Towlid (Woman and the Emancipation of the Forces of Production)*. Tehran: Pishgâm, 1978.

Agaev, S.L. "The Zigzag Path of the Iranian Revolution." *Soviet Sociology* 25.2 (1988): 3–30.

Aghajanian, Akbar. "The Status of Women and Female Children in Iran: An Update from the 1986 Census." *In the Eye of the Storm: Women in Post-Revolutionary Iran*, ed. M. Afkhami and E. Friedl. Syracuse: Syracuse University Press, 1994a.

———. "Family Planning and Contraceptive Use in Iran, 1967–1992." *International Family Planning Perspectives* 20.2 (1994b): 66–69.

Ahmadi Oskoo'i, Marziyh. *Khâterat-e Yek Rafiq: Yâddâshthây-e Cherik-e Fadâ'i-e Khalq (The Memoirs of A Comrade: Notes of A People's Fedaii Guerrilla)*. OIPFG, n.d.

Ahmady Khorasany, Noushin. Az Mahâfel-e Zanâneh tâ Tashakkolhây-e Mostaqell-e Zanân: Râhi beh Souy-e Jâme'eh-ye Madani ("From Women's Cliques to Autonomous Women's Organizations: A Path to Civil Society"). *Farhang-e Towse'eh* (Special Issue on Women) (1998a): 12–18.

Ahmed, Leila. "Feminism and Feminist Movement in the Middle East, A Preliminary Exploration: Turkey, Egypt, Algeria, People's Democratic Republic of Yemen." *Women's Studies International Forum* 5.2 (1982): 153–68.

Akbari, Ali Akbar. *Barrasy-e Chand Mas'aleh-ye Ejtemâ'i (Investigating Some Social Problems)*. Tehran: Sepehr, 1977.

Akhavi, Shahrough. *Religion and Politics in Contemporary Iran*. Albany: State University of New York Press, 1980.

———. "Shariati's Social Thought." *Religion and Politics in Iran: Shi'ism from Quietism to Revolution*, ed. N.R. Keddie. New Haven: Yale University Press, 1983.

'Alâ'i Rahmâni, Fâtemeh. *Zan az Didgâh-e Nahjul Balâgha (Woman According to Nahjul Balâgha)*. Tehran: Sâzeman-e Tabliqât-e Islami, 1992.

Alaolmolki, Nozar. "The New Iranian Left." *The Middle East Journal* 41.2 (1987): 218–33.

Al-e Ahmad, Jalal. *Plagued by the West*. Trans. P. Sprachman. Delmar, NY: Caravan, 1982.

Amin, Shâdi. Ravâj-e Bachchehrobâ'i: Sokoot-e Mardân, E'terâz-e Zanân ("Kidnapping of Children by Their Fathers: Men's Silence, Women's Protest"). *Women in Struggle* 9 (1998): 6–7.

Anderson, Benedict. *Imagined Communities: Reflections on the Origin and Spread of Nationalism*. London: Verso, 1991.

Anonymous. Kâbusi beh Nâm-e Jomhury-e Islami ("A Nightmare Called the Islamic Republic"). *Homan* 13 (1998): 34–35, 39.

Arâni, Taqi. Zan va Mâteryâlizm ("Woman and Materialism"). Rpt. in Arâni, Neveshteh-hây-e 'Elmi, Falsafi va Ejtemâ'i ("Scientific, Philosophical, and Sociological Writings"). *Historical Documents: The Workers' Social-Democratic, and Communist Movement in Iran*, ed. C. Chacqueri. Tehran: Antidote, 1983. (Originally published in *Donya* 6 June-July 1934).

'Arâqi, Ezatullâh. *Hoquq-e Kâr (Labor Law)*. vol. 1. Tehran: Dâneshgâh-e Melli, 1977.

Ardalân, Parvin. Zanân az Sazemânhây-e Siyâsy-e Dâneshju'i Gorizânand, Cherâ? ("Why Do Women Distance Themselves from Political Student Organizations?"). *Zanân* 49 (1998): 2–7.

————. *Zanân* Nashriyât-e Zanân râ Mo'arrefi Mikonad (*"Zanân* Introduces Women's Magazines"). *Zanân* 52 (1999): 2–6.

Âryânpour, Amir Hossein. *Dar Âstâneh-ye Rastâkhiz: Resâleh'i dar bâb-e Dinâmizm-e Târikh (On the Eve of Resurrection: An Essay on the Dynamism of History)*. Tehran: n.p., 1951.

Âyandegân. Shomâ az Re'is Jomhur-e Zan Sokhan Goftid, Pas Hesâr va Divâr Cheh Ma'ni Dârad? ("You Have Talked About a Woman President, Then What Do Fence and Wall Mean?") 6 March 1979.

Az. "The Women's Struggle in Iran." *Monthly Review* 32.10 (1981): 22–30.

Azari, Farah. "Islam's Appeal to Women in Iran: Illusions and Reality." *Women of Iran: The Conflict with Fundamentalist Islam*, ed. F. Azari. London: Ithaca, 1983a.

————. "Sexuality and Women's Oppression in Iran." *Women of Iran: The Conflict with Fundamentalist Islam*, ed. F. Azari. London: Ithaca, 1983b.

Bâhonar, Mohammad Javâd. *Houquq-e Zan dar Islam (Women's Rights in Islam)*. Qom: Qiyâm, n.d.

Bamdad, Badr ol-Moluk. *From Darkness into Light: Women's Emancipation in Iran*. Trans. F.R.C. Bagley. New York: Exposition, 1977.

Banani, Amin. *Modernization of Iran*. Stanford, CA: Stanford University Press, 1961.

Bâqeriân, Mitrâ. Eshteqâl va Bikâry-e Zanân az Didgâh-e Towse'eh ("Women's Employment and Unemployment: A Developmental Perspective"). *Zanân* 1 (1991): 4–10.

Bâqi, 'Emâdudin. *Jonbesh-e Dâneshjo'i Iran: Az Âqâz tâ Enqelâb-e Islami (Student Movement in Iran: From the Beginning to the Islamic Revolution)*. Tehran: Jâme'eh-ye Iraniân, 2000.

Baraheni, Reza. *Târikh-e Mozakkar (Masculine History)*. Tehran: Mohammad Ali 'Elmi, 1972.

————. *Ba'd az 'Arusi Cheh Gozasht? (What Happened after the Wedding?)* Tehran: Nashr-e Nou, 1982.

Bardenstein, Carol. "Raped Brides and Steadfast Mothers." *The Politics of Motherhood: Activist Voices from Left to Right*, ed. A. Jetter, A. Orleck, and D. Taylor. Hanover, NH: University Press of New England, 1997.

Barnstein, Kate. *My Gender Workbook*. New York: Routledge, 1998.

Bashiriyeh, Hossein. *Jâme'eh-ye Madani va Towse'eh-ye Siyâsi dar Iran: Goftârhâ'i dar Jâme'ehshenâsy-e Siyâsi (Civil Society and Political Development in Iran: Essays on Political Sociology)*. Tehran: 'Olum-e Novin, 1999.

Basu, Amrita. "Feminism Inverted: The Gendered Imagery and Real Women of Hindu Nationalism." *Women and Right-Wing Movements: Indian Experiences*, ed. T. Sarkar and U. Butalia. London: Zed Books, 1995.

Bauer, Janet. "Sexuality and the Moral 'Construction' of Women in an Islamic Society." *Anthropological Quarterly* 58.3 (1985a): 120–29.

————. "Demographic Change, Women and the Family in a Migrant Neighborhood of Tehran." *Women and the Family in Iran*, ed. A. Fathi. Leiden: E.J. Brill, 1985b.

Bayat, Assef. *Workers and Revolution in Iran*. London: Zed, 1987.

Beheshti, Ahmad. Hejâb va Arzesh-e Vâlây-e Ân dar Islam ("Hejâb and Its Revered Status"). *Zan-e Rouz* 3 August 1985a: 40–41.

————. Sharâyet-e Mo'sser dar Behbud-e Zendegy-e Zanâsho'i ("Steps to Better Marital Life"). *Zan-e Rouz* 5 October 1985b: 40–41.

Behrangi, Samad. "Poetry and Society." *Critical Perspectives on Modern Persian Literature*, ed. T.M. Ricks. Washington, DC: Three Continents, 1984.

Benería, Lourdes. "Accounting for Women's Work." *Women and Development: The Sexual Division of Labor in Rural Societies*, ed. L. Benería. New York: Praeger, 1982.

Benjamin, Jessica. "The Bonds of Love: Rational Violence and Erotic Domination." *Feminist Studies* 6.1 (1980): 144–74.

Betteridge, Anne H. "The Controversial Vows of Urban Muslim Women in Iran." *Unspoken Worlds: Women's Religious Lives in Non-Western Cultures*, ed. N.A. Falk and R.M. Gross. New York: Harper & Row, 1980.

Bhabha, Homi K. "Are You a Man or a Mouse?" *Constructing Masculinity*, ed. M. Berger, B. Wallis and S. Watson. New York: Routledge, 1995.

Bill, James A. *The Politics of Iran: Groups, Classes and Modernization*. Columbus, OH: Charles E. Merrill, 1972.

————. *The Eagle and the Lion*. New Haven: Yale University Press, 1988.

Binney, Va. "Domestic Violence." *Women in Society*, ed. Cambridge Women's Studies Group. London: Virago, 1981.

Blee, Kathleen. *Women of the Klan*. Berkeley: University of California Press, 1991.

Blumer, Herbert. *Symbolic Interactionism: Perspective and Method*. Englewood Cliffs, NJ: Prentice-Hall, 1969.

Bobbio, Norberto. "Gramsci and the Conception of Civil Society." *Gramsci and Marxist Theory*, ed. C. Mouffe. Boston: Routledge & Kegan Paul, 1979.

Bouhdiba, Abdelwahab. *Sexuality in Islam*. Trans. A. Sheridan. London: Saqi Books, 1998.

Bourdieu, Pierre. *Outline of a Theory of Practice*. Trans. R. Nice. New York: Cambridge University Press, 1977.

Boxer, Marilyn J., and Jean H. Quataert, eds. *Socialist Women: European Socialist Feminism in the Nineteenth and Early Twentieth Centuries*. New York: Elsevier, 1978.

Brooks, Geraldine. *Nine Parts of Desire*. New York: Anchor Books, 1995.

Brun, Thierry, and Rene Dumont. "Iran: Imperial Pretensions and Agricultural Dependence." *MERIP Reports* 71 (1978): 15–20.

Buci-Glucksmann, Christine. "Hegemony and Consent." *Approaches to Gramsci*, ed. A.S. Sasson. London: Writers and Readers, 1982.

Burton, Julianne. "Don (Juanito) Duck and the Imperial-Patriarchal Unconscious: Disney Studios, the Good Neighbor Policy, and the Packaging of Latin America." *Nationalisms and Sexualities*, ed. A. Parker et al. New York: Routledge, 1992.

Butler, Judith. *Gender Trouble: Feminism and the Subversion of Identity*. New York: Routledge, 1990.

————. *Bodies that Matter: On the Discursive Limits of "Sex."* New York: Routledge, 1993.

Byanyima, W. Karagwa. "Women in Political Struggle in Uganda." *Women Transforming Politics: Worldwide Strategies for Empowerment*, ed. J.M. Bystydzienski. Indianapolis: Indiana University Press, 1992.

Center for Women's Participation. *Qavânin va Moqarrarât-e Vizheh-ye Zanân dar Jomhury-e Islamy-e Iran ("Special Laws and Regulations for Women in the*

Islamic Republic of Iran"). Tehran: Center for Women's Participation, Office of the President, 1999.

Chafetz, Janet Saltzman. "Action and Reaction: An Integrated, Comparative Perspective on Feminist and Antifeminist Movements." *Cross-National Research in Sociology*, ed. M.L. Kohn. Newbury Park: Sage, 1989.

Chinchilla, Norma S. "Mobilization of Women: Revolution in the Revolution." *Latin American Perspective* 4.4 (1977): 83–101.

CIS-NU. *Nâmeh-ye Pârsi, Vizheh-ye 8 Mârs, Rouz-e Beynulmellali Zanân (Nâmeh-ye Pârsi, Special Issue for March 8th, International Women's Day)*. 15 (n.d.).

Cohen, Anthony P. *The Symbolic Construction of Community*. New York: Routledge, 1995.

Collins, Randall, and Scott Coltrane. *Sociology of Marriage and the Family*. Chicago: Nelson-Hall, 1995.

Coltrane, Scott. *Gender and Families*. Thousand Oaks, CA: Pine Forge, 1999.

Coontz, Stephanie. *The Way We Never Were*. New York: Basic Books, 1992.

Cornforth, Maurice. *Historical Materialism*. New York: International, 1971.

Cottam, Richard W. *Nationalism in Iran*. Pittsburgh: University of Pittsburgh Press, 1979.

Coulson, Noel, and Doreen Hinchliffe. "Women and Law Reform in Contemporary Islam." *Women in the Muslim World*, ed. L. Beck and N. Keddie. Cambridge, MA: Harvard University Press, 1978.

Dallalfar, Arlene. "Iranian Women as Immigrant Entrepreneurs." *Gender and Society* 8.4 (1994): 541–61.

Davâni, Ali. *Nehzat-e Rowhâniyoun-e Iran (Clerical Movement in Iran)*. Vol. 8. Mashad: Bonyâd-e Farhangy-e Imam Reza, 1981.

Davis, Susan Schaefer. "Changing Gender Relations in a Moroccan Town." *Arab Women: Old Boundaries, New Frontiers*, ed. J. Tucker. Bloomington: Indiana University Press, 1993.

Delphy, Christine. *Close to Home: A Materialist Analysis of Women's Oppression*. Amherst: University of Massachusetts Press, 1984.

DOIW. *Zan dar Jâme'eh-ye Iran (Woman in the Iranian Society)*. Britain: DOIW, 1980.

———. *My Struggle Is My Work*. Britain: DOIW, 1982.

———. *Women in Iran: Five Years after the Revolution*. Tehran: DMO, 1984a.

———. *Women's Oppression in Iran*. DMO, 1984b.

———. *Asâsnâmeh va Barnâmeh (Bylaws and Program)*. DOIW, n.d.

Donzelot, Jacques. *The Policing of Families*. New York: Pantheon Books, 1979.

DuBois, Ellen Carol. "Women's Suffrage and the Left: An International Socialist-Feminist Perspective." *New Left Review* 186 (1991): 20–45.

Dworkin, Andrea. *Pornography: Men Possessing Women*. New York: Putnam, 1981.

Ebadi, Shirin. Negaresh-e Sonnat va Moderniyat beh Barâbâry-e Zan va Mard ("Approaches of Traditionalism and Modernity to Equality between Women and Men"). *Jens-e Dovom*, ed. N.A. Khorasany. Tehran: Nashr-e Towse'eh, 1999.

Elster, Jon. *Sour Grapes: Studies in the Subversion of Rationality*. Cambridge: Cambridge University Press, 1983.

Engels, Friedrich. "The Origin of the Family, Private Property and State." *Selected Works*, Karl Marx and Friedrich Engels. Moscow: Progress, 1970.

Epstein, Cynthia Fuchs. *Deceptive Distinctions: Sex, Gender, and the Social Order.* New Haven, CT: Yale University Press, 1988.

Esfandiari, Haleh. "The Majlis and Women's Issues in the Islamic Republic of Iran." *In the Eye of the Storm: Women in Post-Revolutionary Iran*, ed. M. Afkhami and E. Friedl. Syracuse: Syracuse University Press, 1994.

Eskandari, Mansour. *Mas'aleh-ye Arzi, Jonbesh-e Dehqâni va Siyâsat-e Mâ (The Land Question, Peasant Movement and Our Policy).* Tehran: OIPFG, 1984.

Esposito, John L. *Women in Muslim Family Law.* Syracuse: Syracuse University Press, 1982.

Evans, Richard. *The Feminist Movement in Germany, 1894–1933.* London: Sage, 1976.

Ezazi, Shahlâ. Khoshunat-e Khânevâdegi, Bâztâb-e Sâkhtâr-e Jâme'eh ("Family Violence, a Reflection of Social Structure"). *Zanân* 50 (1999): 48–51.

Faghfoory, Mohammad. "The Ulama-State Relations in Iran: 1921–1941." *International Journal of Middle Eastern Studies* 19.4 (1987): 413–32.

Fahim Kermâni, Mortezâ. *Chehreh-ye Zan Dar Â'ineh-ye Islam va Qoran (Woman's Face in the Mirror of Islam and the Koran).* Tehran: Daftar-e Nashr-e Farhang-e Islami, n.d.

Fallaci, Oriana. *Interview with History.* Boston: Houghton Mifflin, 1976.

Farrokhzad, Pouran. *Daneshnâmeh-ye Zanân-e Farhangsâz-e Iran va Jahân. Zan: Az Katibeh tâ Târikh (Encyclopedia of Women Culture-Makers in Iran and in the World. Woman: From Inscription to History).* Vol. 1. Tehran: Zaryâb, 1999.

Fashkhâmi, Massoud, ed. *Naqsh-e Zan dar Hokumat-e Islami (Women's Role in the Islamic Government).* N.p., 1979.

Fatemi, Parvâneh. Tab'iz-zodâ'i dar Âmouzesh va Parvaresh ("Ending Discrimination in Education"). *Farhang-e Towse'eh* Special Women's Issue (1998): 64–67.

Fazlullâh, Mohammad Hossein. Ezdevâj-e Zoodhengâm ("Early Marriage"). *Payâm-e Zan* December 1998: 50–56.

Floor, Willem M. "The Revolutionary Character of the Iranian Ulama: Wishful Thinking or Reality?" *Religion and Politics in Iran: Sho'ism from Quietism to Revolution*, ed. N.R. Keddie. New Haven: Yale University Press, 1983.

Foucault, Michel. *The History of Sexuality.* Trans. R. Hurley. Vol. 1. London: Allen Lane, 1979.

Friedan, Betty. "Coming Out of the Veil." *Ladies Home Journal* June 1975: 104.

Friedl, Erika. *Women of Deh Koh: Lives in an Iranian Village.* New York: Penguin, 1991.

Gagnon, John H. *Human Sexualities.* Glenview, IL: Scott, Foresman, 1977.

Gamarnikow, Eva et al., eds. *The Public and the Private.* London: Heinemann, 1983.

Geertz, Clifford. *The Interpretation of Cultures.* New York: Basic Books, 1973.

Gellner, Ernest. "Inside Khomeini's Mind." *The New Republic* 18 June 1984: 27–33.

Gerami, Shahin. "The Role, Place, and Power of Middle-Class Women in the Islamic Republic." *Identity Politics and Women: Cultural Reassertions and*

Feminisms in International Perspectives, ed. V.M. Moghadam. Boulder: Westview, 1994.

Gerâmizâdegân, Ashraf. Zamineh-ye Nofuz-e Farhang-e Qarb dar Qeshr-e Zanân ("The Causes of the Influence of Western Culture among Women"). *Zan-e Rouz* 5 September 1996: 3, 62.

Ghandchi-Tehrani, Davoud. "Bazaaris and Clergy: Socio-Economic Origins of Radicalism and Revolution in Iran." Unpublished diss., City University of New York, 1982.

Giddens, Anthony. *Modernity and Self-Identity: Self and Society in the Late Modern Age*. Stanford, CA: Stanford University Press, 1991.

Gilmartin, Christina. "Gender, Politics, and Patriarchy in China: The Experiences of Early Women Communists, 1920–27." *Promissory Notes: Women in the Transition to Socialism*, ed. S. Kruks, R. Rapp and M.B. Young. New York: Monthly Review, 1989.

Golesorkhi, Khosrow. *Siyâsat-e She'r, Siyâsat-e Honar (The Politics of Poetry, the Politics of Art)*. N.p. (Written and originally published in 1971).

Golestan, Sheida. Goftogo'i bâ Farzaneh Ta'idi ("An Interview with Farzaneh Ta'idi"). *Nimeye Digar* 6 (1988): 63–73.

Goode, William J. "Idealization of the Recent Past: The United States." *Family in Transition*, ed. A.S. Skolnick and J.H. Skolnick. Boston: Little, Brown, 1984.

Graham, Robert. *Iran: The Illusion of Power*. New York: St. Martin's, 1979.

Gramsci, Antonio. *Selections from the Prison Notebooks*. Trans. Q. Hoare and G.N. Smith. New York: International, 1971.

Gulick, John, and Margaret E. Gulick. "The Domestic Social Environment of Women in Isfahan, Iran." *Women in the Muslim World*, ed. L. Beck and N. Keddie. Cambridge, MA: Harvard University Press, 1978.

Habibi, Nader. "Allocation of Educational and Occupational Opportunities in the Islamic Republic of Iran: A Case Study in the Political Screening of Human Capital in the Islamic Republic of Iran." *Iranian Studies* 22.4 (1989): 19–46.

Haddâd 'Âdel, Qolâmali. *Farhang-e Berahnegi va Berahnegy-e Farhangi (The Culture of Nakedness and the Cultural Nakedness)*. Tehran: Soroush, 1995.

Haeri, Shahla. "Women, Law, and Social Change in Iran." *Women in Contemporary Muslim Societies*, ed. J.J. Smith. London: Associate University Press, 1980.

———. *Law of Desire: Temporary Marriage in Shi'i Iran*. Syracuse: Syracuse University Press, 1989.

Hajjarian, Saeed. *Jomhouriyat: Afsoonzoda'i az Qodrat (Republicanism: The Demystification of Power)*. Tehran: Tarh-e No, 2000.

Halliday, Fred. *Iran: Dictatorship and Development*. London: Pelican, 1979.

Hammami, Rema. "Palestinian Motherhood and Political Activism on the West Bank and Gaza Strip." *The Politics of Motherhood: Activist Voices from Left to Right*, ed. A. Jetter, A. Orleck, and D. Taylor. Hanover, NH: University Press of New England, 1997.

Hammer, Jalna, and Sheila Saunders. *Well-founded Fear: A Community Study of Violence to Women*. London: Hutchinson, 1984.

Hanson, Brad. "The 'Westoxication' of Iran: Depictions and Reaction of Behrangi,

Al-e Ahmad and Shariati." *International Journal of Middle East Studies* 15.1 (1983): 1–23.

Hardisty, Jean. *Mobilizing Resentment: Conservative Resurgence from the John Birch Society to the Promise Keepers.* Boston: Beacon, 1999.

Hartmann, Heidi. "The Unhappy Marriage of Marxism and Feminism: Towards A More Progressive Union." *Women and Revolution,* ed. L. Sargent. Boston: South End, 1981.

Hegland, Mary E. "Political Roles of Iranian Village Women." *Middle East Report.* January-February 1986: 14–19.

Hélie-Lucas, Marie-Aimée. "Women's Struggles and Strategies in the Rise of Fundamentalism in the Muslim World: From Entryism to Internationalism." *Women in the Middle East: Perceptions, Realities and Struggles for Liberation,* ed. H. Afshar. London: Macmillan, 1993.

Hermansen, Marcia. "Fatimeh as a Role Model in the Works of Ali Shariati." *Women and Revolution in Iran,* ed. G. Nashat. Boulder: Westview, 1983.

Hezârkhâni, Manouchehr. Este'mâr va Farhang ("Colonialism and Culture"). *Nezhâdparasti va Farhang (Racism and Culture).* Trans. M. Hezârkhâni. Tehran: Zamân, 1973.

———. Yâddâshthâ'i Darbâreh-ye Khososiyat-e Yek Farhang-e Dallâl ("Notes on the Characteristics of a Go-Between Culture"). *Jong-e Sahar.* Tehran: n.p., 1977.

Hillman, Michael C. *A Lonely Woman: Forugh Farrokhzad and Her Poetry.* Washington, DC: Mage and Three Continent, 1987.

Hobsbawm, Eric J. "Revolution Is Puritan." *The New Eroticism: Theories, Vogues and Canons,* ed. P. Nobile. New York: Random House, 1970.

Holst-Warhaft, Gail. *The Cue for Passion: Grief and Its Political Use.* Cambridge, MA: Harvard University Press, 2000.

Homâyunpour, Parviz. *Gozâresh-e Nahâ'i: Tarh-e Tajroby-e Savâdâmuzy-e Tâbe'i dar Khedmat-e Pishraft-e Ejtemâ'i va Eqtesâdy-e Zanân-i Roostâ'i (The Final Report: The Experimental Project of Functional Literacy in the Service of Rural Women's Social and Economic Advancement).* Tehran: WOI, 1975.

Hoodfar, Homa, and Samad Assadpour. "The Politics of Population Policy in the Islamic Republic of Iran." *Studies in Family Planning* 3.1 (2000): 19–34.

Hoogland, Mary. 1980-"The Village Women of Aliabad and the Iranian Revolution." *RIPEH—Review of Iranian Political Economy & History* 4–5.2–1 (1981): 27–46.

Hooglund, Eric. "Rural Participation in the Revolution." *MERIP Reports* 87 (1980): 3–6.

Hosseini Tehrani, Mohammad Hossein. *Resâleh-ye Nekâhiyeh: Kâhesh-e Jam'iyat, Zarbeh'i Sahmgin bar Peykar-e Moslemin (On Marriage: Population Reduction, a Severe Blow to Muslims).* Hekmat: n.p., 1994.

———. *Resâleh-ye Badi'ah (New Essay).* Mashad: Allâmeh Tabâtabâ'i, 1997.

Hudson, Michael C. "Islam and Political Development." *Islam and Development,* ed. J.L. Esposito. Syracuse: Syracuse University Press, 1980.

Hufton, Olwen H. *Women and the Limits of Citizenship in the French Revolution.* Toronto: University of Toronto Press, 1992.

Huntington, Samuel P. "The Political Modernization of Traditional Monarchies." *DÆdalus* 95 (1966): 763–88.

Institute for Cultural Studies and Research. *Barrasy-e Nahveh-ye M[ˈ]ârrefy-e Zan dar Kotob-e Darsy-e Dowreh-ye Ebtedâ'i—1368* ("Analysis of Women's Roles in Primary School Textbooks—1989"). *Zanân* 11 (1993): 2–7.

Iran Almanac and Book of Facts. Tehran: Echo Publications, 1970.

———.Tehran: Echo Publications, 1971.

———.Tehran: Echo Publications, 1972.

———.Tehran: Echo Publications, 1973.

———.Tehran: Echo Publications, 1975.

———.Tehran: Echo Publications, 1976.

———.Tehran: Echo Publications, 1977.

Iran Statistical Center. *Sarshomâry-e ʿOmumy-e Nofoos va Maskan, Koll-e Keshvar, Sâl-e 1365 (Census of Population and Housing, 1986).* Tehran: Iran Statistical Center, 1988.

———. *Âmâr-e Âmuzesh va Parvaresh (Educational Statistics).* Tehran: Iran Statistical Center, 1997.

———. *Sâlnâmeh-ye Âmâry-e Iran, 1376 (Statistical Yearbook of Iran, 1997).* Tehran: Iran Statistical Center, 1999.

IRI. "The Bill of Retribution." *In the Shadow of Islam: The Women's Movement in Iran*, ed. A. Tabari and N. Yeganeh. London: Zed, 1982.

ISA-US. *Khânevâdeh dar Jâmeʿeh-ye Sosyâlisti (Family in a Socialist Society).* N.p.: ISA-US, Supporters of the OIPFG, n.d.

Isfahâni, ʿEmâdud-din Hossein (ʿEmâdzâdeh). *Zanân-e Peyqambar-e Islam (Women of Islam's Prophet).* Tehran: Mohammad, n.d.

Jackson, Stevi. *Heterosexuality in Question.* Thousand Oaks, CA: Sage, 1999.

Jahânpanâh, Simindokht. Jomhury-e Islamy-e Iran va Âmuzesh-e Zanân ("The IRI and Women's Education"). *Jâmeʿeh-ye Sâlem.* (1997): 59–67.

Jalali Naeini, Ziba. Majlis va Hozoor-e Siyâsy-e Zanân: Moroori bar Tajrobeh-ye Qânun-e Eʿzâm-e Dâneshju ("Majlis and Women's Political Presence: The Case of State-Sponsored Education Abroad"). *Goft-o-gu* 9 (1995a): 7–15.

———. Dowlati yâ Qeir-e-dowlati? Negâhi beh Tajrobeh-ye Daftar-e Hamâhangy-e Sâzmânhây-e Qeir-e-dowlati Zanân dar Iran ("Governmental or Non-Governmental? Review of the Experience of Women's NGOs Coordinating Office"). *Goft-o-gu* 10 (1995b): 97–105.

———. Dowlati, Qablan Dowlati, Baʿdan Dowlati ("Governmental, Governmental Before, Governmental After"). *Jens-e Dovom*, ed. N.A. Khorasany. Tehran: Nashr-e Towseʿeh, 2000.

Javâdi Âmoli. *Zan dar Â'ineh-ye Jalâl va Jamâl (Woman in the Mirror of Glory and Beauty).* Tehran: Rajâ', 1993.

Jazani, Bizhan. *Capitalism and Revolution in Iran.* London: Zed, 1980.

———. *19 Bahman-e Teʾorik (19 Bahman: Theoretical).* Vol. 6. N.p.: OIPFG, n.d.

Jazani, Mihan. Bizhan: Maʿshuq, Rafiq va Hamsar ("Bizhan: Lover, Comrade, and Husband"). *Darbâreh-ye Zendegi va Âsâr-e Bizhan Jazani (On Bizhan Jazani's Life and Works)*, ed. The Committee for the Collection and Publication of Bizhan Jazani's Works. Paris, France: Khavaran, 1999.

Jeansonne, Glen. *Women of the Far Right: The Mothers' Movement and World War II.* Chicago: University of Chicago Press, 1996.

Jetter, Alexis, Annelise Orleck, and Diana Taylor, eds. *The Politics of Motherhood:*

Activist Voices from Left to Right. Hanover, NH: University Press of New England, 1997.

Johnson, Kay Ann. *Women, The Family and Peasant Revolution in China*. Chicago: University of Chicago Press, 1983.

Joseph, Suad. "Gender and Citizenship in Middle Eastern States." *Middle East Report* 198 (1996): 4–10.

Kandiyoti, Deniz. "Bargaining with Patriarchy." *Gender and Society* 2.3 (1988): 274–90.

———. "Islam and Patriarchy: A Comparative Perspective." *Women in Middle Eastern History: Shifting Boundaries in Sex and Gender*, ed. N. Keddie and B. Baron. New Haven, CT: Yale University Press, 1991.

Kaplan, Temma. "Female Consciousness and Collective Action: The Case of Barcelona, 1910–1918." *Signs: Journal of Women in Culture and Society* 7.3 (1982): 545–66.

———. "Naked Mothers and Maternal Sexuality: Some Reactions to the Aba Women's War." *The Politics of Motherhood: Activist Voices from Left to Right*, ed. A. Jetter, A. Orleck, and D. Taylor. Hanover, NH: University Press of New England, 1997.

Kar, Mehrangiz. Jâygâh-e Zan dar Qânun-e Keyfary-e Islam ("Women's Status in Islam's Punitive Law"). *Zanân* 11 (1993b): 16–25.

———. *Zanân dar Bâzâr-e Kâr-e Iran (Women in Iran's Labor Market)*. Tehran: Rowshangarân, 1994.

———. Takâlif-e Qânuny-e Zan dar Barâbar-e Showhar ("Wives' Legal Obligations to Their Husbands"). *Zanân* 31 (1996): 26–29.

———. *Hoquq-e Siyâsy-e Zanân (Women's Political Rights)*. Tehran: Roshangaran & Women's Studies, 1997.

———. Zanân dar Maqâm-e Qâzy-e Tahqiq, Haqq-e Enshâ-ye Ra'i Nadârand ("As Investigative Judges, Women Have No Right to Write Verdicts"). *Zanân* 40 (1998): 18–21.

———. Barrasy-e Khoshunat ʿAlayh-e Zanân dar Qavânin-e Iran ("Violence against Women in Iranian Law"). *Jens-e Dovom*, ed. N.A. Khorasany. Tehran: Nashr-e Towseʿeh, 1999a.

———. *Rafʿ-e Tabʿiz az Zanân: Moqâyeseh-ye Konvânsyon-e Rafʿ-e Tabʿiz az Zanân bâ Qavânin-e Dâkhely-e Iran (Eliminating Discrimination against Women: Comparing the Convention on the Elimination of All Forms of Discrimination to Women in Iranian Law)*. Tehran: Qatreh, 1999b.

———. *Pazhoheshi darbâreh-ye Khoshounat ʿAlayh-e Zanân dar Iran (A Research about Violence Against Women in Iran)*. Tehran: Roshangaran & Women's Studies, 2000.

Katouzian, Homa. *The Political Economy of Modern Iran, 1926–1979*. New York: New York University Press, 1981.

Kayhan Research Associates. "The Employment of Women in the Higher Echelons of the Public & Private Sectors." Report. Kayhan Research Associates for the Women's Organization of Iran. Tehran: Kayhan Research Associates, 1975.

Kazemi, Farhad. *Poverty and Revolution in Iran: The Migrant Poor, Urban Marginality and Politics*. New York: New York University Press, 1980.

Kazemi, Farhad, and Ervand Abrahamian. "The Non-Revolutionary Peasantry of Modern Iran." *Iranian Studies* 11.1–4 (1978): 259–304.

Kâzemi Khalkhâli, Zeinul'âbedin. *Zanâsho'i: Râz-e Khoshbakhti (Marriage: The Secret to Happiness)*. Tehran: Mohammad, 1991.

Kâzemiyeh, Eslâm. Hejâb-e Islami Chist? ("What Is Islamic Hejâb?"). *Kayhan* 12 March 1979.

Keddie, Nikki R. *Roots of Revolution: An Interpretive History of Modern Iran.* New Haven: Yale University Press, 1981.

Kerber, Linda K. *Women of the Republic: Intellect and Ideology in Revolutionary America.* Chapel Hill: University of North Carolina Press, 1980.

Keyhânniâ, Asqar. *Nojavânân Cheh Miguyand? (What Say Adolescents?).* Tehran: Nashr-e Mâdar, 1997.

———. *Javânân va Ezdevâj (Youths and Marriage).* Tehran: Nashr-e Mâdar, 1998.

Khadivi, Mahin. *Kâjhây-e Zard (Yellow Pines).* Tehran: Sâli Publications, 1999.

Khamenehii, Mohammad. Yek Hadaf Vâhed dar Vâhedi Beh Nâm-e Khânevâdeh ("A Single Goal in a Unit Called the Family"). *Zan-e Rouz* 11 January 1992: 14–15, 53.

Khodâparast, Mehdi. Barrasy-e Emkânât-e Eshteqâl-e Bânovân dar Qâleb-e Sherkat-hây-e Ta'âvoni ("Analysis of Possibilities of Women's Work in Co-operatives"). *Ta'âvon, Zan, Eshteqâl (Cooperatives, Women, Employment),* ed. M. of C. Tehran: Ministry of Cooperatives, 1996.

Khomeini, Rouhullah. *Zan az Didgâh-e Imam Khomeini (Women From Imam Khomeini's Point of View).* Tehran: Muslim Women's Movement, 1981.

———. Dar Jostojooy-e Râh az Kalâm-e Imam ("In Search of the Pathway by Imam's Word"). *Zan (Women)* vol. 3. Tehran: Amir Kabir, 1982.

———. *Towzihul Masâ'el (The Explanations for Problems).* Tehran: Esteqlâl, n.d.

Kibria, Nazli. *Family Tightrope: The Changing Lives of Vietnamese Americans.* Princeton, NJ: Princeton University Press, 1993.

Kimmel, Michael S. *Manhood in America: A Cultural History.* New York: Free Press, 1996.

Koonz, Claudia. *Mothers in the Fatherland: Women, the Family and Nazi Politics.* New York: St. Martin's, 1987.

Koven, Seth, and Sonya Michel. "Womanly Duties: Maternalist Politics and the Origins of Welfare States in France, Germany, Great Britain, and the United States, 1880–1920." *American Historical Review* 95.4 (1990): 1076–108.

Kruks, Sonia, and Ben Wisner. "Ambiguous Transformations: Women, Politics, and Production in Mozambique." *Promissory Notes: Women in the Transition to Socialism,* ed. S. Kruks, R. Rapp and M.B. Young. New York: Monthly Review, 1989.

Lâhiji, Shahlâ. Zanân va Tashakkolhây-e Senfi ("Women and Professional Assemblies"). *Jens-e Dovom,* ed. N.A. Khorasany. Tehran: Nashr-e Towse'eh, 1999.

Lamphere, Louise. "The Domestic Sphere of Women and the Public World of Men: The Strengths and Limitations of an Anthropological Dichotomy." *Gender in Cross-Cultural Perspective,* ed. C.B. Brettell and C.F. Sargent. Englewood Cliffs, NJ: Prentice-Hall, 1997.

Landes, Joan B. "Marxism and the 'Woman Question'." *Promissory Notes: Women* in the Transition to Socialism, ed. S. Kruks, R. Rapp and M.B. Young. New York: Monthly Review, 1989.

Le Monde. "Le commité international du droit des femmes a rendu compte de sa mission." 6 April 1979.

Lewis, Michael. The Culture of Inequality. Amherst: University of Massachusetts Press, 1993.

Lorber, Judith. Paradoxes of Gender. New Haven, CT: Yale University Press, 1994.

Lukes, Steven. Individualism. New York: Harper & Row, 1984.

Ma'sumi, Massoud. Ahkâm-e Ravâbet-e Zan va Showhar va Masâ'el-e Ejtemâ'y-e Ân (Regulations Concerning Spousal Relationships and Social Implications). Qom: Center for Islamic Propaganda Publications, 1998.

Mahdavi, Kefâyat. Khâsteh-ye Zanân-e Kârgar: Tasvib-e Tarh-e Bâzneshastegy-e Pish az Mow'ed ("Working Women Demand Passing the Early Retirement Bill"). Farhang-e Towse'eh, Special Issue on Women (1998): 48–49.

Mahmoodi, 'Abasali. Zan dar Islam (The Woman in Islam). Tehran: Fayzal Kashani, 1981.

Malaki, Gildâ. Zanân dar Â'ineh-ye Âmâr ("Women in Statistics" Pt. 2). Payâm-e Zan March 1998: 14–23.

Marshall, Susan E., and Anthony M. Orum. "Opposition Then and Now: Countering Feminism in the Twentieth Century." Women and Politics: Activism, Attitudes and Office-Holding, ed. G. Moore and G. Spitze. Greenwich, CT: JAI, 1986.

Marx, Karl. Pre-Capitalist Economic Formations. New York: International, 1980.

Marx, Karl, and Friedrich Engels. "The German Ideology." Collected Works. New York: International, 1976.

Matin, Mahnaz, ed. Bâzbiny-e Tajrobeh-ye Ettehâd-e Melly-e Zanân (The National Union of Iranian Women Revisited). Berkeley: Noghteh Books, 1999.

Matini, Jalal. "The Impact of the Islamic Revolution on Education in Iran." At the Crossroads, ed. A. Badran. New York: Paragon House, 1989.

Mattelart, Michele. "Chile: The Feminine Side of the Coup or When Bourgeois Women Take to the Streets." NACLA Report on Latin America and the Empire. 9 (1975): 14–25.

Mazlumân, Reza. Zankoshi dar Lavây-e Qânun ("Woman-Killing Under the Aegis of the Law"). Hoquq-e Zan dar Iran (Women and the Law in Iran), ed. M. Afkhami. Bethesda, MD: Women's Center of the Foundation for Iranian Studies, 1994.

Mehran, Golnar. "Socialization of Schoolchildren in the Islamic Republic of Iran." Iranian Studies 22.1 (1989): 35–50.

Mehri, Homâ. Ezdevâj Mamnu' ("Marriage Forbidden"). Hoquq-e Zan 4 (1998): 18–19.

Melucci, Alberto. Challenging Codes: Collective Action in the Information Age. New York: Cambridge University Press, 1996a.

———. The Playing Self: Person and Meaning in the Planetary Society. New York: Cambridge University Press, 1996b.

Mernissi, Fatima. "Virginity and Patriarchy." Women's Studies International Forum 5.2 (1982): 183–92.

———. Beyond the Veil: Male-Female Dynamics in Modern Muslim Society. Bloomington: Indiana University Press, 1987.

Mesbâh Yazdi, Mohammad Taqi. Jaygâh-e Islam dar Beyn-e Makâteb-e Falsafy-e Konouny-e Jahân ("Islam's Place in Contemporary Philosophical Schools"). *Resâlat*. (Spec. Iss. Commemoration 15th Ann. Ayatollah Motahhari's Death). 1 May 1993: 153.

Meyrowitz, Joshua. *No Sense of Place: The Impact of Electronic Media on Social Behavior*. New York: Oxford University Press, 1985.

Milani, Farzaneh. *Veils and the Words: The Emerging Voices of Iranian Women Writers*. Syracuse: Syracuse University Press, 1992.

Millett, Kate. *Sexual Politics*. New York: Doubleday, 1970.

————. *Going to Iran*. New York: Coward, McCann & Geoghegan, 1982.

Ministry of Cooperatives, ed. *Ta'âvon, Zan, Eshteqâl (Cooperatives, Women, Employment)*. Tehran: Ministry of Cooperatives, 1996.

Ministry of Culture and Higher Education. *Âmâr-e Âmuzesh-e 'Âly-e Iran: 1366–67 (Statistics of the Higher Education in Iran, Academic Year 1987–88)*. vol. 1. Tehran: Center for Statistics and Educational Planning, Ministry of Culture and Higher Education, 1988.

Mirani, Kaveh. "Social and Economic Change in the Role of Women, 1956–1978." *Women and Revolution in Iran*, ed. G. Nashat. Boulder: Westview, 1983.

Mirsepassi-Ashtiani, Ali, and Valentine M. Moghadam. "The Left and Political Islam in Iran: A Retrospect and Prospect." *Radical History Review* 51 (1991): 27–62.

Mirvahabi, Farin. "The Status of Women in Iran." *Journal of Family Law* 14.3 (1975–76): 383–404.

Moallem, Minoo. "Ethnic Entrepreneurship and Gender Relations Among Iranians in Montreal, Quebec, Canada." *Iranian Refugees and Exiles since Khomeini*, ed. A. Fathi. Costa Mesa, CA: Mazda, 1991.

Moghadam, Khadijeh. Ta'âvonihây-e Zanân: Az Harf tâ 'Amal ("Women's Cooperatives: Theory to Practice"). *Jens-e Dovom*, ed. N.A. Khorasany. Tehran: Nashr-e Towse'eh, 2000.

Moghadam, Valentine M. "Socialism or Anti-imperialism? The Left and Revolution in Iran." *New Left Review* 166 (1987): 5–28.

————. "Women, Work and Ideology in the Islamic Republic." *International Journal of Middle East Studies* 20.2 (1988): 221–43.

————. *Modernizing Women: Gender and Social Change in the Middle East*. Boulder: Lynne Rienner, 1993.

————. *Women, Work, and Economic Reform in the Middle East and North Africa*. Boulder: Lynne Rienner, 1998.

Moghissi, Haideh. "Women in the Resistance Movement in Iran." *Women in the Middle East: Perceptions, Realities and Struggles for Liberation*, ed. H. Afshar. London: Macmillan, 1993.

————. *Populism and Feminism in Iran: Women's Struggle in a Male-Defined Revolutionary Movement*. New York: St. Martin's P, 1994.

————. Feminism-e Popolisti va 'Feminism-e Islami': Naqdi bar Gerâyeshhây-e Nomohâfezehkârâneh-ye Feministhây-e Irani dar Qarb ("Populist Feminism and 'Islamic Feminism': A Critique of Neo-conservative Tendencies among Iranian Academic Feminists"). *Kankash: A Persian Journal of History, Culture, and Politics* 13 (1997): 57–95.

Mohammadi, Majeed. *Jâme'eh-ye Madani beh Manzeleh-ye Yek Ravesh (Civil Society as a Method)*. Tehran: Qatreh, 1997.

———. *Jâme'eh-ye Madany-e Irani: Bestarhây-e Nazari va Mavâne' (Iranian Civil Society: Theoretical Bases and Obstacles)*. Tehran: Nashr-e Markaz, 1999.

Mohammadiniâ, Asadullâh. *Âncheh Bayad Yek Zan Bedânad (What A Woman Must Know)*. Qom: Center for Islamic Propaganda Publications, 1992.

Mohseni, Maryam. Vaz'iyat-e Zanân-e Kârgar: Hoquq va Jensiyat ("The Status of Working Women: Rights and Sex"). *Farhang-e Towse'eh*, Special Issue on Women (1998a): 46–47.

———. Kârgarân-e Zan-e Khânegi ("Women and Industrial Homework"). *Negâh-e Zanân*, ed. N.A. Khorasany. Tehran: Nashr-e Towse'eh, 1998b.

Moin, Baqer. *Khomeini: Life of the Ayatollah*. New York: St. Martin's, 1999.

Mokhtâri, Mohammad. *Tamrin-e Modârâ (The Practice of Tolerance)*. Tehran: Vistar, 1998.

Molyneux, Maxine. "Women and Revolution in the People's Democratic Republic of Yemen." *Feminist Review* 1 (1979): 5–19.

———. "Legal Reform and Socialist Revolution in Democratic Yemen: Women and the Family." *International Journal of the Sociology of Law* 13 (1985): 147–72.

———. "Mobilization Without Emancipation? Women's Interests, the State, and Revolution in Nicaragua." *Feminist Studies* 11.2 (1985): 227–54.

Momeni, Djamchid. "The Difficulties of Changing the Age at Marriage in Iran." *Journal of Marriage and the Family* 14.3 (1972): 545–51.

Momeni, Hamid. Nâmeh-ye Hamid Momeni beh Bagher Momeni ("Hamid Momeni's Letter to Bagher Momeni"). *Fasli dar Golesorkh* 1 (1979): 53–54.

Momeni, Mohammad Bagher. *Dard-e Ahl-e Qalam (Writers' Grievance)*. N.p., 1977.

Morgan, David H. J. "Issues of Critical Sociological Theory: Men in Families." *Fashioning Family Theory*, ed. J. Sprey. Newbury Park, CA: Sage, 1990.

Mosaffa, Nasrin. *Moshârekat-e Siyâsy-e Zanân dar Iran (Political Participation of Women in Iran)*. Tehran: Ministry of Foreign Affairs, 1997.

Mosse, George L. *Nationalism and Sexuality: Middle-Class Morality and Sexual Norms in Modern Europe*. Madison: University of Wisconsin Press, 1985.

Mostafavi, Farideh. Imam dar Zolâl-e Khâterehhâ ("Imam in the Stream of Memories"). *Payâm-e Zan* 1.3 (1992): 23–33.

Mostafavi, Hassan. *Âncheh Bâyad Yek Doushizeh Bedânad (What Every Young Girl Must Know)*. 2nd ed. Tehran: Mostafavi, n.d.

Motahari, Mortezâ. *Mas'aleh-ye Hejâb (The Problem of the Hejâb)*. Qum: Sadrâ, 1969.

———. *'Elal-e Gerâyesh beh Mâddigari (The Causes of Turning to Materialism)*. Qom: Sadrâ, 1978a.

———. *Nezâm-e Hoquq-e Zan dar Islam (The System of Women's Rights in Islam)*. Qom: Sadrâ, 1978b.

———. Naqsh-e Zan dar Târikh-e Mo'âser-e Iran ("Women's Role in Iran's Contemporary History"). *Kayhan*, 3 March 1979: 10.

———. *Islam va Moqtaziyât-e Zamân (Islam and the Necessities of Time)*. Tehran: Sadrâ, 1983.

——. Rahbary-e Nasl-e Javân ("Leading the Youth"). *Dah Goftar (Ten Lectures)*. Qom: Sadrâ, 1987a.

——. Farziyeh-ye 'Elm ("The Ordinance of Science"). *Dah Goftâr (Ten Lectures)*. Qom: Sadrâ, 1987b.

——. Mowqaddameh (Introduction). *Osul-e Falsafeh va Ravesh-e Reâlism (The Principles of the Philosophy and Method of Realism)*, ed. M.H. Tabâtabâ'i. Tehran: Sadrâ (Originally written in 1953), n.d-a.

——. Akhlâq-e Jensi dar Islam va Jahân-e Qarb ("Sexual Morality in Islam and the Western World"). *Âshnâ'i bâ Qoran; Jahâd; Akhlâq-e Jensi (Familiarity with the Koran; Jihad; Sexual Morality)*. Qom: Sadrâ, n.d.-b.

——. *Âshnâ'i bâ Qoran (Introduction to the Koran)*. Vol. 3. Tehran: Sadrâ, n.d.c.

Mullaney, Marie Marmo. *Revolutionary Women: Gender and Socialist Revolutionary Role*. New York: Praeger, 1983.

Murray, Stephen O. "The Will Not to Know: Islamic Accommodations of Male Homosexuality." *Islamic Homosexualities: Culture, History, and Literature*, ed. S.O.M.a.W. Roscoe. New York: New York University Press, 1997a.

Nâhid, Abdulhossein. *Zanân-e Iran dar Jonbesh-e Mashrutiyat (Iranian Women in the Constitutional Movement)*. N.p., 1981.

Najjar, Orayb Aref. "Between Nationalism and Feminism: The Palestinian Answer." *Women Transforming Politics: Worldwide Strategies for Empowerment*, ed. J.M. Bystydzienski. Indianapolis: Indiana University Press, 1992.

Naraghi, Ehsan. *Qorbat-e Qarb (The Alienation of the West)*. Tehran: Amir Kabir, 1974.

——. "Iran's Cultural Identity and the Present Day World." *Iran: Past, Present and Future*, ed. J.W. Jacqz. Aspen, CO: Institute for Humanistic Studies, 1976a.

——. *Âncheh Khod Dâsht . . . (What It Owned Itself . . .)*. Tehran: Amir Kabir, 1976b.

Naraghi, Ehsan, and Esmail Khoi. *Âzâdi, Haq, va 'Edâlat (Freedom, Rights and Justice)*. Tehran: Jâvidân, 1977.

Narayan, Uma. *Dislocating Cultures: Identities, Traditions, and Third World Feminism*. New York: Routledge, 1997.

Nashat, Guity. "Women in the Islamic Republic of Iran." *Iranian Studies* 13.1–4 (1980): 165–95.

——. "Women in the Ideology of the Islamic Republic." *Women and Revolution in Iran*, ed. G. Nashat. Boulder: Westview Press, 1983.

Nasr, Seyyid Hossein. *Ideas and Realities of Islam*. London: George Allen and Uniwin, 1966.

Nategh, Homa. Towzihi darbâreh-ye 'Aqabmândegi va Enhetât-e Zan-e Irâni ("Remarks on the Backwardness and Decadence of Iranian Women"). *Arash* 17 (1967): 14–16.

——. *Az Mâst keh bar Mâst (Nobody Else to Blame But Ourselves)*. Tehran: Âgâh, 1975.

——. Rahâ'y-e Zanân az Rahâ'y-e Zahmatkeshân Jodâ Nist ("Women's Emancipation Is Not Separated From Toilers' Emancipation"). *Kayhan* March 1979: 12.

——. Negâhi beh Barkhi Neveshteh-hâ va Mobârezat-e Zanân dar Dowrân-e

Mashrutiyat ("A Review of Some of the Writings and Women's Struggle at the Constitutional Era"). *Ketâb-e Jom'eh* 14 March 1980: 45–54.

———. Sa'id Soltanpour dar Jonbesh-e Daneshjo'i ("Sa'id Soltanpour and the Students' Movement"). *Sosyâlizm va Enqelâb* 2 (1982): 28–36.

———. Mas'aleh-ye Zan dar Barkhi az Modavvanât-e Chap az Nehzat-e Mashruteh tâ 'Asr-e Reza Khân ("The Woman Question in Some of the Writings of the Left From the Constitutional Movement Until the Reza Khan Era"). *Zamân-e Nou* 1 (1983): 10.

Navâbakhsh, A. *Zan dar Târikh (Woman in History).* Raf'at: n.p., n.d.

Nelson, Cynthia. "Public and Private Politics: Women in the Middle Eastern World." *American Ethnologist* 1 3 (1974): 551–63.

Nelson, Cynthia, and Virginia Olesen. "Veil of Illusion: A Critique of the Concept of Equality in Western Feminist Thought." *Catalyst* 10–11 (1977): 8–36.

Nesârizâdeh, Ibrâhim. *Islam va Mavâd-e Sheshgâneh-ye Shah va Mellat (Islam and the Six Points of the Shah and People Revolution).* Tehran: Chehr, 1966.

Nuri, Yahyâ. *Hoquq-e Zan dar Islam va Jahân (The Woman's Rights in Islam and around the World).* Tehran: Farâhâni, 1964.

NUW. "Aims and Objectives." *In the Shadow of Islam: The Women's Movement in Iran,* ed. A. Tabari and N. Yeganeh. London: Zed, 1982.

OIPFG. Tahlili az E'tesâb-e Kârgarân-e Kârkhânejat-e Kafsh-e Melli ("An Analysis of the Melly Shoe Factory Workers' Strike"). *Nabard-e Khalq* 3 (1974): 28–35.

———. *Kourehpazkhâneh (Brick-Kiln).* Tabriz: OIPFG, 1979a.

———. Barrasy-e Koutâhi az Mobârezât-e Demokrâtik-e Dow Sâleh-ye Zanân ("A Brief Review of the Two Years of Women's Democratic Struggle"). *Kar* Special Issue on International Women's Day 8 March 1979b English trans. "A Brief Assessment of the Iranian Women's Democratic Struggles." *Women & Struggle in Iran.* Women's Commission of the ISA-US, Supporters of OIPFG. 1 (1982).

———. Zendegi va Mobârezât-e Zanân-e Turkaman Sahr â ("The Life and Struggles of Turkaman Sahra Women"). *Kar* Spec. Iss. Turkaman Sahra 18 February 1979c: 1–3.

———. Mortaje'in va zedd-e-enqilâbiouni keh Yek Rouz beh Sâzemanhây-e Siyâsi Hamleh Mikonand va Yek Rouz beh Zanân Bâyad Mojâzât Shavand ("Reactionaries and Counter-Revolutionaries Who One Day Attack Political Organizations and the Next Assault Women Should Be Punished"). *Kar* 15 March 1979d: 1–3.

———. Âzâdy-e Zanân az Âzâdy-e Jâme'eh Jodâ Nist ("Women's Emancipation Is Not Separate from the Emancipation of Society"). *Kar* 15 March 1979e: 6.

———. Payâm-e Sâzemân-e Cherikhâ-ye Fadâ'y-e Khalq-e Iran beh Monâsebat-e Hefdahom-e Esfand, Rouz-e Jahâny-e Zan ("The Message of OIPFG on the Occasion of Esfand Seventeenth [March Eighth], International Women's Day"). *E'lâmiyeh-hâ va Bayâniyeh-hâye Sâzemân-e Cherikhâ-ye Fadâ'y-e Khalq-e Iran dar Sâl-e 1357 (The Leaflets and Statements of OIPFG in 1976).* N.p.: OIPFG, 1979f.

———. "Compulsory Veiling Under the Pretext of Fighting Imperialist Culture." *In the Shadow of Islam: The Women's Movement in Iran,* ed. A. Tabari and N. Yeganeh. London: Zed, 1982a (Originally published in *Kâr* 67).

————. "Women's Rights and Islamic Hejâb." *In the Shadow of Islam: The Women's Movement in Iran*, ed. A. Tabari and N. Yeganeh. London: Zed, 1982b (Originally published in *Kâr* 67).

Ommi, Mahboobeh. Madâr-e Harkat-e Zan-e Mosalmân dar Tarikh ("The Axis of the Muslim Woman's Movement in History"). *Zan-e Rouz* (1987): 10, 43.

Ong, Aihwa. *Spirits of Resistance and Capitalist Discipline: Factory Women in Malaysia*. Albany: State University of New York Press, 1987.

Pahlavi, Mohammad Reza. *Mission for My Country*. London: Hutchinson, 1961.

Pakizegi, Behnaz. "Legal and Social Position of Iranian Women." *Women in the Muslim World*, ed. L. Beck and N. Keddie. Cambridge, MA: Harvard University Press, 1978.

Pâknezhâd, Reza. *Avvalin Dâneshgâh va Âkharin Payâmbar (The First University and the Last Prophet)*. Vol. 19: Hejâb (Hejâb). Tehran: Be'sat, 1989.

————. *Avvalin Dâneshgâh va Âkharin Payâmbar (The First University and the Last Prophet)*. Vol. 20: Hejâb. Tehran: Be'sat, 1990.

————. *Avvalin Dâneshgâh va Âkharin Payâmbar (The First University and the Last Prophet)*. Vol. 39: Ravesh-e Shouhardâri dar Islam (An Islamic Guide to Marital Relationship for Women). Tehran: Be'sat, 1991.

Pakzad, Sima. Appendix 1: The Legal Status of Women in the Family in Iran. *In the Eye of the Storm: Women in Post-Revolutionary Iran*, ed. M. Afkhami and E. Friedl. Syracuse: Syracuse University Press, 1994.

Paret, R. "Umma." *The Encyclopedia of Islam*, ed. M. Houtsman. Leiden: E.J. Brill, 1987.

Parker, Andrew et al. Introduction. *Nationalisms and Sexualities*, ed. A. Parker et al. New York: Routledge, 1992.

Peiss, Kathy. " 'Charity Girls' and City Pleasures: Historical Notes on Working-Class Sexuality, 1880–1920." *Powers of Desire: The Politics of Sexuality*, ed. A. Snitow, C. Stansell, and S. Thompson. New York: Monthly Review, 1983.

Peteet, Julie. "Women and the Palestinian Movement: No Going Back?" *Middle East Report* 138 (1986): 20–24.

Peteet, Julie M. *Gender in Crisis: Women and the Palestinian Resistance Movement*. New York: Columbia University Press, 1991.

Peykâr. Pirâmoun-e Jonbesh-e Zanân-e Zahmatkesh ("Concerning the Movement of the Toiling Women" Part II). *Peykâr*, 16 February 1981a.

————. Pirâmoun-e Jonbesh-e Zanân-e Zahmatkesh ("Concerning the Movement of the Toiling Women" Part III). *Peykâr*, 23 February 1981b.

Plan and Budget Organization and the United Nations. *Human Development- Report of Islamic Republic of Iran, 1999*. Tehran: Plan and Budget Organization and the United Nations, 1999.

PMOI. Tahmil-e Jabry-e Har No' Hejâb Nama'qul Ast ("The Imposition of Any Kind of Hejâb Is Irrational"). *Kayhan* 14 March 1979 (23 Esfand 1357).

————. *Zan dar Masir-e Raha'i (The Woman in the Path of Liberation)*. Tehran: PMOI, 1980.

Pooyân, Amir Parviz. Khashmgin az Amperyâlism, Tarsân az Enqelâb ("Outraged against Imperialism, Fearful of Revolution"). *Pishgâm* 3 (1979): 11–20.

Qaffâri Marân, Mozhgân. Farzand-e Nojavân-e Shomâ az Badan-e Khod Cheh

Midânad? ("What Do Your Teenagers Know about Their Body?") *Zan-e Rouz* 14 May 1994: 21, 50–51.

Qâsemzâdeh, Fâtemeh. Naqsh-e Kâr dar Zendegy-e Zanân ("The Role of Work in Women's Lives"). *Jâme'eh-ye Sâlem* 27 (1996): 52–55.

Qâzinour, Qodsi. Beh-Omid-e Rouzi keh Rouz-e Zan, Hoquq-e Zan va Mas'aleh-ye Zan Nabâshad ("May A Day Come in which Women's Day, Women's Rights, and the Woman Question No Longer Exist"). *Kayhan* 12 March 1979: 6.

Qorbâni, Zeynul'âbedin, ed. *Zan va Entekhâbât (Women and the Election)*. Qom: Tabâtabâ'i, n.d.

Quataert, Jean H. *Reluctant Feminists in German Social Democracy, 1885–1917*. Princeton: Princeton University Press, 1979.

Rahman, Fazlur. *Islam and Modernity, Transformation of an Intellectual Tradition*. Chicago: University of Chicago Press, 1982.

Rahnavard, Zahra. *Tolu'-e Zan-e Musalmân (The Dawn of Muslim Woman)*. Tehran: Nashr-e Mahbubeh, n.d.

Rahnema, Ali. *An Islamic Utopian: A Political Biography of Ali Shari'ati*. New York: I.B. Tauris, 1998.

Ramazani, Nesta. "Women in Iran: the Revolutionary Ebb and Flow." *Middle East Journal* 47.3 (1993): 409–28.

Rashvand, Suri. Kârgarân-e Zan, Kârgarân-e Peymâni va Varzesh-e Kârgari ("Women Workers, Contractual Workers, and Exercise in the Work Place"). *Jens-e Dovom*. Ed.N.A. Khorasany. Tehran: Nashr-e Towse'eh, 1999.

Râvandi, Mortezâ. *Târikh-e Ejtemâ'y-e Iran (The Social History of Iran)*. vol. 3. Tehran: Amir Kabir, 1977.

Ray, Raka. *Fields of Protest: Women's Movement in India*. Minneapolis: University of Minnesota Press, 1999.

Razmandegân. *Gozâreshi az Owzâ'-e Eqtesâdi—Siyâsi va Farhangy-e Khalq-e Arab-e Iran (A Report on the Politico-Economic and Cultural Condition of the Arabs of Iran)*. Tehran: Razmandegân-e Âzâdy-e Tabaqeh-ye Kârgar (Fighters for the Liberation of the Working Class), n.d.

Reeves, Minou. *Female Warriors of Allah: Women and the Islamic Revolution*. New York: E.P. Dutton, 1989.

Rice, Clara Colliver. *Persian Women and Their Ways*. London: Seeley, Service & Co., 1923.

Roberts, Ron, and Robert Marsh Kloss. *Social Movements Between the Balcony and the Barricade*. St. Louis: C.V. Mosby, 1974.

Rommelspacher, Birgit. "Right-Wing 'Feminism': A Challenge to Feminism as an Emancipatory Movement." *Women, Citizenship and Difference*, ed. N. Yuval-Davis and P. Werbner. London: Zed, 1999.

Roohizadegan, Olya. *Olya's Story*. Oxford: Oneworld Publications, 1993.

Rosaldo, Michelle Zimbalister. "Women, Culture, and Society: A Theoretical Overview." *Women, Culture, and Society*, ed. M.Z. Rosaldo and L. Lamphere. Stanford, CA: Stanford University Press, 1974.

———. "The Use and Abuse of Anthropology: Reflections on Feminism and Cross-Cultural Understanding." *Signs: Journal of Women in Culture and Society* 5.3 (1980): 389–418.

Rose, Gregory. "*Velayat-e Faqih* and the Recovery of Islamic Identity in the

Thought of Ayatollah Khomeini." *Religion and Politics in Iran: Shi'ism from Quietism to Revolution*, ed. N.R. Keddie. New Haven: Yale University Press, 1983.

Rowhâni, Hamid. *Barrasi va Tahlili az Nehzat-e Imam Khomeini (A Review and an Analysis of Imam Khomeini's Movement)*. Vol. 1. Tehran: Râh-e Imam, 1981.

Saadawi, Nawal El. *The Hidden Face of Eve: Women in the Arab World*. Boston: Beacon, 1981.

Sabbah, Fatna A. *Woman in the Muslim Unconscious*. New York: Pergamon, 1984.

Sâdeqi Ardestâni, Ahmad. Ravâbet-e Zanâsho'i dar Ekhtelâfât-e Khânevâdegi Shomâ Naqsh Dârad ("The Marital Relationship Has a Role in Your Family Problems"). *Zan-e Rouz* 9 July 1988: 42.

———. Shir-e Mâdar Porbarkattarin-e Qazây-e Koodak Ast ("Mother's Milk Is the Most Nutritious Food for the Child"). *Zan-e Rouz* 13 May 1989a: 16, 45.

———. Shir Kheslathâ-ye Nik va Bad râ Montaqel Mikonad ("Milk Transfers Good and Bad Characteristics"). *Zan-e Rouz* 27 May 1989b: 16, 44.

———. Negâhi beh 'Avârez-e Afzâyesh-e Biraviyeh-ye Jam'iyat va Râhhây-e Pishgiri az Ân ("A Glance at the Effects of Uncontrolled Population Increase and its Control" Part 1). *Zan-e Rouz* 26 October 1991a: 10–13, 56–57.

———. Negâhi beh 'Avârez-e Afzâyesh-e Biraviyeh-ye Jam'iyat va Râhhây-e Pishgiri az Ân ("A Glance at the Effects of Uncontrolled Population Increase and its Control" Part 3). *Zan-e Rouz*, 9 November 1991b: 12–13, 58–59.

———. Negâhi beh 'Avârez-e Afzâyesh-e Biraviyeh-ye Jam'iyat va Râhhây-e Pishgiri az Ân ("A Glance at the Effects of Uncontrolled Population Increase and its Control" Part 4). *Zan-e Rouz*, 23 November 1991c: 14–15, 49.

Sadr, Hassan. *Hoquq-e Zan dar Islam va Ourupâ (Woman's Rights in Islam and Europe)*. N.p., 1940.

Safâ'i-Farâhâni, Ali-Akbar. *Âncheh Yek Enqelâbi Bâyad Bedânad (What A Revolutionary Should Know)*. Tehran: Nabard, n.d. (Written and originally published in 1971 by OIPFG).

Safari, Fâtemeh. Jensiyat va Akhlâq ("Sexuality and Morality" Part 3). *Payâm-e Zan* June 1999c: 36–41, 55.

Saghafi, Morad. Haqq-e Ra'y-e Zanân: 1341–1358 ("Voting Rights for Women: 1962–1979"). *Goft-o-gu* 9 (1995): 53–61.

Saheboz-Zamani, Nasseruddin. *Javâny-e Porranj (Suffering Youth: An Analysis of the Problems of Iranian Youths)*. Tehran: 'Atâ'i, 1965.

Sâlehpour, Mersedeh. Zan va Kâr-e Khânegi ("Women and Housework"). *Farhang-e Towse'eh*, Special Issue on Women 1998: 50–63.

Sanasarian, Eliz. *The Women's Rights Movement in Iran: Mutiny, Appeasement, and Repression from 1900 to Khomeini*. New York: Praeger, 1982.

———. "An Analysis of Fida'i and Mujahidin Positions on Women's Rights." *Women and Revolution in Iran*, ed. G. Nashat. Boulder: Westview, 1983.

———. "Political Activism and Islamic Identity in Iran." *Women in the World, 1975–1985 The Women's Decade*, ed. L. B. Iglitzin and R. Ross. Santa Barbara: ABC-Clio Information Services, 1986.

Saney, Parviz. *Law and Population Growth in Iran*. Vol. 21 Law and Population Monograph Series. Medford, MA: Fletcher School of Law and Diplomacy, Tufts University, 1974.

Sarkar, Tanika, and Urvashi Butalia. Introductory Remarks. *Women and Right-Wing Movements: Indian Experiences*, ed. T. Sarkar and U. Butalia. London: Zed, 1995.

Sarti, Cynthia. "The Panorama of Feminism in Brazil." *New Left Review* 173 (1989): 75–90.

Schild, Maarten. "Islam." *Sexuality and Eroticism Among Males in Moslem Societies*, ed. A. Schmitt and J. Sofer. New York: Harrington Park, 1992.

Scott, James C. *Weapons of the Weak: Everyday Forms of Peasant Resistance*. New Haven, CT: Yale University Press, 1985.

Sedgwick, Eve Kosofsky. "Gosh, Boy George, You Must Be Awfully Secure in Your Masculinity!" *Constructing Masculinity*, ed. M. Berger, B. Wallis and S. Watson. New York: Routledge, 1995.

Sha'bâni, Fâtemeh. Naqsh-e Zan dar Fa'âliyat-hâye Eqtesâdi va Ta'âvoni ("Women's Role in Economic and Cooperative Activities"). *Ta'âvon, Zan, Eshteqâl (Cooperatives, Women, Employment)*, ed. M. of C. Tehran: Ministry of Cooperatives, 1996.

Shaaban, Bouthaina. *Both Right and Left Handed: Arab Women Talk about Their Lives*. Bloomington: Indiana University Press, 1991.

Shâditalab, Zhâleh. Towse'eh va 'Aqabmândigy-e Zanân ("Development and Women's Underdevelopment"). *Zanân* 23 (1995): 4–11.

Shâdkâm, Mohammad Ali. *Zan: Fereshteh-ye Rahmat yâ 'Efrit-e Tabi'at (Woman: The Angel of Mercy or the Demon of Nature)*. Tehran: Kânoon-e Enteshârât, 1976.

Shahidian, Hammed. "The 'Woman's Question' in the Iranian Revolution of 1978–1979." Unpublished diss., Brandeis University, 1990.

———. "National and International Aspects of Feminist Movements: The Example of the Iranian Revolution of 1978–79." *Critique: Journal for Critical Studies of Iran and the Middle East* 2 (1993a): 33–53.

———. "The Iranian Left and the 'Woman Question' in the Revolution of 1978–79." *International Journal of Middle East Studies* 26.2 (1994): 223–47.

———. "Islam, Politics, and Problems of Writing Women's History in Iran." *Journal of Women's History* 7.2 (1995): 113–44.

———. "Iranian Exiles and Sexual Politics: Issues of Gender Relations and Identity." *Journal of Refugee Studies* 9 1 (1996): 43–72.

———. "Women and Clandestine Politics in Iran: 1970–1985." *Feminist Studies* 23.1 (1997): 7–42.

———. "Writing Out Terror." Manuscript. University of Illinois Springfield, 1999.

Shâhmorâdi, 'Azizeh, and Maryam Mohseni. Moshkelât-e Zanân-e Kârgar-e Kârgâhhây-e Towlid-e Pushâk ("Problems Facing Workingwomen in Clothing Workshops"). *Negâh-e Zanân*, ed. N.A. Khorasany. Tehran: Nashr-e Towse'eh, 1998.

Shâhmorâdi, 'Azizeh, and Nastaran Moossavi. Taqviyat-e Vâbastegi yâ Tamrin-e Esteqlâl? ("Enforcing Dependency or Practicing Independence?") *Jens-e Dovom*, ed. N.A. Khorasany. Tehran: Nashr-e Towse'eh, 1999.

Shâmbayâti, Giti. Negareshi beh Kâr-e Zan ("Glance at Women's Labor"). *Kelk* 39 (1993b): 88–93.

Shariati, Ali. *Takyeh beh Mazhab (Reliance on Religion)*. Tehran: Abuzar, 1977.

———. Tashaiyo'-e 'Alavi va Tashaiyo'-e Safavi ("Alavite Shi'ism and Safavid Shi'ism"). *Majmou'eh-ye Âsâr (Collected Works)*. Tehran: Ershâd, 1980.

———. *Fatima Is Fatima*. Trans. L. Bakhtiar. Tehran: The Shariati Foundation, n.d.-a.

———. Ummat va Imamat ("Ummat and Imamite"). *Majmou'eh-ye Âsâr (Collected Works)*. Tehran: Ershâd, n.d.-b.

———. Zan dar Chashm va Del-e Mohammad *(Woman in Mohammad's Eye and Heart)*. Tehran: Hosseiniyeh-ye Ershâd, n.d.-c.

Sharoni, Simona. "Motherhood and the Politics of Women's Resistance." *The Politics of Motherhood: Activist Voices from Left to Right*, ed. A. Jetter, A. Orleck and D. Taylor. Hanover, NH: University Press of New England, 1997.

Sherkat, Shahlâ. Sarmaqâleh: Sho'ârhây-e Bozorgdâsht-e 'Zan' râ Bâvar Konim Yâ...? ("Editorial: Should We Believe Slogans Revering 'The Woman' Or...?"). *Zanân* November-January 1994: 2.

Shid, Nâhid. Hefz-e Kiyân-e Khânevâdeh ("Protecting the Constitution of the Family"). *Payâm-e Hâjar* Spec. double Iss. Women's Role in Poverty Alleviation and Sustainable Development 221–22 (1995): 40–48.

Shirazi-Mahajan, Faegheh. "A Dramaturgical Approach to Hejâb in Post-Revolutionary Iran." *Critique: Journal of Critical Studies of the Middle East* 7 (1995): 35–51.

Shoaee, Rokhsareh. "The Mujahid Women of Iran: Reconciling 'Culture' and 'Gender'." *The Middle East Journal* 41.4 (1987): 519–37.

Simon, Roger. "Civil Society, the State, and the Nature of Power." *Gramsci's Political Thought: An Introduction*. London: Lawrence and Wishart, 1982.

Skocpol, Theda. "Social Revolution and Mass Military Mobilization." *Social Revolutions in the Modern World*, ed. T. Skocpol. New York: Cambridge University Press, 1994.

Sâdeq Sabâ Kist? ("Who Is Sâdeq Sabâ?") *Sobh* 74 (1997b): 63.

Soja, Edward W. *Postmodern Geographies: The Reassertion of Space in Critical Social Theory*. London: Verso, 1989.

Solomon-Godeau, Abigail. "Male Trouble." *Constructing Masculinity*, ed. M. Berger, B. Wallis and S. Watson. New York: Routledge. 1995.

Soltanpour, Sa'id. No'i az Honar, No'i az Andisheh *(One Kind of Art, One Kind of Thought)*. N.p., n.d. (Written early 1970s).

Soroush, Lili. Dar Râhpeymâ'y-e Rouz-e 17 Esfand (Rouz-e Jahâny-e Zan) Cheh Gozasht? ("What Happened on the Isfand 17 Demonstration [International Women's Day]?") *Âyandegân* 12 March 1979a.

———. Zanân ra dar Showrây-e Enqelâb Râh Dahid ("Admit Women to the Revolutionary Council"). *Âyandegân* 30 January 1979b.

Stacey, Judith. *Patriarchy and Socialist Revolution in China*. Berkeley: University of California Press, 1983.

Staggenborg, Suzanne. *Gender, Family, and Social Movements*. Thousand Oaks, CA: Pine Forge, 1998.

Stalin, J. V. "Concerning Questions of Leninism." *Works*. Moscow: Foreign Language Publishing House, 1954.

Stanko, Elizabeth. *Intimate Intrusions: Women's Experience of Male Violence*. New York: Routledge, 1985.

Sultânzâdeh. Mowqeʿiyat-e Zan-e Irani ("The Status of the Iranian Woman"). *Historical Documents: The Workers' Social- Democratic, and Communist Movement in Iran*. Ed. C. Chacqueri. Tehran: Elm, n.d.

Supporters of OIPFG—Sistân and Baluchestân. *Zan-e Baluch (The Baluchi Woman)*. n.p.: Supporters of OIPFG—Sistân and Baluchestân, 1984a.

———. Gerâmi Bâd Rouz-e Jahâny-e Zan ("Hail to the International Women's Day"). *Bâmi Estâr* March 1984b.

———. Rouz-e Zan, Sâlrooz-e Jonbesh-e Zanân-e Zahmatkesh-e Jahân Gerâmi Bâd ("Commemorate Women's Day, The Anniversary of The Movement of Toiling Women"). *Bâmi Estâr* March 1985.

Supporters of Peykâr, ed. *'Eshq, Ezdevâj va Khânevadeh az Didgâh-e Marxysm-Leninysm (Love, Marriage, and the Family from the Marxist-Leninist Point of View)*. N.p.: Supporters of Peykâr, 1979.

Swidler, Ann. "Culture in Action: Symbols and Strategies." *American Sociological Review* 51.2 (1986): 273–86.

Tabari, Azar, and Nahid Yeganeh, eds. *In the Shadow of Islam: The Women's Movement in Iran*. London: Zed, 1982.

Tabâtabâ'i, Mohammad Hossein. *Estrâtezhy-e Zan dar Islam (The Strategy of Women in Islam)*. Tehran: Nedây-e Emân, 1979.

Tabatabaie, Kia. "Human Rights of Women." *Farzaneh: Journal of Women's Studies and Research* 7 (1995–1996): 83–91.

Teymouri, Ebrahim. *Tahrim-e Tanbâkoo (The Tobacco Boycott)*. Tehran: Jibi Books, 1971.

Koran. Trans. N.J. Dawood. New York: Penguin, 1988.

Thompson, Kenneth. *Beliefs and Ideology*. New York: Tavistock, 1986.

Thönnessen, Werner. *The Emancipation of Women, The Rise and Decline of the Women's Movement in German Social Democracy 1863–1933*. London: Pluto, 1976.

Tibi, Bassam. *Islam and the Cultural Accommodation of Social Change*. Trans. C. Krojzl. Boulder: Westview, 1991.

Touba, Jacquline Rudolph. "Sex Segregation and Women's Roles in the Economic System: The Case of Iran." *Research in the Interweave of Social Roles: Women and Men*, ed. H.Z. Lopata. Greenwich, CT: JAI, 1980.

Tucker, D.F.B. *Marxism and Individualism*. Oxford: Basil Blackwell, 1980.

Tudeh Party of Iran. Hoquq-e Zan az Didgâh-e Marx va Engels ("Women's Rights According to Marx and Engels"). *Supplement to Nâmeh-ye Mardom* 9 August 1984.

UNESCO. *Statistical Yearbook*. Lanham, MD: UNESCO Publishing & Barnam, 1998.

———. *Statistical Yearbook*. Lanham, MD: UNESCO Publishing & Barnam, 1999.

UNICEF. *The State of Women: Islamic Republic of Iran*. Tehran: UNICEF, 1998.

United Nations. *The World's Women: Trends and Statistics*. New York: United Nations. 1995.

Vahidi, Mohammad. *Ahkâm-e Bânuvân (Edicts Concerning Women)*. Qom: Sisters' Unit of the Bureaus of Islamic Propaganda of the Qom's 'Elmiyeh Center, 1994.

Vajdi, Shifteh, and Reza Fathi. *Barrasy-e Âmâry-e Ezdevâj va Talâq dar Iran (A*

Statistical Analysis of Marriage and Divorce in Iran). Tehran: Women's Organization of Iran, 1978.

Vieille, Paul. "Iranian Women in Family Alliance and Sexual Politics." *Women in the Muslim World,* ed. L. Beck and N. Keddie. Cambridge, MA: Harvard University Press, 1978.

Vogel, Lise. *Marxism and the Oppression of Women: Toward a Unitary Theory.* New Brunswick: Rutgers University Press, 1983.

Vološinov, V.N. *Marxism and the Philosophy of Language.* New York: Seminar Press, 1973.

Walby, Sylvia. *Theorizing Patriarchy.* Cambridge, MA: Blackwell, 1994.

Waters, Elizabeth. "In the Shadow of the Comintern: The Communist Women's Movement, 1920–1943." *Promissory Notes: Women in the Transition to Socialism,* ed. S. Kruks, R. Rapp and M.B. Young. New York: Monthly Review, 1989.

Weber, Max. "The Social Psychology of the World Religions." *From Max Weber: Essays in Sociology,* ed. H.H. Gerth and C.W. Mills. New York: Oxford University Press, 1981.

Weeks, Jeffrey. "Questions of Identity." *The Cultural Construction of Sexuality,* ed. P. Caplan. New York: Tavistock Publications, 1981.

———. *Sexuality.* New York: Tavistock, 1986.

West, Candace, and Don H. Zimmerman. "Doing Gender." *Gender and Society* 1 (1987): 125–51.

Williams, John Alden, ed. *Islam.* New York: George Brazillier, 1962.

Williams, Raymond. "Base and Superstructure in Marxist Cultural Theory." *Problems in Materialism and Culture.* London: Verso, 1982.

WOI. *Women's Organization of Iran.* Tehran: WOI Publications, n.d.

Woodsmall, Ruth Frances. *Women and the New East.* Washington, DC: Middle East Institute, 1960.

———. *Women in the Changing Islamic System.* Delhi: Bimla Publishing House, 1983.

Yeganeh, Nahid. "Women's Struggle in the Islamic Republic of Iran." *In the Shadow of Islam: The Women's Movement in Iran,* ed. A. Tabari and N. Yeganeh. London: Zed, 1982.

Zabih, Sipihr. *The Left in Contemporary Iran.* Stanford: Hoover Institute, 1986.

Zâhedi, Shamsussâdât. Mowqeʻiyat-e Zanân dar Jâmeʻeh-ye Dâneshgâhi ("Women in Universities"). *Zanân* 21 (1995): 2–12.

Zakaria, Fouad. "The Standpoint of Contemporary Muslim Fundamentalists." *Women of the Arab World,* ed. N. Toubia. London: Zed, 1988.

Zamâni, Mostafâ. *Peymân-e Zanâshuʾi (Marital Commitment).* Qom: Payâm-e Islam, 1970.

Zanân. Fâezeh Hashemi Cheh Migooyad? ("What Does Fâezeh Hashemi Say?"). *Zanân* (1996): 8–17.

Zan-e Rouz. 1985. Miz-e Gerd darbâreh-ye Mas âʾel va Moshkelât-e Farhangi, Hoquqi, va Ejtem âʾy-e Khâharân, Qesmat-e Dovom ("Round Table Discussion about Sisters' Cultural, Legal, and Social Problems, Part 2"). *Zan-e Rouz* 16 March 1985: 10–11, 53–55.

———. Fasl-e Garmâ, Badhejâbi dar Khiâbânhâ va Mâjeray-e Dowbareh-ye Dargirihâ ("The Warm Season, Badhejâbi in the Streets, and the Recurring Clashes"). *Zan-e Rouz* 25 April 1987: 4.

———. Pas az Gozasht-e Dah Sâl az Enqelâb dar Mowred-e Mobârezeh bâ Badhejâbi Chârehʾi Joz Eʿmâl-e Feshâr Nadârim ("Ten Years After the Revolution, We Have No Alternative but to Exercise Force Against Badhejâbi"). *Zan-e Rouz* 22 April 1989: 5.

Index

About the Author

HAMMED SHAHIDIAN is Honorary Research Fellow at the Faculty of
Social Sciences, University of Glasgow (2001–2002). He teaches Sociology
at the University of Illinois at Springfield, where he was honored with the
University Scholar Award. He is also a research associate at the UIS Institute for Public Affairs. Focusing mainly on gender and political activism
and Iranians in exile, Shahidian has published in *Qualitative Sociology,*
Current Sociology, Sexualities, Sociological Inquiry, Feminist Studies, and
elsewhere. He serves on the Editorial Board of *Sexualities.*